Teaching French Neoclassical Tragedy

Teaching French Neoclassical Tragedy

Edited by

Hélène E. Bilis and Ellen McClure

The Modern Language Association of America
New York 2021

Library of Congress Cataloging-in-Publication Data

Names: Bilis, Hélène E., editor. | McClure, Ellen, editor.
Title: Teaching French neoclassical tragedy / Hélène E. Bilis, Ellen McClure.
Description: New York : Modern Language Association of America, 2021. | Series: Options for teaching, 10792562 ; vol 55 | Includes bibliographical references. | Summary: "Offers pedagogical techniques for teaching French neoclassical tragedy mainly from the reign of Louis XVI in undergraduate classes. Topics include tragic themes (fate, freedom), political subtexts, postcolonial adaptations and productions, performance, rhetoric, and performance practices. Includes syllabus suggestions and information on editions, reference works, biographies, film adaptations, and online resources"—Provided by publisher.
Identifiers: LCCN 2021004694 (print) | LCCN 2021004695 (ebook) | ISBN 9781603295307 (hardcover) | ISBN 9781603295314 (paperback) | ISBN 9781603295321 (EPUB)
Subjects: LCSH: French literature—17th century—Study and teaching (Higher)—United States. | French drama (Tragedy)—Study and teaching (Higher)—United States. | French drama (Tragedy)—History and criticism.
Classification: LCC PQ63.U5 T43 2021 (print) | LCC PQ63.U5 (ebook) | DDC 840/.71173—dc23
LC record available at https://lccn.loc.gov/2021004694
LC ebook record available at https://lccn.loc.gov/2021004695

Options for Teaching 55
ISSN 1079-2562

Published by The Modern Language Association of America
85 Broad Street, Suite 500, New York, New York 10004-2434
www.mla.org

Contents

Acknowledgments

As we finish preparing our volume for publication amid a global pandemic and the widespread practice of social distancing, the *huis clos* quality of French neoclassical tragedy takes on new relevance. While critics have often reproached neoclassical French tragedy for this suffocating mood—one action, one day, one location, over the course of five acts—the early modern genre speaks to both the intensity and the intricacy of relationships that resonate today when so many find themselves in confinement. We therefore wish to recognize our respective partners, Adam Van Arsdale and Dan Cherry, for their love, support, and patience, and we thank Flora, Anthony, and Vincent, brilliant and resilient actors in an unexpected confinement saga and beyond.

We thank all the contributors to the volume, whose persistence and responsiveness allowed us to complete the project. In particular, we single out Sylvaine Guyot, who was willing to change course from baroque to twenty-first-century theater to help advance the project, and John Lyons, who joined the MLA, despite his reservations, to support his colleagues. We also wish to recognize Julia Prest, who joined us late in the development of the project. We are grateful for the guidance of James Hatch, senior acquisitions editor at MLA, who generously supported the project throughout its many stages. We thank the four anonymous reviewers of the manuscript, for their thoughtful reading and helpful suggestions, as well as the MLA copyeditors, especially Zahra Brown. Finally, it is only fitting that for a project dedicated to teaching in the twenty-first century, we acknowledge the liveliness, curiosity, intellectual energy, and diversity of the students who have inspired the essays that make up this volume. We are grateful that they have been open to trying out new approaches and that they have encouraged us to adopt unfamiliar methods to create connections between the concerns of today and those of old texts.

Hélène E. Bilis and Ellen McClure

Introduction: Teaching Neoclassical Tragedy outside France

Why Neoclassical French Tragedy Now?

We ready this volume for publication in a world ravaged by disease and racism, scourges that are now impossible for anyone to hold at a safe distance. Indeed, we are newly aware of a widespread and willful distancing of violence and the tragic that has become untenable. Juliette Cherbuliez, one of the contributors to this volume, notes in the closing lines of her book *In the Wake of Medea* that art—and the tragic—play a crucial role in "[helping] us face the structures of violence undergirding our lives" (206). Tragedy is indeed, as the editors of *PMLA*'s 2014 special issue on tragedy declared, "a resource with which to think, feel, and perform the urgencies of the times" (Foley and Howard 631). The editors and the contributors to the volume point to the ways in which tragedy speaks to enduring human vulnerabilities and suffering even in the "inhospitable environments" of modernity and postmodernity (618). The *PMLA* volume, which covers a wide range of works from Seneca and Shakespeare to Tony Kushner and the Constitution of the United States, figures among other important works on tragedy that have appeared in recent years, from Terry Eagleton's *Sweet Violence* to Rita Felski's *Rethinking Tragedy* and Blair

Hoxby's *What Was Tragedy?* Tragedy and the tragic—as well as the scholarship surrounding these concepts—seem to be more alive and relevant than ever. Yet what of the subgenre of French neoclassical tragedy, absent from the *PMLA* issue? Is it still relevant as well, or should it be consigned to the role of historic curiosity, a quaint vestige of the political tensions endemic to absolutist monarchy?

In approaching these questions, an appreciation of the outsized role played by French neoclassical tragedy in the French literary canon can be helpful. The plays of Pierre Corneille and Jean Racine occupy a position akin to those of Shakespeare in British and American literary history; taught to every French adolescent, for many generations they constituted the bedrock of French cultural identity. As such, these works have been the object of ideological overinvestment almost ever since their first appearances on the French stage. Deployed by Louis XIV during festivals intended to impress both his subjects and foreign representatives, these plays also served as the battleground for the development of rules adapted from Aristotle and his Italian Renaissance commentators and self-consciously designed to ensure that these productions would achieve a timeless universality that would mirror the glory of the French monarch.

The seventeenth century was dominated by the development of divine-right absolutism, which reached its apogee, at least as a theory if not in practice, during the reign of the Sun King. The establishment of the cult of regularity and order—not only in literature, but also in music, gardens, and architecture, culminating in the palace of Versailles—became a means of forging national unity after the tumultuous, traumatic years of the sixteenth-century religious wars, the assassination of two kings, and the more recent rebellion of the Fronde (1648–53). As a result, the genre of French neoclassical tragedy, which, with the support of the Crown, flourished during this period, became inextricably linked to the historiography of a Grand Siècle, a golden age, characterized by French cultural, military, and diplomatic dominance.

Rejection of the French neoclassical tragic aesthetic therefore became a means of criticizing the political regime under which it thrived. Prominent philosophes writing about theater sought to break with its tradition. For example, Denis Diderot reimagined the role of the actor, arguing for an approach more physical and natural, less pompous, than the formal neoclassical style of declamation. Meanwhile, Jean-Jacques Rousseau rejected outright the social utility of theater, most notably in his *Lettre à d'Alembert sur les spectacles* (*Letter to d'Alembert on the Theater*), where he condemned the morality of Racine and Molière's dramaturgy. Neoclassical tragedies and operas continued to be performed throughout the Revolutionary period, but they also became synonymous with the hierarchical artificiality of the ancien régime.[1]

The outright rejection of the neoclassical aesthetic only intensified during the nineteenth century, as Stendhal's well-known treatise *Racine et Shakespeare* exemplifies. Stendhal peremptorily declares that neoclassical literature, despite its purported aspirations to timelessness, is irrevocably passé:

> Je ne nierai point que l'on ne puisse créer de belles choses, même aujourd'hui, en suivant le système classique; mais elles seront ennuyeuses. C'est qu'elles seront en partie calculées sur les exigences des Français de 1670, et non sur les besoins moraux, sur les passions dominantes du Français de 1824. (87)
>
> I will not deny that one may create beautiful works, even today, by following the neoclassical system, but they will be boring. That is because they will have been in part calculated on the demands of the French of 1670, and not on the moral needs, on the dominant passions, of the French of 1824. (our trans.)[2]

Yet the very vehemence of Stendhal's rejection testifies to the continued cultural prominence of the neoclassical aesthetic. Moreover, Stendhal's argument demonstrates the kinds of questions that neoclassicism almost inevitably provokes—questions that remain at the heart of literary study today: Are emotions and passions universal, or are they historically contingent? What should be the relation between theater and "moral needs," as opposed to a conception of pure pleasure? And, of course, the question at the center of this proposed volume: What could theater written in the 1600s under a strict monarchical regime, and self-consciously in dialogue with its classical antecedents, possibly offer to spectators, readers, and students today?

In the wake of Stendhal's provocative treatise, the answers to these questions usually fell into two distinct categories. On the one hand, neoclassical tragedy's detractors, including major figures like Victor Hugo, presented neoclassicism as an outmoded form of rule and taste, a remnant of a bygone era of constraint and subjugation, an antimodern and dogmatic aesthetic lost in a servile allegiance to the fading tradition of the ancients (see Hugo, *La préface de* Cromwell). On the other hand, neoclassical tragedy's proponents, often writing from the vantage point of academic circles, viewed it as the great legacy of France's heyday, a testament to a history of glory, dignity, and prestige worthy of patriotic pride. Indeed, the works of Corneille and Racine formed the basis for the canon of France's Third Republic, paradoxically celebrated as heroic secular models of civic republican duty (see Albanese, *Corneille*, *Racine*). This mythologizing of French neoclassical works would be carried to new extremes in moments of national crisis, and is perhaps most in evidence in the notorious Nazi collaborator Robert Brasillach's elevation of Pierre Corneille to the essence of the French national genius.[3]

Recent scholarship, much of it conducted in North American universities, has countered ideological claims that describe neoclassical literature as the foundation of a Frenchness that patriotically relishes its own glory and simultaneously aspires to universality. New momentum has come from scholars who probe the fissures and tensions at the heart of the neoclassical aesthetic, thereby ensuring the genre's survival and relevance to audiences, students, and readers today (cf. Braider, *Indiscernible Counterparts* and *The Matter of Mind*; Goodkin, *Birth Marks*, *How Do I Know Thee?*, and *Tragic Middle*; Greenberg; Lyons, *Kingdom* and "Le mythe"; Reiss, *Toward Dramatic Illusion* and *Tragedy*; Stone, *Classical Model* and *Royal DisClosure*). Significantly, Larry Norman, countering any lingering impression that neoclassical tragedy entails a seamless updating of the ancients, has demonstrated that the relationship of seventeenth-century writers and critics to their Greek and Roman counterparts was deeply ambivalent, and characterized by dynamic interaction rather than blind adherence. Across the Atlantic, Hélène Merlin-Kajman, writing deliberately against those who wish to mythologize the French literary tradition, locates seventeenth-century theater and its attendant polemics at the emergence of a literary culture that manages to hold in tension the dream of a totalizing narrative and the forces and voices that point to the impossibility, as well as the dangers, of establishing a univocal community (*L'animal*). In addition to such calls to heed the multiplicity of voices within and around the genre, in recent years exciting developments in the field of performance studies have further contributed to the revitalization of these plays beyond the borders of France (see Guyot; Harris). English-language adaptations, such as Tony Kushner's rewriting of Corneille's *Illusion comique* (*Comic Illusion*) and Joanne Akalaitis's adaptation of Racine's *Phèdre*, demonstrate how the genre remains relevant, in its complexity, to contemporary spectators throughout the world.

The Development and Evolution of French Neoclassical Tragedy

The relatively recent critical exploration of chaos and disorder in seventeenth-century French neoclassical tragedy does not, however, negate the very real concern for the poetic rules and "regularity" that we find in the treatises and prefaces of the period. Codification was seen as a means of helping playwrights distill everyday human experience and emotions into the refined and elevated form of tragedy. Yet for all their reaching toward universality and timelessness, the neoclassical playwrights followed rules that were tightly linked to a narrow historical and political context. Specialists of neoclassical tragedy often divide the genre's evolution into three generations. The first, considered the birth of neoclassicism under Cardinal Richelieu's aegis, begins in the 1630s and runs until 1661, when, following the death of Cardinal Mazarin, Louis XIV decided to rule without a prime minister. This period, the heyday of *le grand Corneille* ("the Great Corneille"), includes the playwright's publication of his complete works, including explanatory prefaces to all his plays and three essays on theater, *Les trois discours sur le poème dramatique* (*Three Discourses on the Dramatic Poem*).[4] These essays amount to Corneille's poetic manifesto, in which he responds at length to the polemics that characterized the rise of French neoclassical tragic conventions. The second generation, considered the golden age of neoclassicism (and of Louis XIV's rule), begins in the 1660s with Racine's great works and a turn toward an aesthetic of gallantry associated with the refinement and youth of Louis's court. Racine's tragic aesthetic, which overshadowed that of *le vieux Corneille* ("the aging Corneille") in this period, culminated with his masterpiece, *Phèdre*, published in 1677, after which the playwright left the public stage to become royal historiographer. This periodization is problematic since it neglects the two biblical tragedies, *Esther* (1689) and *Athalie* (1691), that Racine wrote for the young women of Saint Cyr at the request of Madame de Maintenon, the king's mistress and founder of the school for girls. The third generation is the post-Racine era, usually viewed as the twilight of neoclassicism because the tragedies from this era are not considered canonical works today and rarely figure on syllabi. For all its neatness, this chronological division discounts the popularity of other playwrights of the seventeenth century, most notably Jean Rotrou and Thomas Corneille, and minimizes the success of eighteenth-century tragedians, especially Crébillon père and Voltaire, whose works were enormously lucrative at the Comédie-Française. Such periodization also obscures the elasticity of the tragic genre, including the popularity and influence of adjacent forms, such as the *tragédie en musique* ("musical tragedy") and the *tragédie à machines* ("machine tragedy"), which theater history has often erased from the neoclassical narrative.

The 1630s nonetheless proved to be a decisive period for the development of neoclassical tragedy. Regarding his first play, *Mélite*, performed in 1629, Corneille notes it does not adhere to the neoclassical rules because he did not know there were rules to follow when he wrote it.[5] Georges Forestier has underscored the sudden reversal that occurred in such a short span of time from the genre's lack of popularity in 1628, when not a single play offered to Parisian audiences that year was presented as a tragedy, to its unquestionable renaissance six years later, when Corneille, Rotrou, Jean Mairet, and Georges de Scudéry, all influential playwrights of the period, each published a play they labeled a "tragedy" (*La tragédie française* 29–66). In 1635, Richelieu founded the Académie Française and the same year Corneille wrote his first tragedy inspired by the ancients, *Médée*. The polemic around his tragicomedy *Le Cid* raged from 1636 until the Académie published an official judgment of the play in 1637, which deemed that adherence to poetic precepts and neoclassical forms was of greater importance than satisfying the tastes of spectators.[6] In this decade, Louis XIII and his prime minister invested in and built up the theater as a noble institution, a distinguished art with specific rules and practices meant to display a high style worthy of the most elevated ancient genre (Blocker).

Inspired by Aristotle and Horace's tragic poetics, and further influenced by the numerous ars poeticas of the Italian Renaissance, the members of the Académie Française emphasized the exceptional literary and cultural status afforded to tragedy. Experts known as *doctes* produced a flowering of French poetics in the 1630s and 1640s, translating, explaining, and expanding upon Aristotle's poetic commentary. In the *Poetics*, Aristotle assigned to tragedy the ability to arouse terror and pity and thereby purge excessive and dangerous passions through catharsis. Meanwhile, the Roman Horace insisted on tragedy's crucial capacity to instruct through example and thereby serve a public good. Taking these lessons to heart, the French theorists insisted that the potential social benefits of tragedy depended on mastery of the proper technique, the set rules and methods, needed to create an effective dramatic imitation (*mimesis*) of the world and thus sustain a cathartic illusion.[7]

Jean Chapelain, a founding member of the Académie Française and a key figure in the development of early neoclassicism, published in 1630 the *Lettre sur la règle des vingt-quatre heures* (*Letter on the Unity of Twenty-Four Hours*), arguing for tragedy's essential conformity to Aristotelian precepts. In this period, Chapelain and other *doctes* published poetic treatises meant to serve as how-to formulae for constructing and judging the worthiness of a tragedy. Despite the authority and political power associated with the *doctes*, in many of his prefaces and in the *Trois discours* Corneille responds directly to his erudite critics, especially the formidable François Hédelin, abbé d'Aubignac, engaging them in his own interpretation of Aristotle and the tragic code, and always emphasizing the priority he gave to spectators' pleasure over the rules.[8]

Scholars have often marveled at the speed with which these rules took hold: by the 1640s no Parisian playwright could still claim ignorance of them. It can be disheartening for specialists of the seventeenth century to see the genre so often reduced to its stodgy code, as the tradition of the Romantics has done. Indeed, following John D. Lyons's important study of how the rise of the unities—unity of time, place, and action—in French neoclassical tragedy is connected to scientific, philosophical, and political changes in the same period, recent scholarship has offered more complex interpretations (*Kingdom*). For instance, Richard Goodkin has insisted that the battle over the unities constituted an ethical struggle and "a fight about monitoring the dissemination and interpretation of culture" (*How Do I Know Thee* 59). Ellen R. Welch has analyzed how theatrical modes of representation and reception were crucial to diplomatic culture and practice, and she has argued that the political realm of early modern France cannot be fully understood without a grasp of the theatrical concepts underpinning it. Blair Hoxby has shown how until the 1790s the tragic genre was defined by its poetics more than its themes—the unities, the arrangement of words and scenes, and, for the French, the assumption that a tragic representation entailed reciting the twelve-syllable alexandrine verse. Only at the end of the eighteenth century do writers replace tragedy as a poetic concept with a philosophy of the tragic that identifies the genre with the plight of a hero struggling with the collision of freedom and necessity in human existence.[9]

The study of early modern French neoclassical tragedy can serve to illuminate the questions and conflicts, now neglected if not forgotten, that surrounded the emergence of the modern state and subject. Such an endeavor is particularly worthwhile at a time when the shortcomings of the modern conceptions of autonomy, volition, and freedom are becoming apparent. Indeed, and unsurprisingly, much of postmodern theory emerged in dialogue with seventeenth-century French authors, from Roland Barthes's *Sur Racine* (*On Racine*) to Jacques Derrida's 1967 essay "Force et signification" ("Force and Signification"), an engagement with Jean Rousset's reading of Corneille (*Forme*). And, as Mitchell Greenberg notes in the introduction to his *Racine: From Ancient Myth to Tragic Modernity*, "the seventeenth century seems to function as a seductive fulcrum for Foucault" (11). In *Sur Racine*, Barthes declares the eponymous playwright to be a "commonplace [*lieu commun*] of our literature" (11). He suggests that Racine left as a legacy a sovereign "art of accessibility [*disponibilité*], which permits [the twentieth-century French reader] to remain eternally within the field of any critical language" (11).

Now, more than half a century after Barthes, and more than 350 years after the zenith of neoclassical tragedy, the contributors to this volume have mounted a twenty-first-century claim about the genre's accessibility. We wager that undergraduates hailing from a diversity of backgrounds and studying in a range of academic institutions can feel connected to the mournful beauty of the neoclassical corpus as presented here. We draw attention in the essays to contemporary adaptations and integrations of neoclassical tragedy, building inroads to the seventeenth century from new vantage points for new generations. The dialogue between the present and the neoclassical genre is not new. It appears in French New Wave cinema with *L'amour fou* (*Mad Love*), which includes long scenes of a troupe rehearsing Racine's *Andromaque* and serves as a means for the director, Jacques Rivette, to reflect upon the legacy of neoclassical theatricality for a new brand of French film. The conversation extends across the Atlantic to the Caribbean with Nono Numa's adaptation of Corneille into Creole with *Jénéral Rodrig*. In Numa's loose translation of *Le Cid*, the Haitian playwright adapts the seventeenth-century plot to the twentieth-century Caribbean of Jean-Claude Duvalier. The genre continues to lend itself to fresh forms with other postcolonial adaptations, such as Faustin Linyekula's *Pour en finir avec Bérénice* (*To Put an End to Berenice*) and Wajdi Mouawad's *Une chienne* (*A Female Dog*), loosely inspired by *Phèdre*. Drawing attention to female receptions of neoclassical tragedy, Patricia Mazuy's film *Saint-Cyr* (*The King's Daughters*) is a period drama starring Isabelle Huppert as Madame de Maintenon, who stages Racine's *Esther* in the school she founded for young aristocratic women. Nathalie Azoulai's prize-winning novel *Titus n'aimait pas Bérénice* (*Titus Didn't*

Love Berenice) offers a fictional account of Racine's artistic awakening told alongside the struggles of a modern-day French woman named Bérénice to understand why her boyfriend, Titus, has left her. With the premise that "Racine, c'est le supermarché de l'amour" 'Racine is the supermarket of love,' Bérénice sets out to understand how the bourgeois and provincial seventeenth-century playwright could have written such piercing portraits of female passion (18).[10] Meanwhile, in the comedy *Le goût des autres* (*The Taste of Others*), directed by Agnès Jaoui, *Bérénice* similarly serves as a catalyst for reflection on connections between the seventeenth and twenty-first centuries, but this time the lens is economic, with Racine comically and touchingly illustrating cultural and linguistic divides across French social classes.

In weaving together essays on the historical context and the modern reception of the neoclassical corpus, our volume highlights the creative and intellectual activity that French tragedy has persistently inspired. From the ubiquitous theatrical metaphors in early modern writing to the use of tragedy by monarchs in grand courtly festivities, the genre was an imaginative model for understanding the world in all its aspects, from political science to the metaphysics of the universe to the morality of private life, and even in shaping painting and sculpting under the ancien régime. The poetic conception of the neoclassical genre reveals far more about early modern culture than Stendhal and the Romantic tradition ever imagined.

For instructors and students unfamiliar with the "rules" of neoclassical tragedy, we offer an overview of the genre's codes in the seventeenth century, emphasizing the persistent divide between theory and practice, the lack of consensus on form and content, and, especially, the diversity of texts that fall under the neoclassical label.

The Neoclassical Code

In assessing the values and style of French neoclassical tragedy, we must begin by pointing out that the term *neoclassical* was not used by those to whom it is now applied. In fact, the *neo-* as a gesture of revival or resuscitation does not apply in the French characterization of the period. Rather, the choice of the term *classique* for this vein of tragedy differentiates the French tragic corpus from the Greek and Roman *antique*, whose oftentimes coarse and brutal depictions proved to be challenging models for seventeenth-century playwrights to adopt and adapt (see Norman). The authors associated with this genre never thought of themselves as *classiques*, or as neoclassical; rather, they chose to advance a form with a distinct tradition and feel—*la tragédie régulière*.

When playwrights and theorists speak of tragedy's "regularity," they are referring above all to its respect of the three "unities" of time, place, and action. These principles were said to be drawn straight from the *Poetics*, but in fact the seventeenth-century theorists, influenced by sixteenth-century Italian interpolations of Aristotle, creatively redrew the lines of the genre. An overarching goal advanced by French authors of tragic poetics was that respect for the unities fostered the audience's sense of illusion. The theory hinged on the idea that the more invested in the theatrical action spectators were —that is, the more mimetic it was—the more viewers would experience the positive effects of fear and pity. In contrast to the implausibility and temporal unpredictability of irregular theater such as tragicomedies, neoclassical poetics insisted that the five-act plot should track the audience's sense of belief by presenting intrigues that conform to their understanding of a historical period and action (*vraisemblance externe*) and fortify their sense of illusion (*vraisemblance interne*). To do so, the plot should stay as close to real time as possible, only covering at most one day, as the clock ticks down toward the dénouement over the course of the five acts. Racine is considered to be the master of regular tragedy in his embrace of a twelve-hour clock where "one day" means from dawn to dusk, as in *Iphigénie*, which begins at daybreak in Agamemnon's tent and ends in the evening with a sacrifice at the altar. Corneille, in contrast, is recalcitrant to constriction; he is known for relishing action-packed plots, where the multiple feats of his protagonists press up against the limits of twenty-four hours, as in *Le Cid*, in which the hero duels his beloved's father in the afternoon, battles the invading Moors at night, and enters into a second duel with a rival the next morning.

As for the unity of place, Aristotle does not mention it. It is a norm developed in the early modern era in the belief that just as a spectator's sense of illusion would be thwarted by excessive changes in time, so would a transformation of setting break the audience's focus from one act to the next. In his 1640 tragedy *Horace*, Corneille is once again at pains to adhere to this limitation. In deference to the one-location stage, the king of Rome arrives at the home of the eponymous hero to congratulate him for his military accomplishments, a visit that incurred the indignation of seventeenth-century critical sticklers, who deemed it entirely implausible and a poor conformity to the rule: everyone knows kings summon their subjects to the throne; they do not stop by for an unannounced visit. Here again, Racine stands as the virtuoso in the aesthetics of constriction. His stage captures so effectively the sense of *huis clos* ("no exit") associated with neoclassical poetics, especially in his predilection for staging the plot in pressure-filled royal antechambers. *Britannicus* and *Bérénice* are emblematic of the closed fixity of Racine's stage, as is the Ottoman harem in *Bajazet* or the royal tent in *Iphigénie*. In contrast, Corneille, despite the criticism he received for *Horace*, continued to push the limits of conformity to the rules, adopting the *palais à volonté* ("infinite palace"), a loosely defined location that allows conspirators to plot their rebellion in the same space where the emperor laments the weight of his power.

Finally, unity of action, sometimes referred to as the "unity of peril," is derived most closely among the three from Aristotle. A tragic plot should have a distinct beginning, middle, and end, resulting in a cohesive action. It should not veer off into tangents or intervals that slow the advancement of the plot toward its unraveling or dénouement. A tragic plot should prize a simplicity of action. The archetypal example of neoclassical minimalism is Racine's *Bérénice*, whose plot was based on a single quotation by the historian Suetonius: "Titus reginam Berenicen, cui etiam nuptias pollicitus ferebatur, statim ab Urbe dimisit invitus invitam" 'Titus, who passionately loved Berenice and who was widely thought to have promised to marry her, sent her from Rome, in spite of himself and in spite of herself, in the early days of his empire' (Racine, "La préface" 450). This model of condensing the theatrical plot to its barest and most emotional elements has turned Racine into the exemplar of the neoclassical aesthetic, yet a closer look at the entirety of his eleven-tragedy corpus reveals far more variation and experimentation than literary history has recognized.[11]

Above all, in defining the tragedy of the neoclassical era, playwrights and theorists of the seventeenth century stress the dignity and elevation of the genre. Corneille offers the following definition: "La dignité de la tragédie demande quelque grand intérêt d'Etat, ou quelque passion plus noble et plus mâle que l'amour, telles que sont l'ambition ou la vengeance, et veut donner à craindre des malheurs plus grands que la perte d'une maitresse" 'The dignity of tragedy demands a great matter of state, or a passion more noble and more virile than love, such as ambition or vengeance, and that provokes a fear of afflictions greater than that of losing a lover' (*Les trois discours* 124; our trans.). The playwright deems a tale of love without a crisis of the public realm insufficiently perilous or grave to deserve the tragic label. Although the rise of Racine in the second generation of neoclassicism brings a shift toward increased focus on gallantry and a more natural portrayal of flawed heroes, his characters are still models of noble grandeur. Erich Auerbach describes the men and women who inhabit the world portrayed in neoclassical tragedy as evincing a particular sense of superiority: “Being a prince is much rather a posture, an ‘attitude,’ than a practical function” (377). The population of French tragedy is usually confined to the highest spheres of society, dwelling on the immediate entourage of the king or character associated with sovereign power.

Although Romantic detractors of neoclassical tragedy will fault it for a blind submission to Aristotelian principles, a closer look reveals skepticism toward those precepts even in the heyday of the genre. For instance, Corneille openly doubts the effectiveness of catharsis in his reflections on tragedy’s effects, and Racine makes no mention of the Aristotelian effects but insists on the dignity essential to the genre when offering a definition of tragedy: “[I]l suffit que tout s’y ressente de cette tristesse majestueuse qui fait tout le plaisir de la tragédie” ‘It is enough for [tragedy] to provoke the feeling of that majestic sadness that creates all the pleasure of tragedy’ (“La préface” 450).

Tragedy’s New Chronologies

Because of the centrality of court dynamics within tragic plots, literary historians have emphasized the singular influence of the Académie Française, an institution founded and funded by the monarchy, in dictating the terms of neoclassical poetics. Our volume seeks to understand the evolution of tragedy within a broader context by tying the development of the neoclassical aesthetic more closely to the bloody religious wars (1562–1629) that tore France apart in the sixteenth century and by considering it in relation to other European literatures. A guiding principle of our approach is to resist walling off the Grand Siècle as a self-contained French historical moment. In reaching across the sixteenth-, seventeenth-, and eighteenth-century divides, we are better able both to recognize the complex role played by religion in early modern France and to grasp more accurately how neoclassical tragedy served to revisit and complicate earlier humanistic ideals of free will and mastery.

Our volume arrives, therefore, at a time when the study of neoclassical tragedy calls for wider-angle analytical methods than the narrower interpretative strategies employed by previous generations of scholars. Drawing from the dynamic, eclectic fields of comparative literature, performance studies, gender studies, and the digital humanities, the authors invite teachers and students to redraw the lines that have traditionally delimited the neoclassical genre.

Despite the long-held polarities that pit neoclassicism against the modern, the baroque, the rococo, or the romantic, we take seriously the suggestion Jean Rousset was already making in 1953 that between the baroque and the neoclassical the difference is only a matter of lighting (*La littérature* 7). In the last decade, we have seen scholars work with renewed effort to highlight the "classico-baroque" (Merlin-Kajman, *L'animal*) or the "French trauerspiel" (Bjørnstad and Ibbett) integral to neoclassicism.[12]

For influential playwrights like Rotrou, Tristan L'Hermite, and Mairet, neoclassical tragedy was a literary form always in flux from one play to the next; this is true as well for Corneille and Racine, the genre's most eminent practitioners. Is Racine more neoclassical than Corneille? As we will see throughout the volume's contributions, they are differently neoclassical, for the category is permeable enough to envelop them both. Neither playwright offered a decorporealized theater of talking heads, pace the Romantics, and for both the body plays an essential role in the performance of the tragic (Guyot). Thus, when d'Aubignac asserts that on the neoclassical stage "Parler c'est agir" 'To speak is to act,' his attention to rhetoric and versification should not obscure the ways in which playwrights created hybrid works permeated by multiple cultural forces, fashions, and trends (d'Aubignac 407; our trans.).

Although Corneille authored thirty-seven plays between *Mélite* in 1629 and his last tragedy, *Suréna*, in 1674, his renown as a great tragedian stems from the era of his tetralogy, the four plays published in quick succession between 1637 and 1643. Today they stand as models of French tragic production: *Le Cid* (1637), *Horace* (1640), *Cinna* (1643), and *Polyeucte* (1643). From these tragedies, the key neoclassical notions of the "Cornelian hero," the "Cornelian dilemma," and "Cornelian glory" were forged, terms familiar to generations of French schoolchildren, even those who have not read the plays. First among these canonical works is *Le Cid*, a play notorious for breaking the rules. In fact, *Le Cid*—Corneille's most read and taught play on North American college campuses—was published as a tragicomedy before the playwright relabeled it a tragedy in the 1648 edition of his complete works and in editions thereafter (Bilis). Yet *Le Cid*'s protagonist, Rodrigue, has come to embody the Cornelian neoclassical tragic hero: a man torn between two impossible positions but who chooses honor and glory over the satisfaction of personal desires.[13] For its fluctuations in category of genre, its polemics, and its enduring success,

Le Cid stands as an ideal case study for analyzing the deep imbrication of political and artistic debates in the Richelieu era. The play's famous *querelle* ("quarrel"), in which acrimonious pamphlets vehemently attacked or defended the wildly popular play, attests to the stakes Corneille and other playwrights faced as they challenged tragic precepts and the authority of the ancients—at least as they were interpreted by the Académie Française. We have therefore included several essays devoted to *Le Cid*, each one helping teachers and students grapple with the complicated legacy of this irregular exemplar of neoclassical tragedy.

In thinking about the role *Le Cid* played in shaping subsequent tragic productions, Faith Beasley's scholarship and an earlier MLA Options for Teaching volume have engaged us to look beyond the halls of the Académie Française to consider the impact of how female audiences received the play and participated in the *querelle du Cid* (Beasley, *Salons*, *Options*). Our volume thus acknowledges the imprint of salonnières such as the Marquise de Rambouillet and Madeleine de Scudéry in the formation of French literary culture and the creation of a public sphere beyond the royal court. Women such as these were integral to shaping the key poetic notion of *bienséance*, a sense of decorum within the language and action of tragedy. The playwrights of neoclassical France knew that to be successful, they needed to write for the polished and polite society of Paris, who expected a display of refined gallantry onstage: the true arbiters of *vraisemblance* and *bienséance* were the esteemed women of the salons who did not have to memorize the poetic treatises to discern the all-important *bon goût* (good taste) necessary for a tragedy to succeed.

The playwrights, as well as many of the learned members of the Académie, frequented the salons as they moved between the royal court, royal societies, and the Parisian *hôtels* (large aristocratic residences). This attention to networks reflects recent developments in scholarship that attempt to account for the complexity surrounding the genesis and reception of artworks. Just as the image of the isolated genius has been supplanted by more nuanced conceptions of subjectivity and authorship, so the idea of the text as the expression of a singular nation has been complicated by increased awareness of global contact and influence, aspects that essays in this volume explore through postcolonial francophone adaptations of these works.

We are convinced that despite the sense of irreducible strangeness a student might feel when first encountering French neoclassical tragedy, its piercing relevance to our own troubled and transitional times quickly becomes apparent when the corpus is placed within a framework that speaks to an audience of scholars, undergraduates, and graduates reflective of the diversity and breadth of the Modern Language Association's membership and critical approaches. Our position as teachers of French language and literature in the United States allows us to productively assess the gulf that separates neoclassical tragedy's prominent status in French classrooms from its relative absence on this side of the Atlantic, where most students have never heard of the genre's leading playwrights. We have deliberately geared our volume in a different direction from the many pedagogical editions published in France by French presses that either rely too strongly on patriotic readings of the neoclassical masterpieces or assume previous knowledge of the genre's foundational texts. In so doing, we hope to have established a bidirectional conversation between French literary specialists and nonspecialists that will address these texts against the grain and open this compellingly complex corpus to new perspectives and audiences.

We have grouped the volume's essays into five categories, described below. The astute reader will note, however, that there are many blurred boundaries and cross-pollinations between the sections. This lack of clearly defined, autonomous approaches is itself a testimony to the vibrant dynamism that characterizes current efforts to engage a wide variety of students, including, and perhaps especially, those students whose previous exposure to neoclassical literature, French history, and tragedy and the theater more generally, might be minimal. The contributions recognize this lack of familiarity (and even perhaps interest) and provide detailed and inventive methods for overcoming it and bringing students to an appreciation not just of early modern tragedy but of artistic production and analysis more generally. Indeed, the wide range of theoretical and pedagogical approaches to the material that the authors of the essays propose serves to illuminate these works' poetic distinctiveness and historical context all while underscoring the ways in which they continue to speak to twenty-first-century questions, students, and audiences.

Just as the pedagogical and theoretical approaches on display here defy strict classifications, so the works discussed stretch beyond any narrow conception of neoclassical tragedy. Certainly, the two major figures of Corneille and Racine recur most often, in part because of the immense richness of their works and in part because of their accessibility in recent editions and in translation. Yet, as several of the essays remind us, these writers did not work in isolation—far from it!—and neoclassical tragedy itself did not spring, spontaneously and undefiled, from Aristotle's *Poetics.*

The essays that follow place the standbys of the genre—Corneille's *Le Cid*, Racine's *Phèdre*—in a productive dialogue with other works, authors, theoreticians, and artistic forms. They also expand the frame in which these works have traditionally been considered, both temporally, by enlarging the scope of analysis to include the sixteenth and eighteenth centuries, and geographically, by noting the impact of global concerns on the development of the genre and by tracing the influence and reach of neoclassical tragedy beyond the "hexagon" of mainland France and into francophone areas, past and present.

In broadening the category of the neoclassical, we have chosen to retain the term rather than speak of early modern tragedy in general or enter into often arbitrary designations of baroque versus neoclassical tragedy. If we had opted for either of these alternate designations, we believe the essay submissions would differ from those we have collected here, which all address in one form or another the codes, conversations, and contexts that saw the rise of the "regular" form of tragedy, so defining of France's golden age. In short, to group the diverse and wide-ranging essays together under the label of neoclassical tragedy is a gesture meant to emphasize the pedagogical benefits that stem from applying an elastic definition of the genre. Through this enlarged framework, we hope the essays expand the options available to instructors who wish to integrate these works into their syllabi, whether in a graduate course taught in French, an undergraduate literature survey, or a course on early modern intellectual history. Where possible, the authors of the essays have indicated where translations into English are available; they have also provided ways to modify the material for a variety of audiences and institutions.

Tragic Poetics: Revising Frameworks

The first section of this volume is devoted to restoring some of the dynamism and uncertainty that surrounded the poetics of neoclassical tragedy. These essays invite a reflection on the anachronistic term *neoclassical*, recasting the works of the period as an ongoing conversation with classical models rather than a simple imitation of them, especially as the authors of the time sought to adjust to the tastes and expectations of their French audiences. Larry Norman and David Wray propose an approach to Racine's tragic masterpiece *Phèdre* that enables instructors and students to explore the rich intertextual conversations informing the play and its more recent adaptations. Tracing the implicit and explicit influences of Euripides, Seneca, and Ovid on Racine's work leads students to contemplate the ways in which stories and performances are adapted through time in order to remain alive, provocative, and relevant. John D. Lyons also centers his essay on Racine's *Phèdre*, using it along with Corneille's *Le Cid* as an invitation to students to consider that most essential component of tragic drama: fate. Leading students through a series of activities that draw attention to the use of language connoting fate and destiny by the various characters, Lyons points to the ambiguity surrounding this concept on the early modern stage, including the ways in which it resonates with ongoing debates concerning predestination and free will. Jeffrey N. Peters also alludes to the intellectual turbulence of the period in his astute analysis of place and location in early modern tragic texts. Noting that the unity of location recommended in early modern dramatic theory was the only unity not explicitly mentioned by Aristotle, Peters ties the seventeenth century's theatrical inventiveness concerning location to the evolution of early modern conceptions of space, place, and the cosmos. Faith E. Beasley's contribution offers a road map for introducing students to one of the founding moments of the articulation of neoclassical tragedy: the literary quarrel that followed the tremendous success of Corneille's *Le Cid*, first performed in 1637. Beasley provides a welcome reminder of the crucial role that women played in the play's composition and reception, allowing Corneille to articulate a vision of theater based more upon the pleasure of his audience than on strict adherence to rules that, Beasley suggests, were elaborated in no small part to police precisely the female unruliness on display in the play itself. Andrea Frisch's essay also gestures toward an unexpected source for the seventeenth century's unique tragic aesthetic, based on regularity and restraint, provocatively suggesting that it can be attributed, at least in part, to the influence of the traumatic sixteenth-century Wars of Religion that brought chaos and uncertainty throughout the kingdom. Frisch guides students through a comparative study of Jacques Grévin's *César*, first performed in 1561 on the eve of the wars, and Scudéry's 1634 *Mort de César*, helping them see how the open-ended debates concerning political authority in the former are replaced in the latter by the respect for authority that would become characteristic of absolutism, and how these ideological shifts manifest themselves in theatrical practice. In so doing, she invites students to reflect on the complex relation between history and literature as well as the specificities and limitations of each. Juliette Cherbuliez's essay seizes upon one of the most characteristic strictures of neoclassical tragic poetics—the relegation of violent acts to offstage—to lead students through an examination of hypotyposis, or the description of images in words. Through a series of interactive and provocative exercises geared toward all levels of learners in a wide range of classes, Cherbuliez's students gain an appreciation of the difficulty of verbally representing violent events; consequently, they acquire an ear for the poetry and emotion that characterize such scenes in Racine's theater.

The Performance of Tragedy: On Stage and in the Classroom

As many of the authors in the first section note, French neoclassical tragedy was not meant to be read but staged. The essays in the second and third parts of this volume concentrate on the genre as it was, and is, performed, with much attention paid to the pedagogical opportunities that performance affords to a wide range of classes and students. Like Cherbuliez, Laurence Marie takes as her point of departure the neoclassical rule that violence and extreme events should not be shown but rather recounted verbally. She invites students to consider the evolution of performance styles in the seventeenth and eighteenth centuries, drawing upon theoretical interventions, indications within the dramatic texts themselves, and the visual arts. The result is a historically informed approach that leads students to the realization, as Marie puts it, that realism in performance is not necessarily "the summit of the art," but rather one approach among many, and that "suggestion and stylization may produce a similar, even stronger, effect on the audience." Blair Hoxby similarly focuses on performative theory and practice, using as the base of his course not only contemporary performances of early modern theater and opera but also secondary sources that allow students to appreciate the stylistic and theoretical decisions that render these works living and evolving entities. Jennifer Tamas fully exploits the performative aspects of neoclassical tragedy by drawing students' attention to the centrality, and complexity, of avowal scenes in Racinian drama. She then proposes a series of activities meant to encourage students to interpret these scenes as part of their final projects, integrating the knowledge imparted by primary and secondary sources into a performance informed by decisions concerning stagecraft and twenty-first-century culture.

The next two essays in this section focus on stagecraft in order to expand instructors' and students' knowledge of the wide variety of theatrical performances available to seventeenth-century authors and audiences. John Boitano and Louise Thomas concentrate on the uniquely French *tragédie en musique* as a reminder that the French stage was not populated solely by the great poetic and text-centered tragedies but took root alongside, and in response to, the baroque explosion of music, dance, and song conveyed by this neglected genre. Likewise, Hélène Visentin provides the resources necessary for instructors to introduce students, and themselves, to the exciting and innovative genre of machine plays (*pièces à machines*) that incorporated the scientific advances of the time to enchant seventeenth-century Parisian audiences. Racine in particular conceived his austere dramaturgy in part as a response to the elaborate stagecraft of the *tragédie en musique* and the *pièces à machines* that were so popular during the period. These essays demonstrate that devoting class time to these marginalized genres serves to elucidate the theatrical context in which neoclassical tragedy evolved and flourished all while captivating twenty-first-century students whose sensibilities have been shaped by multimedia and special effects.

The three essays in part 3 chart the expansion of neoclassical tragedy beyond the borders of continental France. Julia Prest presents a variety of pedagogical exercises and resources, including online databases, that expose students to the presence of these works, and others, in the colonial context of eighteenth-century Saint-Domingue. Her approach allows students to explore a variety of sources and texts, offering them credit not merely for the finished product of their research but also for the process of carrying out their project and identifying the questions—answered and unanswered—that it raises. Ellen Welch's contribution centers on twenty-first-century adaptations of the neoclassical corpus as a way of calling attention to how decisions concerning staging, casting, and the text itself transform the plays for current audiences and current concerns. She offers as a case study a multicultural adaptation of Racine's *Andromaque*, presented by the Collectif La Palmera, which transports and translates the play to new audiences inside and outside France. Finally, Sylvaine Guyot explores the Congolese director-choreographer Faustin Linyekula's recent adaptations of perhaps the most text-centered work of the corpus, Racine's *Bérénice*. Linyekula's stagings provide the opportunity for instructors and students to consider the relevance of *Bérénice*, and the neoclassical tragic corpus more generally, in a postcolonial, multicultural world.

Tragedy and Politics: Between the Ancien Régime and the Present

Another distinctive feature of French neoclassical tragedy is its subject matter. Unlike comedy, which presents characters and situations that audience members might reasonably recognize or encounter in their own lives, tragedy focuses on kings, queens, and courts, charting the difficult articulation of royal power. The essays in part 4 offer ways of helping students appreciate the stakes involved in the struggles presented on the early modern stage while encouraging them to make informed connections to the political world today.

Marc Bizer's essay takes students through a consideration of human nature and free will by building a provocative and original comparison of the Abbé de Thélème in Rabelais's sixteenth-century masterpiece *Gargantua* and the troubled Trézène of Racine's *Phèdre*. Drawing on the invocation of the maxim "Fais ce que voudras," or "Do what you will," in both texts, Bizer's juxtaposition serves to complicate the narrative that equates modernity with a unidirectional, progressive growth in human autonomy and reason. The questions at the heart of the discussions that he provokes in his class—are humans essentially reasonable creatures, and do they really possess free will?—are adroitly linked to current dilemmas both in government and in popular culture.

Toby Wikström's essay reaches beyond the canonical tragic corpus to introduce instructors and students to lesser-known dramas that attempt to stage some of the situations and issues stemming from early modern global encounters. Through a reading of Nicolas Chrétien des Croix's *Les Portugais infortunés* (*The Unfortunate Portuguese*) and the anonymous *Tragédie française d'un more cruel envers son seigneur nommé Riviery, gentilhomme espagnol, sa demoiselle et ses enfants* (*French Tragedy of a Moor's Cruelty toward His Lord, the Spanish Nobleman Riviery, and His Lady and Children*), Wikström allows students to appreciate the early modern struggle to depict and make sense of encounters with cultural and racial difference. In the process, he reminds us all of the profound effect of early modern globalization on French cultural production, which arguably persisted long after global tragedies ceded the stage to their neoclassical successors.

Sylvie Romanowski's exploration of *Britannicus* focuses on desire and power as a means of appreciating Racine's work as a commentary, both critical and descriptive, of ancien régime court society. Her essay illustrates how this analysis can be used as a key element of a course on the emergence of Enlightenment ideals where students reflect on notions of sovereignty in a monarchical versus a democratic context, underscoring the relevance of such questions in contemporary European and American political life. Jeffrey Leichman's contribution explores the influence of neoclassical tragic conceptions of kingship, here modeled by Corneille's *Cinna*, on Aimé Césaire's 1964 dramatization of the Haitian revolution,

La tragédie du roi Christophe. Leichman's students are encouraged to make comparisons with English-language tragedies, especially those of Shakespeare, that recount the demise of the monarch. Students are also led to appreciate the way in which the plays' poetics and performance clarify the characters' power struggles and illuminate "the power of language and the language of power."

Explorations in Theory and Technology

While all the essays in this volume demonstrate innovative and creative ways to connect students with early modern French tragedy, the essays in the final section approach the corpus through theoretical lenses and technological and pedagogical innovations that might have been inconceivable only a few decades ago. Jennifer Row's course introduces students both to seventeenth-century drama and to queer theory, encouraging them through secondary sources and class exercises to see the links between the two. Indeed, although the term *queer* is clearly anachronistic to the early modern period, in many ways it serves as a helpful and even accurate description of the ambiguity and uncertainty surrounding identity, power, and desire at the heart of the tragic corpus. Meanwhile, informed by the engaged pedagogy of bell hooks and Paolo Freire, as well as performance and affect theory, Anna Rosensweig provides a model instructors can use to enhance students' involvement with neoclassical tragedies by encouraging them to chart, and eventually share, their emotional reactions to the plays. By explicitly acknowledging the passions that these works were meant to excite in their audiences, Rosensweig challenges the common assumption that students are uninterested in the material and that reason must necessarily take precedence over emotion. Theresa Varney Kennedy and David Jortner illustrate how students can actively engage with the foundational *querelle du* Cid by transforming this vicious and prolonged polemic into a courtroom drama. By enacting the roles of Corneille, his defenders, his attackers, and even his judges, students are led to a deeper comprehension of the issues and stakes involved in arguments over literature and its influence. Finally, Hélène Bilis guides readers through the creative use of digital humanities in the early modern theater classroom. Thoughtfully encouraging students not only to use digital humanities but to reflect on the advantages and disadvantages of digital methods, Bilis goes on to provide concrete lesson plans and exercises that take full advantage of the online resources available to instructors and students today, including the registers of the Comédie-Française. She demonstrates that, undertaken with care and reflection, digital humanities can greatly enrich student engagement and understanding and, moreover, that the French neoclassical corpus is particularly well suited to such an approach.

Notes

1. For precise figures representing the box office success of neoclassical tragedies versus other genres staged at the Comédie-Française throughout the eighteenth century, see the Comédie-Française Registers Project, a digital resource that allows users to consult the attendance records and programming of all plays performed between 1680 and 1791 (cfregisters.org).

2. Stendhal goes on to give the following definition of the seventeenth-century aesthetic: "Imiter aujourd'hui Sophocles et Euripide, et prétendre que ces imitations ne feront pas bailler le Français du dix-neuvième siècle, c'est du classicisme" 'To imitate today Sophocles and Euripides and to say that these imitations will not make a nineteenth-century Frenchman yawn, that's neoclassicism' (44; our trans.).

3. Robert Brasillach's 1938 biography *Corneille* remains an important contribution to Corneille scholarship (it was reedited by Fayard in 2006) even as its celebration of human willpower is darkened by its author's collaboration with the Nazi regime in France, a crime for which he was tried and executed in 1946.

4. Readers of French will find the 1999 Flammarion edition, with a helpful dossier of documents to explain and situate Corneille's writings, particularly useful.

5. "Cette pièce fut mon coup d'essai, et elle n'a garde d'être dans les Règles, puisque je ne savais pas alors qu'il y en eut" 'This play was a first attempt, and I paid no attention to following the rules, because I did not know then that there were rules to follow' ("Examen de Mélite" 5; our trans.).

6. For francophone classrooms, see Civardi, which groups the thirty essays written during the polemic over Corneille's play, including an excellent edition of the two versions (the one published and the one that remained in manuscript) of the Académie Française's official response, *Les sentiments de l'Académie française sur la Tragi-Comédie du* Cid (*The Academy's Opinion Concerning the Tragicomedy* The Cid).

7. For an analysis of the reception of Aristotle's poetics in seventeenth-century dramaturgical circles, especially with regards to the dynamic of pity and fear, and Corneille's critique of catharsis, see Ibbett, pp. 60–97.

8. Both Chapelain and d'Aubignac penned their own tragedies, but neither won sustained success with their creative works, although their theoretical writings carried immense weight and encapsulate the academic investment in defining the proper rules to create the proper effects.

9. This interpretation of tragedy would be reinforced during the nineteenth century through the engagement of Schelling and Hegel with tragedy; see Goldhill.

10. The novel won the Prix Médicis in 2015.

11. Campbell expresses skepticism at the notion of a particular "Racinian tragic" that would be cohesive and defining of his works. He insists instead on the importance of understanding each tragedy in its specific context.

12. Merlin-Kajman writes: "N'importe quel spécialiste de Corneille sait à quel point il a fait œuvre originale en matière de poétique, et à quel point, prenant bien des risques, il a placé l'*extraordinaire* au cœur de son théâtre" 'Any Corneille specialist knows to what extent his works were original in terms of poetics, and to what extent, taking many risks, he placed the *extraordinary* at the heart of his theater' ("Un siècle" 163; our trans.).

13. For an effective historicization of the notion see Lyons, "Le mythe," pp. 433–48.

Works Cited

Akalaitis, Joanne, director. *Phèdre*. Translated by Paul Schmidt, Sept.-Oct. 2002, Court Theatre, Chicago.

Albanese, Ralph. *Corneille à l'école républicaine: Du mythe héroïque à l'imaginaire politique en France 1800–1950*. L'Harmattan, 2008.

———. *Racine à l'école républicaine, ou les enjeux socio-politiques de la tragédie classique (1800–1950)*. L'Harmattan, 2013.

Auerbach, Erich. *Mimesis: The Representation of Reality in Western Literature*. Translated by Willard R. Trask, Princeton UP, 1953.

Azoulai, Nathalie. *Titus n'aimait pas Bérénice*. Edition P.O.L., 2015.

Barthes, Roland. *On Racine*. Translated by Richard Howard, Octagon Books, 1977.

———. *Sur Racine*. Editions du Seuil, 1963.

Beasley, Faith, E. *Salons, History, and the Creation of Seventeenth-Century France: Mastering Memory*. Ashgate, 2006.

———, editor. *Teaching Seventeenth- and Eighteenth-Century French Women Writers*. Modern Language Association of America, 2011.

Bilis, Hélène. "Corneille aux États-Unis, ou quel 'auteur classique' pour les campus américains." *Appropriations de Corneille*, Centre d'Études et de Recherche Éditer/Interpréter, EA 3229, http://publis-shs.univ-rouen.fr/ceredi/index.php?id=847.

Bjørnstad, Hall, and Katherine Ibbett, editors. *Walter Benjamin's Hypothetical French Trauerspiel*. Special issue of *Yale French Studies*, vol. 124, 2013.

Blocker, Déborah. *Instituer un 'art': Politiques du théâtre dans la France du premier XVIIe siècle*. Champion, 2009.

Braider, Christopher. *Indiscernible Counterparts: The Invention of the Text in French Classical Drama*. U of North Carolina P, 2002.

———. *The Matter of Mind: Reason and Experience in the Age of Descartes*. U of Toronto P, 2012.

Brasillach, Robert. *Corneille*. 1938. Fayard, 2006.

Campbell, John. *Questioning Racinian Tragedy*. U of North Carolina P, 2005.

Chapelain, Jean. "Lettre sur la règle des vingt-quatre heures." *Opuscules critiques*, by Chapelain, edited by Alfred C. Hunter and Anne Duprat, Droz, 2007, pp. 222–34.

Cherbuliez, Juliette. *In the Wake of Medea*. Fordham UP, 2020.

Civardi, Jean-Marc. *La querelle du* Cid *(1637–1638): Edition critique intégrale.* Honoré Champion, 2004.
Corneille, Pierre. "Examen de Mélite." *Œuvres complètes*, edited by Georges Couton, vol. 1, Gallimard-La Pléiade, 1980.
———. *Les trois discours sur le poème dramatique.* Edited by Marc Escola and Bénédicte Louvat, Flammarion, 1999.
d'Aubignac, François Hédelin, abbé. *La pratique du théâtre.* 1657. Edited by Hélène Baby, Honoré Champion, 2001.
Derrida, Jacques. "Force et signification." *L'écriture et la différence*, Seuil, 1967, pp. 9–49.
Diderot, Denis. *Le paradoxe sur le comédien.* Editions Mille et une Nuits, 1999.
Eagleton, Terry. *Sweet Violence: The Idea of the Tragic.* Blackwell, 2002.
Felski, Rita, editor. *Rethinking Tragedy.* Johns Hopkins UP, 2008.
Foley, Helene P., and Jean E. Howard, editors. *PMLA*, vol. 129, no. 4, Oct. 2014, pp. 617–33.
Forestier, Georges. *La tragédie française: Passions tragiques et règles classiques.* Armand Colin, 2010.
Goldhill, Simon. "The Ends of Tragedy: Schelling, Hegel, and Oedipus." *PMLA*, vol. 129, no. 4, Oct. 2014, pp. 634–48.
Goodkin, Richard E. *Birth Marks: The Tragedy of Primogeniture in Pierre Corneille, Thomas Corneille, and Jean Racine.* U of Pennsylvania P, 2000.
———. *How Do I Know Thee? Theatrical and Narrative Cognition in Seventeenth-Century France.* Northwestern UP, 2015.
———. *The Tragic Middle: Racine, Aristotle, Euripides.* U of Wisconsin P, 1991.
Greenberg, Mitchell. *Racine: From Ancient Myth to Tragic Modernity.* U of Minnesota P, 2010.
Guyot, Sylvaine. *Racine et le corps tragique.* PU de France, 2014.
Harris, Joseph. *Inventing the Spectator: Subjectivity and the Theatrical Experience in Early Modern France.* Oxford UP, 2014.
Hoxby, Blair. *What Was Tragedy? Theory and the Early Modern Canon.* Oxford UP, 2015.
Hugo, Victor. *La préface de* Cromwell. Flammarion, 2020.
Ibbett, Katherine. *Compassion's Edge: Fellow-Feeling and Its Limits in Early Modern France.* U of Pennsylvania P, 2018.
Jaoui, Agnès, director. *Le goût des autres.* Pathé, 2000.
Kushner, Tony. *The Illusion.* Broadway Play Publishing, 2003.
Linyekula, Faustin, director. *Bérénice.* By Jean Racine, produced by Comédie-Française / Théâtre de Gennevilliers / Studios Kabako, 26 Mar.–7 May 2009, Studio-Théâtre of the Comédie-Française, Paris.
Lyons, John D. *Kingdom of Disorder: The Theory of Tragedy in Classical France.* Purdue UP, 1999.
———. "Le mythe du héros cornélien." *Revue d'histoire littéraire de la France*, vol. 107, no. 2, 2007, pp. 433–48.
Mazuy, Patricia. *Saint-Cyr.* United International Pictures, 2000.
Merlin-Kajman, Hélène. *L'animal ensorcelé: Traumatismes, littérature, transitionnalité.* Ithaque, 2016.
———. "Un siècle classico-baroque?" *Dix-septième siècle*, vol. 2, no. 223, 2004, pp. 163–72.

Mouawad, Wajdi. *Une chienne*. Actes Sud, 2016.

Norman, Larry. *The Shock of the Ancient: Literature and History in Early Modern France*. U of Chicago P, 2011.

Numa, Nono. *Jénéral Rodrig*. Edision Bon Nouvel, 1975.

Racine, Jean. *Œuvres complètes, tome I: Théâtre-Poésie*. Edited by Georges Forestier, Gallimard-La Pléiade, 1999.

———. "La préface de *Bérénice*." *Œuvres complètes*, pp. 450–53.

Reiss, Timothy J. *Toward Dramatic Illusion: Theatrical Technique and Meaning from Hardy to Horace*. Yale UP, 1971.

———. *Tragedy and Truth: Studies in the Development of a Renaissance and Neoclassical Discourse*. Yale UP, 1980.

Rivette, Jacques, director. *L'amour fou*. Cocinor, 1968.

Rousseau, Jean-Jacques. *Lettre à d'Alembert sur les spectacles*. Edited by Marc Buffet, Gallimard-Flammarion, 2003.

Rousset, Jean. *Forme et signification: Essais sur les structures littéraires de Corneille à Claudel*. José Corti, 1962.

———. *La littérature de l'âge baroque en France: Circé et le paon*. José Corti, 1953.

Stendhal. *Racine et Shakespeare*. 1823–25. Le Divan, 1929.

Stone, Harriet. *The Classical Model: Literature and Knowledge in Seventeenth-Century France*. Cornell UP, 1996.

———. *Royal DisClosure: Problematics of Representation in French Classical Tragedy*. Summa Publications, 1987.

Welch, Ellen R. *A Theater of Diplomacy: International Relations and the Performing Arts in Early Modern France*. U of Pennsylvania P, 2017.

Part I

Reframing Tragic Poetics

Larry F. Norman and David Wray

Racine among the Phaedras

What exactly do we mean by "neoclassical" in "French neoclassical tragedy"? How were Greek and Latin authors appropriated and transformed by early modern dramatists? To what degree do such creative adaptations reveal continuity or rupture with ancient tragedy? And what might these metamorphoses of dramatic forms, themes, and characters tell us today about the nature of the tragic and its winding evolution from antiquity to the present?

These are some of the key questions that the two authors, one a specialist of French literature and the other a scholar based in classics, tackled in a broadly interdisciplinary cotaught course focused on Jean Racine's masterpiece *Phèdre*. Designed to appeal to a broad group of undergraduate and graduate students from college majors and doctoral fields such as French, comparative literature, classics, English, and theater and performance studies, the course places the tragedy within a wide-ranging series of adaptations of the ancient myth, from its Greek and Latin sources to contemporary translations and stage adaptations.

Given the broad aims of a course grappling with the very definition of neoclassical theater as a space for reimagining ancient texts, why focus on a single play? First of all, the rich history of diverging versions of the Phaedra story, its essential seriality, makes it an exemplary text for a comparative approach: Racine's tragedy resonates more richly as one among many Phaedras. Secondly, the critical prominence and contemporary accessibility of *Phèdre* are unparalleled. Considered by Racine himself as an experiment testing (and affirming) the adaptability of Euripides in the modern world, the play has since its first performance generated intense critical reflection—from the encomiastic to the acidly polemical—concerning its emulation of the ancients. Celebrated in the Enlightenment, reviled by Romantics, reinvigorated by the moderns, *Phèdre* is one of the most often performed and most frequently translated of French early modern tragedies. And finally, in regard to student interest today, this tale of a woman's forbidden desire also presents a captivating work of theater raising provocative issues of sexuality, gender, violence, religion, and political power.

The authors taught the course in two iterations, first as an undergraduate course and then as a graduate seminar. In both cases the course was taught in English, with French readings available both in translation and, for students with reading knowledge of French, in the original language. The undergraduate and graduate versions were thus cross-listed in departments from French and classics to gender studies.

The undergraduate version focused almost entirely on primary literary readings. In addition to the main focus on Racine's version, these readings included three primary ancient sources: Euripides's *Hippolytus*, Ovid's epistolary poem "Phaedra to Hippolytus" in the *Heroides*, and Seneca's *Phaedra*. To provide early modern French tragic contextualization, the authors chose Corneille's *Le Cid* and *Œdipe* (the latter not available in English translation—but one of the authors made an unpublished English translation) as examples of the heroic style with which Racine is often contrasted. Racine's earlier *Andromaque*, also readily available in translation, offered a framework for probing Racine's rewriting of the ancients to create a modern tragedy of erotic passion, moral ambiguity, and political struggle. Rameau's *Phèdre et Hippolyte* opened up to class discussion a new medium, opera, as did—moving forward to the twentieth century—the film *Phaedra*, directed by Jules Dassin and set in postwar Greece, France, and England. A last text, Sarah Kane's controversially graphic play *Phaedra's Love*, brought class readings to the threshold of the twenty-first century.

For the graduate version, these comparative primary texts were complemented with a range of critical readings. These concentrated on the key issues that traversed both versions of the course: Greek and Roman sources, early modern neoclassical French adaptation and its reception, modern theatrical and cinematic versions, translations and translatability of Racine, and theatricality and performance.

Greek and Roman Sources

One of many advantages of *Phèdre* as the focus of a course of this kind lies in the interest and accessibility of the three principal Greco-Roman texts that Racine took as models and prototypes for his play at every level, from diction and theme to characterization and plot structure. By becoming familiar with Euripides's *Hippolytus*, Ovid's "Phaedra to Hippolytus," and Seneca's *Phaedra* before undertaking the act-by-act analysis of *Phèdre* that occupied the center of the course, students gained a measure of access to the pleasures and challenges of developing as readers of the eruditely allusive dramatic poem that is Racine's tragedy. They learned not only to recognize the presence of intertextual material but to make and support claims about the kinds of work such material is doing at a given point in the target text. While the Phaedras of antiquity occupied only a relatively small portion of the syllabus, nearly every class discussion featured one or more of them, not only as source models for *Phèdre* but also as artifacts for literary comparison. So that such comparisons could begin as early as possible, students were assigned a first read-through of *Phèdre* (in Wilbur's translation) as preparation for studying the Greco-Roman material.

Discussing the *Hippolytus* of Euripides, especially with *Phèdre* fresh in mind, facilitated an introduction to much of the knowledge base and many of the interpretive and contextual issues of the course. It also initiated a conversation that was already as much about Racine as it was about his ancient predecessors. The classical Athenian tragedy is an adaptation of preexisting literary and mythological material no less than the seventeenth-century French one. And Racine does not just imitate and refer to Euripides; he also resembles him, as a poet writing inside a tradition with a very long memory.

For example, when Phèdre begins her confession to her nurse, Œnone, by decrying how the goddess Aphrodite's malice wrecked the lives of her mother and sister (1.3.249–58), Racine is of course running a fairly close replay of his Euripidean model (*Hippolytus* 337–41). He is also, however, here as often, reaching back beyond Euripides into an archaic myth system he knew intimately through philological study. Aphrodite's undying grudge against the Sun, Helios, has its ultimate origin in a scene recounted in the *Odyssey*, where Hephaestus punishes his wife's adultery with Ares by trapping the pair in a golden bag and exposing them to the shaming laughter of the Olympians (8.266–366). The Phaedra myth is a sequel to this story: blaming Helios for spotting her furtive loves with his all-seeing eye and informing her husband, Aphrodite retaliates in kind by driving his female progeny, the solar princesses of Minoan Crete, into disastrous couplings. Pasiphae mates with a bull; Ariadne betrays her father for the young Theseus, who abandons her on an island; and now Phaedra in turn is racked by the vengeful goddess with desire for her stepson, a desire she finds irresistible and abominable in equal measure, and that in Racine's version she imagines as reddening the Sun's face with shame.

The Euripidean Phaedra clearly knows all this mythological material as traumatic family history. But, strangely enough (and this twist may be Euripides's invention), *Hippolytus* presents a public story in which the explicit object of Aphrodite's hatred is not Phaedra but Hippolytus, for his shunning of her cult. This dissonant coexistence of mythological variants is a not uncommon feature of Greco-Roman tragedy. Racine makes it a feature of his own tragedy when, just before she is about to learn from her husband's mouth that she has a rival for the love of his son, Phèdre mounts a desperate (but also petulant, elegiac, Ovidian) prayer to Venus in which she suddenly "remembers" the Euripidean version of her own story, urging the goddess to avenge herself on a man who refuses to worship at love's altar (3.2.813–23). In shaping mythopoetic erudition into a system of figures for psychological depth, Racine arguably outstripped the Greco-Roman depictions of Phèdre's passionately divided interiority and thereby made his heroine a predecessor for characters like Flaubert's Emma Bovary. A course outcome was to enable students to form opinions and arguments about literary historical and comparatist claims of just this kind.

The time allotted to Euripides's *Hippolytus* and its contexts could easily have been expanded. Issues of performance conventions and the social, cultural, and political role of fifth-century Attic tragedy were only briefly touched on, as were discussions of gender and laws governing incest and marriage. Class discussion also unpacked the implications of the fact that the *Hippolytus* we possess is Euripides's second version, composed after an unsuccessful original tragedy in which Phaedra aggressively defended the naturalness of erotic passion and the appropriateness of sexually pursuing her own stepson. In the version we possess, Euripides seems to have tasked himself with testing the limits of just how conventionally honorable an ethical disposition he could lend to a dramatic character who desires her stepson and, once rebuffed, falsely accuses him of raping her.

Ovid, conversely, seems to have tested the limits in the other direction, constructing a Phaedra maximally free of the constraints of shame, or rather using them as goads to a characteristically Ovidian kind of wicked pleasure. Mounting her case with breathtakingly specious rhetoric, the Phaedra of the *Heroides* makes dark threats and wild promises, pleads Love's irresistible divine power, offers her lifetime conjugal fidelity as a kind of second virginity for Hippolytus to deflower, presents Theseus as their common enemy, and even argues that public affection between stepmother and stepson, far from arousing suspicion, will be commended as evidence of a tender affection so rarely found in such relations.

One of the first salient features of "Phaedra to Hippolytus" (no doubt intricately intertextual with many lost versions of *Phaedra*), in the context of this course was how Ovid seems to have insinuated it into the plot of Euripides's second *Hippolytus*, as if to suggest a secret backdrop to that tragedy in which Phaedra, after leaving the stage and before writing the suicide letter accusing Hippolytus of raping her, wrote a first draft (Ovid's poem) making a bid for his love, only to realize its futility immediately upon rereading it. This complex Alexandrian allusive technique, where a later version presents itself as a revisionist correction of an earlier version or an alternative decision considered but rejected by a character, is of course an intertextual mode familiar to students through popular media. Recognizing it in Ovid offers an entryway into appreciating the similarly rich and subtle intertextualities of Racine's *Phèdre*. As with Euripides's version, Ovid's Phaedra raised an overabundance of classroom discussion threads on issues of gender and agency, political and social norms, and related questions, most of which reappeared later during the close reading of *Phèdre*.

Seneca's *Phaedra* is a tragic text that, as students quickly noticed, seems almost to beset the text of *Phèdre* like a guilty secret. Insistent as a structuring model, pervasive as a source text, Seneca is implicitly disavowed by Racine in his preface's claim to be following Euripides—followed by an unattributed citation of the Senecan Phaedra's prevaricating denouncement of Hippolytus for rape. And while Euripides's Phaedra had suicided at her play's midpoint, clearing the stage for a tragic agon between father and son, Seneca models a Phaedra who, like Racine's, lives on to speak both her passion and her detestation of it for five full acts, closing the play in grand operatic style by confessing her guilt and killing herself in public.

Racine's characters seem almost to interact with Seneca's version of their own stories as lived memory, expectation, or hidden desire. Near the end of her *aveu* (confession) to Hippolyte, for example—at the precise dramatic moment where Seneca's Hippolytus had grabbed her hair, pulled her neck back, and drawn his sword to kill her, only to throw it down in disgust and leave it for her to use in her fifth-act suicide—Phèdre first asks Hippolyte to draw his sword, as if to activate the Senecan model. Then, when he refuses, she hurls a shocking cry that breaks decorum ("donne" 'hand it over') and prompts Œnone to rein her mistress back in, as if containing her outburst of Senecan excess and reestablishing the smooth and stately order of Racinian poise. Studying *Phèdre*'s major ancient models and learning to discern their presence gives students, even when reading in translation, a sense of how Racine endows his characters with passionate interiorities that seethe beneath that poise and shudder across its surface.

Racine's Adaptation: Context and Reception

While reading the Greek and Roman versions, students thus briskly delved into the rich mine of comparisons and contrasts with Racine's *Phèdre*. Making sense of the French dramatist's rewriting within its historical and cultural moment, however, provided a new and bracing challenge. In this regard, a good place to start is Racine's own preface to the first edition of the play. The tensions inherent in Racine's description of his choices constitute a powerful motor for classroom discussion. As noted, in the first line of the preface, Racine claims to be inspired entirely by Euripides; as in the preface to his previous tragedy, *Iphigénie*, he praises the Greek tragedian throughout. And yet in the second line Racine immediately qualifies his stated debt to Euripides by acknowledging that he has "taken a somewhat different path" than his venerated predecessor. This deviation, he asserts, is required by the different moral and social norms of the modern Christian world (3).

Transforming the play to suit a contemporary audience, Racine affirms, requires two crucial modifications. Each of these proved effective prompts for classroom discussion, presentations, and papers. First, Racine claims that modern audiences would find shocking Phaedra's baseness in calumniating Hippolytus with the accusation of rape; hence the playwright's decision to place the false accusation in the mouth of Œnone. The next modification is considerably more radical than the first: it alters the entire dramatic structure and moral climate of the play. Claiming that a modern audience would find Hippolyte's emblematic trait in antiquity, his inflexible chastity, too admirably virtuous for the demands of tragedy, Racine justifies his invention of a forbidden love interest for Hippolyte in the character of Aricie.

Discussion can be organized around several rubrics. The first topics concern the fundamental principles of adaptation at play. In this regard, students can consider the relation between theory and practice, between a broadly conceptual and a locally imitative approach to the play's sources. Racine seems to favor the first over the second: he expresses more interest in Aristotle's poetics than in Euripides's plot choices as a dramatist.[1] The playwright is particularly preoccupied by the Aristotelian conception of tragic pathos—the pity and fear inspired by a largely virtuous but nevertheless imperfect character. One might here assign selections from Aristotle's *Poetics*, notably chapters 1–6 (49–64) and 13–15 (75–83). Racine thus claims to rewrite the play driven not by fidelity to the source's plotline or poetic language but by a desire for the play to achieve a certain emotional effect on the audience. Following this logic, the Euripidean Phaedra's act of calumny would appear, Racine argues, too villainous to inspire any pity toward her, while the original Hippolytus's virginity would appear so blameless as to provoke only the audience's indignation at his unjust death at the hands of a monstrously cruel father.

Further classroom discussion compared Racine's own (notoriously unreliable) version of his intentions here with close readings of the play itself. Examinations of Phèdre's active decision-making in Hippolyte's downfall in acts 3 and 4 put in question Racine's mitigation of her guilt. Perhaps most tantalizing, in a development that Racine himself refuses to acknowledge in the preface, the insertion of Hippolyte's love subplot fundamentally alters not only his own character and storyline, but also those of Phèdre. Upon learning in act 4 of Hippolyte's love for Aricie, Phèdre experiences a passion unknown to her Greek and Roman predecessors: jealousy. Does this jealous rage, which temporarily but nevertheless fatally feeds her desire for revenge, make her more culpable than the Phaedras of Euripides and Seneca? Is this new emphasis on jealousy part of a larger Racinian move edging tragedy from concerns with political and family duty toward a focus on inner emotions?

Probing such problems raises questions not just regarding literary and dramatic adaptation but also concerning the play's early modern social and political context. What does Racine's decision to (partially) transfer the guilt of calumny from Phèdre to her servant tell us about changing conceptions of honor and their relation to personal honesty? What are we to make about the class distinctions implied here between a noble "princess" and a subaltern, and their relation to a conception of tragic grandeur? Parallel readings from a Corneille play of heroic passions and duty, such as *Le Cid* or *Horace*, prove particularly useful here, as would reading key passages from Paul Bénichou's classic study, *Man and Ethics*.[2]

The transformation of Hippolyte from chaste hunter to courtly lover also rewards attention to context. As concerns dramatic structure, seventeenth-century French plays, like most early modern European ones, generally feature well-developed subplots and thus often feature two amorous story lines. Hippolyte's love therefore satisfied audience expectations concerning complexly interwoven dramatic action. Furthermore, as indicated by other plays the class might read by Corneille or Racine (or other early modern playwrights), modern tragedy generally grants an important place to love. The French in particular prided themselves on a sophisticated and highly refined form of courtly love then labeled as *galant*. This is the language employed in Hippolyte's deferential courting of Aricie in acts 2 and 5. The circumlocutious elegance of such idealized amorous discourse, seen as building upon and surpassing the earlier models of medieval chivalry and Petrarchan poetry, was lauded at the time as a hallmark of an advanced modern civilization, one that had risen above sexual brutality and embraced respect toward women. The softness and courtly formalism of such *galanterie*, however, was already decried in the next century as deflating tragic grandeur, and it became nothing less than an embarrassment for the Romantics, who condemned what they saw as its saccharine conventionality.

Given the depth and breadth of Racine's modernization of the Phaedra tale, one might ask what remains of the Greek and Roman plays he claims to emulate. Critical attention to the question can help nourish reflection here. While Bénichou sees in Racine a fundamentally modern author ensconced in the pessimistic neo-Augustinian Christian antiheroism of the Jansenists who raised him, George Steiner, in his landmark study of the tragic tradition, views Racine as one of only a small handful of modern playwrights who have captured the essence of Greek tragedy (45–105). The debate, fortunately for us, lives on in the classroom.

Modern Versions: Jules Dassin, Sarah Kane

Jules Dassin's film *Phaedra* and Sarah Kane's one-act play *Phaedra's Love* are two modernizing adaptations that, while not explicitly intertextual with Racine in significant ways, can extend and broaden class discussions around issues of adaptation. In addition, they can open up new perspectives on gender, sexuality, power, agency, and related categories that students find engaging but current scholarship on *Phèdre* tends not to emphasize.

Set in contemporary Greece, London, and Paris, Dassin's film features Melina Mercouri, the star of Dassin's *Never on Sunday*, as Phaedra and Anthony Perkins, who had recently won fame for his performance in Alfred Hitchcock's *Psycho*, as her stepson. Thanos, a Greek shipping mogul, sends his wife, Phaedra, to London in hopes that she will dissuade his son, Alexis, from pursuing a career as an artist. Instead, the two fall in love in a sequence of scenes including a visit to the British Museum, where Greek statues and sculpted reliefs serve as backdrop to the mounting sexual tension. From there they make their way to Paris for a campily stereotypical cinematic lovers' getaway. At length they return to Greece, where, after some reveals and confessions and outbursts, Alexis takes his Alfa Romeo (a gift from his father) out for a high-speed drive, blasting the music of Johann Sebastian Bach and giving voice to existential angst until an oncoming truck runs him off the road to his traditionally grisly death.

Kane's play is set in an imagined but still recognizably British "royal palace" and peopled with graphic acts of sex and violence. Hippolytus is an overweight prince who, when not exercising his uncanny sex appeal, mostly watches television while eating potato chips and masturbating into dirty socks. Phaedra's confession of love includes performing oral sex on him, her suicide comes near the play's midpoint, and the action concludes with Hippolytus torn apart by an angry mob.

While these two dramatic texts seem geared toward very different aims—middlebrow culture box office success and artistic shock value, respectively—they nonetheless share in common an engagement with their own spatiotemporal conditions of production that puts them at an interesting and productive remove from both Racine's early modernity and the antiquity of his Greco-Roman predecessors. In addition to generating lively discussion, these updated versions prompted revisiting Euripides and Seneca, as well as Racine, in regard to questions about the kind of consumer each of those texts seems to construct and expect, and what presuppositions each seems to embody in regard to ideas like male chastity, feminine agency, parental authority, class hierarchy, moral norms, and the nature of sexual desire. Other versions of this course could obviously omit either or both of these texts, but both proved engaging and successful in the graduate iteration.

Translations and Translatability: Wilbur, Hughes

A course of this kind, by its broadly cross-disciplinary scope, attracts a wide range of students with various backgrounds and levels of preparation, including students outside the humanities. Obviously, this entails a classroom experience where some students can read and appreciate Racine's French alexandrine verse while others have to rely on translations either as trots for working through the original or as outright substitutes. And yet, far from being a hindrance, the necessary presence of different versions of *Phèdre* (and the Greco-Roman texts) in the room can serve, if thematized and theorized, as material for discussion not just about translation theory and the evaluation of individual translations but also about canonicity, reception, world literature, and the particular status of Racine's acclaimed masterpiece in all these regards.

A usefully provocative launching pad for discussion on this topic is George Steiner's strong claim that neoclassical French drama, and especially Racine, is fundamentally untranslatable as drama. Steiner insists that Racine's untranslatability makes *Phèdre* into a special case that cries out for explanation, as a dramatic poem of world-class literary caliber whose range has remained parochially national. *Phèdre*'s reception outside its own language community puts it in stark contrast with canonical summits like *Oresteia*, *Hamlet*, and *Faust*. While their "essential poetry" may indeed be untranslatable, those texts have been rendered into other languages effectively enough to garner the status of "world possessions" (46). Steiner musters a catalogue of reasons for this anomaly: Racine's systematic "thinning out" (49) of everything superfluous (and therefore more readily translatable); neoclassical French poetry's distant remove from popular and folkloric elements and energies; that "noble intricacy of seventeenth-century speech" (105), with its courtly understatement (what Spitzer called the dampening effect, the Racinian *sourdine* [2–4]) that Steiner finds to be both radically essential to Racine's depiction of life and a "wine" that "will not travel" (46); and the claim that Racine was a "presenter of reality in language alone" who "invested his words with such responsibility that no other words will conceivably do the job," with the result that even the best translations bring "dispersal and dissolution to the tightness of Racine's style" (102).

Two impressive and strikingly different poetic translations of *Phèdre* into English that have appeared since (and in spite of) Steiner's discouraging pronouncements are readily available for classroom use. Richard Wilbur's *Phaedra* achieves the rather astonishing result of a more or less line-by-line rendering into American English heroic couplets that, if never tight like Racine's alexandrines, are everywhere both readable and stageworthy, as dramatic readings in class can readily demonstrate. Ted Hughes's *Phèdre*, conversely, is a free verse script that prioritizes speed and intensity of impact over reproducing the poetic form, the dictional register, and sometimes the literal sense of its source text. While the Wilbur translation seemed the more obvious pedagogical choice for the standard reference text in discussion (not least because of the line-for-line correspondence with the original), the two translations studied together made interesting material for the kinds of investigations into Racine's dramatic poetry and its reception that it would have been hard to have otherwise.

Comparing sets of sample passages proved an effective means of highlighting the differences between these two English translations in ways that sparked interesting discussion. In a passage like the beginning of Phèdre's confession to Thésée in act 5, scene 7, where dramatic intensity is coupled with stark dictional simplicity, even students with little or no French can get a sense of how each of these two translations manages to render a different subset of the effects in the original. Wilbur renders the experience of a dramatic poem where prosodic regularity, the inevitability of rhyme, and dignity of utterance constitute the rarefied atmosphere in which Racine's characters live and move and have their being. Hughes, on the other hand, gives us very little of the form of the original but conveys a strong sense of the stark ferocity of its affect and tone. Sharing their impressions of a particular translated passage in two different versions can offer students an engaging and memorable experience of collective close reading.

Theatricality and Performance

While questions concerning stage performance are more central to other contributions in this volume, the comparative emphasis of our approach offers some fruitful avenues for investigating theatrical adaptation and practices. In the undergraduate version, this included collaboration with our university's program on theater and performance studies in order to organize workshop sessions in campus studio spaces, allowing students to engage in scene study with theater practitioners. The serial and iterative nature of our Phaedra texts here stimulated rich interplay: students improvised scenes based on their close reading of the different Phaedra texts and thus probed in a newly creative and intuitive fashion the variations in character motivations and dramatic dynamics. Students then wrote short analyses of their experiences.

In the graduate version of the course, the focus on performance was primarily critical and historical rather than experiential. Beginning as early as the eighteenth century, Racine was often considered above all the master of French verse rather than a man of theater, an exalted literary poet rather than a genius of stagecraft. The past several decades, however, have given renewed attention to the theatrical power of his plays. In this sense, the comparison with Seneca proves illuminating: while the Roman playwright's tragedies were also long considered closet dramas, their theatricality has recently been revived.[3] A comparative study of the repression—and the return—of the "theatrical" can thus serve to stimulate broader examinations of the shifting fortunes and interpretations of the Phaedra drama.

Finally, Racine's relation to his classical sources—both his fidelity and his infidelity to ancient models—is also a subject of theatrical and performance history. Despite the rich references and allusions to Greek and Latin authors in the play's poetic and dramatic construction, the original staging of *Phèdre* included minimal ancient local color: the costumes and decor were largely those of the modern French court, with a few nominal Greco-Roman accents. The end of the eighteenth century, however, saw a new neoclassical stage aesthetic applied to Racine, whose plays' performances were re-Hellenized in both costume and sets throughout the nineteenth century. The class studied the visual manifestations of this reclassicization through reproductions of the sumptuous engravings by Jacques-Louis David's student Girodet in the monumental 1801 Didot edition of Racine's *Œuvres.* A comparison between these austerely sculptural illustrations—striking for their elegant Greco-Roman robes, statuary allure, and pared-down décor—and the baroque and painterly exuberance of the original swirling frontispiece engravings for Racine's first editions by Chauveau and Le Brun (interspersed throughout vol. 1 of *Œuvres complètes*) allows students to examine the relation of modernity to antiquity, of Racine to Euripides or Seneca, not as a static concept, but instead as an ever-shifting aspect of historical evolution.

In conclusion, this course, like the many versions of the Phaedra story it probes, is best understood in an iterative and evolving fashion. Endless possibilities beyond those cited here are of course available. The authors offer it as a kind of menu from which future syllabi of widely varying natures may choose items à la carte. To give one example, at the University of Chicago the course helped pave the way for a Seneca-Racine *Phaedra* module in one of the sequences of the college-wide first-year humanities core. May the Phaedras multiply!

Notes

1. One might also discuss here Racine's above-noted refusal to acknowledge Seneca's version in the preface's homage to the ancients. Is this due to Racine's desire to echo Aristotle's authoritative praise of Euripides? It is certainly true that Racine—as a partisan of the ancients in what came to be known as the quarrel of the ancients and moderns—wished to construct an image of himself as the inheritor of the Greeks.

2. In particular the chapters titled "Racine" (138–67) and "The Destruction of the Hero" (98–115).

3. Studies useful in this regard include David Maskell for Racine and Helen Slaney for Seneca.

Works Cited

Aristotle. *Poetics*. Translated by S. H. Butcher, Hill and Wang, 1961.

Bénichou, Paul. *Man and Ethics: Studies in French Classics*. Translated by Elizabeth Hughes, Anchor, 1971.

Dassin, Jules, director. *Phaedra*. Jorilie Melinafilm, 1962.

Euripides. *Hippolytos*. Translated by Robert Bagg, Oxford UP, 1992.

Homer. *The Odyssey of Homer*. Translated by Richmond Lattimore, Harper and Row, 1967.

Kane, Sarah. *Phaedra's Love*. 1996. Methuen, 2008.

Maskell, David. *Racine: A Theatrical Reading*. Clarendon Press, 1991.

Ovid. "Phaedra to Hippolytus." *Heroides*, translated by Harold Isbell, Penguin Classics, 1990, pp. 28–38.

Racine, Jean. *Œuvres complètes, tome I: Théâtre-Poésie*. Edited by Georges Forestier, Gallimard-La Pléiade, 1999.

———. *Œuvres de Jean Racine*. Didot, 1801. *The Met*, Metropolitan Museum of Art, 2020, www.metmuseum.org/toah/works-of-art/58.635.1(1)/.

———. *Phaedra*. Translated by Richard Wilbur, Harvest, 1987.

———. *Phèdre*. Translated by Ted Hughes, Farrar, Straus and Giroux, 1998.

Rameau, Jean-Philippe. *Hippolyte et Aricie*. Conducted by William Christie, performed by Les Arts Florissants, Erato, 2012. CD.

Seneca. *Phaedra*. Translated by Frederick Ahl, Cornell UP, 1986.
Slaney, Helen. *The Senecan Aesthetic: A Performance History*. Oxford UP, 2015.
Spitzer, Leo. "Racine's Classical Piano." *Essays on Seventeenth-Century Literature*, edited and translated by David Bellos, Cambridge UP, 1983, pp. 1–111.
Steiner, George. *The Death of Tragedy*. Alfred A. Knopf, 1961.

John D. Lyons

Fate, Freedom, and the Tragic World

What role does "fate" play in tragedy? This is a question likely to arise in an undergraduate course on French tragedy or in an undergraduate survey course on European tragedy, whether focused on early modern theater or offering a broader historical overview of tragedy since antiquity. In my experience, college students and even many graduate students arrive with firmly held notions of what a tragedy should be. These include the idea of a "tragic hero," of "the tragic flaw," and of "fate." Here, I propose to take "fate" as a way into the study of tragedy, first, providing an approach that makes use of students' already formed but limited conceptions of the tragic, and, second, helping students develop habits of thinking and investigation that can be used for many other domains of literary study. It is therefore up to the students to answer the question posed above. The general purpose of the direction that I propose is to give students the active role in thinking about "fate" in tragedy. But why bring up the question in the first place? Clearly such a question is weightier and more significant than one about the role of, for example, food in tragedy—even though that would be a really interesting one, especially if we extend "food" to include drink, and thus poison. But still, food, drink, weapons, and letters are only instruments, whereas "fate" and "fatality" suggest a force behind appearances that impacts the whole of the plot and thus the nature of tragedy at the most important level: why do things happen? Why do people in tragedy do things?

Many students in the United States are first introduced to tragedy in an English course or in a humanities or great books course heavily influenced by a tradition in the teaching of Shakespeare (and then projected onto ancient tragedy) that derives from German Idealism and entered the English-speaking world at the dawn of the twentieth century through A. C. Bradley's *Shakespearean Tragedy* (see Hoxby, Billings). While Bradley does not endorse a "fated" plot for tragedy, the term appears on page after page, with the result that it seems that in order to talk about tragedy, one needs to talk about fate and fatality, even if in the end fatal causation is rejected in favor of human freedom. In talking about *King Lear*, Bradley writes that the play is plotted in such a way that "it startles and terrifies by suggesting that the folly of Lear and the ingratitude of his daughters are no accidents or merely individual aberrations, but that in that dark cold world some fateful malignant influence is abroad, turning the hearts of the fathers against their children and of the children against their fathers" (262).

Once the question of whether tragedy does or does not represent humans in the grip of fate has been introduced, a preliminary class discussion can allow students to get their own initial views on the table before a homework assignment invites them to see what the scholarly world has produced in the way of opinions. Students' inclination will probably be simply to google—a good start, but we can show them some more refined search tools, such as dictionaries that reveal historical strata in the use of terms such as *destin*, *fatalité*, and *sort* (here is a chance for students to negotiate the *Dictionnaires d'autrefois* [*Dictionaries of the Past*; artfl-project.uchicago.edu/content/dictionnaires-dautrefois] as well as the *Trésor de la langue française* [*Treasure of the French Language*; atilf.atilf.fr] online). While some students volunteer or are assigned to check out the lexicon, others may be assigned to explore the *MLA Bibliography* and *JSTOR* for articles and books about "tragedy and fate." Even the French *Wikipedia* would be a very good starting point for some students, especially for courses that are taught in French. The current article on *destin* (destiny), for instance, gives a good overview of the concept ("Destin") as well as links to other *Wikipedia* articles and bibliography on related concepts such as *déterminisme* (determinism), *libre arbitre* (free will), and *tyché* (chance).

This is not the point in the course to make any conclusions about fate *in tragedy*, of course, but the assignment has three benefits: first, the students confront the effort of defining terms; second, they practice using reference and research tools; third, they can see that the issues under discussion have a history, that other people have worked seriously to understand them.

A quick search of books and articles combining the terms *tragedy* and *fate* and related ones such as *destiny* or *fatality* turns up a fair number of publications. Students will notice that fate is mentioned with particular frequency in connection with Racine. They will probably come across J. P. Short's "The Concept of Fate in the Tragedies of Racine" and Jean Gooder's "'Fixt Fate' and 'Free Will' in *Phèdre* and *Macbeth*." In the process, students will find that French tragedy of the seventeenth century is often described as "Aristotelian" or "neo-Aristotelian"—though the contradiction, or at least the paradox, that this raises will not yet be apparent.

This is a good moment to read the *Poetics*, where students will discover that with regard to fate, Aristotle specifically *excludes* transcendent causes from the ideal tragedy. In chapter 9 of the *Poetics*, the philosopher insists on the careful plotting of cause and effect, so that "things occur contrary to expectation yet still on account of one another" (42). In the following chapter Aristotle says that recognition and reversal (two plot modules that one finds in the very best tragedies) "should arise from the intrinsic structure of the plot, so that what results follows by either necessity or probability from the preceding events: for it makes a great difference whether things happen because of one another, or only *after* one another" (42). And Aristotle's condemnation of plots that are resolved by a god suddenly appearing gives us the well-known term *deus ex machina* (47–48). So there seems to be a conflict, or at least a tension, between Aristotle's insistence on an immanent causality, in which there would be no need for seeking a supernatural influence, and definitions of fate or destiny, such as "Puissance extérieure à la volonté humaine, qui, selon certaines croyances, régirait l'univers, en fixant de façon irrévocable le cours des événements." 'Power external to human will, which, according to certain beliefs, would control the universe, determining in an irrevocable manner the course of events' ("Destin" [*Trésor*]). On the other hand, they will discover that critics and even theater directors often invoke Racine's education in the Jansenist schools of Port-Royal as grounds for interpreting his plays as structured around the intervention of divine predestination—a Christian version of "fate"—in human life. English playwrights and German playwrights could find similar ideas in Calvinistic or Lutheran circles.

At this point it seems appropriate to invite students to focus primarily on materials close to the production of the French tragedies themselves. Three approaches might be suggested. The class can consider what the theorists of tragedy like Pierre Corneille; François Hédelin, abbé d'Aubignac; and Hippolyte-Jules Pilet de La Mesnardière say about fate in the various commentaries, prefaces, treatises of playwriting, and so forth (see for example Corneille, *Trois discours*). What recommends this approach? The writers in question are contemporaries of the works and thus are presumed to have an extensive and culturally based (or ideologically based) knowledge we do not have. Such an approach also has its weakness: some of the writers of treatises are not the authors of the best or most-remembered tragedies, and the playwrights who write about tragedy may use such writings as polemical forms or marketing devices rather than giving a frank description of their own tragedies. Do such writings distort their readers' view of the play itself?

A second approach is similar but slightly broader. Outside of the narrow world of dramatic theory, what did early modern French people think about fate and predestination? Viewers with such topics on their minds might interpret plays through the lens of their philosophical and religious expectations. This seems like a promising approach, particularly if we adopt the view that each literary work (or other cultural production) necessarily reflects the worldview that dominated at the time of its production. But can we be sure that everyone, each playwright and every member of the audience, shared the same worldview? Can a writer challenge society's views?

A third approach is to look at the texts of the dramatic works themselves. This is the core of the course and no doubt the most enjoyable part for both teacher and students. What do the characters say about fate, destiny, and human freedom?[1] Do these questions arise as clearly in plays by Corneille as in plays by Racine, for instance? This seems like the most direct approach to questions about fate, but here, too, there are complexities. Who in the play talks about fate? Since each character has an individual voice and perspective, can we reach a conclusion about the playwright's view of fate? Does it matter? And what motivates each character to speak about fate? It is likely, I think, that very frequently characters who could be described as having brought about some catastrophe by their own actions will be the ones who complain that an irresistible external power is responsible for their situation. Moreover, this approach requires a constant self-examination on the part of the reader of the play in order to be aware of any modern projection of assumptions about freedom onto the early modern text.

As examples of the various ways the constellation of terms for fate appears in frequently taught tragedies of the seventeenth century, let us consider Corneille's *Le Cid* and Racine's *Phèdre*. These are almost certain to be on the reading list of a course in seventeenth-century French literature, and they have the advantage of being excellent case studies for the themes of fate and freedom. Of course, one important lesson is that the simple presence of terms for fate does not tell the whole story. This is a particularly important point in an age when we all have at our fingertips (through online databases, word mining tools, and basic Internet search), the ability to find word frequencies and to locate words within specific texts. But it is precisely this ease that can be a good starting point for a student paper or for a class discussion.

In *Le Cid* the noun *destin* appears six times, the adjective *destinée* (in the plural) once, and the noun *sort* ten times. The noun *fatalité* does not appear, though the adjective *fatal* occurs four times. All of these terms are distributed fairly evenly among the main characters. It is not the case, then, that one character is obsessed with seeing the situation through the lens of predestination. For example, in the case of *destin*, it is Don Diègue, the hero's father, who first uses the term, when he calls on his son to avenge the insult that he has received at the hands of Chimène's father. Don Diègue says that he is "[a]ccablé des malheurs où le *destin* me range" '[c]rushed by the woes that Fate hath laid upon me' (1.5.289; emphasis added here and below).[2] Next, Rodrigue, facing almost certain death as he challenges the Comte, emphasizes the unequal nature of the combat: "Les palmes dont je vois ta tête si couverte / Semblent porter écrit le *destin* de ma perte" 'The palms wherewith / Thy brow are crowned would seem to bear inscribed / The promise of my doom' (2.2.413–14). Later in the second act Don Diègue deplores the ravages of old age, noting that heroic (*généreux*) men find "[a]u bout de leur carrière, un *destin* malheureux" '[a] miserable fate old age prepares / For noble-minded men before their end!' (2.8.700). The term does not reappear until the last act of the play, when three female characters each say it once. The Infante in a soliloquy laments, "Pour me punir le *destin* a permis / Que l'amour dure même entre deux ennemis" 'Since destiny, to punish me, decrees / That they shall still love, although enemies' (5.3.1595–96). And in an exchange in the following scene, Elvire tries to show Chimène the bright side of things: "Et quoi que le *destin* puisse ordonner de vous, / Il soutient votre gloire, et vous donne un époux" 'Whate'er it be that destiny may decree, / Thy fair fame will be safe, and thou shalt wed' (5.4.1655–56). After that, Chimène in an apostrophe first renounces vengeance and then hopes that Rodrigue will not be vanquished in a duel. Addressing destiny, she says, "Et toi, puissant moteur du *destin* qui m'outrage, / Termine ce combat sans aucun avantage, / Sans faire aucun des deux ni vaincu ni vainqueur" 'Away with you! Ye have no charms for me / At such a price as this. And thou, almighty / Dispenser of my grievous destiny' (5.5.1665–67). What can we draw from carefully looking at the use of this word?

One rather obvious commonality is that destiny is not intrinsically cheerful but rather associated with bad news, bad outcomes, and menace. The only case in which this is not clear-cut is Elvire's concessive comment that whatever happens, Chimène will end up with her reputation intact and with a husband. But even in this instance, *destin* is on the negative side of a ledger with two columns. Elvire seems to be saying that (1) there may be some bad things in the situation, but (2) there are the good things that seem most certain.

In several of the cases *destin* seems simply to mean "situation" or "predictable pattern." This is clearly the case both times that Don Diègue speaks of destiny. He finds himself in a bad situation because of the Comte's insult in act 1; then, in the following act, he points out that heroic warriors get old and lose their strength. Similarly, when Rodrigue speaks with the Comte before their duel, the *destin* is simply the probable outcome of an unequal combat between an inexperienced young man and a powerful, seasoned warrior in his prime. The Infante and Chimène, on the other hand, seem to use the term *destin* as a substitute for *God*—this is particularly clear in Chimène's apostrophe to the *puissant moteur du destin* ("powerful motor of destiny"; my trans.). Since most students are quite used to the idea of praying to God, and since they may know that France was an officially Catholic country in the seventeenth century, this usage may occasion some interesting discussions. It seems a paradox that a Catholic playwright (educated by the Jesuits and author of religious poetry) writing for a mostly Christian audience would avoid explicit mention of the Christian God. Here we can point out the tense and unstable relationship between the established church and the theater, and talk with students about the compromise by which the exclusion of direct references to "God" (in the singular) was not a sign of irreligion but rather of respect. By not mixing religion into a profane (secular) play, Corneille could avoid censure.

Looking still more closely at Chimène's apostrophe, we can see that *destin* in this case also has the sense of "situation" or "what happens" rather than the sense of a power that *causes* things to happen. An argument in favor of a non-predestined vision of life in Corneille may come from the great attention that the characters attach to making decisions about what to do. A celebrated formal feature of *Le Cid* is the use of *stances*, passages strikingly different in meter and rhyme, on two occasions. These are the soliloquies during which first Rodrigue, at the end of act 1, and later the Infante, in the last act, consider their difficult situations. Both speakers assume that they must choose carefully how to act because their decision matters and will have consequences. In other words, they reason within a horizon of immanent cause and effect and perceive the situation they are in as the outcome of a series of human events. It is not surprising that the critical tradition has not generally seen in *Le Cid* a vision of life determined by external, transcendent powers.

When we turn to our other example of a seventeenth-century French tragedy, Racine's *Phèdre*, we find a much more substantial field of inquiry, nourished not only by the text of the play itself but by centuries of commentary that focuses precisely on the theme of fatality. It is particularly stimulating for both teachers and students to have to discern and articulate the complex web that Racine has constructed with the threads at his disposal: references to the ancient Greek gods, the tragic characters' comments on their own self-perception in relation both to the gods and to their own ancestors (sometimes these *are* gods), and the implicit seventeenth-century social-political-religious context that was known to the playwright's contemporaries and that has subsequently been extensively described by critics, particularly in the second half of the twentieth century. In approaching this background in a college course, the teacher needs to decide whether to give the students right away a preview of the critical debate or start with the text, as we did for *Le Cid*.

Whether we start or finish with the debate among critics and among *metteurs en scène* (directors), we know that there are strong opinions, and that critics divide into two camps. First, there are those who believe that Racine's conception of the tragedy was shaped by a Jansenist (or Augustinian) doctrine of predestination, with the implication that the Greek gods function as symbolic stand-ins for an all-determining Christian God who decrees all that is to happen (the word *fate*—Latin *fatum*—derives from the verb *for, fari*, meaning "to say," hence to decree). What God says, happens. The other camp rejects the view that Racine's early education with the Jansenists had anything to do with *Phèdre*, except that the future playwright got an excellent education in Greek from the *petites écoles* of Port-Royal. There are a number of nuances in the anti-fate camp, but globally its view is that Racine creates a foreboding atmosphere through the characters' own beliefs or claims about the gods, which they—the main characters—project onto the fictive world (see Campbell, Forestier, Goldmann, Toczyski).

Here, from the critic and director Christian Biet, is a vigorous statement of the view that Racinian tragedy portrays a world entirely determined by fatality (the gods) and without room for human freedom:

> Deux ans après *Mithridate*, lorsqu'il est temps de revenir à l'Antiquité grecque, la souffrance vient directement des Dieux, puisqu'ils l'exigent. Il est donc certain que la douleur convient aux hommes même si les hommes ne savent jamais comprendre ce que veulent exactement les Dieux. S'il pouvait encore y avoir, à Rome ou en Orient, l'ombre d'un choix pour l'homme devant son destin, *Iphigénie* et *Phèdre* indiquent qu'il n'en est plus rien. L'homme n'est pas libre, les destins doivent être accomplis et rien ne peut les repousser, ni les erreurs d'interprétation des décrets divins, ni les ruses—on ne ruse pas devant Dieu—, ni les plaintes. Il est donné à l'homme de souffrir parce qu'il est homme, marqué par la faute, et les dieux sont là pour le lui rappeler. (Biet 140)
>
> Two years after *Mithridate*, when it is time to come back to Greek antiquity, suffering comes directly from the Gods, because they demand it. It is thus certain that suffering befits mankind, even if humans never understand exactly what the Gods want. If there could still be, in Rome or in the East, the faintest opportunity for mankind to make a choice in the face of destiny, *Iphigénie* and *Phèdre* show that this is just not true. Man is not free, destinies must be accomplished, and nothing can prevent them, neither errors in interpreting divine decrees, nor trickery—one does not trick God—nor lamentations. It is man's lot to suffer because he is human, marked by fault, and the gods are there to remind him. (my trans.)

Here, on the other hand, is a statement by Gonzague Truc of a quite different view, that fate plays little or no role in *Phèdre*:

> Il faut, pour apprécier exactement *Phèdre*, se débarrasser d'abord de quelques opinions préconçues. . . . [S]i l'on suivait la critique traditionnelle, on irait jusqu'à voir dans la pièce un morceau d'apologétique janséniste. [Les critiques] ont su trouver en des lieux communs sur la fatalité de l'amour des arguments pour ou contre l'efficace ou la suffisance de la grâce et le pouvoir prochain. (Truc 107)

> First of all, to appreciate *Phèdre* properly, one must get rid of preconceived opinions. . . . [I]f one followed the traditional criticism, one would go so far as to see the play as a piece of Jansenist propaganda. [The critics] were able to take commonplaces about the fatal nature of love and point to them as arguments for or against efficacious grace, sufficient grace, and *pouvoir prochain*. (my trans.)

What Truc suggests is that purely internal, psychological factors drive the characters' actions, but that the characters themselves interpret what is happening to them by supposing that their feelings are coming from some supernatural force:

> Ce n'est pas par image qu'elle attribue à la vengeance ou au caprice des Immortels la malédiction dont elle souffre ainsi: une telle fatalité est plus qu'humaine et quand nous la devons subir, nous cherchons, étonnés encore, d'où elle nous vient. Pareil aux autres fléaux, l'amour ne semble jamais naître tout seul et, dès que nous le devons recevoir, nous recherchons avec une crainte superstitieuse quelle puissance, quelle magie a bien pu nous l'imposer et quelle faute inconnue nous expions sous les tortures raffinées que seul il sait départir. (113)
>
> It is not as a figure that she thus attributes the damnation that she suffers to the vengeance or the whim of the Immortals: such a fate is larger than life, and when we must suffer it, we seek, astonished, where it comes from. Like other plagues, love never seems to come to life all by itself, and when it comes upon us, we seek, with a superstitious fear, what power, what magic, could have set it upon us and for what unknown fault we are paying in the exquisite tortures that love alone can deploy. (my trans.)

The views of these two critics give a good idea of the range—almost always a polar opposition—between the view that transcendent, supernatural forces determine the action in *Phèdre*, and the view that references to divinities are allegorical projections, by the characters themselves, of their entirely immanent feelings of desire, guilt, and shame (see Toczyski).

Whether the students hear about this conflict of interpretations at the outset of discussion or later, it is important to look closely at some of the evidence. In the case of Racine, the concepts in play appear within an extensive lexical context. Alongside *destin* (twice), and *destinée* (three times), and the adjective *fatal(e)* twelve times, there are extensive references to the gods—together *dieu* and *dieux* appear fifty-six times, and *déesse* twice. Although *destin* in one instance seems simply to mean "what happened" ("J'ignore le *destin* d'une tête si chère" 'I have not heard / Of my dear father

Theseus' destiny' [1.1.6; emphasis added]),[3] in most cases the speakers use these terms to designate some active, malevolent, force that inflicts misery on humans. Hippolyte mentions *dieux* (gods) thirteen times, Oenone and Thésée ten times each, Phèdre sixteen times (and *déesse*—goddess—twice), Aricie and Ismène together three times, and Théramène four times. Venus is named seven times; Phèdre herself names or calls upon the goddess five of those times, and she also mentions her ancestor, the sun, twice. The gods, in other words, are massively present in the discourse of the tragedy. What stands out from this simple and rather mechanical survey is that Phèdre is the one who most often mentions destiny, the gods, and specifically Venus.[4] The characters repeatedly ascribe what happens to them and even what they feel to the gods or to destiny. Thésée, for instance, as we have seen, hearing that Hippolyte has raped Phèdre, blames it on an active, malicious destiny: "Avec quelle rigueur, destin, tu me poursuis" 'How harshly you pursue me, destiny.' (4.1.1003). Phèdre asserts that Venus cursed her mother and herself: "O haine de Vénus ! O fatale colère ! / Dans quels égarements l'amour jeta ma mère" 'O hate of Venus! Anger-laden doom! / Into what dark abyss love hurled my mother!' (1.3.249–50).

The critics who see Racine's play as a decisive representation of the overwhelming domination of supernatural forces over human freedom seem to win the argument. Phèdre and Thésée say this, and Théramène—the philosopher of the play—seems to agree, saying that Hippolyte's disfigured body is only a "[t]riste objet, où des Dieux triomphe la colère" 'A tribute to the anger of the gods' (5.6.1569). Certainly many students will concur and will have good textual evidence on their side. Or will they? Is Racine's play such a clear representation of a transcendental, predestinatarian causality? Who, after all, is making these claims? And what are they actually saying? The first scene of the play already provides evidence against a transcendent, supernatural reading. When Hippolyte reluctantly admits to his tutor that he is in love with Aricie, against his father's orders, Théramène's reply seems on its face to be a cogent statement that a supernatural destiny drives our lives: "Ah! Seigneur, si votre heure est une fois marquée, / Le ciel de nos raisons ne sait point s'informer" 'Ah! when your hour has once but struck, my lord, / Heaven of our reasons takes but little heed' (1.1.114–15). Destiny seems to rule: each event in our life is "marked" (noted—precisely the origin of *fatum*: said, decreed) by powers beyond our control. Score a point for predestination! But Théramène proceeds to give a very nontranscendent explanation of why his charge is in love with Aricie: she is the forbidden fruit, designated as desirable by Thésée himself: "Thésée ouvre vos yeux en voulant les fermer; / Et sa haine, irritant une flamme rebelle, / Prête à son ennemie une grâce nouvelle" 'Theseus opens your eyes despite yourself. / His hatred of Aricia has fanned / Your passion and has lent her added grace' (1.1.116–18). In other words, there is a perfectly normal combination of adolescent (hormonal) development and Oedipal psychology at work—deterministic forces, to be sure, but purely *immanent*, biological and psychic pulsions. A similar observation could be made about many of Phèdre's references to Venus, the gods, and divine vengeance; for example, "Objet infortuné des vengeances célestes" 'The hapless victim of heaven's vengeances' (2.5.677). Consider Phèdre's description of her own torment of desire, when she cannot end her obsession with her stepson: "Ce n'est plus une ardeur dans mes veines cachée: / C'est Vénus tout entière à sa proie attachée" 'The fire no longer slumbers in the veins. / Venus in all her might is on her prey' (1.3.304–05). On one hand, this seems like an excellent, figurative evocation of the intensity of a love that has become pathologically uncontrollable—a feeling that afflicts people in every epoch. On the other hand, Phèdre attributes the feeling to an outside, transcendent, supernatural force, rather than to inherent natural drives.

At this point in the discussion, it is probably worthwhile to return to the starting point, to the definitions of terms like *fate*, *destiny*, *fatality*, and so forth, with a renewed attention to distinctions like immanent and transcendent, internal and external, natural and supernatural. Yet rather than considering these concepts in the abstract, in a purely metaphysical way, we can ask ourselves whether the fact that it is Phèdre herself who principally attributes her state to the goddess is an important factor. Is she, as Truc suggests, simply giving voice to the amazement and distress of a feeling that exceeds anything that she ever thought could come from nature itself?

One of the most salient features of Racine's theater, one that accounts for its staying power with audiences and readers, is the way it provides plausibly for a double vision: one view based on a purely natural and immanent set of causes and another view that accommodates a transcendent explanation. To illustrate this concept of a double vision, permitting both transcendent and immanent explanations, let us consider the moment of Hippolyte's death. Does the young hero die because a god answered (in a perhaps deliberately malicious way) Thésée's call to kill Hippolyte: "Un Dieu vengeur te suit, tu ne peux l'éviter" 'A god of vengeance follows hard on you' (4.4.1160)? Or did he die for easily discernible, natural reasons—for instance, that he neglected the training of his horses because he was so lovesick over Aricie? Théramène, recounting Hippolyte's encounter with the monster that surged out of the sea and frightened the horses, points toward the possibility of divine intervention in human affairs: "On dit qu'on a vu même, en ce désordre affreux, / Un Dieu qui d'aiguillons pressait leur flanc poudreux" 'In this wild tumult, it is even said, / A god appeared, goading their dusty flanks' (5.6.1540). Did Neptune, god of horses, drive the horses so that they would not obey Hippolyte? Here it seems that the case for divine and fatal intervention is strong. And yet Racine provides support for the opposite view as well. After all, Théramène did not see this himself, and the testimony seems to have come from an unknown, undesignated source, perhaps at several removes: "*On* dit qu'*on* a vu . . ." '*Someone* said that *someone* saw (emphasis added; my trans.).

The themes of fate and freedom—of ineluctable divine control of human life on the one hand and, on the other hand, of human decision and responsibility—offer ample opportunities to engage students in the active exploration of tragedy. And the discussion of tragedy, fate, and freedom can in turn lead to further readings and discussion about why we should care about moral action, prudence, and justice, and considerations about the value of human life itself.

Notes

1. It is possible to use the very current word *agency* rather than to speak of human freedom. The drawback to *agency* is its fundamental ambiguity. Some use it to mean the human ability to act with intention, while others seem to use it to mean the human ability to act effectively (i.e., to reach the intended goal). In the first sense, we can say that Sophocles's Oedipus depicts the protagonist's agency; in the second sense, Sophocles depicts the failure of the protagonist's agency.

2. All English translations of Corneille are taken from Lockert.

3. All English translations of Racine are taken from Cairncross.

4. Phèdre mentions destiny twice, the sun twice, Venus five times by name and twice as the *déesse*, the gods sixteen times—and these are only the most explicit mentions or apostrophes.

Works Cited

Aristotle. *The Poetics of Aristotle: Translation and Commentary.* Translated by Stephen Halliwell, U of North Carolina P, 1987.

Biet, Christian. *Racine, ou la passion des larmes.* Hachette, 1996.

Billings, Joshua. *Genealogy of the Tragic: Greek Tragedy and German Philosophy.* Princeton UP, 2017.

Bradley, A. C. *Shakespearean Tragedy; Lectures on* Hamlet, Othello, King Lear, Macbeth. Macmillan, 1910.

Campbell, John. *Questioning Racinian Tragedy*. North Carolina Studies in the Romance Languages and Literatures, 2005.

Corneille, Pierre. *Le Cid*. *Œuvres complètes*, edited by Georges Couton, vol. 1, Gallimard, 1980, pp. 711–77.

———. *Trois discours sur le poème dramatique*. Edited by Bénédicte Louvat and Marc Escola, Garnier-Flammarion, 1999.

"Destin." *Wikipédia: L'encyclopédie libre*, Wikimedia Foundation, 19 Feb. 2020, fr.wikipedia.org/wiki/Destin.

"Destin, Subst. Masc." *Trésor de la langue française*, CNRS / Université de Lorraine, atilf.atilf.fr.

Forestier, Georges. *Jean Racine*. Gallimard, 2006.

Goldmann, Lucien. *Le dieu caché*. Gallimard, 1959.

Gooder, Jean. "'Fixt Fate' and 'Free Will' in *Phèdre* and *Macbeth*." *Cambridge Quarterly*, vol. 28, no. 3, 1999, pp. 214–31.

Hoxby, Blair. *What Was Tragedy? Theory and the Early Modern Canon*. Oxford UP, 2015.

Lockert, Lacy. *The Chief Plays of Corneille*. Princeton UP, 1957.

Racine, Jean. *Iphigenia; Phaedra; Athaliah*. Translated by John Cairncross, Penguin Books, 1963.

———. *Phèdre*. *Œuvres complètes, tome I: Théâtre-Poésie*, edited by Georges Forestier, Gallimard-La Pléiade, 1999, pp. 820–76.

Short, J. P. "The Concept of Fate in the Tragedies of Racine." *Studies in French Literature Presented to H. W. Lawton by Colleagues, Pupils, and Friends*, edited by J. C. Ireson et al., Manchester UP, 1968, pp. 315–29.

Toczyski, Suzanne. "Teaching *Phèdre*: Desire and the Phenomenology of Action." *Racine et/ou le classicisme*, edited by Ronald W. Tobin, Gunter Narr Verlag, 2001, pp. 321–32.

Truc, Gonzague. *Jean Racine, l'œuvre, l'artiste, l'homme et le temps*. Librairie Garnier frères, 1926.

Jeffrey N. Peters

Place and Space in Neoclassical Tragedy

For English-speaking students accustomed to the rich materiality of Shakespeare's Dover cliffs and Scottish heath, the relatively austere settings of French neoclassical tragedy can be baffling. What, after all, is the function of place in a theater tradition whose dramatic situations often seem disconnected from the locations in which they occur? When a Roman hero, fresh from victory on the battlefield, suddenly murders his sister in Pierre Corneille's seminal *Horace*, for instance, the shocking, but dramatically central, event unfolds offstage, beyond the gaze of the spectator. Corneille and his contemporaries withheld direct portrayal of this and other disturbing scenes in part for often ambiguous reasons of decorum, but also because when violent upheavals of this sort are set apart, out of view, the visible place of the stage is reserved for what Corneille describes as the spectator's affective investment in the unique presentness of dramatic conflict. It matters little, Corneille wrote of his tragedy *Cinna*, that the single unadorned chamber set on stage figures simultaneously, and therefore incongruously, both the palace apartment of the emperor Auguste and the home of the conspirators who plot to overthrow him. As long as its emotional response to what is happening is suitably managed, an audience will choose to ignore obvious spatial and logical contradictions (*Discours* 189).

Because the sense of reality conveyed by tragedy is a visceral one, derived from the powerful emotions its spectators are impelled to feel, scenic place is relieved of its mimetic responsibility. The dramatic force of neoclassical tragedy lies in an appeal to an inward reality immanent to, but distinct from, a stage space characterized by its visual economy: local color is banished, the particularities of setting are effaced, and even identifying set decor, as Corneille himself insisted, was to be minimized (*Discours* 189). The result is what seventeenth-century poets and commentators referred to as the *unité de lieu* ("unity of place"), a principle of scenic placing that eschewed the naturalistic representation of a concrete world, excluded the spectator from the world of the characters, and rigorously limited dramatic action to a single visible location. In this sense, place assumes the near-allegorical features of an abstract drama occurring elsewhere, somehow above or beyond the present events set visibly on stage before the theater audience.

In this essay, I propose a set of readings intended to give instructors the tools they need to help students identify the problems raised by the depiction of the physical world in the theater, discover that issues of place and location exemplify the dramatic stakes of neoclassical tragedy, and situate the aesthetic questions raised by place, location, and setting in French tragedy of the seventeenth century in the broader intellectual tradition concerning physical space in early modern natural philosophy. These readings would be appropriate, with some modification, for undergraduate and graduate students, and could serve either as the historical backdrop to a unit on dramatic place in a course on tragedy or a French literature survey, or as the framework for a much broader course on French tragedy as an expression of early modern European thought. In what follows, I introduce some of the most important theoretical writing from the period concerning the problem of location in the theater and then turn briefly to several tragedies by Corneille (*Médée*; *L'illusion comique*; *Horace*), Jean Racine (*Bérénice*), and, in passing, Jean Rotrou (*Le véritable Saint Genest*), which, taken collectively, reveal how during the seventeenth century a notion of infinite space dislodged the tightly fitting places that had earlier described the Aristotelian understanding of cosmic being.

The Contrivances of Dramatic Place

Spectators of Corneille's *Horace* encounter the following lines in act 4:

> La victoire entre eux deux n'était pas incertaine,
> L'Albain percé de coups ne se traînait qu'à peine,
> Et comme une victime aux marches de l'Autel,
> Il semblait présenter sa gorge au coup mortel. (4.2.1135–38)
>
> Between them victory was not in doubt.
> Pierced with wounds the Alban could hardly move,
> and like a victim brought before the altar,
> he seemed to offer his throat to the deadly blow.[1]

Here Valère, a Roman soldier, describes Horace's stunning victory over three brothers chosen to represent the city of Alba in battle against Horace and his own two brothers, representing Rome. In Corneille's tragedy, we are not witness to this tense and bloody scene, which is dramatically intricate and requires some narrative detail. We are given only Valère's words, pronounced subsequent to, and in a place distant from, the events themselves, a situation that immediately raises a host of difficulties pertaining to the seventeenth-century dramatic *unité de lieu*. In seventeenth-century theaters as in today's, stage actors and audience members both are and are not in the same place. On the one hand, actor and spectator, together with every usher and stage technician, share the same physical location—the same theater house or performance site. At the same time, and on the other hand, we usually—though not always—think of performers and spectators as belonging to quite different places. When they speak and move, and wherever they speak and move, actors formulate an imaginary, fictional place that belongs to an entirely separate world of performance (Biet and Triau 75–129). This dramatic place may lie, present, before the spectator or extend, unobserved, beyond the agreed-upon performance site (e.g., the stage) depending on whether it is visible or invisible to the spectator.

In either case, audiences are usually asked to imagine a place that is different from the one they can see. Accordingly, some places are more concrete than others. A theater stage is alternately and all at once a material thing sharing real location with the spectator, a concrete but imagined fictional place different from the place of the stage (say, a palace chamber, visible to the audience), and a place set in a spatiotemporal world entirely unlike the spectator's—ancient Rome, for example. We owe much of our understanding of location in the theater to a broader distinction we are accustomed to making between place and space. We generally assume that *places* are those concrete sites which may be topologically identified in their specificity (e.g., Rome), whereas *space* describes an open-ended region, volume, or distance to be physically or conceptually embraced through travel or the imagination (e.g., the area between, or encompassing, Rome and Constantinople, or indeed between an interior palace chamber and a battlefield beyond the palace walls) (Ubersfeld 1: 113–49; Lyons, *Kingdom* 147–59 and "Unseen Space"). In the specific environment of the theater, we often suppose that place becomes space when it is abstracted through fiction, when it becomes a field of dramatic engagement: we may call it "Rome" (a place), but the stage before us is also a site of the poetic (a performance space where Corneille's *Horace* is given voice).

That early modern debates around place and space should offer crucial insights into the French tradition of neoclassical dramatic art may come as some surprise to students of tragedy. But the mutual entailment of theatrical and natural philosophical understandings of physical location is instructive with respect to neoclassical tragedy in two key ways. First, the specific relative qualities of place and space are closely bound up with central principles of dramatic representation in seventeenth-century France. It is, for example, instructive that the French *unité de lieu* is the only unity not to be found in Aristotle's *Poetics* but was instead derived from the related Aristotelian unities of time and action in the late sixteenth century by the Italian Ludovico Castelvetro. The *unité de lieu* is therefore necessarily inseparable from basic matters pertaining to the invention—in the Latin rhetorical sense of *inventio*—of dramatic plot. Second, the unique presentation of physical space, as contrasted with place, in neoclassical tragedy is inseparable from developments in astronomy and cosmology in early modern Europe. Dramatic poets in this period did not distinguish between place and space in the same ways we do today. Because there was no word in any Romance or Germanic language for *space* prior to the fifteenth century (Zumthor, "Lieux et espaces" 4 and *La mesure du monde*), the vehemently contested philosophical understanding it described—an empty, infinite, oriented field of relative location—was therefore also relatively recent. Early modern dramatic poets were concerned not with the essential qualities distinguishing place from space so much as they were concerned with making their stories dramatically compelling by locating them in plausible ways. The narrative strategies these poets devised not only paved the way for a renewal and consolidation of tragedy in France during the early decades of the seventeenth century but also formulated a means of imagining a physical cosmos thrown recently into crisis by the Columbian explorations and the humanist dissolution of Thomist-Aristotelian tradition (see Aït-Touati; Panofsky; Ramachandran).

There are a number of short, accessible theoretical texts from early in the seventeenth century available to instructors who want to explore with students the centrality of place to an aesthetics of neoclassical tragedy. As agreement among dramatic poets about the literary value of tragedy began to coalesce around 1630, debates concerning the specific requirements of imitation in art, in the specific sense given to the concept of mimesis in antiquity, necessarily encountered the challenges posed by the representation of place, on and off the stage. The crux of the matter during these debates, as students will discover from this reading, lay indeed with the authority of ancient example: To what degree should rigid faithfulness to ancient aesthetic principles take precedence over modern innovations and tastes (Forestier, "De la modernité anti-classique")?

The first recommended text is *La généreuse Allemande, ou le triomphe d'amour* (*The Noble German Lady; or, Love's Triumph*), by André Mareschal. In the preface to his *Généreuse Allemande*—statements of aesthetic principles from this period are almost always found in prefaces—Mareschal defends his own violation of the so-called rules of literary procedure by prioritizing the artful imitation of truth over the imitation of ancient prescriptions. If part of his tragicomedy occurs in Bohemia and part in Silesia, as Mareschal freely admits, it is because his play adheres to the more rigorous constraints of what the seventeenth century called *vraisemblance*, or dramatic plausibility (in other words, what usually happens). The freedom Mareschal asserts with respect to the depiction of place is part of what, polemically, he calls "pleasing defects" (*des vices agréables*) that are in keeping, as he puts it, with the French taste for aesthetic pleasure.

The second recommendation is Jean Chapelain's "Lettre sur la règle des vingt-quatre heures" ("Letter Concerning the Twenty-Four-Hour Rule"). In this key text, Chapelain develops an argument quite similar, though not identical, to Mareschal's, drawing also on the depiction of place as a central feature of *vraisemblance* in the theater. Whereas, however, Mareschal promotes a kind of total imitation of history or world, which in his view authorizes in the name of truth the presentation of multiple places onstage, Chapelain locates audience pleasure in what he calls perfect imitation, a correspondence between representation and represented story (Forestier, "Imitation"). The spectator's pleasure emerges in this case not from the so-called truth of imitation but from the presentation of events that, when artfully rearranged by poetic adjustment, seem to occur, located, in front of the audience (Chapelain 115). Chapelain's perspective has the force of paradox. What constitutes audience pleasure is the consistency and plausibility of the spectacle, which is contrived by the poet so as to convince viewers that the events they see unfolding are in fact present before them. The effect of these contrivances is to give poetic spectacle a plausibility that derives from its conceptual, as distinct from its imitative, presence. Events seem true precisely *because* they are dissociated from material place.

Finally, in the preface to his play *La Silvanire* (*The Wood Nymph*), "Préface en forme de discours poétique" ("Preface in the Form of a Discourse on Poetry"), the playwright Jean Mairet extends Chapelain's statement on imitation and presence by explicitly connecting it to the value and necessity of audience pleasure. Mairet returns to Chapelain's language of proximity, but he does so through an emphasis on the pleasure provoked by the impression of dramatic presence (484). Unlike history, which Mairet describes in Aristotelian terms as the simple narration of objective events, theater is a poetic art designed specifically to please the imagination. What is notable about Mairet's discussion, however, is that dramatic pleasure is inseparable from the artificial compression of space and time (485). Dramatic pleasure derives for Mairet, as for Chapelain, not only from the convincing correspondence of spectacle and story, but from the specific presence of events in front of—in the same place as—the spectator. This kind of proximity is available to the spectator under, again, two specific conditions: the depiction of place must be concentrated through adjustment and contrivance, and it must be given dramatic shape as the product of poetic modification.

Place in Corneille

One way to make these fairly abstract developments more concrete with students is to illustrate them by turning to an important trio of plays by Corneille that frame in dramatic terms these debates about place. These are Corneille's first tragedy, *Médée*; the hybrid comedy *L'illusion comique* (*Comic Illusion*); and *Horace*, often understood to usher in Corneille's canonical period. In general terms, these plays chronicle a period of five years, from 1635 to 1640, during which Corneille applied what we might call a centripetal force to the presentation of dramatic place. In *Médée*, for example, the sorceress threatens Corneille's tragedy with the possibility that her violent crimes, strewn throughout the Mediterranean world during her distant travels, will be brought into view in the present of dramatic spectacle. How, Corneille asks in his own later reflections on the dramatic construction of *Médée*, is spatial distance, embodied here in the form of Médée's elemental, monstrous excess, to be portrayed onstage? Throughout the first half of the play, Médée's violence is kept at a distance, described by Jason, then by Créon, then by Médée herself in a series of dramatic narrations (*récits*). Only at the end of the play will the threatened danger—that the cosmic scope of Médée's monstrosity will poison the place of the stage—come into visible being during the violent deaths of both Créon and Créuse. The deadly dress Médée gives Créuse is described in terms that emphasize how Médée's travels in distant lands will be brought here, literally to the stage where they may be seen. This movement is captured by the snakes who, in the form of the venom she has gathered from them, come from Africa to Corinth to the stage where Jason and the spectators will see their deadly effect.

Médée emplots a transition from a primarily verbal mode of dramatic depiction to one that emphasizes the problems posed by visual place in the theater. The concentrating force of *Médée* compresses the distant geography of travel into the consuming spectacle of Créuse's suffering and death. The former is narrated; the latter is shown. But if spectacle is the mode of portrayal with which narration is replaced, Corneille is also ill at ease, as demonstrated by his own subsequent writing about the tragedy, with the multiple stage places shown to the spectator in the play, and therefore with the play's inadequate concentration of geographic distance.

In the experimental *L'illusion comique*, place is an element central both to the plot itself and to principles of dramatic portrayal Corneille was formulating during that period of his career. The work is triply staged as a play within a play within a play: theater audiences watch characters who, beginning in the second act, themselves watch a play, which is later revealed to contain within it a third play. *L'illusion comique* may be read in these terms as a dramatization of spatial compression. What begins outside, in a pastoral setting appropriate to the work in the play of the conjurer Alcandre, moves into a cave, which Alcandre describes as a theater. The shift from outside to inside the cave mirrors spatially a primary thematic concern of the play, namely, what is the most effective way to portray things occurring far away, in distant places? A worried father named Pridamant has come to consult Alcandre and ask him to locate his wayward son. The magician tells Pridamant that instead of telling him about his son, he will show him where he is by means of the dramatic spectacle he has prepared for him, his audience (and for us, Corneille's audience), in his cave-theater (situated on Corneille's stage). What ensues is the story of a series of mostly preposterous adventures concerning Pridamant's son and a ridiculous soldier named Matamore who claims to have traveled throughout the world, from Mexico to Iceland to Japan, and to be even a kind of cosmic being living in the heavens. Despite the absurdity of his claims, Matamore is not unlike Médée, whose distant navigations must somehow be brought to the stage.

Alcandre's play within a play rejects Matamore's narrative reporting and makes him a figure of the priority Alcandre gives to visual depiction. Telling becomes showing as distant place is set visibly onstage in Alcandre's cave. Geographic expansion is brought under the centripetal force of dramatic spectacle when the action moves inside the cave and, again, when the play within a play within a play begins and Matamore's boastful speech is replaced by a tragedy that constitutes act 5 of the play. It is in this final act that Corneille presents the principle of dramatic place that he will bring fully to bear on the seminal formulations of the tragedy *Horace* (Peters 92–101). For *Horace* is the very play Corneille turns to in two other indispensable statements on the nature of tragic place in theater of the 1630s and 1640s, the *Discours des trois unités d'action, de jour et de lieu* (*Discourse on the Three Unities of Action, Time, and Place*) and the *Discours de la tragédie* (*Discourse on Tragedy*). (Corneille's *Discours* are at least partly in dialogue with yet another important statement on the nature of dramatic place in the seventeenth century, *Pratique du théâtre* [*The Practice of Theater*], by François Hédelin, abbé d'Aubignac). In this treatise, Corneille binds the contrivances required of place in the neoclassical theater to a broader concept of dramatic plausibility. The unity of place is, among other things, a problem of visual perception. Modern audiences, Corneille suggests, cannot be expected to believe, as Sophocles's audiences were, that the physical place they see before them embodies multiple places simultaneously, especially given that what they see before them is already double: it is at once the literal, physical stage and the abstract site of dramatic fiction. Correspondingly, if the unity of place is accommodated by setting the action of a play in, as Corneille puts it, a single city, then it is equally impossible to show the entire city on the stage. Changes to the quality of the place imagined to lie visibly before the audience must *necessarily* (*de nécessité*, in Corneille's insistent emphasis) be made.

Corneille's solution, required by the structural imperfections of *Médée*, is first presented in the final act—the mini-tragedy—of *L'illusion comique* and subsequently brought to fruition in *Horace*. Though it tells the story of an adulterous affair between Pridamant's son Clindor, who turns out to be an actor playing a role, and Princesse Rosine, act 5 of *L'illusion comique* is fundamentally about believing in—becoming affectively invested in—what one sees despite knowing that it is an illusion. The proliferating distances characteristic of both Médée's and Matamore's worlds are compressed in the final act of *L'illusion comique* into a single space held inside a double play, itself narrowly framed by Alcandre's cave on Corneille's theater stage. This is the artificially contrived place of dramatic, rather than mimetic, plausibility (of *vraisemblance*). When Clindor's (fictional) wife Isabelle tells him, "[Q]ue j'aide bien à m'abuser moi-même! / Je vois qu'on me trahit, et je crois que l'on m'aime" 'Let me deceive myself! / I see that I am betrayed and I believe that I am loved' (5.3.1513–1514), she is telling us that dramatic place in tragedy is the site of necessary artifice. It is what Corneille tells us about *Horace* in the *Discours des trois unités* when he writes that the unity of place requires narrative and perceptual contradictions that may only be solved by tricking the spectator ("Cela aiderait à tromper l'auditeur,"), engaging in theater contrivances ("des fictions de théâtre") that emphasize the audience's affective investment in the action of the play. Tragic place does not imitate real places. Instead it sets the conditions for the narration of places in plausibly structured dramatic plots whose pleasing artfulness is designed to turn audiences away from the "peu de justesse" 'lack of accuracy' characteristic of the depiction of place on stage (189). Characters have substance—being, in poetic terms—not because they have location, but because they and the situations they embody are contrived so as to be dramatically coherent, and therefore to touch and entertain their audiences. They are the conceptual product of a locating, rather than located, force of becoming that in dramatic terms we call plausibility, and that in modern cosmological terms we call space.

Early Modern Space and Racinian Tragedy

Corneille's tragic theater is of a piece with contemporaneous transformations in natural philosophical concepts of physical space. The cosmological revolution brought about by Nicolaus Copernicus, Giordano Bruno, Galileo Galilei, and Johannes Kepler was only the most radical culmination of a set of medieval debates by scholastic philosophers and church fathers over the nature of divine creation and the location of the God in the cosmos (see Hallyn; Seidengart). How, scholars like Thomas Aquinas and Nicholas of Cusa asked, could the infinity of God's creative agency be reconciled with the Aristotelian postulation of a geocentric, finite universe? For Aristotle, place (topos) was the primary quality of all things that exist. To have being meant to be located in place. Aristotle demonstrates in book 4 of the *Physics* that place is an a priori condition of all things. And because all things that exist have place, or are in place, place must itself be a thing in place in order to exist. As such, it preexists the bodies it contains and persists beyond them if those bodies cease to exist. Further, the universe is itself a kind of super-place composed of tightly packed topoi allowing of no void between or within them (4.213a11–216b20). Place, then, in the Aristotelian conception, which would dominate philosophical accounts of the universe up through much of the European Middle Ages, is inseparable from being.

Throughout the Middle Ages and Renaissance, Aristotle's concepts of place and void were vigorously debated and increasingly challenged. The most immediate problem for medieval theologians was the status of the divine in a cosmology predicated upon the absence of a creator exterior to the concentric spheres of the universe. In other words, where was the Christian God to be located in a cosmos determined by the finite, tightly fitting places? Moreover, how could the phenomenon of motion be explained if place is by nature immobile, in Aristotle's view, and if there is nothing beyond the world and the outermost sphere itself has no place (Grant 61–185)? How could bodies move without room in which to move? By the early fifteenth century, scholars such as Nicholas of Cusa began to challenge Aristotle's topos seriously and posit the necessity of infinite interstitial space (Jammer 52–88; Nicholas 107). Indeed, by 1606, the French lexicographer Jean Nicot would define space as the "intervalle de temps et lieu entre deux extrémités" 'the interval in time and space between two extremes,' whereas nearly a century later, and in far more epistemologically radical terms, Antoine Furetière would write that space "est l'intervalle qui est entre les trois dimensions, longueur, largeur et profondeur, quand même le corps qui . . . l'occupe serait détruit et qu'il serait entièrement vidé" 'is the interval between the three dimensions, length, width, and depth, even when the body that occupies it is destroyed and when it has been emptied out.' No longer a defining, ontologically primary principle of being and identity, as it had been in Aristotle, space becomes the sometimes empty, potentially infinite, force defined only in terms of what it is not, in terms of what becomes in and from it (Ropars-Wuilleumier 72–79).

In the wake of Corneille's innovations, and in the light of the natural philosophical transformations that informed them, the depiction and function of physical location in early modern French tragedy evolved in crucial ways. In *Le véritable Saint Genest* (*The True Saint Genest*), Jean Rotrou derived an important dramatic conceit from the radical proliferation of real and imagined places (e.g., 1.5.297–306; 2.7.477–532) only to reveal that place has functioned over the course of the play not as a principle of location but as a generating function of—the condition of possibility for—a far more abstract event: the hero's conversion to Christianity. But it was Jean Racine, several decades later, who would explore the dramatic implications of a locating universe that could no longer be relied on to provide either the reassuring emplacements of Aristotelian physics or the optimistic continuities of humanist Christianity. In his secular tragedies, Racine does not depict the world in its being so much as he offers dramatic accounts of its active becoming. The Racinian stage is less—or not only—a closed and inviolable place, an emblem of psychical oppression, as scholars have often suggested (e.g., Barthes 20), than it is a borderless field of passing-through. In Racine, Aristotelian place-as-being gives way to post-Copernican space-as-becoming (Peters 113–26).

A brief, concluding look at *Bérénice* allows us, students and teachers, to see why the handling of dramatic space in neoclassical tragedy should draw our attention to the developments of early modern natural philosophy. Just as spatial distances are compressed in Corneille's theater in the late 1630s, the vast expanses of the Mediterranean world, to which both *Bérénice* and the earlier *Andromaque* make detailed reference, are concentrated in a narrowly delimited stage space—a single chamber of Pyrrhus's palace in *Andromaque* and the famously minimalist *cabinet*, or small room, of *Bérénice*. But if the visible setting of *Bérénice* exemplifies, on the one hand, the dramatic conditions required by the neoclassical unity of place, it also illustrates, on the other, how the apparent absence of the material world in the tragic theater of this period offers a powerful reflection on the creative force of recent concepts of space. When he summarizes Pierre Gassendi's physics in his *Abrégé de la philosophie de Gassendi* (*Epitome of Gassendi's Philosophy*), François Bernier emphasizes both the immateriality and the specifically receptive character of cosmic space, which he defines as "une pure étendue immatérielle et une pure capacité à recevoir les corps, laquelle n'est ni substance, ni accident, ni rien de tout ce qui est capable d'agir ou de pâtir" 'a pure incorporeal extension, a pure capacity to receive material bodies which is itself neither a substance nor an accident nor anything that is capable of acting or suffering' (1: 12). Bernier's statement foregrounds the creative void space characteristic of Epicurean atomism, a body of natural philosophical speculation with which Racine and his contemporaries were very familiar (Darmon 5–26), and it seems to find a poetic echo in an astonishing statement Racine makes in the preface to *Bérénice*. Responding to critics of early performances who complained, in essence, that nothing happened in the play, Racine writes that in composing *Bérénice* he had challenged himself to bring forth the new from a kind of poetic void. Some commentators, Racine emphasizes, do not understand that literary invention "consiste à faire quelque chose de rien" 'consists of making something from nothing' (451). In this statement, Racine aligns himself with the heroes of his tragedies: *Bérénice*, in this case, is a poem about characters who seek ways to bring language into being from silence, to create something from nothing.

In an important sense, the apparent absence of represented material space in *Bérénice* is an ideal test case for the notion that students may discover fundamental principles of neoclassical drama in the encounter with early modern debates around cosmology. By the late seventeenth century, space had replaced place as the primary principle of material location (Casey 3–22): where Aristotelian and medieval place had *location*, early modern space *located*. Space had become a principle of orientation without directly perceptible being (Miller 1–26). As they posited the existence of void space and derived the principle of infinity from mathematical abstraction, philosophers in the early modern period proposed a concept of the universe available only to a conceptual theater of the mind (Fricheau 224–26). In Racine, as in natural philosophy, depicted space does not describe the emplacement of material bodies and worlds. Instead, its creative, indeed poetic, force describes worlds and events coming into being, even as it is itself immaterial and imperceptible (Peters 115). To read book 4 of Aristotle's *Physics* alongside the first several chapters of Bernier's presentation of Gassendi's natural philosophy gives students unique insight into the dramatic situations expressed in the French neoclassical tragic theater. As natural philosophers offered new ways of thinking the situatedness of the material world, dramatic poets such as Corneille and Racine formulated new responses to the question,

What does it mean to be, to have location, to be located in an often unknowable cosmos?

Note

1. All translations in this essay are mine.

Works Cited

Aït-Touati, Frédérique. *Contes de la lune: Essai sur la fiction et la science modernes.* Gallimard, 2011.

Aristotle. *Physics. The Complete Works of Aristotle*, edited by Jonathan Barnes, vol. 1, Princeton UP, 1984, pp. 315–446.

Barthes, Roland. *Sur Racine*, Seuil, 1963.

Bernier, François. *Abrégé de la philosophie de Gassendi.* Anisson et Posuel, 1678. 8 vols.

Biet, Christian, and Christophe Triau. *Qu'est-ce que le théâtre?* Gallimard, 2006.

Casey, Edward S. *The Fate of Place: A Philosophical History.* U of California P, 1998.

Chapelain, Jean. "Lettre sur la règle des vingt-quatre heures." 1630. *Opuscules critiques*, by Chapelain, edited by Alfred C. Hunter and Anne Duprat, Droz, 2007, pp. 222–34.

Corneille, Pierre. *Discours des trois unités, d'action, de jour, et de lieu. Œuvres complètes*, vol. 3, pp. 174–90.

———. *Horace.* 1640. *Œuvres complètes*, vol. 1, pp. 831–901.

———. *L'illusion comique.* 1635. *Œuvres complètes*, vol. 1, pp. 611–88.

———. *Médée.* 1635. *Œuvres complètes*, vol. 1, pp. 533–94.

———. *Œuvres complètes.* Edited by Georges Couton, Gallimard, 1980–87. 3 vols.

Darmon, Jean-Charles. *Philosophie épicurienne et littérature au XVIIe siècle en France: Etudes sur Gassendi, Cyrano de Bergerac, La Fontaine, Saint-Evremond.* PU de France, 1998.

Forestier, Georges. "De la modernité anti-classique au classicisme moderne: Le modèle théâtral (1628–1634)." *Littératures classiques*, no. 19, 1993, pp. 87–128.

———. "Imitation parfaite et vraisemblance absolue: Réflexions sur un paradoxe classique." *Poétique*, vol. 82, 1990, pp. 187–202.

Fricheau, Catherine. "Savoirs, techniques et esthétiques de l'espace à l'âge classique." *Histoire de la France littéraire, tome 2: Classicismes XVII–XVIIIe siècles*, edited by Jean-Charles Darmon and Michel Delon, PU de France, 2006, pp. 215–90.

Furetière, Antoine. *Le dictionnaire universel.* 1690. SNL-Le Robert, 1978.

Grant, Edward. *Planets, Stars, and Orbs: The Medieval Cosmos, 1200–1687.* Cambridge UP, 1996.

Hallyn, Fernand. *La structure poétique du monde: Copernic, Kepler.* Seuil, 1987.

Jammer, Max. *Concepts of Space: The History of Space in Physics.* Harvard UP, 1954.

Lyons, John D. *Kingdom of Disorder: The Theory of Tragedy in Classical France*. Purdue UP, 1996.

———. "Unseen Space and Theatrical Narrative: The 'Récit de Cinna.'" *Yale French Studies*, no. 80, 1991, pp. 70–90.

Mairet, Jean. "Préface en forme de discours poétique." 1631. *Théâtre du XVIIe siècle*, vol. 1, edited by Jacques Scherer, Gallimard, 1975, pp. 479–88.

Mareschal, André. *La généreuse Allemande, ou le triomphe d'amour*. Pierre Rocolet, 1631.

Miller, David Marshall. *Representing Space in the Scientific Revolution*. Cambridge UP, 2014.

Nicholas of Cusa. *De docta ignorantia*. Yale UP, 1954.

Nicot, Jean. *Le thresor de la langue francoyse*. David Douceur, 1606.

Panofsky, Erwin. *Perspective as Symbolic Form*. Translated by Christopher S. Wood, Zone Books, 1996.

Peters, Jeffrey N. *The Written World: Space, Literature, and the Chorological Imagination in Early Modern France*. Northwestern UP, 2018.

Racine, Jean. *Bérénice*. 1670. *Œuvres complètes, tome I: Théâtre-Poésie*, edited by Georges Forestier, Gallimard, 1999, pp. 447–509.

Ramachandran, Ayesha. *The Worldmakers: Global Imagining in Early Modern Europe*. U of Chicago P, 2015.

Ropars-Wuilleumier, Marie-Claire. *Ecrire l'espace*. PU de Vincennes, 2002.

Rotrou, Jean. *Le véritable Saint Genest*. *Théâtre du XVIIe siècle*. 1647. Edited by Jacques Scherer, vol. 1, Gallimard, 1975.

Seidengart, Jean. *Dieu, l'univers et la sphère: Penser l'infinité cosmique à l'aube de la science Classique*. Albin Michel, 2006.

Ubersfeld, Anne. *Lire le théâtre*. Editions sociales, 1977. 3 vols.

Zumthor, Paul. "Lieux et espaces au moyen âge." *Dalhousie French Studies*, vol. 30, 1995, pp. 3–10.

———. *La mesure du monde*. Seuil, 1993.

Faith E. Beasley

Accounting for Taste: Corneille and the Power of the Female Spectator

In 1702, M. de Vigneul-Marville penned an intriguing description of Pierre Corneille's creative process: "Quand il avait composé un ouvrage, il le lisait à Mme de Fontenelles sa soeur, qui en pouvait bien juger. Cette dame avait l'esprit fort juste" 'When he had composed a work, he would read it to his sister, Mme de Fontenelles, who could judge it well. This lady had a very accurate mind' (156).[1] Vigneul-Marville alludes to a world in which women were integrated into the Republic of Letters and helped shape neoclassical theater. His observation, however, clashes with conventional literary histories of the great canonical writers, which are devoid of women's participation and influence. An examination of Corneille's authorial practices confirms this alternative history and illuminates the ways in which women exerted unprecedented influence on literature as writers, as critics, and, in the specific case of theater, as members of a public that sought to shape the genre at a critical moment of its elaboration in France.[2]

One of Corneille's most famous plays, *Le Cid*, illustrates especially well the impact women had on the genre of neoclassical theater, promoting a new literary taste that writers increasingly recognized as valid and authoritative. *Le Cid* was Corneille's first triumph and also his most controversial work, sparking a literary debate that spanned decades. He was still revising and commenting on his play in 1660, almost a quarter century after its first appearance. In what follows, I will describe an approach to teaching *Le Cid* that illuminates France's unique literary culture. This approach can be profitably used in introductory survey courses on French literature, those focused on the seventeenth century, and advanced seminars on the role of conversation in France, the Republic of Letters and its networks, and salon culture. My goal is to teach students how neoclassical tragedy developed; the roles authors, critics, and spectators played in its elaboration; and especially the gender dynamics that were particular to France during this time. The various versions of *Le Cid*, the documents of the quarrel, and Corneille's commentary on and revisions to his play illuminate the century's battles to come to terms with the emerging force of a worldly public whose roots were in salon culture, a world created and dominated by women. When studied through the lens of gender, Corneille's *Le Cid* and the quarrel it provoked reveal a battle over differing concepts of literary taste and values, and the use of theater to convey these values and shape society.

Reconstructing the context necessary for this reading of *Le Cid* and the quarrel requires dismantling a number of preconceptions twenty-first-century students often have about authorship, spectatorship, theatrical performance, and the relation between literature and society. Many students imagine Corneille as a genius producing a work in solitary reflection that is then performed in a public space before an elite audience. But these conceits do not correspond to seventeenth-century French literary culture. I thus begin with a lecture in which I focus on an essential difference between our world and Corneille's—namely, the collaborative nature of both literary invention and its reception during this period—and lay the groundwork to allow students to perceive the larger questions *Le Cid* and the quarrel will evoke: What influence does the public exert on the composition and the reception of a work of theater? What role does theater play in the public sphere? How is literary innovation viewed? How do critics establish their authority? Who determines what is acceptable to present to a public and what needs to be censored?

As Roger Chartier and others have persuasively shown, dramatic works such as *Le Cid* existed in oral form before finding a second existence in print. In my opening lecture I stress that in seventeenth-century France, plays were often elaborated in gatherings such as the *ruelles* later known as *salons*, an institution created and dominated by women. Drawing on works such as Chartier's, I evoke a world in which literary creation and consumption were often communal, collaborative activities. I focus on the evolution of the French public and on how literary texts were produced and received, and suggest that in many respects the public can be considered collaborators in literary production rather than simply consumers.[3] Conversations about a work played a critical and influential role in its reception and shaped the mindset of the period.

In my overview of Corneille's literary context, I describe the emergence of different, often competing, publics. Corneille produced *Le Cid* in the decade that saw the founding of the Académie Française, a body that is associated with a *docte*, or scholarly, primarily male, public. Richelieu's august body was determined to assert its primacy and its normative, restricting vision for the theater. For the Académie, the legitimate rules governing literary invention and reception are those emanating from a traditional education that privileged texts such as Aristotle's *Poetics*. During the same period, an alternative public associated with the worldly (*mondain*) milieu of the salons was emerging as a competing critical authority, a public whose taste and values were not tethered to the scholarly criteria of the *doctes*. *Le Cid* and the ensuing quarrel bear witness to the development of this powerful *mondain* public. Corneille uses *Le Cid* to enter his society's debates over the authority of this worldly public and its often competing literary values. Teaching *Le Cid* and the ensuing quarrel as illustrative of seventeenth-century French debates over literary values, reception, and authority allows me to bring a distant history to life using issues, such as freedom of expression, female agency, and social networking, that today's students find relevant and intriguing.

I focus students' attention on elements that will enable them to understand Chimène, the main character in *Le Cid*, and her reception, because the treatment of this female protagonist during the quarrel illuminates the gendered dynamics of the work's literary context. Corneille created a lively and engaged conversation with his female, worldly public and was especially intent on sanctioning a taste women were instrumental in developing. I present the criteria associated with the *mondain* taste developed in the salons and contrast it with the scholarly or *docte* criteria that playwrights used to compose "regular" tragedies.[4] In the 1630s, when Corneille was producing this work, there was a growing movement among the *doctes* to promote standards derived from Aristotle's *Poetics*. In 1630, for example, Jean Chapelain produced his *Lettre sur la règle des vingt-quatre heures* (*Letter Concerning the Twenty-Four-Hour Rule*), illustrating the move toward standardization based on classical models. But a playwright who wished to have popular success had increasingly to conform to a worldly taste elaborated outside the scholarly milieu using different criteria. Most important in this formulation of literary taste was that a play be pleasing; adherence to regulations such as the *trois unités* ("three unities") of place, time, and action was of secondary importance.[5] Corneille took the increasing power of the worldly public—a public that pointedly included women—seriously, sought to obtain its approbation, and composed his *Cid* to adhere to its values. The documents of the quarrel, composed by the more traditional *doctes*, constitute a direct repudiation of the power of this new public and its values, and served as an attempt to exclude this public and its literary taste from the Republic of Letters.

Our first discussion of *Le Cid* is oriented toward understanding the creation of the text with the ensuing quarrel in mind.[6] Students read Corneille's original 1637 version because it sparked the debate.[7] I provide study questions to guide their readings and ask the class to pay particular attention to Chimène and to how Corneille negotiates the various expectations for neoclassical theater. We discuss possible reasons why Corneille might have decided to use a particular version of this story, Guillén de Castro's 1621 Spanish play *Las Mocedades del Cid* (*The Cid's Early Years*), as his source. In this rendition of the legend, Chimène is in love with Rodrigue before the dispute between their fathers that complicates their union. It is possible to attribute Corneille's attraction to this Spanish version of *Le Cid* to its emphasis on Chimène and love as opposed to the political heroics and the traditional themes of honor and duty embodied by the title character.[8]

From an initial encounter with the play itself we move to excerpts from the quarrel.[9] We start by reading passages from *Excuse à Ariste* (*Apology to Ariste*), a poem Corneille composed following the initial success of *Le Cid*. The poem can be read as a provocation as well as a preemptive strike against Corneille's detractors, whose critiques must have already been circulating in oral form. We focus on passages that reveal Corneille's awareness of and relationship to his contemporary publics, especially the newly influential worldly public, and try to re-create the conversations that surrounded the work. We read aloud from the play and the poem in order to underscore how texts were received differently in the early modern period. This exercise heightens students' awareness of the differences between the seventeenth-century literary world and their own, and foregrounds the importance of recognizing that Corneille's public would not have engaged with *Le Cid* solely as a published text, as students usually do in a classroom. To return to Chartier's formulations, texts were often first experienced communally and orally; encounters with the printed text usually occurred afterward if at all.

Corneille's poem allows us to revive the conversations about literature during the period that I had evoked in the introductory lecture. In the *Excuse*, Corneille articulates the stakes of the debate and provides the precise context for interpreting the other texts of the quarrel. He provokes his critics by articulating a question that was circulating throughout erudite and worldly circles: Who has the authority to pronounce judgment on a literary work? In a bold move, he substitutes himself for Parnassus, rejecting the authority of the *doctes*, and explains that the criteria advocated by such critics have been supplanted by a new set of values and a new sense of who can determine a composition's value and what a literary work should do. He writes, "Je sais ce que je vaux, et croy ce qu'on m'en dit" and "Je satisfais ensemble et peuple et courtisans" 'I know my worth and I believe what people tell me . . . I satisfy both commoners and the court' (780). *Le Cid* must be deemed a success because it pleased the public, a public understood as the *mondain* public who applauded his creation because it conformed to their literary taste. Corneille further allies his work with worldly values when he identifies love for a particular woman as the source of his success: "Charmé de deux beaux yeux, mon vers charma la Cour, / et ce que j'ai de nom je le dois à l'amour" 'Charmed by two beautiful eyes, my verse charmed the court / And whatever reputation I have, I owe to love.' This self-congratulatory poem is equally a defense of the right of an author to compose a work whose principal value lies in its ability to please a worldly public as opposed to a slavish adherence to abstract rules such as the three unities that Corneille's contemporaries derived from Aristotle's *Poetics*.

The texts of the quarrel reveal that contemporaries recognized immediately Corneille's transgressive valorization of pleasure over other criteria for poetic invention as well as his anointing of a new worldly public as legitimate arbiters of literary taste. Students read excerpts from the two most important contributions: Georges de Scudéry's *Observations sur* Le Cid (*Observations on* The Cid), which launched the attack, and the response by the Académie Française, the *Sentiments sur la Tragi-Comédie du* Cid (*Opinion Concerning the Tragicomedy* The Cid), composed by Jean Chapelain. I also include Corneille's *Lettre apologétique* (*Letter of Apology*), his 1637 response to Scudéry, and his *Examen du* Cid (*Examination of* The Cid), penned for the revised 1660 edition of the play. We read these texts to understand the dynamics of the literary field. The *doctes*' reception of Corneille's *Cid*, and their ultimate condemnation not only of the play but also of the public's approbation, illuminate the ways Corneille was perceived as disruptive and why. The quarrel over *Le Cid* is as much about literary creation in general as it is about the play. Scudéry's and the Académie's attack on *Le Cid* are efforts to establish the authority of a more traditional public that judged according to scholarly standards and moral codes. They condemned Corneille's decision to prioritize the values associated with *mondain* salon culture.

One passage from Scudéry's diatribe illustrates particularly well that the *doctes* perceived Corneille's principal transgression to be his authorization of the worldly public to impose its own taste, and for literature to convey new values associated with this sphere. Scudéry denounces the same public whose admiration Corneille used in his poem to defend his creation, writing:

> Tout ce qui brille n'est pas toujours précieux . . . souvent l'apparence du bien se fait prendre pour le bien même. Aussi ne m'étonnai-je pas beaucoup que le Peuple qui porte le jugement dans les yeux, se laisse tromper par celui de tous les sens, le plus facile à décevoir: Mais que cette vapeur grossière, qui se forme dans le Parterre ait pu s'élever jusqu'aux Galeries, et qu'un fantôme ait abusé le savoir comme l'ignorance, et la Cour aussi bien que le Bourgeois, j'avoue que ce prodige m'étonne. . . . (782)
>
> Everything that shines is not always valuable . . . often the appearance of value is mistaken for value itself. Thus I am not surprised that commoners, who judge by their eyes alone, allow themselves to be fooled by this sense, which is the easiest to deceive. But that this unrefined fog, which develops in the cheapest seats, could have reached the heights of the most expensive seats, and that this ghost could have encroached on knowledge as well as ignorance, and the court as well as the bourgeois, I admit that this extraordinary event does shock me. . . .

Corneille's fellow playwright is astounded by the fact that a "vapeur grossière" 'unrefined fog' has risen from its habitual place in the lowly, uneducated "Parterre" and clouded the judgment of those who should be better able to assess a play's value, the court and the bourgeoisie in the "Galeries." To Scudéry's amazement, this supposedly more knowledgeable and discerning public also applauded Corneille's creation. Scudéry advocates for judging the play's value using the criteria that he believes will dispel this "fog"; namely, the scholarly rules associated with the *doctes* and, more generally, a moral code that would have no place for a woman like Chimène. The lengthy diatribe against Corneille's popular play is an effort to reassert the authority of a learned, educated public composed of experts such as himself. Scudéry specifies what the reaction of a "reasonable" public should be, stressing that spectators must allow themselves to be guided by traditional learned arbiters and their definition of what is reasonable.

Given that one of my objectives is to tease out the role gender and women in particular play in the literary sphere, I direct students' focus toward Scudéry's critique of Chimène and the emotionally charged vocabulary he employs. Scudéry characterizes Chimène as "cette dénaturée" 'that unnatural woman' and "ce monstre" 'that monster' (792). He condemns her because in his opinion she chooses love over honor or "honnêteté" 'decency' (789). She is a "mauvaise fille" 'bad daughter' who dishonors her father (788). Scudery takes on the role of judge, pronouncing Chimène "criminelle" 'criminal' and "indigne de la lumière" 'unworthy of the light of day' for refusing to reject her fiancé, Rodrigue, after he kills her father (789). In putting this "monstre" on stage, Corneille offers a character who is "contre la raison et la bienséance" 'against reason and propriety' and who as such clearly cannot serve as a positive example (788). In Scudéry's estimation, Chimène has no place in a theatrical work that must first and foremost instruct the public.

Read in their seventeenth-century context, Scudéry's vitriolic attacks on Chimène, which will be echoed by the Académie Française, emanate from various threats to the *doctes*' authority.[10] Corneille's *Le Cid* does not obey the rules the Académie wants to impose: the playwright makes a mockery of the three unities and, even more disturbingly, his protagonist flouts the *doctes*' concept of acceptable female behavior. Worst of all, the play and its heroine are a success; they please the worldly public, which in turn is empowered to pronounce on literary value. According to Scudéry and the *doctes*, theater must serve as a tool to shape and promote cultural norms. The public's approbation of *Le Cid* is proof that neither the worldly public nor its criteria can be allowed to determine the merits of a literary work. Corneille's Chimène knows her own mind and succeeds in her quest for happiness by remaining emotionally faithful to someone she has chosen. *Doctes* like Scudéry refuse to accept such a woman as morally believable, not because she couldn't exist, but because she shouldn't exist. In Scudéry's estimation, an opinion that the Académie Française will endorse in its response, the public should not be allowed to find pleasure in such a morally defunct character because pleasure can lead to emulation. Scudéry condemns pleasure that is not in the service of conveying a "reasonable" moral code and plausibility, especially for women. In his desire to please this public, Corneille has upended norms governing poetic composition. He separates pleasure from its traditional function, which is to make moral instruction in a dramatic work more acceptable.

In creating a character who pleases the wrong public for the wrong reasons, Corneille allies himself squarely with the worldly audience. He embraces this position in his written response to Scudéry and defies a more conventional poetics that views theater as necessarily in the service of the creation of a moral society. He defends his public's freedom to find Chimène's story acceptable and grants legitimacy to their approbation. The premise of his defense is simple: the play is pleasing to the worldly public, so it must be good. He defends Chimène by reminding Scudéry that "les plus vertueuses Dames de la Cour" 'the most virtuous women of the court' approved of her:

> Ne vous êtes-vous pas souvenu que *Le Cid* a été représenté trois fois au Louvre et deux fois à l'Hôtel de Richelieu: Quand vous avez traité la pauvre Chimène d'impudique, de prostituée, de parricide, de monstre; ne vous êtes-vous pas souvenu, que la Reine, les Princesses et les plus vertueuses Dames de la Cour et de Paris, l'ont reçue et caressée en fille d'honneur? (*Lettre* 803)
>
> Did you not remember that *The Cid* was staged three times at the Louvre and twice at the Hôtel de Richelieu: when you called poor Chimène shameless, a prostitute, parricidal, a monster; did you not remember that the Queen, the Princesses, and the most virtuous women of the court and of Paris fawned over her as a woman of honor?

Corneille rejects those traditionally charged with determining literary value in favor of a new critical body, the worldly public, which includes women as legitimate arbiters of literary taste.

Richelieu found the stakes of this quarrel over *Le Cid* so important that he ordered the Académie Française, which he had founded only two years earlier, to intervene and settle the dispute. The Académie's *Sentiments sur la Tragi-Comédie du* Cid reveals Richelieu's intention to use the quarrel to establish the Académie as the official arbiter of literary taste and value, using criteria as defined by the *doctes* and not the worldly public. Richelieu recognized that literature could be a tool to advance a particular set of values and can be viewed as having founded the Académie in part to develop this mindset. Audiences, especially women, who were uneducated in the traditional literary values and the conventionally accepted function of literature in society needed to be excluded from the process of literary accreditation. While some salon habitués like Jean Chapelain were also "immortels," as Académie members are called, no woman was an "immortel" until Marguerite Yourcenar's election in 1981. Richelieu considered the Académie's arbitration of the quarrel over *Le Cid* so critical that he rejected numerous drafts until Chapelain could produce one that expressed the group's-cum-Richelieu's official and authoritative opinion adequately.

Students are especially struck by the difference between the original reception of *Le Cid* and their initial reading of the play when they learn that the Académie sided with Scudéry instead of defending what they might view as an author's freedom of expression. In the opening lines, Chapelain takes the same anti-pleasure, pro-rules position as Scudéry, declaring that the purpose of the Académie's intervention is to "regarder pas tant si elle avait plu, que si en effet elle avait dû plaire" 'not to determine if the play *was* pleasing but if it *should have been* pleasing' (809; my emphasis). In the Académie's response, only one public, the scholarly public, has the expertise and the authority to answer that question, because pleasure must be generated by adherence to scholarly rules and advance a particular moral code. As in Scudéry's critique, the discussion is gendered: the *doctes* are the male arbiters whose taste is formed through a traditional education and illustrates a particular view of the world. The worldly public, however, judges the value of a work according to different standards. This milieu has developed a literary taste that does not associate pleasure only with meeting conventional guidelines for composition—guidelines often used to convey a certain traditional code of what behavior is acceptable. In its response, the Académie, guided by Richelieu's heavy hand, rejects such worldly taste in favor of its own. In the Académie's estimation, "on doit plaire selon les règles" 'one must please according to the rules':

> [N]ous pouvons dire tous ensemble qu'une pièce de théâtre est bonne quand elle produit un contentement raisonnable . . . nous ne dirons pas sur la foi du peuple, qu'un ouvrage de poésie soit bon parce qu'il l'aura contenté, si les doctes aussi n'en sont contents. Et certes il n'est pas croyable qu'un plaisir puisse être contraire au bon sens, si ce n'est le plaisir de quelque goût dépravé. (808)[11]

> [W]e can unanimously state that the play is good when it produces a reasonable satisfaction . . . we will not say that a literary work is good

> because it pleased the people, if it did not also please the *doctes*. And to be sure it is unbelievable that pleasure could be contrary to good sense, unless it is pleasure derived from some kind of depraved taste.

"Good sense" as defined by the *doctes* must emanate from a literary work; therefore, an author's task is to convey this "bon sens" in an acceptable manner (810). The Académie agrees with Scudéry and finds that Chimène defies "reason" by not displaying the qualities of a proper woman, or moral values (810); she is not "natural" (809). In their estimation no woman would accept in marriage her father's murderer, much less on the same day of his death, unless she were "la plus dépouillée d'honneur et d'humanité" 'the most bereft of honor and humanity.'[12] Scudéry and the Académie judge Chimène to be a "furie" 'shrew' because she refuses to stop loving Rodrigue even after he kills her father. The errant public that Corneille uses to defend his play must be corrected by the "experts" and the true "préceptes de ces arts" 'precepts of these arts,' to which Corneille has only superficially adhered in creating his version of *Le Cid*.[13]

After having studied the texts of the quarrel, we turn to a second analysis of the play to see how Corneille actually provoked the controversy and crafted *Le Cid* to enter this gendered war over literary invention and criticism. We observe how Corneille constructed his version of *Le Cid* to find favor with the worldly public and to authorize this new arbitrating body for literature and its worldly taste. His choice of this particular story is in itself provocative: it would appear impossible to argue that the plotline offers an acceptable model of female behavior. But the play is carefully constructed to justify Chimène's actions and to encourage the public to applaud her as an honorable woman and daughter (702). Corneille chooses to open his version of *Le Cid* with Chimène's father's approval of Rodrigue as his future son-in-law, thus enabling the public to view Chimène first as a dutiful daughter. After speaking with the Comte, Chimène's *suivante*, or lady-in-waiting, Elvire, reports to her mistress that her father supports her love for Rodrigue. In the 1648 version, Corneille goes even farther and underscores Chimène's qualities as the dutiful daughter, saying that her father was especially impressed that Chimène was willing to allow him to choose her spouse: "Ce respect l'a ravi, sa bouche et son visage / M'en [Elvire] ont donné sur l'heure un digne témoignage" 'He welcomed this respect. His words and looks / At once bore witness to his joy at it' (1.1.21–22).[14] Corneille removes the Comte from the opening scene in order to focus attention entirely on Chimène and her obedience. All his versions of *Le Cid* thus open with the Comte's approval of the union in order to elevate Chimène and affirm her judgment in her attraction to Rodrigue. To compound this recognition of Rodrigue's intrinsic merit, the third scene (the second scene in the later versions) is devoted to the Infante's own love for Rodrigue.

Having established Chimène as the dutiful daughter, and the young couple as honorable and acceptable, Corneille then presents what he portrays as the egotistical argument between the couple's fathers, who come to symbolically represent an old order.[15] Rodrigue becomes the innocent son who has no choice but to obey his father's demands to avenge him after the Comte's attack on his honor. The couple's union, previously legitimized by both fathers, is threatened by an old order that obliges a son to avenge his father. Chimène, too, is portrayed as a victim to what Corneille intimates is this outmoded code of honor. Through the character of Chimène Corneille suggests that a different behavior, one that follows the code of love, is more logical. By creating a protagonist who questions what reasonable behavior is and devising an alternative plot that supplants the old order represented by the fathers, Corneille reconceptualizes "bon sens," or good sense. In act 2, Chimène recognizes the trap Rodrigue has been forced into, just after her father's long soliloquy, which is designed to display his arrogance and to eliminate any positive feelings spectators might have for him. Even the King criticizes the Comte. Through the structure and language of his play, Corneille reorients his public's perspective on its moral landscape. He justifies Rodrigue's actions and renders Chimène's response logical and even morally acceptable. Corneille creates a strong affinity between the couple and the play's spectators before the fateful duel commanded by Rodrigue's father. After Rodrigue kills the Comte, Chimène runs to the King to demand retribution, a move that allows her to be viewed as a dutiful daughter in the traditional sense.

Corneille's character building in acts 1 and 2 prepares the public to accept his more daring and controversial act 3, which Scudéry and the Académie single out for condemnation even while acknowledging that this act received the most applause from the public. Act 3 illustrates Corneille's desire to ignite a debate over taste and to test the rules of poetic composition. In scene 3, Chimène shockingly admits that she is still passionately in love with Rodrigue even though he has just killed her father. To underscore the heresy of such passion and compound its powerful effect, Corneille has Elvire exclaim, "Il vous prive d'un père, et vous l'aimez encore!" 'You love him still, he who deprived you of a father?' to which Chimène responds, "C'est peu de dire aimer, Elvire, je l'adore" 'I love, Elvira, nay, I worship him' (3.3.819–22). Corneille continues to push the boundaries of acceptable behavior in this scene. Elmire understands and justifies Chimène's shocking feelings: "Madame, croyez-moi, vous serez excusable / de conserver pour vous un homme incomparable" 'Lady, believe me, you're excusable / For having failed to hound the man you love' (3.3.847–48).[16] In order to further solidify his worldly public's acceptance of Chimène, Corneille sets this conversation in private rather than requiring his heroine to flout convention in the public sphere. Chimène explains her plan to Elvire: "Pour conserver ma gloire, et finir mon ennui, / Le poursuivre, le perdre, et mourir après lui" 'Preserve my glory, finish my despair / Procure his doom and die when he is dead' (3.3.857–58). Corneille's heroine will seemingly choose honor over love; only Elvire will know her true feelings. Chimène's decision can also be interpreted by the public, who is privy to this conversation, as privileging love over duty since she will join Rodrigue immediately in death. Corneille thus juxtaposes two different notions of "reasonable" behavior, one founded on traditional duty and a second that valorizes love. Chimène's decision to continue to love Rodrigue, albeit in death, is legitimized by Corneille and can be found pleasing by his public even though it is an outright contradiction to neoclassical norms that require duty to take precedence over love. Corneille's Chimène justifies Rodrigue's actions as she redefines "duty" by transforming its object: the lovers are obeying a duty to each other, not simply to their fathers. Act 3, scene 4, is a glorification of love, and a condemnation of an old order that would require Chimène and Rodrigue to abandon their love in order to pay for the sins of the fathers.

Scudéry recognized Corneille's daring transgression and chastised him for only superficially advancing behavior that the *doctes* would consider "reasonable." The quarrel reveals that, while Corneille would agree with Scudéry that the theater must represent seriously things "as they should be" 'les choses comme elles devraient être,' what is really in dispute is what this moral landscape should be, what actions are to serve as models (89). In the world Corneille constructs, love is the ultimate value and replaces sentiments, such as filial honor and duty, that the *doctes* considered to be the primary motors of neoclassical tragedy. *Le Cid* ends with the King himself elevating love over a traditional sense of duty, adhering to new norms of reasonable behavior, and substituting a new order founded on love: he orders Chimène to marry Rodrigue. It is indeed her duty to obey the King, since to kill this hero would be a blow to the state and could even be considered treasonous.

Corneille's decision to privilege love over duty, to offer a daring female protagonist, and to please the worldly public attests to the growing power of this public and its taste. Corneille's public did not applaud *Le Cid* only because of its emphasis on love and its depiction of a new order and a strong heroine. They also recognized that Corneille was validating their criteria for literary critique, their taste, as he offered a new definition of an acceptable work of theater. Corneille pleased his public by offering a world that reflected worldly taste and values. In *Le Cid*, he redefines honor and duty, which are no longer associated only with the male sphere of patriarchs and duels, but have become entwined with emotions such as love. These emotions are also to be honored and can be used to motivate actions that might have been considered unacceptable, such as marrying one's father's murderer. Corneille's *Le Cid* helps us discover other voices, other influences, especially of those who have been marginalized in traditional literary histories of this canonical period. The voices of Chimène, Corneille's sister, and "the women of the court and Paris" resurface as the important influences they were during this vibrant, dynamic period.

Notes

1. All translations are my own except the lines from *Le Cid*, which are quoted from the Cairncross translation.

2. For an overview of salon culture of the early modern period, see Beasley, Introduction and "Salons."

3. Depending on the level of the students and the context of the course in which I'm teaching *Le Cid*, I either provide the necessary background material in a lecture or I assign students selections from cultural critics and historians that elucidate the various networks and the circulation of ideas during this period. Key texts include works by Nicolas Dew, Alain Viala, Joan DeJean, Roger Chartier, Erica Harth, and Norbert Elias on notions of public and private space. I also use Hélène Merlin's work on the public to show the standard interpretation of this public as configured as male.

4. For a succinct overview of the development of the theoretical underpinnings of neoclassical tragedy at the time of *Le Cid*'s composition see Serroy's preface, pp. 8–17.

5. In *Salons*, I analyze the development of this taste and examine *Le Cid* in this context (100–14). It is important to stress that the *doctes* and the salon public were not completely separate entities. Jean Chapelain, for example, was an active salon participant as well as the first secretary of the Académie Française.

6. My students read the play before reading selections from the quarrel, but I orient this first reading of the text to focus attention on the characteristics that will provoke the quarrel.

7. Serroy's edition reproduces the 1637 text and provides a useful appendix that includes Corneille's changes from 1648 and 1660, as well as his *Examen du* Cid and an excellent critical apparatus devoted to the quarrel. Most modern editions and English translations reproduce the 1648 and 1660 versions.

8. See Jean Serroy's illuminating introduction for a discussion of Corneille's relationship to his sources and the development of Chimène as a character, especially pp. 17–24. As Serroy explains, in later versions Corneille weakens this sentimental plot in order to make *Le Cid* conform more to the scholarly expectations for a tragedy (20–21). In fact, he changes the subtitle to "tragedie," eliminating "comédie" altogether, in the 1660 edition (16).

9. There are two editions of the complete documents of the quarrel, which instructors can draw from in teaching; the first, edited by Armand Gasté in 1899, was reissued in facsimile by Forgotten Books in 2017. The second is edited by Jean-Marc Civardi and was published by Champion in 2001. Georges Couton in the *Œuvres complètes* of Corneille offers all the documents in a useful synthesis, and I have used Couton's edition here. The texts of the quarrel are only available in French. I provide translations of some key passages from these texts in my analysis of the quarrel in *Salons*, pp. 102–14.

10. Many commentators maintain his critique arose out of jealousy because he never enjoyed the kind of success Corneille garnered with *Le Cid*. Scudéry was never embraced with as much enthusiasm by the salon public as Corneille, despite the fact that his sister, Madeleine, had her own salon and was arguably the most popular novelist of the century.

11. Interestingly, a more mature Corneille, at the height of his power, abandons this provocative stance. In his *Examen du* Cid, which served as a preface to the 1660 edition of his play, Corneille writes that he has revised his play to respect these rules founded upon Aristotle.

12. The Académie does not address the fact that this dubious timing occurs only because Corneille is adhering to the traditional three unities required by the *doctes*.

13. Corneille's bow to the twenty-four-hour rule magnifies Chimène's transgression and contributes to making her totally unacceptable in the eyes of his critics. Corneille thus points to the artificiality of this constraint.

14. I am using John Cairncross's blank verse translation. Other translations reproduce the alexandrine verse, but I opt for Cairncross's translation because I believe it preserves the spirit of the play while appealing more to students, though it does not convey the beauty of Corneille's verse.

15. In order to further devalorize such traditional values, Corneille emphasizes that the Comte's death occurs as the result of a duel. Duels had recently been banned in France, so both fathers are portrayed as representing an old order that engages in actions that are now deemed treasonous.

16. The literal translation of this line is even more provocative: "Madame, believe me, it is excusable to keep for yourself such an incomparable man."

Works Cited

Beasley, Faith E., editor. Introduction. *Teaching Seventeenth- and Eighteenth-Century French Women Writers*, Modern Language Association of America, 2011, pp. 1–16.

———. "Salons and Innovation." *Teaching Seventeenth- and Eighteenth-Century French Women Writers*, Modern Language Association of America, 2011, pp. 64–75.

———. *Salons, History, and the Creation of Seventeenth-Century France: Mastering Memory*. Ashgate, 2006.

Chapelain, Jean. *Les sentiments de l'Academie française sur la Tragi-Comédie du* Cid. Corneille, *Œuvres complètes*, pp. 809–20.

Chartier, Roger. "Loisir et sociabilité: Lire à haute voix dans l'Europe moderne." *Littératures classiques*, no. 12, Jan. 1990, pp. 127–47.

Civardi, Jean-Marc, editor. *La querelle du* Cid. Champion, 2001.

Corneille, Pierre. *Le Cid*. Edited by Jean Serroy, Gallimard, 1993.

———. *The Cid*. *The Cid; Cinna; the Theatrical Illusion*, translated by John Cairncross, Penguin Books, 1976, pp. 23–112.

———. *Examen du* Cid. *Œuvres complètes*, pp. 699–707.

———. *Excuse à Ariste*. *Œuvres complètes*, pp. 779–81.

———. *Lettre apologétique du sieur Corneille, contenant sa response aux observations faites par le Sieur Scuderi sur* Le Cid. *Œuvres complètes*, pp. 800–03.

———. *Œuvres complètes*. Edited by Georges Couton, vol. 1, Gallimard, 1980.

DeJean, Joan. *Tender Geographies: Women and the Origins of the Novel in France*. Columbia UP, 1991.

Dew, Nicholas. *Orientalism in Louis XIV's France*. Oxford UP, 2009.

Elias, Norbert. *La société de cour*. 1969. Calmann-Lévy, 1974.

Gasté, Armand, editor. *La querelle du* Cid*: Pièces et pamphlets*. H. Welter, 1899.

Harth, Erica. *Cartesian Women: Versions and Subversions of Rational Discourse in the Old Regime*. Cornell UP, 1992.

Merlin, Hélène. *Public et littérature en France au XVIIe siècle*. Les Belles Lettres, 1994.

Scudéry, Georges de. *Observations sur* Le Cid. Corneille, *Œuvres complètes*, pp. 782–99.

Serroy, Jean. Preface. Corneille, *Le Cid*, pp. 7–39.

Viala, Alain. *Naissance de l'écrivain: Sociologie de la littérature à l'âge classique*. Minuit, 1985.

Vigneul-Marville, M. de. *Mélanges d'histoire et de littérature*. Vol. 1, Rotterdam, 1702.

Andrea Frisch

Tragic Aesthetics: Humanist Uncertainty vs. Neoclassical Inevitability

This essay will explore ways in which teachers and students can examine the evolution of the relation between politics and aesthetics in the theatrical tragedy of early modern France. It presents a juxtaposition of two theatrical tragedies on the death of the Roman emperor Julius Caesar—Jacques Grévin's *César*, and Georges de Scudéry's *La mort de César*—that highlights differences in structure, content, and style that can be linked to the sociopolitical context of each play, with the intervening French Wars of Religion (1562–1629) as the central point of historical reference. Through this comparison I aim to give students the tools with which to reflect on the specific impact that the Wars of Religion might have had on the adaptations of the story of Caesar's assassination in early modern France; to model a method of historicizing literary analysis that students can apply to a range of other texts; and to facilitate a broader discussion of the relationship between history, both as subject and as context, and literature. The execution of this program would require four to five one-hour class meetings at the undergraduate level, or two three-hour meetings at the graduate level.

The examination of two plays on the same subject allows students to focus more precisely on the particularities of *how* the plot is conveyed and the characters drawn in the respective works, and also makes room for the transmission of information about political conditions in France at the time the plays were composed. Since neither play is available in English translation, their use requires that students possess at the minimum a good basic reading knowledge of French.[1] Many will know the general plot from having studied Roman history or Shakespeare (whose *Julius Caesar* could also be brought into the discussion if appropriate for the course). The foregrounding of form and structure in this approach, moreover, means that many details of archaic vocabulary need not necessarily be addressed in order for the analysis to succeed.

The reading of Scudéry's 1634 play is situated against the political backdrop of Louis XIII's defeat of the last Protestant stronghold at La Rochelle in 1629 and the establishment of the Académie Française in 1635 by Richelieu, to whom Scudéry's play is dedicated.[2] It is predicated on a narrative with which scholars of seventeenth-century France are well familiar—the so-called rise of absolutism—but it is hoped that the juxtaposition with Grévin's play will help draw attention to the rhetorical scaffolding upon which that narrative was built under Louis XIII. Grévin's play was published at the other end of the religious wars, on the eve of the Massacre at Wassy. For the purposes of this discussion, the period of the wars should be approached through the figure of the monarch with a particular focus on the instability of the monarchy in the context of religious conflict after the death of Henri II in 1559.[3] Protestant and Catholic factions both sought to influence Henri's son and successor, the young François II, who died of illness at age sixteen after only seventeen months on the throne. François II's brother Charles IX was crowned at age ten in the year Grévin's *César* appeared; he also died of illness at a young age (twenty-four), less than two years after the Saint Bartholomew's Day massacres of 1572, on the occasion of which thousands of Protestants were murdered, and in the planning and execution of which Charles himself was implicated. The third son of Henri II to accede to the throne, Henri III, though not himself a supporter of the Protestant cause, engineered the assassination of two powerful Catholic extremists (the Duke and Cardinal of Guise) in 1588 for political reasons, and was himself assassinated by a Catholic friar in 1589. Henri de Navarre, a Protestant, was next in line for the throne but was not crowned until 1594, after he agreed to convert to Catholicism in the wake of a series of violent military conflicts with the French Catholic League. As Henri IV, he promulgated the Edict of Nantes, which established a modicum of official religious tolerance in 1598, but was in his turn assassinated by a zealous Catholic in 1610.[4]

As can be easily imagined from this summary, the character of the king and the moral authority of the monarchy was a subject of active and indeed violent controversy as France absorbed the impact of the Protestant Reformation, and led to a series of events that were qualified as "tragic" in a range of contemporaneous sources. As it happens, political and social unrest intensified just as sixteenth-century French playwrights were beginning to revive ancient tragedy as part of the self-conscious imitation of ancient literature promoted by Joachim du Bellay in his famous 1549 manifesto, the *Deffense et illustration de la langue françoyse* (*The Defense and Illustration of the French Language*). The protagonists of Greco-Roman tragedy, unlike those of medieval French theater, are, precisely, the monarch and the political elite. My claim is that the intersection of political ancient tragedy with a period in sixteenth-century French history specifically characterized as "tragic" by contemporaries led French playwrights of the period to use tragedy as a means to engage in ongoing, open-ended political reflections. For Grévin (as for Robert Garnier—whose three Roman plays, *Cornélie*, *Porcie*, and *Marc Antoine*, orbit closely round, but never represent, Caesar's assassination), the staging of Roman history affords an opportunity to explore a range of political questions, but this exploration does not yield any clear moral resolution or definitive political message.[5] *César*, therefore, like the Roman tragedies of Garnier, uses a suspenseful plot and unstable characters, in what I call here an "aesthetics of tragic uncertainty," as a means to invite ongoing reflection on the political issues raised by the assassination of Julius Caesar.

In stark contrast, Scudéry's *La mort de César* casts the stability and predictability that flow from a firmly held, unquestioned political ideology on the part of a privileged few as aesthetically pleasing, thereby applying the patina of the beautiful to Richelieu's program of cultural absolutism and to Louis XIII's violent suppression of religious and political dissent. Scudéry's play stages a closed world of heroic, self-confident figures whose trajectory never wavers, and who neither engage in nor invite moral or political debate. Rather than invite reflection on the political debate between Brutus's Republicanism and Caesar's ambition to rule alone, or even a discussion of the moral qualities of its two main characters, *La mort de César* constructs its tragic conflict out of the confrontation between two equally noble and heroic central figures far removed from the common herd (see

Michel). Instead of tracking the uncertain movements of self-doubting characters who deliberate inconclusively, Scudéry's play hews to a straight line that traces an inevitable collision between two idealized figures who speak in what the author proudly calls a "style pompeux" 'pompous style' (6). The privileging of an aesthetics of unity and propriety—what I will here term an "aesthetics of tragic inevitability"—goes hand in hand with a lack of suspense on the level of plot that consolidates Scudéry's tragedy as a site of moral certainty rather than its contrary.

Preparatory Discussion

In order to highlight the importance of generic form, preparatory discussion could explore the relation between tragic poetry and historiography. Given that both genres frequently draw on the same material, what might be gained, or lost, by presenting the figure of Julius Caesar in a tragic poem, rather than in a prose history or biography?[6] How do these two genres of writing differ? Responses to these questions should generate a set of notions that students already associate with tragedy (e.g., unhappy ending, fate, highly wrought language, performance, audience, Greek setting) and historiography (e.g., important, actual, past events; chronological format; dry style; boring details) as well as some key terms from the source texts that the instructor should bring out: in his own description of tragedy (included in Foster's edition), Grévin states that it is a "représentation de quelque *faict illustre et grand de soymesme*" 'a representation of an illustrious and grand fact' (46; emphasis added here and below) and a "représentation de *vérité*, ou de ce qui en ha apparence" 'a true representation, or one of something that has the appearance of truth' (47). At the outset of his note to the reader, by contrast, Scudéry announces that tragic poetry "n'a pour objet que *d'émouvoir les passions*, et de *donner l'horreur* et *la pitié*" 'has as its aim to move the passions and to provoke horror and pity' (6). The relative weight given to the *content* of the historical source by Grévin, and to the *emotional impact* of the tragic poem by Scudéry, can be used to hypothesize a move away from a focus on political debate and toward the privileging of aesthetic pleasure in French tragedy over the period from 1560 to 1640. This shift will be a primary object of investigation as reading of the plays progresses.

A reading from the prefatory material of the two plays can further the discussion of the relation between history and tragedy and help prepare students to read the respective first acts on their own. Grévin's extremely succinct presentation of his play in terms of a plot of the tragic reversal of fortune of a "brave guerrier" 'brave warrior' (143) offers a stark contrast to Scudéry's much longer account of tragic aesthetics, in which he assures the reader that his play respects the three unities (6). This contrast underlines a disparity between Grévin's preoccupation with the didactic potential of the historical material and Scudéry's concern for "beauté" 'beauty,' "plaisir" 'pleasure,' and "proportion" 'symmetry.' This contrast can be further amplified by way of a collective reading of the first few lines of each play to conclude the first class session: whereas Grévin's tragedy opens with César alone onstage, anxiously deliberating about the nature of his reputation in reaction to a creeping fear that he might be killed (see e.g. lines 1–28), Scudéry's opens with Brutus, whose first words, spoken to his coconspirator Cassius, are "Ne délibérons plus" 'Let us cease deliberating,' and who has no doubt that the act he is planning is "juste" and "beau" (1109, 1115).[7] The atmosphere of uncertainty in Grévin's play, conveyed by Caesar's staged internal debate, crystallized in his subsequent remark to Marc Antoine, "c'est peu d'avoir vaincu, puisqu'il faut vivre en doute," 'it is a small thing to have emerged victorious, when one must live in uncertainty' (151), creates suspense on the level of plot, since we have very little idea of what awaits in terms of action, and since we are unsure about the true character of the central figure, whose lingering doubts are left open to interpretation. The first few verses of Scudéry's play, by contrast, offer a "jeune et vaillant héros" 'young and valiant hero' (so says Cassius [119]), confident of his plan to kill Rome's tyrant, an act described as a "grand coup" 'a grand strike' (111) all but destined by Brutus's family history. Brutus and Cassius both allude to the overthrow of the Roman emperor Tarquinius in the sixth century BCE, in which Lucius Junius Brutus was instrumental. Our role is simply to watch this beautifully overdetermined action unfold.

Reading Assignment 1: Acts 1 and 2

Study questions for a reading of the first two acts of the two plays should draw attention to overall form and structure. The first act of Grévin's play can be read as an internal debate about a historiographical topic that, importantly, yields no clear conclusion. César's initial deliberatory speech covers a vast stretch of historical ground and engages several of the well-known controversies surrounding his legacy: if he were to die that day, would he be remembered as a brilliant general or as a power-hungry dictator? As is typical of sixteenth-century French tragedy, the monologue includes a large number of *sentences* ("aphorisms"), signaled by quotation marks in Foster's edition, that set out contrasting points of view, a technique also used as the debate is pursued with Marc Antoine, and that tend to disperse rather than consolidate a psychological notion of character. When, in line 211, César suggests they stop the discussion and prepare for the upcoming meeting of the Roman Senate, the debate remains open. The subsequent appearance of a chorus made up of a group of César's soldiers who are waiting for their next glorious deployment reinforces the open-ended structure of the plot, since, entangled in the circumstances themselves, they offer no bird's-eye view of what is to come.

Grévin's act 2 also opens with a long internal monologue, presenting a Brutus who is trying to goad himself into action. Repeatedly addressing himself in the third person, he offers a number of perspectives that question his own character. Brutus's hesitation is in fact explicitly thematized by his coconspirators. As act 2 of Grévin's *César* concludes, a mood of hesitation still lingers over the assassination plot. After the conspirators fall silent at the end of act 2, the debate about César's character is taken up again by the chorus of soldiers, who are no longer so sure what to think about César's grandiose exploits. As readers or spectators, we are invited to enter the world of *César* alongside characters who are subject to profound doubt, who debate but reach no firm conclusions about what they should do next, and who are therefore mainly waiting to see what Fortune will bring. We are, in short, immersed in a multifaceted historical moment that appears to allow for multiple possible outcomes, and it is this profound uncertainty that produces the play's "tragic" atmosphere.

In stark contrast to this, Scudéry's first act, from its very first line, forecloses doubt and debate on every level, and foregrounds characters framed as decisive agents who have "always already" made up their minds. Suspense—let alone surprise—is extremely attenuated in Scudéry's tragic universe, since the actions of its protagonists flow predictably from their clear-cut character. Nothing that happens in the play will change their outlook, cast their beliefs in a new light, or cause them to question their actions. Whereas Grévin's César initially decides not to go to the Senate at the urging of his wife, Calpurnie, in the wake of her ominous dream (759–60), only changing his mind when Decimus Brutus taunts him for listening to a woman (761–778), Scudéry's César, offended at the very idea of staying home, immediately rejects his wife's entreaties.

Reading Assignment 2: Act 3

The postulate that Scudéry's tragedy proffers an aesthetics of certainty and inevitability *in place of* a site for deliberation about political and moral virtue is confirmed in scene 1 of act 3, when César condemns Antoine's harsh call for violence against his enemies only to propose a more cynical and insidious politics (675–80). In Scudéry's tragic universe, César's plot to "tromper le peuple" 'fool the people' does not compromise his heroic stature in the least; indeed, his strategy for seducing the Romans into giving up their liberty is vindicated at the end of the play, when Brute and his companions find themselves rejected by César's subjects (1139–40). "Je ne vois pour nous que la seule vertu" 'We have only virtue on our side,' concludes Brute (1144), and indeed, while he does not hesitate to depict César as cunning and self-interested, Scudéry emphasizes the virtuous allegiance to a higher principle on the part of César's assassins.

If all this appears to square uneasily with Scudéry's professed disdain for Brutus, it sits well enough with his conception of the aesthetics of tragedy as he enunciates them in his note to the reader (6–7). By privileging both the grandeur and the constancy of all his characters, by employing a consistently elevated language, and by constructing a very tight unity of plot, Scudéry produces a harmonious tragic universe whose aesthetic qualities effectively drown out the political conflict the play supposedly recounts, unperturbed by notes of moral ambiguity. Meanwhile, Grévin's third act offers an extended representation of César's hesitation in the face of Calpurnie's dream. Even after Decime Brute taunts him, he confesses to feeling torn between his wife's entreaties and his desire to go to the Senate to seek absolute power (779ff). Once again Grévin concludes on a note of uneasy uncertainty, leaving us to question the wisdom of César's decision to place his honor above his life, as the chorus of soldiers discuss the inconstancy of Fortune and their apprehensions about what might happen next based on Calpurnie's vision, which they compare to the prophecies of Cassandra.

Reading Assignment 3: Acts 4 and 5

It is imperative to note at this point that while Scudéry's act 4 stages the direct confrontation between César and his assassins, right up until the very moment in which César dies in scene 8, Grévin sets the assassination entirely offstage in between acts 3 and 4. Rather than represent César's death in the mode of heroic pathos, as Scudéry does, Grévin chooses in act 4 to dwell with the devastated Calpurnie. The messenger who reports César's death to her refers to him as "le pauvre César" 'poor Caesar' (913), and she experiences nothing but grief at his passing. The whole affair provokes pity among the chorus of soldiers, who ultimately conclude that César's fate is that of all humans, one that even a prince cannot escape (1010–14). The message is clear here: Grévin's César is subject to forces beyond his control, just as all humans are. Through their very hesitation and indecision, then, Grévin's tragic characters invite us to identify with them in all their—human—vulnerability and uncertainty.

Scudéry, by contrast, portrays a César who exists on an entirely different plane from most mortals. Shortly before he dies, Scudéry's César suggests that the historical circumstances of his death—and, consequently, the dramatic action of *La mort de César*—are ultimately irrelevant to his fate, and thus, one presumes, to the moral thrust of the play. Rather than deliberate about the morality of his conduct, Scudéry's César scoffs at the notion that the manner of his death will have any bearing on his "essence immortelle" 'immortal essence,' which transcends history. In addition to foreclosing any kind of discussion about the legitimacy or appropriateness of specific political actions, Scudéry's staging of a character conceived as glorious from the outset robs César's death of any real *dramatic* significance: the protagonist's serene confidence in his immortality drains his death of its tragic sting, rendering it a trivial detail rather than a climax or a dénouement. The plot remains unified to the point of immobility. In addition to draining the play of any real suspense, this way of imagining Caesar's route to death foregrounds the power of human agency, thereby robbing Fate of its power to constrain free will—a central topic for class discussion that can be linked to other literary, philosophical, and theological works according to the reference points available to a given group of students.

At the end of Scudéry's play, someone brings news that he has seen a vision of César becoming a star. Upon hearing this, Marc Antoine announces his plan to build a temple to César in order to tell all the world "QUE L'ILLUSTRE CÉSAR, EST AU NOMBRE DES DIEUX" 'that illustrious Caesar / Is now among the gods,' the play's final lines. This conclusion takes us straight out of the realm of politics and into the ahistorical world of immortal glory, where no meaningful revenge is possible. The earthly revenge sought by Marc Antoine and his troops allows for the possibility of a subsequent play, but we know that nothing that ensues could threaten the immortality of Scudéry's César, whose deification finds its perfect vehicle in Scudéry's tragic aesthetics. Though the unity of plot and the constancy of character may provoke "horreur et pitié," they do not incite doubt or invite moral or political deliberation.

Scudéry's aesthetics of tragic inevitability leaves no room for historical contingency; yet historical contingency is the very engine of tragedy for Grévin. Students will not be surprised to discover that the end of Grévin's play solicits precisely the open-ended moral and political deliberation that Scudéry's play precludes. Providing no reassurance to those who would presume that their situation is secure, the final lines, spoken by one of the soldiers, read as follows: "Ceste mort est fatale / Aux nouveaux inventeurs de puissance Royale" 'this death is fatal / to new inventors of royal power' 1102–03). In the last scene of *César*, Marc Antoine joins the chorus of soldiers to exact revenge for the death of César, opening the play out onto the Roman civil wars that were to follow, thereby further deferring any kind of conclusion regarding the moral and political conflict between César and his Republican adversaries, and situating Grévin's play within a potentially endless sequence of human tragedies.

As Scudéry's prefatory statements about *La mort de César* make clear, his aim in the play is to create purely aesthetic effects. Grévin's *César*, I have been suggesting, shows us what Scudéry's particular aesthetic leaves behind: with its scenes of inconclusive deliberation and its privileging of doubt and suspense, Grévin's *César*—despite its title—subordinates character to plot, and plot to a Fortune "qui entre ses mains / Va pesle-meslant les humains" 'that manipulates humans willy-nilly' (576) rather than ordering their lives according to any discernible design. In one sense, Grévin's aesthetics of tragic uncertainty can be said to reflect the political instability of his time; but by constructing his tragedy as a site for political deliberation, the sixteenth-century dramaturge casts tragedy as an instrument of political intervention, and not merely as a poetic recreation of his own historical context. Scudéry's aesthetics of tragic inevitability, by contrast, result in a play with no political teeth. The legacy of Scudéry's César is settled before the play even begins; the play is therefore simply an extended account of his gloriousness, and his steadfastness in the face of his assassination at the hands of the unfailingly virtuous Brute offers only a further confirmation of the same. This predetermined moral outcome obviates the need for any real deliberation on the part of the reader or spectator, whose attention is instead drawn to the grandeur of the characters and the eloquence of the poet who makes them speak. Offering more than the mere representation of a strong ruler, Scudéry's play elaborates an aesthetics of tragedy that no longer privileges the genre as a site of open-ended political deliberation.

The contrast between these two plays lays the ground for several broader discussions: in a course focused on early modern France, one could ask whether the two works are representative of larger trends in France in their respective periods; in a course focused on tragedy as a genre, one could juxtapose the aesthetics of Grévin and Scudéry with those of tragic authors in other times and places; and in a course focused on literature as a social discourse, one could use Grévin's uncertainty and Scudéry's inevitability as terms by which to evaluate the political potential of a wide range of literary (and non-literary) texts.

Notes

1. Grévin's play has the advantage of being relatively short, which is an important consideration given that it is only available in sixteenth-century orthography. Two editions of *César* appeared in the 1970s: the first by Ellen Ginsberg and the second by Jeffrey Foster. Foster's straightforward presentation is best for classroom use, and I will refer to this edition throughout. (See also Foster's doctoral thesis, César *de Jacques Grevin*, which is essentially the typescript of the published edition). Scudéry's play is available in a critical edition prepared by Evelyne Dutertre and Dominique Moncond'huy, last reissued in 2012. Moncond'huy offers a substantial introduction to the play (195–280), and Dutertre recounts the many and varied phases of Scudéry's poetic career, of which *La mort de César* represents only one (xiv–xxii). *La mort de César* also appears on the Théâtre Classique Web site in a lightly annotated transcription with modernized orthography prepared by Ernest Gwénola and Paul Fièvre in 2015. Since this online edition is easily accessible and very well suited to classroom use despite a fair number of typos, I will refer to it in the present essay.

2. My dating of the play follows Moncond'huy (196).

3. My presentation here will necessarily be schematic. For the details of this turbulent period, see Mariéjol.

4. One effective way to convey the contrast I am trying to bring out here is to prepare a slide with portraits of all the French kings of the sixteenth century (seven, from Louis XII to Henri IV) on one side and those of the seventeenth on the other (three including Henri IV, but if one takes the fall of La Rochelle as a turning point, as I do, only Louis XIII and Louis XIV).

5. Gillian Jondorf has studied this dimension of Garnier's theater in *Robert Garnier and the Themes of Political Tragedy in the Sixteenth Century*.

6. Plutarch's *Life of Julius Caesar* is readily available in English; sections 63–68 should be required at the graduate level, where historiographical style should

also be historicized, and could be optional at the undergraduate level, both as a prose comparison to tragic poetry and as a reminder of the basic course of events.

7. English translations are my own.

Works Cited

Grévin, Jacques. *César*. Edited by Ellen Ginsberg, Droz, 1971.

———. *César*. Edited by Jeffrey Foster, Nizet, 1974.

———. César *de Jacques Grévin: Édition critique avec introduction et des notes par Jeffrey Alan Foster*. Edited by Jeffrey Foster, 1968. Rice U, PhD dissertation, scholarship.rice.edu/bitstream/handle/1911/14435/6815620.PDF ?sequence=1&isAllowed=y.

Jondorf, Gillian. *Robert Garnier and the Themes of Political Tragedy in the Sixteenth Century*. Cambridge UP, 1969.

Mariéjol, Jean-Hippolyte. *La réforme et la Ligue: L'édit de Nantes, 1559–1598*. Tallandier, 1983. *Gallica*, visualiseur.bnf.fr/ark:/12148/bpt6k9864n.

Michel, Lise. "Régicide et dramaturgie dans la tragédie française, de *La mort de César* de Scudéry (1636) à la *Rosemonde* de Baro (1651)." *Littératures classiques*, vol. 67, no. 3, 2008, pp. 115–29.

Plutarch. *The Life of Julius Caesar*. *Lives*, translated by Bernadotte Perrin, vol. 7, Loeb Classical Library, 1919. Transcribed by William E. Thayer, penelope .uchicago.edu/Thayer/E/Roman/Texts/Plutarch/Lives/Caesar*.html.

Scudéry, Georges de. *La mort de César*. Edited by Ernest Gwénola and Paul Fièvre, Théâtre Classique, 2015, www.theatre-classique.fr/pages/pdf/ SCUDERY_MORTDECESAR.pdf.

———. *La mort de César*. *Le prince déguisé; La mort de César*, edited by Evelyne Dutertre and Dominique Moncond'huy, S.T.F.M., 1992.

Juliette Cherbuliez

The Microdrama of Vivid Description: Hypotyposis as a Pedagogical Tool

Contrary to its reputation—cultivated perhaps even by some of its champions—neoclassical tragedy can be taught at a range of curricular levels, in a variety of courses, to many different kinds of audiences, and by instructors who are neither specialists of the period nor already convinced of its relevance or interest. Instead of addressing how to teach a specific play, theme, approach, or element, I treat a feature of the literary that is so fundamental to poetic expression that its rich pedagogical potential is often overlooked: that of description. Seventeenth-century tragedies incorporated descriptive forms to convey events not performed in front of the audience (occurring before the start of the play or beyond the location of the stage), to expose crucial background information, and often to mobilize audience sympathies toward one interpretation of the action.

The structure and form of description lends itself to this approach. Descriptive moments in theater tend to convey discrete events or reactions of a distinct time and a different place that complement the situation in which they appear. Thus, they can be easily excerpted and studied in-depth, whether students read the whole play or not. Additionally, learning how to think about and draw from tragic description is a skill that can be honed from class to class and level to level. I first show the broader implications of teaching description, with an example from a survey course taught in translation to students with no assumed knowledge of literature, theater, or French culture. Building on those pedagogical techniques, I turn to advanced grammar courses before considering introductory literature classes and advanced seminars focused on tragedy or political theater. By demonstrating that description can be a fundamental teaching tool adaptable to increasingly complex pedagogical contexts, I show how instructors can incorporate neoclassical tragedy in many kinds of classes and with varying degrees of intensity and depth.

My focus will be on one particular form of description: hypotyposis, generally understood to mean "vivid description." Categorized in rhetorical manuals as a form of *demonstratio* (description) and closely linked to, even interchangeable with such terms as *evidentia*, *sub oculos subiectio*, and *enargeia*, hypotyposis appears within a constellation of many figures catalogued by rhetoricians, from Horace through Cicero and Quintilian to Bernard Lamy and other neoclassical writers, who debated the relative merits of words' appealing to the mind's eye and to the ear. Hypotyposis distinguishes itself not just by creating mental images, but by fostering in auditors a position of astonished fascination at what they imagine and what they then feel, effecting a kind of rhetorical seduction (Le Bozec, "L'*hypotypose*" 5). Neoclassical playwrights drew upon the rhetorical tradition to craft a style of theater addressing the demands of their culture. Jean Racine's hypotyposes were often drawn from his classical sources (Declercq 73–74); they function to convey information, dramatize characters' dilemmas, account for events that happen elsewhere, and respect the cultural constraints against violence and bloodshed that shaped the neoclassical tragic form. As Marc Fumaroli has said, hypotyposes "rend imaginable l'inimaginable et vraisemblable l'invraisemblable" 'makes the unimaginable imaginable and the implausible plausible,' thus stretching the limits of what neoclassical theater could adequately convey to its audience (678–79).

I will underscore three qualities of hypotyposis that are particularly interesting for teaching neoclassical tragedy: its conversion of words into images, its persuasive capacity, and its affective strategy. Generally, hypotyposis is meant to impose a vision, convincing audiences of things they have not witnessed, therefore causing them to feel something they would not otherwise have felt. It relies on great detail, hyperbolic or hyperprecise vocabulary, and artful organization. It also adopts the speaker's point of view, necessarily shifting the perspective toward that character. By artfully providing evidence of a thing not apprehended by an audience, hypotyposis moves beyond narration and into acting; in the seventeenth century especially, hypotyposis may be said to mobilize the passions of both the orator and the audience (Noille-Clauzade 13–14; Spica 18).

Some of the most memorable tirades and soliloquies in neoclassical descriptions may be considered hypotyposes: from Racine, the account by Ulysse of Calchas's revelation and the deus ex machina that saves Iphgénie and condemns Eriphile (*Iphigénie* 5.5), or, of course, Théramène's account of Hippolyte's death (*Phèdre* 5.6). While Racine's corpus is particularly rich in such descriptions, hypotyposis also appears in the works of other authors: the account of the multiple bad omens by Tyrésie in Rotrou's *Antigone* (5.5.1582–612) and, in Corneille's *Le Cid*, Chimène's account of her father's murder (2.8.675–80), which Braider calls "a masterpiece of forensic hypotyposis" (56).

While instructors will find that the pedagogical structures I discuss can be applied to all of these examples and many more, I will draw primarily from two exemplary hypotyposes, one often taught in undergraduate courses that treat tragedy, and one very much overlooked. First, *Andromaque*'s "Songe, songe, Céphise" (3.8) demonstrates the dynamics of vivid description as an entrée into tragedy. Even if a class has never read Racine's tragedy or any other rendering of the Trojan War or its aftermath, Hector's widow's memory of the defeat of Troy is a touchstone for considering the powerful presence of the past through description.

My second example comes from Racine's last play, his 1691 Christian tragedy *Athalie*. I focus on the eponymous queen's twenty-one-line account of a dream in which her mother's ghost warns of her downfall. Referred to as "Le songe d'Athalie," these verses were for two hundred years lauded, cited, and anthologized, from Voltaire through Chateaubriand to Proust. Today, however, *Athalie* seems to have little to recommend it thematically to most undergraduate curricula. The play's drama recounts the reinstatement of the Jews under the young king Joas after they overthrow and kill the pagan queen Athalie (2 Kings 8:16–11:16). Unlike *Phèdre*, *Horace*, or *Andromaque*, which treat questions of power and its abuse, internal struggles, and incommensurable desires, *Athalie*'s dilemmas appear at first blush as inaccessible to American undergraduates. They need a great deal of historicizing since their context is doubly distant from us: written for a premodern European Christian monarchy, the tragedy treats a pagan queen in ninth-century Jerusalem and addresses the fate of the Jewish people, whose Judaism is figured as proto-Christianity. It would be an understatement to observe that its pressing questions are not easily mapped onto contemporary issues. What is the currency of biblical history? How do we speak of the role of providence in shaping faith? How do we discuss a vision of Jews and Judaism whose antiquated philo-Semitism reads as blatant anti-Semitism today?

It may come as a surprise, then, that "Le songe d'Athalie" can be taught like most seventeenth-century dramatic hypotyposes: it needs only a little context to be readily accessible to audiences. While we might hope that the Trojan War, the backdrop to *Andromaque*, is still a common reference point for undergraduates, Athalie's dream demands no prior knowledge to be compelling: it is a ghost story. Generally, as narrative poems told from a specific point of view, tragic descriptions are astonishingly accessible, and hypotyposes are marvelously self-contained and particularly portable (see Combel). Given an appropriate amount of context, and depending on what connections we make beyond the play (to history; to theoretical concepts; to the neoclassical genre; to theoretical, philosophical, and political issues of storytelling, persuasion, and witnessing), hypotyposes can be a gateway into an extremely rich engagement with neoclassical tragedy.

Situating Description between Account and Testimony

Vivid description is a compelling way to introduce tragedy to diverse learners. It allows a glimpse into the alterity of early modern art and culture, and a taste of what the humanities can offer students pedagogically: its tolerance and even promotion of ambiguity, and direct access to the benefits of what Jennifer Roberts has explored in her piece on using art-historical methods to "slow down" the pace of our lives elsewhere and otherwise. As Roberts observes, "It is commonly assumed that vision is immediate," but given three hours in front of a painting, students learn "that in any work of art there are details and orders and relationships that take time to perceive." Likewise, working on a small snippet of verse, especially one that calls into question the power of vision and the attendant values of witnessing, as well as of telling and listening, affords participants a moment of self-reflection on why they often believe images over words. I've created an exercise that ties tragic description to the power of testimony and questions of objectivity, the history of the eyewitness (and perceptions of credibility), the transmission of memory, and, perhaps most significantly, the role of words in our image-driven culture. I often use it in guest lectures or alumni sessions, to introduce the concept of description as a motivated, imaginative mode of witnessing.

In this forty- to ninety-minute exercise, we begin with the adage "a picture is worth a thousand words," asking what it means and under what circumstances it is true. Students tend to respond affirmatively to the first question: images are "more powerful" and "more immediate," even "more faithful" or trustworthy in their transmission, needing no "translation." The 2016 controversy on *Facebook* regarding the Associated Press photographer Nick Ut's 1973 photo of the nine-year-old Phan Thị Kim Phúc fleeing naked alongside other children after having torn her burning clothing off during a napalm attack of her town, Trảng Bàng, troubles this evaluation. The site's algorithm flagged and censored the image as pornographic, an action that was widely criticized (Scott). *Facebook* covered the story about its own mistake, as did *The New York Times*, and both outlets published comments from readers. We trace the connections between one image—here an iconic photo—and different kinds of words, observing first how an image can be completely misunderstood without its story, and how the image itself spawns more words: readers' own histories with the image or the war for which it came to stand.

In the second part of this exercise, we address tragedy. Racine's *Andromaque* allows me to evoke the Trojan War, a subject of which some participants will have at least a passing understanding. I sit students in facing pairs so that one half of the class sees the projection screen while their partners, with their backs toward the screen, cannot. I offer the following instructions: to recount, in as much detail as possible, the projected image, in sentences beginning, "There is [or are] . . . I see . . ." The unseeing partners listen attentively, sketching what they understand. For this exercise, I have used a Robert Laurie print based on Gavin Hamilton's eighteenth-century painting of the fall of Troy. A mammoth, somewhat caricatural Achilles triumphantly looms on his chariot, ready to drag Hector's body around the city walls. Among the spectators, a fainting Andromache stands on the ramparts.

Describers struggle to observe without injecting their skepticism or bemusement. This is in part because many do not recognize the image's context, but it is also because they cannot position themselves in any relation to the image. Then I change the conditions: now the describers are instructed to begin their sentences, "I saw." This subtle change in the prompt compels them, without realizing it, to adopt a much more intimate relation to the action of the image, as if they had been there. The emotions explode, and so do the stories. Some even go so far as to invent a backstory, and many locate themselves precisely in time and or place. They frequently take a stand, decrying the injustice or the violence of Achilles, or mocking the swooning Andromache. Afterward, we discuss how witnessing involves personal reaction, emotion, and invention. Participants marvel at the difference between detached and motivated descriptions: when the describers act the part of an eyewitness, they don't have any more information or greater insight, but their attachment to the scene and clear stakes in its transmission lend emotion, pathos, and therefore a certain undeniable credibility.

We then turn to the hypotypotic version from Racine's *Andromaque*:[1]

> Dois-je les oublier, s'il ne s'en souvient plus?
> Dois-je oublier Hector privé de funérailles,
> Et traîné sans honneur autour de nos murailles?
> Dois-je oublier son père à mes pieds renversé,
> Ensanglantant l'autel qu'il tenait embrassé?
> Songe, songe, Céphise, à cette nuit cruelle
> Qui fut pour tout un peuple une nuit éternelle.
> Figure-toi Pyrrhus, les yeux étincelants,
> Entrant à la lueur de nos palais brûlants,
> Sur tous mes frères morts se faisant un passage,
> Et de sang tout couvert échauffant le carnage.
> Songe aux cris des vainqueurs, songe aux cris des mourants,
> Dans la flamme étouffés, sous le fer expirants.
> Peins-toi dans ces horreurs Andromaque éperdue:
> Voilà comme Pyrrhus vint s'offrir à ma vue;
> Voilà par quels exploits il sut se couronner;
> Enfin voilà l'époux que tu me veux donner.
> Non, je ne serai point complice de ses crimes;
> Qu'il nous prenne, s'il veut, pour dernières victimes. (3.8.992–1010)
>
> Must I forget them, if he no longer remembers them?
> Must I forget Hector, deprived of a burial,
> Dragged without honor around our city walls?
> Must I forget his father dashed at my feet,
> Bloodying the altar which he clutched?
> Remember, remember, Céphise, that cruel night,
> Which was for an entire people an eternal night,
> Picture Pyrrhus, eyes blazing,
> Entering under the gleaming flares of our burning palace,
> Picking his way through the bodies of my dead brothers,

> Covered in blood, inciting more carnage.
> Remember the cries of the victors, remember of the cries of the dying
> Stifled by the flames, extinguished by the sword.
> Imagine amid these horrors Andromaque cowering:
> That is how Pyrrhus presented himself to my eyes;
> These are the deeds by which he crowned himself;
> This is the spouse you want to give me.
> No, I will not be an accomplice to his crimes;
> Let him take us, if he so wishes, as his final victims.[2]

I first establish the more immediate context for Andromaque's dilemma in the drama. We examine what makes this version of the defeat of Troy different from the image. Starting with point of view, we contrast the multiple perspectives that an image can allow with Andromaque's single perspective. Tracing the themes of burning and fire, the tension between Hector's dead body and Pyrrhus's march over the corpses, the students identify how such features of the poetry strengthen the argument behind the memory. Observing the repetition of "Dois-je oublier" 'Must I forget,' followed by the injunction, "Songe, songe," 'Remember, remember,' they identify the motivation behind Andromaque's memory. Once they notice that Andromaque has a reason for telling this story, they want to trace the argument, even consulting the French to ask about the translation or noticing rhymes that are accessible (such as *cruelle* and *éternelle*, *crimes* and *victimes*). This exercise has been very successful in situations like alumni weekends or student recruitment events, where the classroom might include people with very diverse interest in French literature. "Songe, songe, Céphise" raises questions of eyewitnessing and much-debated ideas of credibility and objectivity, alongside the idea of pathos.

These sessions have also given me renewed license to risk far more complex engagement with tragedy in my French language classes. This engagement in turn has allowed me to address a problem I see in current language curricula. American approaches to language learning, dominated by proficiency models, divide communication skills into discrete actions: speaking therefore is divorced from listening. They also divide language learning from interpretation and analysis. Offering a more holistic approach with greater integration of skills, Steven Shapiro introduces images of seventeenth-century figures into his first-semester French class, engaging students with the politics of royal portraiture as sources of basic description. Both Shapiro's approach and my hypotyposis strategy work "hand in hand with reconsidering the functional model of language learning . . . and pushing students towards dealing with concepts and abstractions early on" in their study. Hypotyposis offers a kind of verbal portrait of an event, allowing more practiced students to trace both concrete and abstract meaning through engagement with grammar, point of view, and basic poetics.

Hypotyposis in Fifth-Semester French

I integrate tragic hypotyposis into fifth-semester French classes with goals similar to those of Shapiro, with the conviction that performance- and rhetoric-based pedagogies should be as integral to foreign-language learning as those of visual literacy, thereby contributing to a multiliteracies framework of foreign-language learning. Moving beyond traditions of language proficiency as measured by literacy within discrete skills, the paradigm of multiliteracies situates language within "socially complex multimodal contexts" (Warner and Dupuy 117). One of the corollaries to this integrated framework is a resistance to hierarchies of content or learning such as those often instantiated in departments of foreign languages (Paesani, "Think Globally" 434). Albeit in a perverse way, word-based descriptions taken from the high literature of tragedy provide an apt platform for resisting such hierarchies; they offer opportunities for what Kate Paesani has called the "spiraling of language and content": the simultaneous learning of grammar and more abstract forms of meaning ("Exploring" 1278). In developing competency in teaching description, instructors enable students to engage with the multiple meanings of a text, its embedded nature within a greater context, refusing the idea of "culturally neutral" texts (Warner and Dupuy 122).

While working with alexandrines with students in fifth-semester French may seem daunting, it is not. Most fifth-semester French students I have taught conjugate verbs and recognize verb tenses, can write casual French, and are adept at interpreting visual matter. They are often double majors, with French representing a love but not a career. Their commitment to language is expressed through enthusiasm for communication, and not necessarily for history, philosophy, or aesthetics. Nevertheless, tragic hypotyposis speaks to them. Generally, these students are eager to practice speaking and want to feel more comfortable with complex sentence structure. Neoclassical French has the virtue of having a highly limited vocabulary, and hypotyposes are particularly fun to teach because they can engage students' bodies, voices, and imaginations. Using a performance-based approach, we spend one to two class sessions working on "Le songe d'Athalie" ("Athalie's Dream"):

Mais un trouble importun vient, depuis quelques jours,
De mes prospérités interrompre le cours.
Un songe (me devrais-je inquiéter d'un songe?)
Entretient dans mon coeur un chagrin qui le ronge.
Je l'évite partout, partout il me poursuit.
C'était pendant l'horreur d'une profonde nuit.
Ma mère Jézabel devant moi s'est montrée,
Comme au jour de sa mort pompeusement parée.
Ses malheurs n'avaient point abattu sa fierté.
Même elle avait encor cet éclat emprunté,
Dont elle eut soin de peindre de l'orner son visage,
Pour réparer des ans l'irréparable outrage.
Tremble, m'a-t-elle dit, fille digne de moi.
Le cruel Dieu des Juifs l'emporte aussi sur toi.
Je te plains de tomber dans ses main redoutables,
Ma fille. En achevant ces mots épouvantables,
Son ombre vers mon lit a paru se baisser.
Et moi, je lui tendais les mains pour l'embrasser.
Mais je n'ai plus trouvé qu'un horrible mélange
D'os et de chair meurtris, et traînés dans la fange,
Des lambeaux pleins de sang, et des membres affreux,
Que des chiens dévorants se disputaient entre eux. (2.5.485–506)

But an intrusive agitation has, for a few days now,
Interrupted this state of prosperity.
A dream (should I worry about a dream?)
has fed a worry that gnaws at my heart:
While I flee it everywhere, everywhere it follows me.
It was during the horror of a deep dark night.
My mother Jezabel appeared before me,
Dressed as on her death day, splendidly.
Her sorrows had not felled her pride.
She even had that borrowed brilliance
From having painted and decorated her face,
To repair the unstoppable ravage of years' decay.
"Tremble," she said to me, "my worthy daughter,
The Jews' cruel God has marked you too.
I fear that you might fall into his fearsome grasp,
My daughter." And, finishing these frightful words,
Her shadow seemed to lean toward my bed,
And me, I reached out my arms to embrace her
But found only a horrible mess
Of bones and putrid flesh dragged through the mud,

Shreds of blood-soaked skin and horrible limbs,
Over which devouring dogs fought one another.

Their guided examination of the description engages listening, reading, partial grammatical parsing, analysis of rhetorical forms and of argumentative structure, and performance. Our goal is not to understand the literary prowess of Racine's alexandrines or the symbolism of nightmares in a premodern context but to engage multiple facets of vivid description.

For preparatory homework, students read the text while listening to a recording of it ("Le songe funeste"). I ask them first to listen to determine where the rhythm changes, where the speaker adds emphasis, and how. They affirm that the speed of French speech and its use of pauses are the most evident forms of emphasis, in contrast to English. Second, they determine who is speaking and to whom, and also identify verb tenses. They have a synopsis giving context to this account: Athalie is a pagan queen whose mother, Jezabel, persecuted the Jews and was murdered. At this level, the big story of the tragedy, the neoclassical context, and even the "rules" of tragic poetry are secondary; essential is that this is a play and that in this sense it is Athalie who is narrating. This realization changes their apprehension of the description's aims—it is told from a certain perspective. Further, most students, tracing the verbs, are relieved to realize that the "songe," an exemplar of the dynamics of past narration, combines *imparfait* and *passé composé*, with only one instance each of the *conditionnel* and *passé simple* tenses. Through these straightforward prompts, they engage with the basics of the text and gain a good deal of confidence about how to read and listen to such material.

In class, we begin with another listening exercise: we listen to three or four different recitals of the "Songe d'Athalie" (Madore). Reinforcing an earlier unit on the syllabus that addresses the history and diversity of the French language, we include a version that recovers seventeenth-century pronunciation. Through these recordings, students discover that this is poetry! They then see the rhyme structure, and I show them that every line has twelve syllables; they are introduced to the difference in how French and English syllables are determined in poetry. Reading out loud also emphasizes how the alexandrine reinforces pronunciation. I dig gently into the structure of an alexandrine, often by spending a concentrated amount of time on the line, "Un songe (me devrais-je inquiéter d'un songe?)" 'A dream (should I worry about a dream?).' Noting the repetition of "songe," we investigate its *champ lexical* (a group of words that refer to a dominant notion or theme, similar to a semantic field in linguistics) through a dictionary and synonym-finding exercise. We end by exposing the tirade's *champ sonore* (or sound field, referring to the oral landscape of the poetry), the repetitions of plosives and the tension between *m*'s and *t*'s, and diving into a few other choice alexandrines whose structure, vocabulary, and sounds work together to create the horror that Athalie experiences.

In one memorable session with a class of students whose levels of comprehension and preparation of the text were particularly diverse and divergent, I gave small groups each a section of the room's whiteboard on which to draw a picture of the narration. One group, surreptitiously seeking inspiration from the others, realized that no two images were alike; none had fully understood the concatenation of time and space in the account. That group came to understand that the passage is not just a description of a dream in which a mother turns into a ghoul; it is an account by a queen in a temple, of a dream she had in her bed, of her murdered mother issuing a warning before turning into a dismembered corpse. The cartoon this group drew, cribbed from their classmates' work, demonstrated the mise-en-abyme structure of this description and the necessity of interpreting the stage directions, set, and audience. It was a dramaturgical interpretation of the piece rivaling the visual architecture of sophisticated graphic novels.

I always ask a few brave souls to recite the text. Exposed previously only to contemporary realia in their French classes, students are astonished not only to be able to read and understand seventeenth-century poetry, but, in acting it out, to find it moving. Theater pedagogy also works to allow students interpretive license of the text; some emphasize the alexandrines we have studied closely, while others seize on elements they have studied in their groups. The results are a group of truly divergent yet sound interpretations of a single text.

Students' last exercise is to compose a memory of a major event. One tenet of my class is that no one should feel compelled to bare their soul or share their life in class; I actively encourage students to invent stories. Highlighting their immediate classroom experiences, including recently acquired vocabulary and grammatical structures, I offer the semester's syllabus and suggest that they narrate an event we have learned about, doing so as if they had witnessed it. Students come out of the exercise with a renewed attention to the internal frame of persuasive writing; they can identify some of these techniques in other texts we examine and even apply them to their own writing. Some use rhetorical devices such as those we see used in Athalie's dream—repetition, oxymoron, and so on—without ever identifying them. Many imitate the overblown style of hypotyposis and expand their vocabulary and poetic voice by seeking florid language. Not all of it is successful or accurate, but the skills they develop are foundational.

Hypotyposis as Microdrama

My syllabi for surveys of francophone literature used to introduce the literature and poetry of the seventeenth century through *Phèdre* or *Horace*. Both exemplify neoclassical tragedy: they can be taught for their respect of the *trois unités* (three unities of time, place, and action) as well as *vraisemblance* (seemliness) and *bienséance* (decorum). In the light of recent research on tragedy in theater and literary history (see Guyot; Hoxby), however, I have turned my attention away from confirming nineteenth-century conceptions of neoclassical tragedy. While continuing to teach plays in their entirety, I now include a focus on hypotypotic moments. This approach works well with a variety of plays commonly appearing on Introduction to French Literature syllabi and many that do not often make the cut. It also works if one is taking an anthologized approach; as I have discussed above, hypotyposes work well excerpted.

Traditional approaches to tragedy emphasize the reestablishment of Aristotelian rules restricting performance options to what was socially acceptable. Hypotyposis can demonstrate these rules. Scenes of exposition use description to offer background to the crisis at hand, describing the historic foundations that have led to the present moment and so guarantee the *unité d'action* (Andromaque's memory of Pyrrhus's triumph in "Songe, songe, Céphise"). Descriptions of events occurring in other locales preserve the constrained space that is also the hallmark of classical tragedy, the *unité de lieu* (as in Théramène's récit in *Phèdre* 5.6), and accounts of events happening before the action of the play maintain the *unité de temps* (Cinna's description of convincing his coconspirators, 1.3; which is also a description of a description). Description clearly can be seen to help respect both *vraisemblance* (Eriphile's death, *Iphigénie* 5.6) and *bienséance* (Valère's account of the battle in *Horace* 4.2). Hypotyposis, emphasizing a motivation behind the description and a privileged perspective of the teller, always adds pathos and increases the tension in the action. We can therefore see hypotyposes as "microdramas": discrete, structured moments of tension and resolution.

Athalie's dream functions very well as a microdrama within the larger tragedy. Structurally, the *songe* offers a scene of exposition (explaining why Athalie has come to the temple), exposes the history at stake, and forebodingly suggests a certain future. It raises interesting questions around *vraisemblance*: Does this account of a ghost appearing as a mangled corpse, derived from the historical record, fit the bill? Similarly, it appears doubly *bienséant* in that a terrible event—the death of Jézabel—occurs at a triple remove: occurring not just offstage and in the past, it is also told through a dream.

We begin the investigation with an understanding of the paradoxes that frame this soliloquy. Why is Athalie telling this story at this moment? Students ask the basic "who," "what," "when," "where," "why" questions, establishing the strange situation of a pagan queen confessing her dreams in a Jewish temple. Connecting the hypotyposis to the *unités* of time, place, and action as Racine delineated them underscores the paradox of Athalie's dream being both within the time of the play and completely "out of time" as a dream sequence that evokes both the past and the present. We establish the parallel between Athalie's disruptive and unwelcome arrival in the temple and the play's first lines, spoken by Abner, "Oui, je viens dans son Temple adorer l'Éternel. / Je viens, selon l'usage antique et solennel, / Célébrer avec vous la fameuse journée, / Où sur le mont Sina la Loi nous fut donnée" 'Yes, I come to his Temple to adore the Eternal God. / I come according to the traditional and solemn customs, / Celebrate with you this famous day when on Mount Sinai the Law was given to us' (1.1.1–4). Finally, we recall Racine's own synopsis, in the preface, of the play's central action, "Elle a pour sujet Joas reconnu et mis sur le trône; . . . Athalie y joue un personnage si considérable, et que c'est sa mort qui termine la pièce" 'Its subject is Joas recognized and placed on the throne . . . Athalie plays such a considerable role and it is her death that ends the play' (1009).

The question about Athalie's motivation, "Why does she tell this story?" remains unresolved, however. In order to work out the motivation behind this microdrama, we delve into the poetic devices and rhetorical structure of the description. We review figures of speech (see *Silva Rhetoricae* [rhetoric.byu.edu]) and identify those used; in Athalie's dream alone we find hypallage, alliteration and assonance, chiasmus, comparison, oxymoron, and metaphor. This is also an excellent way to teach versification. We can take the same alexandrine that I explore in fifth-semester French, delving deeper into the poetry by noting the ways the repetition of "songe" bookends and frames the "je," or the inverse use of the repeated "partout" two lines later, which structures that line's chiasmus, in which Athalie is at first subject and then object of the "chagrin" of the dream.

We also trace the flow of the whole account, dividing it into five portions. The first two lines ("Mais un trouble importun vient, depuis quelques jours, / De mes prospérités interrompre le cours" 'But an intrusive agitation has, for a few days now, / interrupted this state of prosperity') describe not only Athalie's state of being but the very act of her entrance into the temple and the state of her words: all interruptions. Second, she begins to tell the dream ("C'était pendant l'horreur d'une profonde nuit" 'It was during the horror of a deep dark night'), an interruption that is linked to her state of mind through the alliterative *p*'s (*partout, poursuit, pendant, profonde*). In the third moment, the narration builds and the alliteration switches to *m*'s, and a careful examination of "Ma mère Jézabel devant moi s'est montrée" 'My mother Jezabel appeared before me' offers up the mother as primary symbol while highlighting Athalie through the "ma" and "moi" as objects of the mother's appearance, "s'est montrée." These different *m*'s—the mother, the *moi*, and the issue of what is shown, *montrée*—guide the rest of what Athalie sees: her mother, whose appearance is first ghastly not because she is dead or a vision, but because she uses makeup paradoxically to repair the "irréparable outrage" 'unstoppable ravage' of aging. Students identify other paradoxes, wondering about the possibility of an "éclat emprunté" 'borrowed brilliance,' for example. The narrative switches again in the fourth section, once Athalie voices her mother ("Tremble, m'a-t-elle dit, fille digne de moi," 'Tremble, she said to me, daughter worthy of me'), with another paradox: if Athalie is *digne* of her mother, should she tremble? Or is the situation so extreme that even Jézabel quakes? Jézabel's warning, that her daughter will fall to the Jews as she did, is punctuated with "Ma fille," a *rejet*, a form of enjambment that highlights, through isolation at the beginning of the line, the syntactical remainder from the preceding line. With Jézabel's silence comes the conclusion, where the *m*'s and *p*'s of the earlier sections create their own "horrible mélange" 'horrible mess' filled with the sensorial contradiction of a child reaching for its mother's embrace and finding only her shredded remains (Cherbuliez, *In the Wake* 183–85).

This close poetic reading of Athalie's dream should also be contextualized, however, within the history of the play's performance. Students are astonished to hear about this play's first staging, at Saint-Cyr, Mme de Maintenon's school for impoverished noble girls (Forestier). Through attention to this description, we confront the problem that many students have regarding the paradox of the printed play, a challenge that is particularly acute for neoclassical tragic drama: this very long and difficult poem was meant to be acted out. This notion counters all suppositions about the role of theater as entertainment, and especially about the specific roles of audience and players. At the same time, it underscores neoclassical tragedy's importance in so many facets of its culture.

Advanced Classes on Tragedy

More advanced students can use the building blocks of hypotyposis to interrogate the genre itself. With honed analytical skills and more experience interpreting texts, students are able to investigate how the poetics of tragedy can become a means of inquiry into the very limits of a highly regulated genre. In advanced classes, I build on the "microdrama" approach I use in more introductory levels. I have experimented successfully with reading the hypotyposis before even starting the play. Because I firmly believe that students should not read tragedies for suspense or plot, but with as much familiarity as possible with the central tensions, characters, and events, I always distribute a synopsis of the play in advance. Students then can concentrate on how tensions unfold, perhaps accessing a small part of the pleasure that early modern audiences would have taken in already knowing how a tragedy ends, and so relishing the unfolding of the inevitable. When we begin with Athalie's *songe* or Rodrigue's account of his victory over the Moors (*Le Cid* 4.3.1267–339), students reorient away from suspense and toward connections, interpretations, and a more holistic understanding of the drama.

In more foundational classes I tend to teach the classical rules of tragedy without great contextualization or critique. In contrast, in an advanced class I will offer a more rigorous understanding of the mythology of neoclassical "rules." Hypotyposis again serves as an excellent example of how tragedy can be understood not just as a highly constrained genre, but also as one that repeatedly violates these tenets. Zeroing in on the work of vivid descriptions reveals that they are often, if not always, accounts of violence unseen by the audience. In a course including *Athalie*, this is confirmed by comparing other hypotypotic moments, such as Josabet's tirade recounting the massacre during which she saves the baby Joas (1.2.235–64). Athalie's dream and Josabet's account of "un poignard à la main l'implacable Athalie" 'a dagger in hand, the implacable Athalie' during the massacre at the temple, are both historical events. They are nevertheless foundational to the action at hand and provide insight into why the characters are so divided. Both recount graphic violence, the kind that might be thought of as unseemly or precisely that which other rules of *bienséance* would disallow. Why does the tragic form make room for these descriptions? The argument about historical background does not suffice. Even such brief hypotypotic moments as Chimène's personification of her father's wound and her account of the conversation it has with her are portraits of violence and its effects. Neoclassical tragedy wants to conjure up spectacle for its audience and creates moments where an audience can not only see but also feel it (Cherbuliez, "Et que méconnaîtrait"). The exception here also proves the rule; a class that includes Corneille's *Polyeucte* might consider the surprising lack of either performance or description of the eponymous character's conversion. As Christopher Semk has shown, this absence avoids making the character's body "the object of a curious, prurient, or indiscriminating gaze and thereby evacuat[ing] its theological significance" (93). Here, the lack of a spectacular performance, whether on stage or in words, confirms the sacred nature of the event.

In contrast, description is at the crux of the action in *Horace*, where the outcome of the battle is told repeatedly, first in Julie's account (3.2) of the army's refusal to fight, then in her description of Rome's victory and of Horace's presumed flight from the battlefield (3.6), and later in Valère's revised version explaining Horace's ruse and his victory (4.2.1101–22). This last hypotyposis detailing the death of the three Curiaces is as close to a report as a hypotyposis can get. It only becomes violent and motivated when Horace arrives back onstage, proudly exhibiting his heroism and the swords of the three dead Curiaces. Camille's offstage killing is what confirms both the veracity of Valère's extraordinary tale and the deadly, cold-blooded courage of its hero. Seemingly respecting the *unités*, *Horace* nevertheless oozes violence and injustice.

This approach to the play compels us, therefore, to reconsider our understanding of how tragic discourse regulated and even eliminated violent behavior from the stage. We use Athalie's *songe* as a lens through which to examine the whole play as performance. Building on our close readings of the hypotyposes, we first consider the gender politics of the play given its unique literary history and its portrait of the mother-daughter relationship as recounted by Athalie. We evoke the singular importance of generation—both in terms of legacy and of reproductivity—to a story about the near extinction of a people. We connect Athalie's concern in her dream with the portentous role of history in the play, and think about how dreams offer the means to link past and future. Occasionally we even question the limits of hypotyposis as it relies upon the visual, in a play that elevates the unseeable nature of the divine (Le Bozec, "Les frontières" 30).

A close examination of hypotyposis allows students to appreciate and test the extraordinary richness of poetry in performance while considering the social and political stakes of the hypotypotic moment. We see how a moment of rupture offers a key intervention in the dominant narrative. Learning how hypotyposis necessarily breaks with the action around it, how it forms the character who is speaking as well as the addressee, and how it can push its audience to envision scenes of violence that have been excluded from the performance repertoire in which it has flourished, we can also better debate the ethics of violence and the necessity of its witnessing.

Whether as the focus of single class sessions in translation or as one approach among many in advanced literature courses, hypotyposis is a dynamic and flexible pedagogical tool. Learning about and teaching this figure of speech can be beneficial for seasoned instructors of neoclassical tragedy as well as for those who are not fully acquainted with the genre's poetics, whether one is teaching a course devoted to Racine or Corneille or wishes to offer a single intervention into the politics of witnessing.

I began my own study of hypotyposis in order to better understand French neoclassical tragedy specifically. It has led me to rethink in large part my pedagogical practices and teaching philosophy. As a result, my classrooms are generally oriented toward embodied and performance-based pedagogies, while I am also increasingly committed to giving students skills that empower them. It might have surprised me originally to even consider that hypotyposis might be one of these skills, but I also believe that it has led many students to consider more seriously the power of the imagination, as well as our capacity to convince others to picture the truths we have witnessed.

Notes

1. This hypotyposis has a rich critical history, and instructors can begin by referring to the classic essays by Barthes, Spitzer, Starobinski ("Memoire," "Racine"), and Gomot.

2. All translations are mine. *Andromaque* and *Athalie* are both available in translation, *Athalie* most recently in an edition by Geoffrey Argent. Tim Chilcott's translations of both plays are available in a student edition suitable for classroom

use; for this exercise, I have preferred a more literal translation that eschews rhyming for repetition of certain images. Jim Knight's older translation of these plays uses iambic pentameter to convey the theatricality of Racine's poetry, but is not available in a student edition.

Works Cited

Barthes, Roland. *Sur Racine*. 1963. Seuil, 1991.

Braider, Chris. *Indiscernible Counterparts: The Invention of the Text in French Classical Drama*. U of North Carolina P, 2003.

Cherbuliez, Juliette. "'Et que méconnaîtrait l'œil même de son père': Les limites du savoir oculaire dans la description tragique." *Littératures classiques*, vol. 82, no. 3, 2013, pp. 173–86, doi:10.3917/licla.082.0173.

———. *In the Wake of Medea: Neoclassical Tragedy and the Arts of Destruction*. Fordham UP, 2020.

Combel, Valérie. "L'hypotypose chez Racine." *XVIIe siècle*, no. 188, July–Sept. 1995, pp. 495–503.

Corneille, Pierre. *Le Cid*. *Œuvres completes*, pp. 711–77.

———. *Cinna*. *Œuvres complètes*, pp. 913–69.

———. *Horace*. *Œuvres complètes*, pp. 845–901.

———. *Œuvres complètes*. Edited by Georges Couton, vol. 1, Gallimard-La Pléiade, 1980.

Declercq, Gilles. "A l'école de Quintilien: L'hypotypose dans les tragedies de Racine." *Revue de littératures française et comparée*, no. 5, 1995, pp. 73–88.

Forestier, Georges. "Notice." Racine, *Oeuvres complètes*, pp. 1709–29.

Fumaroli, Marc. *L'âge de l'éloquence: Rhétorique et "res literaria" de la Renaissance au seuil de l'époque classique*. 1980. Albin Michel, 1994.

Gomot, Guillaume. "Une seconde Troie." *Carnets*, vol. 2, no. 5, 2015, doi:10.4000/carnets.358.

Guyot, Sylvaine. *Racine et le corps tragique*. PU de France, 2014.

Hoxby, Blair. *What Was Tragedy? Theory and the Early Modern Canon*. Oxford UP, 2015.

Le Bozec, Yves. "Les frontières de l'hypotypose: Le songe d'Athalie et la prophétie de Joad." *L'information grammaticale*, no. 100, 2004, pp. 26–30, doi:10.3406/igram.2004.2585.

———. "L'*hypotypose*: Un essai de definition formelle." *L'information grammaticale*, no. 92, 2002, pp. 3–7.

Madore, David. "Le songe d'Athalie." 17 June 2002, www.madore.org/~david/lit/athalie.html.

Noille-Clauzade, Christine. "La figure de la description dans la théorie rhétorique classique." *Pratiques: Linguistique, littérature, didactique*, nos. 109–110, 2001, pp. 5–14. *Persée*, doi:10.3406/prati.2001.1909.

Paesani, Kate. "Exploring the Stylistic Content of 'Exercices de style.'" *The French Review*, vol. 82, no. 6, May 2009, pp. 1268–80.

———. "Think Globally, Act Locally: An Alternative Proposal for Effecting Change in Language Education." *Modern Language Journal*, vol. 101, no. 2, 2017, pp. 433–36.

Racine, Jean. *Andromaque. Œuvres complètes*, pp. 193–256.

———. *Athaliah*. Translated and edited by Geoffrey Argent, 2012. *The Complete Plays of Jean Racine*, vol. 4, Pennsylvania State UP, 2010–.

———. *Athalie. Œuvres complètes*, pp. 1009–84.

———. *Four Greek Plays: Andromache; Iphigenia; Phaedra; Athaliah*. Translated by Jim Knight, Cambridge UP, 1982.

———. *Iphigénie. Œuvres complètes*, pp. 695–763.

———. *Œuvres complètes, tome I: Théâtre-Poésie*. Edited by Georges Forestier, Gallimard-La Pléiade, 1999.

———. *Phèdre et Hippolyte. Œuvres complètes*, pp. 815–76.

———. *Three Plays: Andromache; Phaedra; Athaliah*. Translated by Tim Chilcott, Wordsworth Editions Limited, 2000.

Roberts, Jennifer. "The Power of Patience." *Harvard Magazine*, Nov.–Dec. 2013, harvardmagazine.com/2013/11/the-power-of-patience.

Rotrou, Jean. *Antigone. Théâtre complet*, edited by Bénédicte Louvat et al., vol. 2, Société des textes français modernes, 1999, pp. 228–334.

Scott, Mark, and Mike Isaac. "Facebook Restores Iconic Vietnam War Photo It Censored for Nudity." *The New York Times*, 10 Sept. 2016, B1, nytimes.com/2016/09/10/technology/facebook-vietnam-war-photo-nudity.html.

Semk, Christopher. *Playing the Martyr: Theater and Theology in Early Modern France*. Bucknell UP, 2017.

Shapiro, Stephen. "The Grand Siècle in the Language Classroom." Society for Interdisciplinary French Seventeenth-Century Studies 36th Annual Conference, 2–4 Nov. 2017, Mills College.

"Le songe funeste d'Athalie." *iBibliothèque*, Éditions Garnier, 2011–18, www.ibibliotheque.fr/athalie-jean-racine-rac_athalie/promenade-sonore/page1.

Spica, Anne-Élisabeth. "Le traitement de la description dans les manuels de rhétorique à l'usage des élèves au XVIIe siècle." *Pratiques: Linguistique, littérature, didactique*, nos. 109–110, 2001, pp. 15–33, *Persée*, doi:10.3406/prati.2001.1910.

Spitzer, Leo. "L'effet de sourdine dans le style classique: Racine." 1931. *Études de style*, Gallimard, 1993, pp. 208–335.

Starobinski, Jean. "Mémoire de Troie." *Critique*, vols. 687–88, no. 8, 2004, pp. 725–53.

———. "Racine et la poétique du regard." *L'œil vivant*. 1957. Gallimard, 2008, pp. 71–92.

Warner, Chantelle, and Beatrice Dupuy. "Moving toward Multiliteracies in Foreign Language Teaching: Past and Present Perspectives . . . and Beyond." *Foreign Language Annals*, vol. 51, 2018, pp. 116–28.

Part II

The Performance of Tragedy: On Stage and in the Classroom

Laurence Marie

Performing Neoclassical Tragedy: Between Text and Image

When I was a student in France in the 1990s, I was taught drama as a literary text to be read rather than a dialogue to be performed. This persistent conception was certainly inherited from the French interpretation of Aristotle in the seventeenth century, which considered performance to be secondary, and the entire meaning encompassed within the poetic text. Fortunately, today this approach belongs to the past, and most printed editions of plays now provide sections emphasizing the multifaceted aspects of performance.

In this essay, I aim to show how French neoclassical tragedies of the seventeenth and eighteenth centuries are a valuable means for introducing students to what is at stake in performance, considered both in its essence and in its historicity. These plays were written in a transitional period, in which modern performance became the subject of experimentation and tragic acting theory started to be written. The debate between telling and showing in the tragic genre and, more broadly, between a theater of the text and a theater of the image, provides particular insight into this evolution. One may therefore want to use the following questions as a common theme for the course: Should dramatists describe violent actions by way of narrative to engage the imagination, or should they stage them to strike the eyes? And do alternatives exist?

The analysis and examples proposed here are destined for flexible usage in class. I have tested them in various undergraduate settings. They may be incorporated, in part or in full, into sessions devoted to neoclassical tragedy in an introduction to literary studies, or in a survey course on the early modern period. They may also be extended into a full course devoted to theater in performance.

The primary corpus intertwines theater and the visual arts. It is composed of plays, written documents (commentaries, parodies, anecdotes), and images (paintings, engravings, drawings). Racine's *Iphigénie*, Voltaire's *Sémiramis*, and Ducis's *Macbeth* may be read in full, since they each embody specific ways of dealing with the issue at stake. But they may also be excerpted, with a focus on scenes occasioning challenges for performance. Unless otherwise noted, all the documents mentioned here are accessible online.

The pedagogical objectives of this course are as follows: to engage students in the analysis of drama in performance, and in particular in the identification and description of contrasting ways of writing and performing the same scene; to foster visual literacy of an image, in relation to the dramatic text and the stage; and to gain digital skills through practice, using digital tools related to early modern drama. It is my hope that emphasizing performance's various aspects will reinforce inclusivity in the classroom by both incorporating visual material and generating assignments that further encourage students' creative impulses.

Performances in the Seventeenth Century

I generally start by asking students about their experience with theater. Most of them have read very few plays in extenso, even fewer have been to the theater, and usually no one has attended a performance of a neoclassical tragedy. What may appear remote to French students often feels even more distant to Americans.

To arouse students' interest, we start with the fascination for theater at Versailles and in Paris in the seventeenth and eighteenth centuries. We begin in medias res with the opening scene of *Iphigénie*, one of Racine's most popular tragedies in the eighteenth century, and we study the play in the light of its first performances. The students read the dialogue aloud in pairs to familiarize themselves with the rhythm of the alexandrines. Then they identify internal stage directions and, in particular, words that refer to time and space, and at the same time to the conditions of performance, in exposition scenes. The words "reconnais la voix qui frappe ton oreille" 'Is my voice so hard to recognize?' and "à peine un faible jour vous éclaire et me guide" 'Its feeble rays could scarcely light your way' underscore that the play starts at dawn (1.1.5).[1] They encourage us to recall that, following Aristotle, a tragedy of this period unfolded between sunrise and sunset, but also that, on a stage dimly lit by candles, the actors' faces could appear indistinct, which made listening all the more important. We point to the setting, through "Le spectacle pompeux que ces bords vous étalent; / Tous ces mille vaisseaux, qui, chargés de vingt rois" 'The triumphant sight this shore displays? / A thousand ships, by twenty monarchs manned': the impossibility of reproducing it as such onstage underlines that performances relied on conventions accepted by the audience (1.1.26–27). Similarly, whereas the fable notes that silence reigned ("Avez-vous dans les airs entendu quelque bruit" 'Has any sound disturbed the slumbrous air?'), the French theater was noisy, whether at Versailles or at the Comédie-Française, where people standing in the parterre were boisterous (1.1.5–6).

The students are then invited to imagine the ways the scene could be staged by paying attention to the setting and to the actors' dress, positioning, movement, vocal delivery, facial expressions, and body language. When each group shares its ideas with the class, the students realize how diverse the interpretations can be. Next, we turn to *Iphigénie*'s first performances, whose setting varied according to the location. We put the play's grandiose premiere, at Versailles on 18 August 1674, with Marie Champmeslé in the title role, into context with help from the online pedagogic file designed for the 2016 exhibition *Fêtes et divertissements à la Cour* (Château de Versailles). The spectacular setting (part real and part trompe-l'oeil), designed to celebrate the king's conquests, was described by the art historian André Félibien as consisting of a long green alley framed by basins, grottoes, and statues, with camp tents in the background (20–21). By contrast, *Athalie* was presented in 1691 without setting, costume, or orchestra at the Saint-Cyr school, presumably not to a lesser effect ("*Athalie*").

Then we evoke *Iphigénie*'s resumption at the Hôtel de Bourgogne from December 1674 through March 1675. We read the first scene of Molière's *L'impromptu de Versailles* (*The Impromptu at Versailles*), which mocks tragic acting, in the context of the rivalry between the Hôtel de Bourgogne's and the Palais Royal's troupes. We reflect upon the relative notion of "natural acting" and on the fact that even Molière's comic acting would probably seem very artificial to us today. We then examine Antoine Watteau's painting *Les Comédiens-Français*. In a "palais à volonté" (literally a "palace at will"), figured by imitation classical columns, three actors, two female and one male, dressed in heavy faux-ancient costumes, are aligned as though in a bas-relief and face the audience like orators; they express grief stiffly, from balletic poses. Actors at the time were generally hemmed in by benches in the acting space (not visible in the painting), where socially privileged spectators (*petits-maîtres*) could sit.[2] The actors' arms are contained in the space between the belt and the shoulders, abiding by the rules of rhetorical decorum. Their postures are similar to the frontispiece of *Iphigénie*'s first edition in 1674, and to François Nivelon's engraving "Standing" in *The Rudiments of Genteel Behavior* (plate 1). One may recognize the passion of "sadness" as rendered by the history painter Charles Le Brun, who drew a series of expressive heads for conferences he gave to the Académie in 1668. Action on stage being signified by speech, the actor was considered an orator, a conception derived from the French interpretation of Aristotle, who believed that "the tragedy realizes its goal even without help and without actors" (6.50b15). Performance thus remained a blind spot of seventeenth-century theory. The actor was dealt with marginally in oratory treatises (and gendered male by default). Declamation followed strict rules that made it close to singing (see Green [audio CD]).[3]

At this stage, students should certainly be made aware of a key methodological point: early modern theater iconography should not be treated as an objective document, even if several details appear to realistically reproduce the stage conditions. Watteau's aforementioned painting looks like it was copied from the actual stage; however, the two comic actors in the background have been added to contrast the two styles; and the artist has left aside the stage benches and the two soldiers who were probably standing on each side of the stage to prevent misbehavior.

Action and Tableau Aesthetics

I ask students to list the pros and cons they identify in narrative and visual action, and we proceed to the historic shift that took place in the early eighteenth century. We read excerpts of Voltaire's writings from the 1730s, at a moment when he and others criticized performances of tragedy for being cold and artificial, and for following the rules too literally instead of giving priority to the effect produced and to the audience's pleasure. Voltaire, who had discovered English theater when exiled in London from 1726 to 1728, regretted that French tragedies were "plutôt des conversations qu'elles ne sont la représentation d'un événement" 'more conversations than representations of an event' and encouraged dramatists to "donner beaucoup plus à l'action" and "parle[r] plus aux yeux," 'give much more to action' and 'speak more to the eyes,' without shedding blood onstage ("Discours" 164). Visual spectacles were distrusted in the seventeenth century because they were deemed to be stronger than effects upon the ears (Boileau 170); ironically, by the beginning of the eighteenth century they were being promoted for the same reason.

Stemming from the call for new visual illusions, several innovations allowed the stage's space to become more divided from the audience's: benches were removed from the Comédie-Française's stage in 1759, thanks to the intervention of Voltaire's friend the Count of Lauraguais, who financially compensated the actors for the loss of premium tickets; the lighting was perfected, costumes resembled more closely the era represented by the play, and acting tended to involve the whole body (Marie, *Inventer* 76–79). These elements helped frame the stage like a painting and create an invisible fourth wall: "Imaginez sur le bord du théâtre un grand mur qui vous sépare du parterre, jouez comme si la toile ne se levait pas" 'Imagine on the edge of the stage a great wall that separates you from the pit, act as if the curtain was not rising' (Diderot, *De la poésie* 1310). The objective was to absorb viewers into the scene: being ignored by the actors let spectators feel that they were watching unseen, helped them forget about the divide between fiction and reality, and ensnared them in the illusion, through a process that Michael Fried analyzed for eighteenth-century painting. However, despite repeated calls in favor of more "vérité" 'truth,' this conception never approached Émile Zola's naturalism or what would now be called realism; it was concerned with illusionistic effect rather than an exact resemblance to reality (Frantz 167–82).

Voltaire's *Sémiramis* exemplifies the new kind of neoclassical tragedies that culminated in spectacular "tableaux" 'paintings' described through elaborate stage directions. I ask students to compare the description of the play's early staging, with benches on stage, and its resumption after their removal. At first, the effect failed completely because characters had to cross a row of spectators (Marmontel, *Mémoires* 159). But in September 1759, the scene could be staged like a dramatic painting: the queen Sémiramis, surrounded by her numerous courtiers, was viewed watching the ghost of her husband Ninus exiting his tomb accompanied by thunder and lightning (Marmontel 200; Marie, *Inventer* 74–77). One may usefully complement the analysis of the fascination with stage paintings with Barnabé Farmian de Rozoi's adaptation of Shakespeare's *Richard III* (in particular act 5, which multiplied painting-like attitudes described by stage directions) and its parody by Pierre-Germain Parisau, *Richard*, which in scene 19 staged a "Dessinateur" 'Drawer,' who asked characters to pause their movement so that he could draw it (45).

The new model was based on a shift from formal delivery to a more visual, body-centered type of performance. The English actor David Garrick was the great model of the natural acting style that extended expression to the whole body. Several images may be contrasted with Watteau's painting. William Hogarth's *David Garrick as Richard III* shows the actor still absorbed in the nightmare from which he has just awoken, expressing horror from head to toe: his eyes are fixed on images from his dream; one hand clutches his sword and the other is raised in front of him, with palm facing out and fingers stretched; the angles of his legs and feet suggest that he has just jumped from his bed. Other aspects of the scene evoke what did, and will, happen, stretching the single moment that painting is limited to (in contrast with drama): notably, the painting of Christ on the cross symbolizes the innocence of those persecuted by Gloucester; the sword, the armor in the foreground, and the military camp in the background signify that the king is about to fight the Battle of Bosworth Field, where he will lose his horse and be killed by Richmond.

Jean-Louis Fesch and Whirsker's gouache miniature paintings embody the French adoption of this new acting style. *Mlle Dumesnil dans le rôle de Phèdre* (*Mlle Dumesnil in the Role of Phaedra*) strikingly contrasts with Watteau's painting: the actress, one arm high above her head, the other holding what looks like a scarf, expresses a violent passion (anger? despair?); she ignores the viewer and is shouting, perhaps at a character who is not visible. The painting appears to condense three moments from act 1, scene 3: Phèdre removing the veils that weigh on her, blushing with shame, then exploding with anger when Œnone pronounces Hippolyte's name. Here, following decorum is less important than expressing passions, and the picture illustrates words attributed to the actor Michel Baron: "Les règles défendent de lever les bras au-dessus de la tête; mais si la passion les y porte, ils feront bien: la passion en sait plus que les règles" 'Rules forbid one from raising one's arms above the head; but if passion leads them there, they will do right: passion knows more than the rules' (Marmontel, *Éléments* 323).

The Debate over *Iphigénie's* Ending

In the new theatrical context of the eighteenth century, the opposition between telling and showing was epitomized by one fascinating example that constitutes an excellent case study: the debate around *Iphigénie*'s ending, and on the limits of visual representation.[4] The arguments developed by the following commentators may be the subject of an assignment composed of an analysis of excerpts, followed by a personal essay on the respective merits of showing and telling (the passages are quoted at length in Cronk and in Bret-Vitoz 180–82).

In Diderot's *Entretiens sur* Le fils naturel (*Conversations on* The Natural Son), Dorval, when evoking Racine's ending, differentiates between actions that are simple enough to be shown (such as Orosmane about to stab his beloved in Voltaire's tragedy *Zaïre*) and those too complex to represent. For him, complex actions should be described by a narrative that will draw out the imagination (1175), since it is easier to move the imagination than the senses (1179). Quoting Ulysses evoking Calchas, "L'oeil farouche, l'air sombre, et le poil hérissé, / Terrible, et plein du dieu qui l'agitait sans doute" 'Eyes flashing, stern-browed, hair in disarray, / Full of the God within' (Racine, *Iphigénie* 5.6.25–26), Dorval argues that no actor can make his hair stand on end or portray the larger-than-life effects characteristic of tragic poetry (1175–76).

Other commentators disagreed. Nicolas Bricaire de la Dixmerie hoped to bring to neoclassical tragedies what he called "progrès" 'progress.' Declaring that Racine should have staged *Iphigénie*'s ending visually, he imagined the progression of the scene, closely following the images conveyed by the hypotyposis (12–13). An editor of Racine, Pierre-Joseph-François Luneau de Boisjermain, regretted that the playwright had not composed his play at a time when the stage was free of benches: if he had, argued Luneau de Boisjermain, he would undoubtedly have replaced his narrative with visual action (209–10).

On 31 July 1769, the playwright Germain-François Poullain de Saint-Foix had the ending performed as a "tableau" at the Comédie-Française. He did not risk letting the audience listen to the narrative while watching its representation: he eliminated most of the text and replaced it with a silent pantomime, using stage directions that underscored sound and visual effects, such as thunder and lightning (406–10). The ending in action was only performed once. The audience didn't applaud, and asked for "la pièce telle qu'elle est" 'the play as it is' ("Comédie-Française").

The critical reception was no better. According to Nicolas-Edme Rétif de la Bretonne, Saint-Foix should have only offered a glimpse of the action in the background, in semidarkness (114). Voltaire judged the subject better fitted for painting, because it showed a single moment; staged as a theatrical scene that had to last, however, it was necessarily "cold and ridiculous," twenty characters being forced to remain standing in the same attitude, like tapestry figures. Indeed, Voltaire, after being among the first to advocate for action, walked back his argument when the aesthetic of the spectacular invaded the stage, insisting that the image should support the poetic text and not supplant it: "Il ne faut jamais sacrifier l'élocution et le style, à l'appareil et aux attitudes" 'Elocution and style should never be sacrificed to apparatus and attitudes' (*Correspondance* 143). Another commentator, Jean-Marie-Bernard Clément, insisted that Racine would have put the ending into action had he considered it a good idea, which he did not, because he knew that the denouement was too complex to be staged (458). Clément thus highlighted the idea that neoclassical aesthetics resulted from deliberate decisions rather than being the default arrangement necessitated by limited stage possibilities.

Theater managers in francophone Saint-Domingue (today's Haiti) did not read these arguments or else were simply not sensitive to them. Saint-Foix's ending in action was performed in Le Cap in 1781. The ad published by the *Affiches américaines* (*American Notices*), the local newspaper, described the staging:

> Le récit que l'Auteur a mis dans la bouche d'Ulisse au cinquième acte, est mis en action. Le dénouement par un coup de théâtre subit représentera Iphigénie défendue en vain par Achille, prête d'expirer sous le couteau sacré, toute l'Armée attendant le sacrifice avec la plus grande impatience, et Calchas par une inspiration subite substituant à cette Princesse une autre victime dont le sang répandu par elle-même apaisera la colère celeste. (Advertisement)

> The narrative that the Author placed in the mouth of Ulisse at the fifth act is put into action. The denouement by a sudden coup de theatre will represent Iphigenia defended in vain by Achilles, about to expire under the sacred knife, the whole Army waiting for the sacrifice with the greatest impatience, and Calchas, by a sudden inspiration, substi-

tuting to the Princess another victim whose blood shed by herself will appease celestial wrath.

Even though the colonists used the French stage as their model, they chose to show an ending that had been performed only once, but had been much written about. They likely did so to attract local audiences, who were partial to visually striking scenes (see Marie, "Writing").

The Limits of What May Be Staged: Shakespeare Adapted

Growing attention to visual imagery also affected the writing and performance of new tragedies in the eighteenth century.[5] Theorists and dramatists wished to regenerate the French stage with spectacular visions and "déchirer les entrailles du spectateur" 'tear the spectator's entrails' (Diderot, *Entretiens* 1138). They sought inspiration from English tragedies, which, unconstrained by neoclassical dramaturgy's unities and decorum, based their effects on visual actions and bodily eloquence.

To investigate this issue in class, we consider different ways of writing and performing violent deaths. Crime raises a specific problem of representation, since neoclassical dramaturgy followed Horace in prohibiting bloodshed on stage (Horace, lines 185–188). Through selected scenes, we explore the use of narrative to fuel an economy of frustration, and various alternatives to the binary opposition between telling and showing.

In his adaptations of Shakespeare, Jean-François Ducis experimented with different options from play to play and within the same play, writing alternate versions and proposing variants in the printed editions. Ducis, who did not know English, worked on free translations by La Place and Le Tourneur to transform Shakespeare's plays into neoclassical tragedies in five acts and alexandrines, abiding by the three unities. However, he kept part of the subversive power of his source and experimented with different ways of rousing the audience's emotions. Rewriting Shakespearean crimes was key.

In his first adaptation, *Hamlet*, performed at the Comédie-Française in 1769 with François-René Molé in the title role, Ducis used a device common in the eighteenth century: the stopped gesture. He replaced the play within the play with a scene in which Hamlet confronted his mother with an urn containing his father's ashes, asking her to swear that she was not guilty of her husband's death (4.4). In the first version performed, Hamlet, as the ghost of his father come to call for revenge, raised a dagger against his mother, thinking her guilty of his death, but ran off in pursuit of Claudius without murdering Gertrude (Ducis, Manuscript). The scene was a "tableau comble" 'apogee-painting' (Frantz 167) designed to make the audience shudder within the limits of what might be shown. Like a sketch, it used the power of suggestion, requiring the viewer to complement and complete the image. Praised by Diderot (*Entretiens* 1175), unfinished gestures aimed at avoiding the laughter caused by a badly performed crime, and at producing a strong terror effect without getting to horror, defined as the "caricature" of terror by Baculard d'Arnaud (xxii). An anonymous engraving displaying François-Joseph Talma and Catherine-Joséphine Duchesnois in *Hamlet* underscored the spectacular dimension of the gesture, through Talma's bulging eyes and an elaborate symmetry of limbs: the stylization reinforced the effect while keeping violence at bay by containing it within a painting frame (*Talma*).

In *Macbeth*, created in 1784 at the Comédie-Française, Ducis pushed the limits further. With extensive stage directions, he described Lady Macbeth / Frédégonde's restless sleepwalking. After putting her dagger back in its sheath, Frédégonde performed "le geste d'une femme qui porte plusieurs coups de poignard dans les ténèbres" 'the gesture of a woman who stabs several times in the darkness.' Then she repeatedly scratched her hands, uttering long sighs and moving quickly "de la plus profonde douleur à la joie et à la plus vive espérance" 'from the deepest pain to joy and to the strongest hope.' The directions indicated that, thinking she was walking straight to the heir to the crown's bed, she murmured, "C'est l'instant de frapper" 'It's time to strike,' then "tir[a] son poignard et se retir[a], toujours dormant, sous l'une des voûtes" 'pulled her dagger and left, still sleeping, underneath one of the vaults.' In the next scene, the audience could understand that she had committed a murder backstage because she came back "égarée, échevelée" 'disorientated, disheveled,' having realized that she had mistaken her own son for the prince. In other words, Frédégonde's blank gesture condensed two crimes: it evoked her previously murdering a counselor to make him appear responsible for the regicide, and it announced the infanticide she would commit offstage. A printed variant staged a cradle bearing the corpse of Frédégonde's son: Frédégonde pulled the crib's curtains and "palp[a]" 'felt' the invisible baby's body before killing herself (5.7.132–135). The horrid gesture materialized the little corpse: suggestion here appears to be more efficient than the sight of an infanticide would have been (see Marie, "Gestuelles"; "Les premières adaptations"). The scene may be compared to Carle Vanloo's famous painting of *Mlle Clairon en* Médée (*Mlle Clairon as* Medea), from Longepierre's adaptation from Euripides, which showed the magician fleeing on her chariot, after stabbing her two children, whose corpses lay in the foreground. By contrast, Medea's expression is neutral, almost peaceful: this paradoxical choice, perhaps designed to reduce the horror of the vision, may also refer to the cold mastering of passions for which Clairon, Diderot's model in the *Paradox of Acting*, was famous, by opposition to her rival Mlle Dumesnil, whose style was characterized as being impulsive and unrestrained.

Various midterm or final assignments may be proposed. Creative writing could consist of rewriting a scene, opting for a narrative or stage directions, staging and acting it; or choosing a theatrical image and describing it, drawing inspiration from the small narratives in Diderot's *Salons*, Daniel Arasse, or Paul Veyne. Essays on contemporary issues could deal with the use of telling, showing, visual and sound suggestion in horror movies; or to what extent the dialectic between showing and telling is still relevant today, analyzing various documents: Py's article about the opposition between images and words at the 2005 Avignon Festival; Viala's descriptions of Racine's contemporary stagings, characterized by an "oscillation . . . entre un théâtre de la parole . . . et un théâtre de la chair" 'an oscillation . . . between a theater of the word . . . and a theater of the flesh' (1151); and the Institut National de l'Audiovisuel online archives for short filmed excerpts of performances (ina.fr).

Students may also select one tragedy and research its performances in the seventeenth and eighteenth centuries by gathering images from *César: Calendrier électronique des spectacles sous l'Ancien régime et sous la Révolution* (*Digital Calendar of Spectacles in the Ancien Régime and in the Revolution* [cesar.huma-num.fr/cesar2/]) and the Comédie Française's *La Grange Database* (www.comedie-francaise.fr/en/la-grange-database),[6] figures and statistics from the *Comédie-Française Registers Project* (cfregisters.org), and possibly accounts of a colonial reception from the *Saint Domingue Theater Database* (theatreinsaintdomingue.org). Students could then write painting labels and curate a small exhibition to be displayed in the department.

I have seen that students, even those specializing in drama studies, often consider realistic performances and films as the summit of the art, unaware that other approaches may exist. Their first reaction when they realize that suggestion and stylization may produce a similar, even stronger, effect on the audience is amazement. And at the end of the semester, their course evaluations most often express satisfaction at having been able to think outside the box of theater realism. It is my hope that the few examples developed here will contribute to expanding students' horizons.

Notes

1. Translations of *Iphigénie* are by Geoffrey Alan Argent. All other translations are my own.

2. Several comical anecdotes staging the interferences of people sitting on the benches with the action of the play may be studied in class or as an assignment (Chaouche 72–73, 87, 94, 104–05).

3. A presentation of the concrete conditions of neoclassical tragedies' performances in seventeenth-century France may be drawn from Pierre Pasquier and Anne Surgers's edited volume.

4. Students may enjoy reading an excerpt from John Crowne's 1675 English rewriting of *Andromaque*, which displayed the crime scene (Lecercle 152–62). The example highlights the major role English aesthetics played in the debate between telling and showing, since the aesthetic of showing was dominant, reflecting the influence of neoclassical dramaturgy, even in seventeenth-century England.

5. To develop this aspect, instructors may want to use recent editions of eighteenth-century tragedies that insist on the various aspects of performance and comment on developments in the staging of spectacular scenes: Pierre Laurent Buirette de Belloy's *Le siège de Calais* (*The Siege of Calais*), Antoine-Marin Lemierre's *Guillaume Tell*, Michel-Jean Sedaine's *Maillard, ou Paris sauvé* (*Maillard, or Paris Saved*), Voltaire's *Œdipe*. They may also want to explore new genres that exploit the tragic outside the forms of tragedy, such as Pierre-Augustin Caron de Beaumarchais's *La mère coupable* (*The Guilty Mother*) or Jacques-Marie Boutet de Monvel's melodrama *Les victimes cloîtrées* (*The Cloistered Victims*).

6. See also Sylvie Chevalley; André Blanc; Joël Huthwohl; Agathe Sanjuan.

Works Cited

Advertisement for *Iphigénie*. *Affiches américaines*, 1 Sept. 1781, p. 9.

Arasse, Daniel. *On n'y voit rien: Descriptions*. Gallimard, 2003.

Aristotle. *La poétique*. Translated by Roselyne Dupont-Roc and Jean Lallot, Le Seuil, 2011.

Baculard d'Arnaud, François-Thomas-Marie. *Fayel*. Lejay, 1770.

Beaumarchais, Pierre-Augustin Caron de. *La mère coupable*. Edited by René Pomeau, Flammarion, 1993.

Belloy, Pierre Laurent Buirette de. *Le siège de Calais*. Edited by Logan J. Connors, Modern Humanities Research Association, 2014.

Blanc, André. *Histoire de la Comédie-Française: De Molière à Talma*. Perrin, 2007.

Boileau. *Art poétique*. *Œuvres complètes*, edited by Françoise Escal, Gallimard, 1966, pp. 151–85.

Bret-Vitoz, Renaud. *L'espace et la scène: Dramaturgies de la tragédie française, 1691–1759.* Voltaire Foundation, 2018.

Bricaire de la Dixmerie, Nicolas. *Lettre sur l'état présent de nos spectacles.* Duchesne, 1765.

Chaouche, Sabine, editor. *La scène en contrechamp: Anecdotes françaises et traditions de jeu au siècle des Lumières.* Champion, 2005.

Château de Versailles. "*Fêtes et divertissements à la Cour*: Ressources Pédagogiques." www.chateauversailles.fr/decouvrir/ressources/fetes-divertissements-cour-ressources-pedagogiques.

Chevalley, Sylvie, editor. *Album théâtre classique.* Gallimard, 1970.

Clément, Jean-Marie-Bernard, and Joseph de La Porte. *Anecdotes dramatiques.* Veuve Duchesne, vol. 1, 1775.

"Comédie-Française Registers Project—R130 Feux 3—1768–1770." 31 July 1769. *Comédie-Française Registers Project*, flipbooks.cfregisters.org/R130_3/index.html#page/241/mode/1up.

Cronk, Nicholas. "L'*Iphigénie* de Saint-Foix et l'esthétique du tableau: Réécrire Racine en 1769." *La réception de Racine à l'Âge classique*, edited by Cronk and Alain Viala, Voltaire Foundation, 2005, pp. 133–44.

Diderot, Denis. *De la poésie dramatique. Œuvres de Denis Diderot*, pp. 1273–350.

———. *Entretiens sur* Le fils naturel. *Œuvres de Denis Diderot*, pp. 1131–90.

———. *Œuvres de Denis Diderot, tome 4: Esthétique-Théâtre.* Edited by Laurent Versini, Laffont, 1996.

Ducis, Jean-François. *Hamlet. Œuvres de J.-F. Ducis*, pp. 19–40.

———. *Macbeth. Œuvres de J.-F. Ducis*, pp. 113–35.

———. Manuscript of *Hamlet.* Archives Comédie-Française, MS 267, Bibliothèque-Musée de la Comédie-Française, Paris.

———. *Œuvres de J.-F. Ducis suivies des œuvres de M. J. de Chénier.* Ledentu, 1839.

Félibien, André. "Les divertissements de Versailles, donnés par le roi à toute sa cour au retour de la conquête de la Franche Comté en l'année mille six cent soixante-quatorze." 1674. *Les fêtes de Versailles*, Dédale-Maisonneuve et Larose, 1994.

Fesch, Jean-Louis, and Whirsker. *Mlle Dumesnil dans le rôle de Phèdre.* ca. 1770–1788. Gouache, ink and gold highlights on vellum. Comédie-Française, Paris.

Frantz, Pierre. *L'esthétique du tableau dans le théâtre du XVIIIe siècle.* PU de France, 1998.

Fried, Michael. *Absorption and Theatricality: Painting and Beholder in the Age of Diderot.* U of California P, 1980.

Green, Eugène. *La parole baroque.* Desclée de Brouwer, 2001. Book with audio CD.

Hogarth, William. *David Garrick as Richard III.* 1745, Walker Art Gallery, National Museums Liverpool.

Horace. *Art poétique. Épîtres*, edited and translated by François Villeneuve, Les Belles Lettres, 1934.

Huthwohl, Joël. *Costumes et comédiens des Lumières.* Bleu Autour, 2011.

Le Brun, Charles. *Bowles's Passions of the Soul: Represented in Several Heads;*

Engraved in the Manner of Drawings in Chalk, from the Designs of the Late Celebrated Monsieur Le Brun. Carington Bowles, 1780?, http://access.bl.uk/item/viewer/ark:/81055/vdc_100051005831.0x000001.

Lecercle, François. "Andromaque et ses adaptations anglaises." *Réécritures du crime: L'acte sanglant sur la scène (XVIe–XVIIIe siècle)*, edited by Lecercle et al., *Littératures classiques*, no. 67, 2008, pp. 147–62.

Lemierre, Antoine-Marin. *Guillaume Tell.* Edited by Renaud Bret-Vitoz, PU de Rennes, 2005.

Luneau de Boisjermain, Pierre-Joseph-François. *Œuvres de Jean Racine, avec des commentaires.* Vol. 4, Louis Cellot, 1768.

Marie, Laurence. "Gestuelles du crime shakespearien sur les scènes française et anglaise de la seconde moitié du XVIIIe siècle." *Littératures classiques*, vol. 3, no. 67, 2008, pp. 201–18.

———. *Inventer l'acteur: Emotions et spectacle dans l'Europe des Lumières.* Sorbonne UP, 2019.

———. "Les premières adaptations de Shakespeare à la Comédie-Française: Expérimentations sur les limites du théâtre visuel mimétique." *Théâtre et imaginaire: Images scéniques et représentations mentales (XVIe–XVIIIe siècle)*, edited by Véronique Lochert et Jean de Guardia, Editions universitaires de Dijon, 2012, pp. 257–64.

———. "Writing about Theater in Saint-Domingue (1766–1791): A Public Voice on a Public Space." *On History's Stage*, edited by Jeffrey Leichman and Karine Bénac-Giroux, Voltaire Foundation, forthcoming.

Marmontel, Jean-François. *Éléments de littérature. Œuvres de Marmontel*, vol. 4, Belin, 1819.

———. *Mémoires.* Edited by Jean-Pierre Guicciardi et Gilles Thierriat, Mercure de France, 1999.

Molière. *L'impromptu de Versailles.* 1663. *Œuvres complètes*, edited by Georges Forestier, Gallimard, 2010.

Monvel, Jacques-Marie Boutet de. *Les victimes cloîtrées.* Edited by Sophie Marchand, Modern Humanities Research Association, 2011.

Nivelon, François. *The Rudiments of Genteel Behavior.* London, 1737. Folger Shakespeare Library, folgereducation.files.wordpress.com/2015/04/poem pocket-cv.jpg.

Parisau, Pierre-Germain. *Richard, parodie de Richard III, en vaudevilles.* Thomas Brunet, 1781.

Pasquier, Pierre, and Anne Surgers, editors. *La représentation théâtrale en France au XVIIe siècle.* Armand Colin, 2011.

Py, Olivier. "Avignon se débat entre les images et les mots." *Le monde*, 29 July 2005.

Racine, Jean. "*Athalie.* Notice." *Œuvres complètes*, p. 1714.

———. *Iphigenia.* Edited and translated by Geoffrey Alan Argent, 2011. *The Complete Plays of Jean Racine*, vol. 3, Pennsylvania State UP, 2010–.

———. *Iphigénie.* 1674. *Œuvres complètes*, pp. 702–63.

———. *Œuvres complètes, tome I: Théâtre-Poésie.* Edited by Georges Forestier, Gallimard-La Pléiade, 1999.

Rétif de la Bretonne, Nicolas-Edme. *La mimographe*. Slatkine Reprints, 1980.
Rozoi, Barnabé Farmian de. *Richard III, tragédie en cinq actes*. Brunet, 1782.
Saint-Foix, Germain-François Poullain de. "*Dénouement d'Iphigénie.*" *Œuvres complètes*, vol. 2, Duchesne, 1778, pp. 339–45.
Sanjuan, Agathe, editor. *La Comédie-Française s'expose au Petit Palais*. Paris Musées, 2011.
Sedaine, Michel-Jean. Maillard, ou Paris sauvé *et* Raymond V, comte de Toulouse. Edited by John Dunkley, Modern Humanities Research Association, 2015.
Talma, rôle d'Hamlet et Mlle Duchesnois rôle de Gertrude, dans la Tragédie d'Hamlet de Ducis. 1807. *Gallica*, gallica.bnf.fr/ark:/12148/btv1b9006693w.item.
Veyne, Paul. *Mon musée imaginaire ou les chefs d'oeuvre de la peinture italienne*. Albin Michel, 2012.
Viala, Alain. "Les mises en scène modernes de Racine." *Théâtre complet*, by Jean Racine, Classiques Garnier, 2014, p. 1172.
Voltaire, François-Marie Arouet. *Correspondance*. Edited by Théodore Besterman, translated by Frédéric Deloffre, vol. 6, Gallimard, 1981.
———. "Discours sur la tragédie à Mylord Bolingbroke." *Œuvres de 1728–1730*, edited by John Renwick, pp. 163–66. *Œuvres complètes de Voltaire*, vol. 5, Voltaire Foundation, 1998.
———. *Œdipe, tragédie de Voltaire suivie de Œdipe travesti, parodie de Dominique*. Edited by Isabelle Degauque, Editions Espace 34, 2002.
———. *Sémiramis*. Edited by Robert Niklaus. *Œuvres de 1746–1748 (I)*, edited by Karlis Racevskis et al., pp. 39–195. *Œuvres complètes de Voltaire*, vol. 30A, Voltaire Foundation, 2003.
Watteau, Antoine. *Les Comédiens-Français*. ca. 1720. *The Met*, www.metmuseum.org/art/collection/search/437925.

Blair Hoxby

A Comparative Approach to Teaching Neoclassical Tragedy

Few first-year college students expect to major in subjects such as French or English these days. Even at elite universities, a good share of the incoming class may be narrowly preprofessional and may hold pessimistic views of the financial returns on majoring in the humanities, based on crude and misleading analyses promoted in the press—and in some cases accepted by state governors and university administrators.[1] So, many courses offered in the humanities must be designed with the question in mind, Why would a student who intends to major in a STEM field and who hopes to work on Wall Street or in Silicon Valley or the Research Triangle want to study this?

My first response is that audiences at the theater, the ballet, and the opera are filled with adults who work in these fields. After all, attending the theater is one of the great pleasures of life. Yet it is an acquired pleasure that becomes more intense as one's knowledge of the theater becomes more refined. An ancillary answer is that many incoming students are uncomfortable with the sorts of formal reading and writing assignments that they believe to be de rigueur in humanities courses and cite these as a reason for steering clear. They prefer creative assignments, group work, or other forms of "active" learning. By focusing on performance, I can teach interpretation and aesthetic appreciation in a way that taps into students' creative and collaborative impulses. I therefore offer a class pitched to first-year students called Theatrical Wonders from Shakespeare to Mozart.

The title is a flexible one that allows me to adjust the syllabus to the live performances and simulcasts that are available in any given year. I have found that in a semester of twelve weeks or longer it is feasible to introduce students to four distinct performance traditions: for example, those of the Globe, the Spanish theatrical courtyards, the French neoclassical stage, and the opera house. In a ten-week quarter, I restrict myself to three of these, allowing two to three classes per work for a total of about eight texts.

What remains constant, regardless of the texts, is my focus on performance. I make extensive use of theater plans, scene designs, acting manuals, film clips, and, when possible, live performances to analyze how these dramas were written with particular performance conditions in mind, yet can continue to live and evolve in the different playing conditions of our own day. I stress that performance is a form of interpretation.

Because I place a premium on live performances, the syllabus constantly changes. If the *Revenger's Tragedy* were being staged, I might commence the course with *Hamlet*. If Mozart's *Die Zauberflöte* (*The Magic Flute*) were being performed, I would start with Shakespeare's *The Tempest*. If Christoph Willibald Gluck's *Iphigénie en Tauride* (*Iphigenia on Tauris*) were on offer, I would be sure to include Jean Racine's *Iphigénie*. If a production of Mozart's *La clemenza di Tito* (*The Clemency of Titus*) were being mounted, I would include Pierre Corneille's *Cinna*. If Giuseppe Verdi's *Otello* (1887) were being produced, I would not scruple to assign a work written long after Mozart's death in 1791. And if Sergei Prokofiev's *Romeo and Juliet* (1935) were being staged, I might venture well into the twentieth century. That said, texts that I assign regularly include Shakespeare's *Romeo and Juliet*, *Othello*, *Macbeth*, *Antony and Cleopatra*, and *The Tempest*; Pedro Calderón de la Barca's *Il principe constante* (*The Constant Prince*) and *La vida es sueño* (*Life Is a Dream*); Corneille's *Le Cid*, *Horace*, and *Cinna*; Racine's *Andromaque*, *Iphigénie*, *Phèdre*, and *Athalie*; and Mozart's *Idomeneo*, *Le nozze di Figaro* (*The Marriage of Figaro*), *Don Giovanni*, and *Die Zauberflöte*. My reason for gravitating toward the French texts in this list is twofold: I want plays that will allow me to discuss displays of the passions on the early modern stage and that will pair well with a Shakespearean tragedy or a later opera.

I teach all texts in English, but I encourage students who know Spanish, French, Italian, or German to read in them. Although I was initially concerned that students who did not know certain languages might feel insecure if their peers referred to passages in the original, I find them to be quick to applaud one another's skills and happy to learn from one another. Indeed, while I like to think that my students learn something from me, they often seem to pay special attention to their peers when they speak with any kind of authority. This atmosphere of display, admiration, and praise has attendant benefits, for at least a minority of my students—I would guess between ten and twenty percent—declare a desire to acquire a new language while at college and follow through by taking classes and, in many cases, studying abroad.

A few decades ago, a course emphasizing live performance might have seemed feasible only in metropolitan areas, but today, the ready availability of clips on *YouTube* and of full-length, live simulcasts from the world's great theaters have made such classes plausible for all. I do not wish to understate the magic of truly in-person performance: if I am able to secure good seats at the San Francisco Ballet or Opera for my students, they consider that experience—dressing up, driving downtown, mingling with more mature adults in the lobby, being confronted by moving and talented performers on stage—qualitatively different from virtual performances. Nevertheless, I have seen plenty of tears drawn from the eyes of students attending simulcasts. The number of companies looking to expand their following through simulcasts is increasing every year, but I am always sure to check the calendars of the Comédie-Française, the National Theatre, the Metropolitan Opera, the Royal Opera House, and the Bolshoi Ballet—all of whom offer simulcasts (or delayed transmissions or reprises of live performances) of a very high quality for prices that do not much exceed the cost of a ticket to the movies. Because these simulcasts feature close-ups from various angles, they offer an experience that differs from, and in certain respects exceeds, that of sitting in a fixed seat in a theater. A course that combines some truly live theater experiences with such simulcasts affords plenty of opportunities to discuss the essence of a theatrical experience. Because it is desirable that such experiences be open to all students, I seek educational discounts from the performance companies and subventions from the university so that students can attend at no expense.

Although this is not the place for a long excursus on financial support for the humanities, I have observed from conversations with university administrators and donors that, while one side or the other—sadly, more often the administrators than the donors—may resist funding the humanities, the performing arts are a near neighbor on which they can often agree. In my view, the creative arts are no substitute for traditional fields such as history, philosophy, and literature and languages, but attaching humanities classes to the arts can sometimes be a useful way of conveying to administrators and donors the appeal of what we do.

One might suspect that my emphasis on performance would do no favors to French neoclassical tragedy, which relies, to a greater extent than most other traditions, on the economy of its plots and the energy of its verse to sway the passions of the audience. But in practice, students find it interesting to consider the different means that can be used to imitate an action and move the passions. Comparing, say, a *tirade* (declamatory speech) from a tragedy by Racine with a rage aria from an opera by Mozart increases their appreciation of both art forms. How can one prepare students to undertake such a comparison? One answer is a sequence of assignments that can feed classroom discussion.

For the first assignment, I ask students to analyze a speech as a rhetorical performance meant to be recited. Which words should be emphasized? Why? Are they the most important words? Are there words that are placed in opposition to each other, or that are arranged in a climax? Where should the speaker pause? What figures of speech (drawn from a short list that I supply) are being employed? I draw excerpts from handbooks for orators, such as Thomas Sheridan's *A Course of Lectures on Elocution*, that are stored in databases such as *Eighteenth-Century Collections Online* (*ECCO*).

For this exercise, I find Sheridan's fourth lecture, "Of Emphasis," especially useful. Sheridan makes two important points: first, that emphasis "ennobles the word to which it belongs, and presents it in a stronger light to the understanding"; and, second, that emphasis marks the rank that words should hold in our mind and their relation to each other (57). He illustrates this with a simple example. The question, "Shall you ride to town tomorrow?" can seek completely different answers, depending on where you lay the emphasis. Are you asking for confirmation? Do you want to know who will go? The means of transportation? The direction? The destination? The timing? The emphasis reveals all.

Sheridan then proceeds to various passages from the Bible and from Shakespeare. When I ask students to read the passage in *Othello*, "Put out the light, then put out the light," they usually emphasize "light" in both clauses. Sheridan notes how much more effective it is to say, "Put out the light, then put out *the* light" (65). In this case, stressing the article indicates the difference between the candle and life. Many actors, he says, are inclined to say, "Perdition catch my soul but I do *love* thee," but the vehemence of Othello's passion is better emphasized by stressing *do*, which makes it an auxiliary verb rather than a mere expletive (66). In the case of these lines from *All for Love*, Sheridan suggests three emphases: "The fault was mine, / To place thee *there*, [pause] where *only*, Thou, *could'st* fail" (67). These three emphases bring out Antony's admission that he placed his admirable friend in the one situation where he was destined to fail.

If one were to assign a passage to be declaimed in French, one might still ask students to analyze periodic structures, rhetorical figures, and emphases. But in the case of French declamation, it is more important to introduce ideals such as harmony and modulation because emphasis is indicated more often by a modulation of pitch or the lengthening of a syllable than by a simple stress. The rules of French declamation can be daunting, especially for nonnative speakers, but many of them are clearly described in Patricia M. Ranum's *The Harmonic Orator*. Although her book is intended to be of service to singers, its central thesis—that French song is a heightened form of oratory—means that it contains a wealth of information about French rhetoric and declamation. For example, she discusses poetic harmony and modulation; the oratorical period; long and short syllables; the doubling of consonants for emphasis; accents and articulations; masculine and feminine speech rhythms; rhythmic figures of speech; the expressive energies of tempos, modes, and chords; and basic French speech melodies. The book contains extensive excerpts from French treatises, quoted both in the original and in English translation. It should prove especially useful for any class that attempts to integrate the study of French drama with *tragédie en musique* ("musical tragedy"), for it stresses the common principles of declamation, recitative, and the singing of airs. A primary text of particular value for this assignment is Jean Léonor le Gallois de Grimarest's *Traité du recitative* (*Treatise on Recitative*), which contains advice on the proper declamation of rhetorical figures such as interrogation, apostrophe, antitheses, gradation, and irony (95–106).

For the next assignment, I ask students to produce an affective script in the margin of a speech on the model of James Burgh's *The Art of Speaking*, whose lessons typically begin with a heading that consists of a series of passions, then reproduce passages from Virgil, Shakespeare, John Milton, Alexander Pope, and others, with marginal notes on the specific passions that the orator should be personating as he utters the lines. Another useful source for this assignment is Grimarest on the proper declamation of the passions (79–95). For example, Grimarest maintains that there are three modes of declamation appropriate to love, depending on whether it makes one feel "la douceur" 'sweetness,' "la joie" 'joy,' or "ses peines" 'one's pain.' The first kind should be expressed with a voice "flateuse et tendre" 'flattering and tender,' as in the exchange of Chimène and Rodrigue in Corneille's *Le Cid* in which they trade half-formed imaginings of what might have been: "Rodrigue, qui l'eût cru? / Chimène, qui l'eût dit? / Que notre heure fût si proche et sitôt se perdît" 'Roderick, who would have thought . . . ? / [Chimène, who would] have foretold / That [Roderick resumes] bliss so near us would so soon be lost!' (3.4.987–88; *The Cid*). Joyous love, like that felt by the queen at the end of the second act of Racine's *Bérénice*, should be expressed in a gay voice: "Rassurons-nous, mon cœur, je puis encor lui plaire. / Je me comptais trop tôt au rang des Malheureux. / Si Titus est jaloux, Titus est amoureux" 'I deemed that I was the most miserable / Of mortals too quickly. Yes if he / Is jealous, he is still in love with me' (2.5.664–66; *The Cid*).

A love infused with suffering, like that expressed in the dying words of Hippolyte in Racine's *Phèdre*, should be expressed in tones that are plaintive and weighed down:

> Le Ciel, dit-il, m'arrache une innocente vie.
> Prends soins après ma mort de la triste Aricie.
> Cher Ami, si mon Père un jour désabusé
> Plaint le malheur d'un Fils faussement accusé,
> Pour apaiser mon sang et mon ombre plaintive,
> Dis-lui qu'avec douceur il traite sa Captive,
> Qu'il lui rende . . . (5.6.1561–67)
>
> Heaven [he says] tears from me a blameless life.
> Care for Aricia, forsaken by my death.
> Dear friend, my father may be undeceived
> One day, and sorry for this son accused
> Unjustly. Say my blood and mournful shade
> Will be appeased if he is gentle with
> His captive, and restores to her . . . (Edmunds 192)

Grimarest produces such passages to illustrate the proper tone of voice to adopt for any given passion.

I typically teach French neoclassical tragedy in the middle of my term, so this assignment is likely to line up with French texts read in translation or in the original language. Although Burgh does not use examples from

French tragedies, I value his production of long affective scripts, and I find that his lessons drawn from epic narrative map well onto some messenger's speeches, such as Valère's report of the battle of the Horatii and the Curiatii in *Horace* (4.1.1102ff.). Furthermore, some of the soliloquies that Burgh glosses, such as Claudius's private prayer in Shakespeare's *Hamlet* (3.3.36–72; Burgh 213–14) or Cato's last thoughts before his suicide in Joseph Addison's *Cato* (5.1.1–40; Burgh 141–42), are sufficiently similar to a monologue or *récit* that one can ask students to apply the method to a passage that develops several affective states to the point of fullness, thus creating a sequence of tableaux, or a gallery of monuments to the passions. Passages by Corneille that lend themselves to this assignment include Don Rodrigue's *stances* (stanzas) in *Le Cid* (1.7.293–352) and Sabine's "Prenons parti, mon âme, en de telles disgrâces" 'Let us take part, dear soul, in such disgraces' (my trans.) in *Horace* (3.1.711–64). Examples by Racine include Andromaque's "Ah! De quel souvenir viens-tu frapper mon âme?" 'Ah, with what memories you pierce my heart!' (*Andromaque* 3.8.1014–38; Edmunds) or the monologues of Antiochus or Titus in *Bérénice* (1.3.19–50; 4.1.987–1040).

In a third assignment, I ask students to identify an appropriate sequence of facial expressions and gestures that will honor the rhetorical structure and affective sequence of a passage. Joseph Roach's *The Player's Passion* and Blair Hoxby's "Passions" and *What Was Tragedy?* provide general accounts of the centrality of the passions and the importance of expression and action to early modern theories of drama and acting. For nuts-and-bolts illustrations, I turn to primary texts such as Fermín Eduardo Zeglirscosac's *La expresión de las pasiones* (*The Expression of the Passions*), Johann Jacob Engel's *Ideen zu einer Mimik* (*Ideas for Facial Expression*), Gilbert Austin's *Chironomia*, and Henry Siddons's *Practical Illustrations of Rhetorical Gesture and Action*. Sometimes, I begin with Dene Barnett's omnibus *The Art of Gesture*, which distills principles of stage action from a wide array of acting manuals dating from the late seventeenth to the early nineteenth centuries and which includes many photographs of actors attempting to follow neoclassical principles of gesture.

Since my object is not to teach students how to perform neoclassical drama but to show them how to appreciate the grace and persuasiveness of classical drama in performance as knowledgeable spectators, I do not get too hung up on technicalities. First, I introduce them to some of the ideals of neoclassical performance, which Barnett discusses under the headings "nobility" (137–38), "idealization and imitation of nature" (139–45), "clarity and precision" (146–48), "variety in gestures" (149–52), "ornament, beauty, and ceremony" (153–57), and "repose" (158–60). Clips from older productions by the Comédie-Française, from the pantomime sections of classical ballets, or even from newer productions, such as Robert Wilson's staging of Gluck's *Alceste*, can, in their different ways, get students accustomed to the peculiar grace and power of neoclassical gesture. Then, I introduce them to the hierarchy of gestures that descends from the epic to the plain style, emphasizing the importance of epic gestures to tragic performance. Austin's comparison of these gestural styles to the wing beats of different birds seems to make intuitive sense to students:

> Perhaps much of the characteristic difference in the styles of gesture will be found in the manner of sustaining the action, something analogous to the flight of birds if it may be permitted to draw from thence an illustration. The transition from gesture to gesture with the arms long displayed and seldom falling to rest, is analogous to the soaring and graceful flight of certain greater birds, whose extended wings do not close for a considerable time, though they vary their movements, and change their rapidity. The flight of the hawk, and the soaring of the eagle, whose motions are both powerful and swift, and magnificently sustained, and boldly terminated, present the image of high tragic and epic gesture. . . The orator [in contrast] seems to fly on the wings of the dove, "rapid, strong, and light." For a time he ascends in towering elevation, but he does not long hover among the clouds, he rather descends to adorn the more interesting domestic scene. (459–60)

My students are intrigued by Austin's drawings of the gestures that Sarah Siddons employed when delivering specific speeches (495–96; Barnett 328–29), even if they do not wish to take the time to learn the complex notation system that Austin employs to record the transition from one gesture to another with the flow of the text. For this exercise in delivering a passage with gestures, I find it best to focus on only three kinds: emphasis, gestures that accompany figures of speech (such as thesis and antithesis, or climax), and gestures that express the passions. (Commencing, indicative, and terminating gestures are important too, but students are already inclined to use these without giving them any thought: they are second nature.) Barnett is an excellent resource on all of them. This third exercise should reinforce lessons learned in the first two. Indeed, it is possible to loop back to the same models (such as Cato's speech before his suicide) because the appropriate gestures for such speeches are detailed by authorities such as Burgh and recorded by Barnett.

Once students are equipped to consider a speech as a performed utterance, they can compare a Racinian *récit* such as Ulysse's account of the sacrifice in *Iphigénie* (5.5.1727–90) or Théramène's report of Hippolyte's death in *Phèdre* (5.6.1498–570) with a fully staged operatic scene—say, the death of Hippolyte in Jean-Philippe Rameau's *Hippolyte et Aricie* (which requires the use of a cloud machine, recitative, and choral lament), the averted sacrifice of Oreste in Gluck's *Iphigénie en Tauride*, or the appearance of Neptune in Mozart's *Idomeneo*. You can also ask them to compare a lament or a *tirade* in a declaimed tragedy by Corneille or Racine with a lament or a rage aria in Mozart.

I favor manuals of elocution written in English (hence my many references to Sheridan, Burgh, and Austin) for two reasons. First, I pitch my course to English-speaking students, so these manuals are easier to read and more likely to contain examples drawn from Shakespeare. Second, they tend to be more concrete than French manuals such as Hippolyte Jules Pilet de La Mesnardière's *La poétique* (*Poetics*), the Abbé d'Aubignac's *La pratique du théâtre* (*The Practice of Theater*), Michel Le Faucheur's *Traité de l'action de l'orateur* (*Essay upon the Action of an Orator*) Grimarest's *Traité du récitatif*, Joseph-Antoine-Toussaint Dinouart's *L'éloquence du corps* (*The Eloquence of the Body*), or Larive's *Cours de declamation* (*Course in Declamation*). Of these, I find Grimarest to be the most useful, though Le Faucheur has the advantage of being available in a contemporary translation.

This difference between English and French manuals may lead some to ask to what extent principles of elocution and stage action were considered transferrable from one national tradition to another and from declaimed drama to opera. On the one hand, almost all early manuals of oratory, no matter what their national origin, take as their point of reference classical rhetorical manuals such as Cicero's and Quintilian's and anecdotes about the crucial interventions that famous actors made in the lives of orators such as Demosthenes and Cicero, transforming them, according to Plutarch's *Lives*, from failures to brilliant successes by training them in principles of elocution and gesture. These texts borrow very freely from each other across languages. Moreover, there is strong evidence to support the notion that declamation, recitative, and song existed on a continuum. For example, it is said that when Jean-Baptiste Lully was developing his style of recitative, he studied the way Racine coached Marie Champmeslé, who triumphed in her interpretations of Andromaque, Bérénice, Monime, Iphigénie, and Phèdre, to enunciate her speeches pitch (*ton*) by pitch (Rosow

473). Conversely, when Voltaire was asked how actors and actresses had spoken in his youth, he replied that the truest record of their style lay in the recitative of Lully (Rosow 476). On the other hand, the historical record is replete with testimonials to the differences between the theatrical and musical tastes of the English, the French, and the Italians. Until at least the mid eighteenth century, many Frenchmen considered English play-acting and Italian music to be expressive to the point of bad taste; at about this time, however, French reformers such as Denis Diderot, Jean-Jacques Rousseau, and Stendhal began to argue that the French could learn something from the English and the Italians.

How should one address this complex relation in the classroom? Most of my students have read at least one or two plays by Shakespeare and may have seen one or two films based on them. Very few of them have had any exposure to neoclassical drama in any language or to opera of any period. Therefore, I take it as my first duty to get them accustomed to early modern and neoclassical drama, without worrying about the finer distinctions between national traditions or between declaimed and sung drama. To make a comparison: if you are dealing with students whose soundscape is formed by techno-pop and hip-hop, it is folly to leap right into the difference between an Italian madrigal and a French air. To be sure, those differences exist, but the first thing that will register with them is the difference between what they usually listen to and what you are inviting them to hear. After a few weeks, it becomes easier to discuss differences in national taste. For example, students are often struck by the number of words and scenes in Shakespeare that violate French rules of decorum: the banquet scene in *Macbeth*, the handkerchief and strawberries of *Othello*, the crab in *Hamlet*, Othello's mention of his thigh (Pemble 69–117). Such little examples point to the important differences between national traditions without undermining the enterprise of comparative performance studies.

In addition to these short exercises that can be presented and criticized in class, I ask students to submit a more formal close reading of a passage, to write a critical review of a performance, and to respond creatively to one of the texts on the syllabus. In preparing them to write a close reading of a passage, I normally assign Cleanth Brooks's "The Naked Babe and the Cloak of Manliness" and a clip of Ian McKellen discussing how to deliver the "Tomorrow, and tomorrow, and tomorrow" soliloquy word by word in an acting workshop. My focus on Shakespeare's *Macbeth* for this assignment is largely an accident of chronology: the play comes early in my course, and I want students to write a close reading earlier rather than later. The basic idea of the assignment—coupling a fine example of close reading with an interesting discussion of acting as a form of close reading—should be easy to replicate using many different texts. When writing critical reviews of a performance, most of my students gravitate to whatever we have seen live—in many cases comparing that performance to another production available on DVD. I have received some interesting essays comparing a relatively classic production from the Comédie-Française (e.g., Pierre Jourdan's *Phèdre*) with a more recent production (e.g., Patrice Chéreau's) that might—in its graphic display of stage violence—be responding to both Shakespearean conventions of stagecraft and to the more recent ideal of a theater of cruelty.

As a formal, creative assignment, most of my students prefer to perform a speech. They are usually drawn to Shakespeare, but a few tackle Racine or Calderón. I have also had students sing arias, choreograph and perform lost dances, design costumes for a production of an opera, write "missing" speeches (such as a soliloquy for Desdemona), and set monologues to music (think Calderón sung to Handel). I have even had students write short stories or abridged sonnet sequences responding to one or more texts on the syllabus. My hope is that this more formal sequence of assignments deepens students' appreciation for the contributions made by authors, directors, and performers, and thus transforms them into, or reaffirms them as, lifelong devotees of the theater. My primary aim is to promote the cultural or rounded intellectual and emotional development of my students. Such courses may also extend the life expectancy of our field, for the students we teach today will be the parents, decision-makers, and donors of the future.

Note

1. Two online resources that have received press attention are Carnevale and Sigelman. Such sources typically report the average earnings of majors ten years after graduation without controlling for the high school achievement of students, the selectivity of their colleges, their sex, or their growth in earnings over a lifetime—all factors that significantly shrink the gap between the returns to humanities and engineering majors. For representative press coverage of the returns to majors and the "crisis in the humanities," see Cohen; Dorfman; Douglas-Gabriel; Eilperin; Jaschik; McGurn; Schmidt; Selingo ("Business," "Six Myths"); Supiano; Tabarrok. On the recent trend of eliminating traditional majors such as English, philosophy, and mathematics from curricula, see Cook. I thank Sarah Turner for references.

Works Cited

Austin, Gilbert. *Chironomia; or, A Treatise on Rhetorical Delivery.* T. Cadell and W. Davies, 1806.

Barnett, Dene. *The Art of Gesture: The Practices and Principles of Eighteenth-Century Acting.* Carl Winter, 1987.

Brooks, Cleanth. "The Naked Babe and the Cloak of Manliness." *The Well-Wrought Urn,* Harcourt, Brace and Company, 1947, pp. 22–49.

[Burgh, James]. *The Art of Speaking.* T. Longman et al., 1761.

Carnevale, Anthony P., et al. *The Economic Value of College Majors.* Center on Education and the Workplace, Georgetown University, 2015, cew.georgetown.edu/cew-reports/valueofcollegemajors.

Chéreau, Patrice, director. *Phèdre.* Written by Jean Racine, performances by Dominique Blanc et al., ARTE France, 2003.

Cohen, Patricia. "A Rising Call to Promote STEM Education and Cut Liberal Arts Funding." *The New York Times,* 2 Feb. 2016, nytimes.com/2016/02/22/business/a-rising-call-to-promote-stem-education-and-cut-liberal-arts-funding.html.

Cook, Emily E. "Competing Campuses: An Equilibrium Model of the U.S. Higher Education Market." U of Virginia, PhD dissertation, 2019.

Corneille, Pierre. *Le Cid.* 1637. *Œuvres complètes,* pp. 689–829.

———. *The Cid. Chief Plays of Corneille,* translated by Lacy Lockert, Princeton UP, 1957, pp. 51–108.

———. *Horace.* 1640. *Œuvres complètes,* pp. 831–901.

———. *Œuvres complètes.* Edited by Georges Couton, vol. 1, Gallimard, 1980.

d'Aubignac, François Hédelin, abbé. *La pratique du théâtre.* 1657. Edited by Hélène Baby, Honoré Champion, 2001.

Dinouart, Joseph-Antoine-Toussaint. *L'éloquence du corps dans le ministère de la chaire, ou L'action du prédicateur.* C. Hérissant Fils, 1754.

Dorfman, Jeffrey. "Surprise: Humanities Degrees Provide Great Return on Investment." *Forbes,* 20 Nov. 2014, forbes.com/sites/jeffreydorfman/2014/11/20/surprise-humanities-degrees-provide-great-return-on-investment/#1cb0ba622031.

Douglas-Gabriel, Danielle. "What's More Telling for Future Earnings, Your College or Your Major?" *The Washington Post,* 7 Dec. 2015, washingtonpost.com/news/grade-point/wp/2015/12/07/whats-more-telling-for-future-earnings-your-college-or-your-major/.

Edmunds, John, translator. *Four French Plays: Cinna; The Misanthrope; Andromache; Phaedra.* By Jean Racine, Penguin Books, 2013.

Eilperin, Julie. "Obama Takes a Shot at a Key Part of His Base—Art History Majors." *The Washington Post,* 30 Jan. 2014, washingtonpost.com/news/post-politics/wp/2014/01/30/obama-takes-a-shot-at-a-key-part-of-his-base-art-history-majors/?arc404=true.

Engel, Johann Jacob. *Ideen zu einer Mimik.* Auf Kosten des Verfassers und in Commission bey August Mylius, 1786.

Grimarest, Jean Léonor le Gallois de. *Traité du recitatif: Dans la lecture, dans l'action publique, dans la déclamation, et dans le chant.* 1707. P. Goss, 1760.

Hoxby, Blair. "Passions." *Early Modern Theatricality*, edited by Henry S. Turner, Oxford UP, 2013, pp. 556–86.

———. *What Was Tragedy? Theory and the Early Modern Canon*. Oxford UP, 2015.

Jaschik, Scott. "Obama vs. Art History: President Joins the Ranks of Politicians Who Suggest Liberal Arts Disciplines Don't Lead to Jobs." *Inside Higher Education*, 31 January 2014, insidehighered.com/news/2014/01/31/obama-becomes-latest-politician-criticize-liberal-arts-discipline.

Jourdan, Pierre, director. *Phèdre*. Written by Jean Racine, performances by Marie Bell et al., Ancinex , 1968.

La Mesnardière, Hippolyte Jules Pilet de. *La poétique*. 1640. Slatkine reprints, 1972.

Larive, Jean Mm. de. *Cours de declamation*. Paris, 1804–10.

Le Faucheur, Michel. *An Essay upon the Action of an Orator, as to His Pronunciation and Gesture: Useful Both for Divines and Lawyers, and Necessary for All Young Gentlemen, that Study How to Speak Well in Publick*. Nich. Cox, [1680?]. *Eighteenth-Century Collections Online*, gale.com/primary-sources/eighteenth-century-collections-online.

———. *Traité de l'action de l'orateur: ou de la prononciation et du geste*. Chez A. Covrbé, 1657.

Lockert, Lacy. *Racine's Mid-Career Tragedies*. Princeton UP, 1958.

McGurn, William. "Is Majoring in English Worth It?" *The Wall Street Journal*, 9 Sept. 2019, wsj.com/articles/is-majoring-in-english-worth-it-11568068987?mod=searchresults&page=1&pos=2.

Pemble, John. *Shakespeare Goes to Paris: How the Bard Conquered France*. Hambledon and London, 2005.

Racine, Jean. *Andromaque*. 1667. *Œuvres complètes*, pp. 199–256.

———. *Bérénice*. 1670. *Œuvres complètes*, pp. 454–509.

———. *Iphigénie*. 1674. *Œuvres complètes*, pp. 702–63.

———. *Œuvres complètes, tome I: Théâtre-Poésie*. Edited by Georges Forestier, Gallimard-La Pléiade, 1999.

———. *Phèdre*. 1677. *Œuvres complètes*, pp. 820–76.

Ranum, Patricia M. *The Harmonic Orator: The Phrasing and Rhetoric of the Melody in French Baroque Airs*. Pendragon Press, 2001.

Roach, Joseph R. *The Player's Passion: Studies in the Science of Acting*. U of Delaware P, 1983.

Rosow, Lois. "French Baroque Recitative as an Expression of Tragic Declamation." *Early Music*, vol. 11, no. 4, 1983, pp. 468–79.

Schmidt, Benjamin. "The Humanities Are in Crisis: Students Are Abandoning Humanities Majors, Turning to Degrees They Think Yield Far Better Job Prospects. But They're Wrong." *The Atlantic*, 23 Aug. 2018, theatlantic.com/ideas/archive/2018/08/the-humanities-face-a-crisisof-confidence/567565/.

Selingo, Jeffrey J. "Business Is the Most Popular College Major, But That Doesn't Mean It's a Good Choice." *The Washington Post*, 28 Jan. 2017, washingtonpost.com/news/grade-point/wp/2017/01/28/business-is-the-most-popular-college-major-but-that-doesnt-mean-its-a-good-choice/.

———. "Six Myths About Choosing a College Major." *The New York Times*, 3 Nov. 2017, nytimes.com/2017/11/03/education/edlife/choosing-a-college-major.html.

Sheridan, Thomas. "Of Emphasis." *A Course of Lectures on Elocution*, W. Strahan for A. Millar et al., 1762. *Eighteenth-Century Collections Online*, gale.com/primary-sources/eighteenth-century-collections-online.

Siddons, Henry. *Practical Illustrations of Rhetorical Gesture and Action.* Richard Phillips, 1807.

Sigelman, Matthew, et al. "Majors That Matter: Ensuring College Graduates Avoid Underemployment." Burning Glass Technologies, 25 Oct. 2018, burning-glass.com/wp-content/uploads/underemployment_majors_that_matter_final
.pdf.

Supiano, Beckie. "What Are You Going to Do with That? For the First Time, Researchers Analyze Earnings Based on 171 College Majors." *The Chronicle of Higher Education*, 24 May 2011, chronicle.com/article/Whats-a-Degree-Worth-Report/127612.

Tabarrok, Alex. "College Has Been Oversold." *Investor's Business Daily*, 19 Oct. 2011, investors.com/politics/commentary/college-has-been-oversold.

"Tomorrow, and tomorrow—Ian McKellen Analyzes Macbeth Speech (1979)." *YouTube*, uploaded by Kris Joseph, youtube.com/watch?v=zGbZCgHQ9m8. Accessed 5 February 2019.

Wilson, Robert, director. *Alceste.* Music by Christoph Willibald Gluck, conducted by Sir John Eliot Gardiner, performed by Anne Sofie von Otter and Paul Groves, Théâtre Musicale de Paris—Châtelet, EMI, 1999.

Zeglirscosac, Fermín Eduardo. *La expresión de las pasiones en el teatro del siglo XVIII: El Ensayo sobre el origen y naturaleza de las pasiones del gesto de la acción teatral.* Edited and translated by Fernando Doménech Rico et al., Editorial Fundamentos, 2011.

Jennifer Tamas

To Speak or Not to Speak: Racine's Lessons on Communicative Strategies

As a French person, I grew up with the works of Jean Racine, Pierre Corneille, Molière. Now, as a specialist in seventeenth-century theater teaching in a public American institution where nobody has heard about *my* authors, I have to face a double challenge: first, judging by enrollment numbers, French and the humanities in general are becoming less and less attractive to students; second, even if a few students remain interested in learning French, they will be probably more captivated by gastronomy, haute couture, or French cinema than by seventeenth-century French tragedies.

Most of the undergraduate students who take my advanced literature courses do so to fulfill a requirement. When I look at my evaluations, I am always surprised to see that sixty percent of the students select "disagree" as their response to the statement, "I had a strong prior interest in the subject matter and wanted to take this course." As a firm believer in the power of rhetoric, I always start the course with a warning based on the *éloge paradoxal*, a rhetorical device that consists of praising what everyone dislikes. I tell students that I am honored and eager to be the professor who will teach them the literature that everybody hates especially because "it is old, it is written in a very difficult style, and it is not relevant to our society since it has been written by a bunch of old white male authors who lived in a time of monarchy and patriarchy." Formulating these prejudices out loud makes the students feel relieved: they know I know most of them are not particularly enchanted to take my class. Then I challenge their expectations by telling them that this class presents them with a wonderful opportunity to discover powerful and beautiful texts that will become part of them forever and will help them communicate better in their daily life. In this way I use the first ten minutes of the course to teach the suspension of disbelief, a key notion for studying seventeenth-century theater, since *vraisemblance* (plausibility) plays such an important role. By encouraging my students to put aside their skepticism for just a few hours per week, I engage them to look at the texts for what they have to say.

Since most of my courses involve reading seventeenth-century plays, the strategies I share here are used for intermediate to advanced theater courses, or surveys for which I usually have ten to twenty students per class. I derive this approach from my experience in teaching the French theatrical canon, especially Racine (*Phèdre*, *Esther*), Corneille (*Le Cid*), and Molière (*Tartuffe*). I will focus mainly on what Racine can teach our undergraduates and why it is useful to read him (a key adjective because most of our students and their parents want to know why they are being asked to spend money on reading seventeenth-century French tragedies). I guide students' inquiry by claiming that each Racinian play stages the revelation of something unacceptable and impossible to articulate. Characters are tortured by their silence, but once they start to speak, everything worsens. In order to link tragic speech and fatality, we focus on avowal scenes (*Phèdre*, 1.3 and 2.5; *Esther*, 3.4). My goal is to provide students with historical and cultural knowledge of French tragedies, but also to develop their communicative strategies and foster their capacity to lead a conversation and understand the manipulative dynamics which structure any dialogue.

Overview of the Assignment

At the first class meeting, I explain the options students will have for their final evaluation. Most of the time, the first option—a ten-page research paper in French with a bibliography—inclines students favorably toward the unannounced second option. When I explain that they can instead perform a scene (to be memorized and staged with costumes, music, and lighting), they become even more daunted. I assure them that I will help them with any of their choices throughout the semester.

If they choose to write a research paper, I ask them well in advance to think about a theme. When we agree on a specific topic, we work one-on-one on the introduction, the *problématique* (the research question), the outline, and a list of resources they can use.

If they prefer to perform a scene, I draw their attention to the theatricality of such an assignment: the semester will conclude with a show consisting of a series of student performances. Whether or not they decide to perform, all students must attend to honor their classmates' hard work. I open the performance to the students' friends and to fellow professors, and I encourage students to advertise the event on social media.

I explain that during the course of the semester students will learn how to master the theatrical and rhetorical tools to understand their scene in great detail; analyze the scene within the entire play to see how it fits into the dynamic of the tragedy; discover the aesthetic and dramaturgic effects of the scene within the plot; and construct a vision of the scene, which means interpreting and imagining the setting, the music, the costumes, the body language, and so forth. After learning these techniques, eighty percent of the students choose to perform a scene for their final assignment.

The Theatrical Dialogue

When we start working on a play, most students lack the vocabulary with which to analyze a scene in French. They cannot express their impressions of how or why the characters converse, who speaks more and who less, who is leading the discussion, in what manner and to what end. I distribute a list of technical terms to help them search for the words they need to speak about phenomena for which they do not yet have a name. In addition to providing straightforward vocabulary such as *didascalies* (stage directions), *quiproquo* (mistake), *aparté* (aside), I stress the difference between an *aparté* and a *monologue* to emphasize the aesthetic and emotional effects of an intimate speech performed alone in front of an audience (*monologue* and *double enonciation*) or performed with an interlocutor in front of an audience (*aparté* and *double énonciation*). A short and easy role-playing exercise gives them firsthand experience of these effects. I ask students to work in groups on something personal they want to say (it can be make-believe, of course) and to test it in pairs (for an *aparté*) or alone (for a *monologue*), while one of their peers represents the audience. They find the *aparté* much easier to perform and the monologue quite difficult and embarrassing. A little summary of J. L. Austin's theory of performative speech helps them make some connections between neoclassical theater and modern theory, using both traditions to understand how words can empower the one who knows how to use them.

In order to shore up students' knowledge of linguistic terms and make certain they do the readings for each class, I assign portions of the play as well as guiding questions on the course learning system that allows me to access and correct online exercises. This virtual tool is precious because it allows me to gauge what students do and do not understand, how they write, how much time they have spent on their assignments, which students are behind, and which are involved. I encourage participation in the online discussion by weighting it as thirty percent of the final grade. The students' responses help me determine what I need to stress and elaborate upon in class and when the class is ready for the next concept. Once the students develop critical skills to analyze how characters interact, we can look for what characters are hiding and consider what they attempt or achieve by their silence.

Silence and the Avowal Scene

The avowal scene is key to our analysis of French theater, not only because students can relate to the deep and familiar feelings it triggers (shame and guilt associated with a voluntary or a forced confession), but also because this particular scene represents the climax of many neoclassical tragedies. In Greek tragedies (especially Euripides), I explain, everything has been foreseen when the play starts. An oracle has spoken (the term *prédiction*, or prediction, etymologically means what has been *pré dit*, already said) and characters will try to elucidate the oracle's message because it remains unclear. In staging free will, in contrast, neoclassical tragedies aim at renewing the Greek tradition. The enigmatic premonition professed by an oracle becomes a secret kept by a character who has the choice to speak or to remain silent. To speak or not to speak is often the question: silence reinforces inaction and freezes the plot, whereas speech can suddenly accelerate human fate.

This dilemma is particularly accurate within the theater of Racine, a playwright known for staging deadlock situations where characters are entrapped by their own speech. As long as they remain silent, nothing can go wrong, but their fate changes as soon as they speak. Indeed, each of Racine's plays stages the revelation of a situation unacceptable and impossible to articulate: The Emperor Titus has to tell Bérénice he is leaving her, in spite of his unflinching love; Phèdre has to reveal an incestuous love; Esther has to declare her Jewish identity to her husband, a king who has condemned all Jews living on his land to death. According to the Aristotelian theory, the avowal scene can coincide with the recognition scene, which reinforces the strong pathetic effects. For instance, Iphigénie perceives Agamemnon as her persecutor, not solely as her father, once he confesses his decision to kill her. The recognition and the declaration occur simultaneously.

When students are asked to identify the avowal scene, they can usually locate it quickly, but they have difficulty interpreting its complex meaning because they do not realize that such a revelation has an impact at three different levels of the play—in the dialogue itself, in the act where it occurs, and the play as a whole. An efficient analysis should combine dramaturgic, rhetorical, and aesthetic tools. Instead of taking some distance, students usually stay fixated on the dialogue and explain it by paraphrasing. Superficial comments serve as a good starting point, however, as they signal that everybody understands the basic argument upon which we need to build a deeper interpretation and diversify our analytic tools.

Let's consider one of the avowal scenes in Racine's *Phèdre*, when Phèdre discloses her love to her confidant, Œnone (1.3). The difficulty of confessing passionate love comes to the fore and strikes the reader for the second time. In the tragedy's preface, the playwright states that Phèdre "préfère mourir que de le déclarer à personne" 'would rather die than speak' (my trans.), and the strong connection between death and speech should draw students' attention. They will keep in mind this obscure link when Œnone comes to Phèdre and goads her into speaking. Act 1, scene 3, is rather long and difficult because of the alexandrine verse and the expanded lines, and students' first task is to grasp the main idea: Phèdre reveals to Œnone that she loves Hippolyte. Since Œnone is Phèdre's confidant, students do not find this kind of intimate conversation surprising. They relate to Phèdre as someone whose secret weighs heavily on her, and they compare Œnone to a maternal figure or a loving friend with whom it feels good to speak. The most advanced students also comment that such a revelation is necessary to the dynamic of the plot. However, almost no one considers this dialogue as a forced confession where Œnone uses her maternal role to manipulate her speech partner and force her to reveal her secret. In order to change my students' perceptions, I divide the class into a few groups for an activity.

The first group is in charge of looking at the *volumétrie des tirades* (number of lines) in order to identify who speaks the most and decide if it is a sign of empowerment or a sign of weakness. They also analyze the *concaténation des répliques*, or how the dialogue is progressing. Do the characters use the same words, or do they rephrase questions as they answer them? Does the dialogue develop along the lines of its original ideas, or is there a meaningful shift? Do the characters provide satisfactory answers, or do they try to focus their partner's attention on another topic? Do they answer using abstractions, adjectives, personal or impersonal forms; do they employ developed or short sentences? Do they answer by posing another question?

The second group examines the rhetorical devices, the verbs and their linguistic forms (tense, mode, person). In order to guide their findings, I suggest focusing on the rhetoric usually associated with denial, difficulty, shame, or refusal to speak. This is when most students encounter for the first time *prétérition* (paralipsis), *périphrase* (periphrasis), *aposiopèse* (aposiopesis), *litote* (litotes), *euphémisme* (euphemism). As they search for these rhetorical tools, they view the text with new eyes. For instance, they notice that Phèdre twice uses the same *aposiopèse* ("J'aime . . .") to convey a powerful feeling that prevents her from revealing the name of the person she loves. *Périphrases* represent a safe way to give hints about the person she loves without disclosing his full identity: "Ce Fils de l'Amazone" 'The son of the Amazon,' "Ce Prince si longtemps par moi-même opprimé" 'The prince I have for so long harshly oppressed' (2.5.262–63; my trans.). Students grasp that Phèdre confesses her love step by step, starting with abstract ideas before arriving at concrete feelings: "je sentis tout mon corps et transir, et brûler" 'I felt my entire body altogether icy and burnt' (1.3.276; my trans.). The dialogue evolves radically when the name of the beloved is revealed. At first, Phèdre provides Œnone with indirect answers that guard her secret: "Ô haine de Vénus! Ô fatale colère!" 'O hate of Venus and its fatal wrath!' (1.5.249; my trans.). A long narration on the birth of her love, however, soon enlightens Œnone, as well as the spectator by the means of the *double énonciation*, and puts an end to the dialogue.

Meanwhile, the third group has the difficult task of imagining the staging of such an avowal. This is challenging because it requires two different abilities: trusting their imagination but also carefully reading the text in order to discern the intention of the playwright. This type of exercise represents a great opportunity to introduce the difference between *didascalie interne* and *didascalie externe* (implicit versus explicit staging directions). The *didascalie externe* is the more obvious because it appears in the text in italics. For this scene, there is just one stage direction ("elle s'assied" 'she sits down'). The implicit *didascalies* are harder to perceive because students need to pay particular attention to the text. This exercise teaches them that staging a play represents a way of interpreting it. The simple mention "she sits" is far from being simple: How will Phèdre sit? Where? How far from Œnone? In which posture (eyes closed, head bent, sighing)? How can a queen convey elegance as she shows fatigue? Will she remain seated during the rest of the dialogue? Will her body stay still? How? Which parts of the body will manifest her emotion, and how? During the brainstorming session, I invite students to consult the video clips I have posted on the discussion board: the staging by Chéreau, for instance, will provide them with ideas about costumes, sets, lights, and music.

This group work leads students to comment more in depth on the scene. Instead of saying, "Phèdre is confessing her love," they can now explain how. Although at this stage students become more sensible to the nuances of the text, they are not yet capable of fully evaluating the pragmatic impact of such a confession. In order to understand how this revelation participates in the tragic progression of the plot, they need to experience the effects of such a personal confession. Therefore, I organize a writing activity before analyzing Phèdre's second avowal: the declaration of her love to Hippolyte in person (2.5).

How to Write the Unsaid

In this group activity I ask students to work in pairs. First, they must imagine something shameful for a character to confess and techniques to make the confession audible. Next, they must write a dialogue focusing on the following tension: A wants, but fears, to say something to B, who is directly concerned with A's confession. Finally, they must think about the consequences of such an avowal.

In crafting such a dialogue, students often imagine adulterous love or passionate crimes. In order to help them materialize the tension between wanting and fearing to speak, I emphasize realistic means of shaping the dialogue: interruptions, rhetorical questions, sighs, silence. I explain how the failures of a dialogue ("les ratés de la parole," as Catherine Kerbrat-

Orecchioni terms them in *La conversation*) are precisely what makes the dialogue powerful and effective on stage (see Fournier). This exercise is also an engaging way for students to review the rhetorical devices they have learned and draw from them to put a theoretical approach into action.

For this exercise, students are welcome to use interdisciplinary and diachronic works. Introducing philosophical texts demonstrates the use of rhetoric in a field other than literature and helps students focus on technique rather than fixating on content. Borrowing from the field of law enforcement, I suggest that students work on police interviews: some police officers use theatrical techniques, such as the "good cop, bad cop" dynamic, that students will be able to identify. I encourage students interested both in law and literature to watch famous trials with great lawyers, such as Badinter on abolishing the death penalty, or Vergès on Klaus Barbie, and have them consider renowned defense speeches (see Biet). This interdisciplinary approach represents an ideal occasion to stress the importance of literature, a field integral to all the subfields of the humanities.

The writing process accentuates the differences and the resemblances between theatrical dialogue and real conversations (see Kerbrat-Orecchioni, "Dialogue"). If the aesthetic effects are particular to the theatrical form, the communicative strategies, the challenge of overcoming fear, and the consequences of shameful speech are particularly enthralling for students.

Once the students have written their own dialogue, they act it out, which puts them in a natural performance situation. The aspiration to disappear, to hide, or even to die after a scandalous confession generates an opportunity for a new class discussion on the effects of words. Ideas of shame, reputation, and prejudice permeate their daily interactions and inform their understanding of the damage caused by written words. Since they are often averse to open conflict, frank criticism, and *scenes d'explication* (arguments), they tend to find the performance of their own writing very challenging. However, when we return to the play, they perceive the second avowal scene (2.5) from a fresh perspective. They understand the dialogue between Phèdre and Hippolyte not only as passionate discourse, but also as a battle replete with guilt, shame, and power games.

Students are now confident in commenting on a theatrical text; they are ready to present a neoclassical scene on their own. For their midterm, an oral presentation represents the best option. I choose *Phèdre* in particular because of its many avowal scenes. *Bérénice* represents another good option because the entire plot revolves around Titus's silence. The emperor prefers to be mute rather than explain why he must end his relationship with Bérénice. In *Esther*, the eponymous character's decision is even weightier, because revealing her Jewish identity may result in her death. Her declaration occurs at the center of the play and changes the course of events. Students are compelled by the deadlocked situation since religious wars and identity quests are topics they easily relate to. The parallels between ancient texts and modern events are all the more striking in the students' performances.

Silence to Kill: The Theatrical Effects

By the final weeks of the course, most of the students are involved and motivated enough to perform a scene they have learned to like. They can relate to a character who has moved them and for whom they feel some compassion. In other words, they are ready to expose themselves—their body, their reputation, their pride—to perform a difficult task. As the semester comes to an end, I stress the importance of making our last session a public one. I design a program listing the names of all the artists involved (including credit for costumes, lighting, and sound), and I provide refreshments to be shared after the performance. When students give their authorization, I record the performance and send it to them as a souvenir.

Now, all this may sound like barrels of fun, and I hope it is, but it also constitutes a scary experience for most students, because they have to experience in the flesh the danger linked to representation and acting bodies. In most avowal scenes, the protagonist encounters a borderline situation in which death represents a possible solution to the deadlock. Phèdre is tempted by death during the entirety of the play and ultimately commits suicide. As a pious protagonist, Esther cannot choose death, but she faints as soon as she sees her husband, to whom she must make her fateful avowal. Fainting can be perceived as a symbolic death through which a character may escape the fearful confrontation. In *Bérénice*, the lovers' separation is far from trivial: on the contrary, it constitutes such a challenging situation for all the characters that they wish to commit suicide. Solving the tragedy without spilling blood represents Racine's tour de force.

In their performances, the students must convey not only their interpretation of the text, but also the scene's relation to modern life. They are welcome to use clothing, media, and music they judge appropriate. Successful performances have called on rap, hip-hop, or classical music to stress a particular aspect of the scene. For instance, one student used an excerpt from "Castle Walls," by TI and Christina Aguilera ("TI ft Christina Aguilera"), to begin and end her staging of Phèdre's declaration of love to Hippolyte (2.5). According to the student, the song resonates with Phèdre's loneliness and passion and ultimately illustrates her defeat. In Racine's tragedy, Hippolyte runs away, leaving Phèdre alone and desperately holding his sword. Much commentary has been made about the phallic symbolism of the weapon, but this student interpreted the sword as a new metonymy of the body: it does not so much represent the most intimate part of Hippolyte's body but rather the most exterior part and the only remains of him that Phèdre can hope to touch. Instead of reaching his inside, Phèdre can only grasp the outside.

Not all performances are as compelling. The constraints of budget and time in a public institution where most students work part-time outside of class in order to pay for their studies make it difficult to accommodate busy and incompatible schedules. Most of the work takes place during class sessions, where I always encourage students to act out the text as they explain it—and set an example by doing so myself. I push their boundaries, exhorting them to use their bodies, their breath, their youth. They feel challenged and sometimes embarrassed. However, even the shyer students find this experience rewarding because they did not expect a literature class to be so down-to-earth. Because acting allows students to take risks, it actually promotes their ability to speak a foreign language.

A particular difficulty of teaching French performance studies in the United States stems from cultural differences regarding physical expression in public. In France, people are more willing to touch each other than in the United States, where people respect a certain personal space and rarely cross that imaginary line. Yet it is challenging to perform dramatic scenes without physical contact. Indeed, it is nearly impossible to interact on a stage while conforming to prevailing notions of personal space, a concept that did not exist in the seventeenth century, when spectators and actors mingled together (see Ravel).

Another challenge is to create a course that is both demanding and accessible. I intend my classes to be serious and fun. I encourage performance as a final evaluation, even though it is time-consuming and hard to organize, knowing that this activity always brings enthusiasm to the classroom and a feeling of achievement to students. I find it especially rewarding as a pedagogical tool, because it fosters students' imagination while consolidating their theoretical knowledge about neoclassical theater, performance, and communication strategies. It also represents a privileged moment for sharing and connecting. Students cherish these memories. I discovered that the *Facebook* group French at Rutgers had posted pictures of students rehearsing on the grass near our classroom.

I conclude the course with a few words on the importance of literature and its power to affect our daily life: sharing this belief is one of my goals in teaching. In the semester's last class, I add two categories to the university's student evaluation sheet. I ask students if the class changed their vision of French culture and if they think that literature will have a new impact on their life. Most note that the course material has opened them to new concepts and led them to appreciate subjects they would like to study further in graduate school. In this sense, teaching neoclassical tragedy built confidence and success while fostering fresh interest in literature.

Works Cited

Austin, J. L. *How to Do Things with Words.* Harvard UP, 1962.

Biet, Christian. *Droit et littérature sous l'ancien régime: Le jeu de la valeur et de la loi.* Champion, 2002.

Fournier, Nathalie. "L'aparté dans la tragédie racinienne." *Mélanges de langue et littérature française offerts à Pierre Larthomas*, École normale supérieure de jeunes filles, 1985, pp. 175–93.

Kerbrat-Orecchioni, Catherine. *La conversation.* Seuil, 1996.

———. "Dialogue théâtral vs conversations ordinaires." *Cahiers de praxématique*, no. 26, 1996, pp. 32–49.

Racine, Jean. *Bérénice.* 1670. *Oeuvres complètes*, pp. 447–509.

———. *Esther.* 1689. *Oeuvres complètes*, pp. 943–99.

———. *Oeuvres complètes, tome I: Théâtre-Poésie.* Edited by Georges Forestier, Gallimard-La Pléiade, 1999.

———. *Phèdre.* 1677. *Oeuvres complètes*, pp. 820–76.

Ravel, Jeffrey S. *The Contested Parterre: Public Theater and French Political Culture, 1680–1791.* Cornell UP, 1999.

"TI ft Christina Aguilera—Castle Walls." *YouTube*, uploaded by TheSweetyLove1000, 13 Dec. 2010, youtube.com/watch?v=9ujMXM5uDWQ.

John Boitano and Louise Thomas

Teaching *la Tragédie en Musique* across the Curriculum

In French and francophone undergraduate and graduate course catalogs we find abundant offerings on Corneille, Molière, and Racine, but rarely do we find *la tragédie en musique*, also called *la tragédie lyrique* or simply *opera*. This is all the more remarkable when one considers that the *tragédies en musique* were the most widely attended and popular performances of the ancien régime. Buford Norman notes, "A new opera could have a run of as many as 150 performances, at least three times a week over a period of almost fifty weeks. By comparison, Racine's tragedies rarely had a first run of much more than thirty, and the greatest box office success of the century, Thomas Corneille's *Timocrate*, only had about eighty" (*Touched by the Graces* 9). When Jean-Baptiste Lully and Philippe Quinault composed the first *tragédie en musique*, *Cadmus et Hermione*, in 1673, they launched a new and uniquely French performing art that delighted the Sun King and his court and created an insatiable desire for more such works. The beauty of the musical poetry, the spectacular costumes and staging, the dazzling choreography, and the lively and fanciful intrigues all combined with Lully's extraordinary music to captivate the spectator and to create a frenzy for this new art form that lasted until the

French Revolution. If the great Racine, Jean de La Fontaine, and so many other distinguished literary figures all aspired to become Lully's librettist, how is it possible that undergraduate- and graduate-level French courses or classes on world literature have completely overlooked this significant genre? When one adds to the equation that each of Lully and Quinault's *tragédies en musique* provides fascinating insights into Louis XIV's court, this oversight becomes all the more problematic.

In studying *la tragédie en musique* alongside neoclassical French theater, and not in isolation, a more complete and nuanced picture of the diversity of performances of the old regime emerges. The differences between *la tragédie en musique* and neoclassical tragedy form a direct link to the two competing aesthetic visions of the century, the neoclassical and the baroque. Norman, William Brooks (*Philippe Quinault*), Catherine Kintzler and others, however, have noted that *la tragédie en musique* is an integral part of French neoclassicism:

> Loin d'être un objet atypique au sein du classicisme français, l'opéra en porte au contraire les caractères et en souligne l'amplitude: non seulement il est un élément régulier du système politique, non seulement il prend sens et forme selon les lois générales qui gouvernent le théâtre classique notamment tragique, mais encore il se présente ouvertement et il est perçu explicitement comme absolument original au sein des productions européennes. (Kintzler, *Poétique* 22)
>
> Far from being an atypical object within French neoclassicism, opera carries on the contrary all of its characteristics and emphasizes its amplitude. It is not only a regular component of the political system; it also takes on its meaning and form according to general laws which govern neoclassical and more notably tragic theater. It manifests itself openly and is explicitly seen as absolutely original within European productions. (our trans.)

The opposing and complementary elements of this aesthetic would lead to what became known as the *querelle des anciens et des modernes* ("quarrel of the ancients and the moderns"). Lully and Quinault's second *tragédie en musique*, *Alceste, ou le triomphe d'Alcide* (*Alceste; or, The Triumph of Alcide*), would ignite this feud as the ancients (Boileau, Racine, La Fontaine) proclaimed the supremacy of the great authors of antiquity, whereas the moderns (Jean de La Bruyère, Quinault, Charles Perrault) postulated the contrary. Norman writes that, "[g]iven this coexistence of two forms of tragedy within the same aesthetic, it should be obvious that one cannot fully appreciate one without the other" ("Remaking a Cultural Icon"

225). The *tragédie en musique* deliberately did not adhere to the neoclassical unities of time (one day), place (one location), and action (one plot); and yet, as Lully and Quinault refined the genre, the spectacles became increasingly serious. The widespread use of *le merveilleux* (the supernatural) in the *tragédie en musique* not only incurred the ire of the ancients; it was at the foundation of a baroque aesthetic, which expanded the notion of neoclassical tragedy beyond the constraints of Aristotelian poetics to include this new performing art. Norman points out that Boileau softened his initial criticism of Quinault, and that Voltaire saw Quinault as the second greatest French poet after Racine (Norman, *Touched by the Graces* ix–x).

The presupposition that only an instructor with musical training and background could teach such a class is no longer valid. When Norman published *Touched by the Graces: The Libretti of Philippe Quinault in the Context of French Classicism* in 2001, he made it possible for instructors without a musical background not only to understand these beautiful performances but also to contemplate developing and teaching curricular offerings on the subject. Thomas Verner and Jean Duron translated Norman's groundbreaking book into French in 2009 with the title *Quinault, librettiste de Lully: Le poète des Grâces.* Norman had previously published a two-volume critical edition of all of Lully and Quinault's libretti in 1999. His informative Web site *Philippe Quinault* (www.quinault.info) contains all the libretti with modern French transcriptions. The Web site is open-source and offers information on CD and DVD recordings and updates on upcoming performances and publications.

In *Touched by the Graces,* Norman defines in clearly understandable language and illustrates with examples essential operatic concepts such as aria (*l'air*) and recitative (*le récitatif*), the role and function of the operatic prologue, and the nature and function of the balletic *divertissements* that occur at the end of the prologue and of each act. He also offers enlightening analysis of the poetry of Quinault's libretti and Lully's music. Arranged in chronological order, the chapters each focus on a given *tragédie en musique* and examine the rich historical context in which it was written and its subtle references to the politics of the Sun King's court. The initial chapters should be assigned during the first two weeks of a semester-long class focused solely on Lully and Quinault's *tragédies en musique* in order to provide students with a basic understanding of the underlying components of opera before they view, listen to, read, and appreciate the works on their own. For a class segment, which might feature just one of Lully and Quinault's *tragédies en musique*, Norman's preface and introduction should provide students with sufficient background information.

A brief background on the birth of opera serves to familiarize students with the rich history of the performing art. This course segment notes that Italian philosophers and artists in Florence attempted to revive the combination of poetry, music, and stage visuals that they believed characterized the theater of ancient Greece. They did not have a name for this new art form—putting all the arts on stage at the same time—so they called it "work" (*opera*). A new multimedia art form was born, rather like the birth of the movies in the twentieth century. Opera soon spread from Florence to all of Italy and then to the court of Louis XIV in France, as audiences thrilled to the magic of music and poetic drama against the backdrop of beautiful stage pictures. Many feature films like *Tous les matins du monde* (*All the Mornings of the World*), *Vatel*, *Le roi danse* (*The King Dances*), and others bring the captivating music, dance, and history of the period to life for students (see appendix).

The stories of the operas are drawn mostly from classical mythology and the history of ancient Greece and Rome. And the poetic theme is almost always eros—the joy of love possessed and the sorrow of love lost. The most commonly told of all the opera stories is that of Orpheus and Eurydice: Orpheus and Eurydice are in love; Eurydice dies, and Orpheus descends into the underworld to restore her to life. This kind of pattern—joy, sorrow, glory—is explored in thousands of operas composed during this period.

This segment of the course also provides students with a basic understanding of Lully's innovative musical movements, which serve as fruitful juxtaposition to neoclassical tragedy's structure. Lully first developed the "French overture" (*l'ouverture*) during the middle baroque period in his ballets (prior to his opera compositions). Later baroque composers would widely use this form. The structure consists of two divisions, complementary in style: the first part generally slows in majestic dotted rhythms, and the second, faster in canonic or fugal style. The first ends with a half-cadence (i.e., on a dominant harmony) that requires an answering structure with a tonic ending. The second section often ends with a brief recollection of the first, sometimes even repeating some of its melodic content. When playing the overture to *Cadmus et Hermione*, the instructor can ask students to identify this structure, which becomes increasingly apparent to them as they go on to study additional *tragédies en musique*.

The class segment or the introductory portion of the dedicated course should also present the important work of Kintzler, who explains the unique nature of the operatic poetics of *la tragédie en musique* and its diverse components (i.e., music, libretto, dance, and staging).

For Kintzler, operatic dance is a fundamental part of this new poetics: "Cette réduction de la musique au concept de matière poétique musicale permet d'y inclure, dans les mêmes conditions, la danse. La participation de la danse au texte poétique s'appréhende en effet à travers la matière musicale" 'This reduction of the music to the concept of musical and poetic matter provides for the inclusion of dance in the same conditions. The participation of dance within the poetic text is effectively understood through the musical matter' (*Poétique* 15; our trans.). Ideally, a student would be able to identify the component parts of a *tragédie en musique* as illustrated by the following hypothetical example, which Kintzler provides: "Le héros se lamente: il n'est pas aimé (air). —Un personnage sacré vient lui révéler une destinée glorieuse (récitatif accompagné) et le soumet à une scène d'initiation (ballet) au cours de laquelle il lui remet un objet magique (chœur) . . ." 'The hero laments that he is not loved (aria). A sacred character reveals to him his glorious destiny (accompanied recitative) and submits him to a scene of initiation (ballet) during which he is given a magical object (chorus). . . .'

So as to further demonstrate these structural components of the *tragédie en musique*, the instructor can play selected scenes from *Cadmus et Hermione*, *Atys*, *Persée*, or *Armide* (see appendix for recommended recordings that include subtitles in the original French and in English translation). As students progress with their readings and viewings, this interactive in-class activity allows them to become quite adept in a relatively short period of time at recognizing and interpreting these component parts. The instructor can play a segment and ask students to determine whether they are hearing a recitative or an aria. To identify a recitative, students need to be able to perceive the singer's uses of the rhythms of ordinary speech. The recitatives move the narrative along quickly and don't repeat lines of text as arias do. The recitatives of the *tragédie en musique* are usually accompanied by harpsichord (*le clavecin*), which students become increasingly able to identify. To recognize an aria, students become aware of the composer's response to both the dramatic situation at hand and the poet's or librettist's formal choices. The aria segments usually have a bass line organized in regular patterns and supporting consonant harmony.

Often the first lines or entire sections of music are repeated. Verbal or melodic phrases may also be repeated or answered by parallel phrases, higher or lower, in sequences. Arias convey the raw emotions of the characters. As students are exposed to more operas, they readily and easily can distinguish recitative from aria.

The following examples serve to illustrate the recitative in Lully and Quinault's first four *tragédies en musique*.[1] In the prologue to *Cadmus et Hermione*, the Sun itself restores order by destroying a monstrous serpent named Python as the diabolical character of Envie jealously laments in his recitative:

Envie
Tu triomphes, Soleil? Tout cèdes à ton pouvoir?
Que d'honneurs tu vas recevoir!
Ah quelle rage! Ah quelle rage!

Envy
You triumph, Sun? Everything yields to your power?
What honors you are going to receive!
Ah! What rage! What rage!

In *Alceste*, a lovesick Hercules, who goes by his first name of Alcide, enters the underworld in act 4, scene 4; gives Cerberus a mighty blow with his club; and brings Alcestis back, turning her over to King Admète and thereby vanquishing love.

Pluton
Qu'on arrête ce téméraire,
Armez-vous, amis, armez-vous,
Qu'on déchaîne Cerbère,
Courez tous, courez tous.
(On entend aboyer Cerbère.)

Alecton
Son bras abat tout ce qu'il frappe.
Tout cède à ses horribles coups.
Rien ne résiste, rien n'échappe.

Pluto
Arrest this reckless man,
Arm yourselves, my friends, arm yourselves,
Let Cerberus loose,
Get yourselves ready, get yourselves ready.
(Cerberus can be heard barking.)

Alecto
His arm brings down everything he strikes.
Everything gives way to his terrible blows.
Nothing resists him, nothing escapes him.

The verses' sharp *k* alliterations ("**q**u'on" and "**c**ourez) and *a* assonances ("son br**a**s **a**b**a**t tout ce qui fr**a**ppe") work to create a frenetic scene on stage as Alcide takes on any and all adversaries.

In perhaps the most widely known segment in all of Lully and Quinault's *tragédies en musique*, Alcide almost sinks Charon's ferryboat in the fourth act. Charon's recitative in scene 1 provides some comic relief as he laments his arduous job and the feebleness of the human condition.

Charon
Il faut passer tôt ou tard,
Il faut passer dans ma barque.
On y vient jeune ou vieillard,
Ainsi qu'il plaît à Parque:
On y reçoit sans égard
Le berger, et le monarque.

Charon
You have to cross sooner or later,
You have to cross in my ferryboat.
Whether young, or old,
Whatever pleases Fate:
We take you whether you are
Shepherd or monarch.

Then, in scene 2, Alcide forces his way across the Styx without furnishing the required coinage.

Alcide, sautant dans la barque
Sortez, Ombres, faites-moi place,
Vous passerez une autre fois. . . .

Charon
Ah! ma barque ne peut souffrir un si grand poids!

Alcide, stepping into the ferryboat
Get out, Shadows, make room for me,
You can cross another time. . . .

Charon
Ah, my ferryboat cannot take such a heavy weight!

Thésée features the maniacal character of the sorceress Médée, who, consumed with love and jealousy, brings down the palace in act 5, scene 6:

> *Medée, sur un char tiré par des dragons volans*
> Je n'ay point preparé la pompe de ces lieux
> pour servir au bonheur d'un amour qui m'outrage;
> je veux que les enfers destruisent mon ouvrage,
> c'est ainsi qu'en partant je vous fais mes adieux.
>
> *Medea, in a chariot pulled by flying dragons*
> I have not prepared the festivities in this place
> To celebrate a love which is an outrage to me;
> I summon Hell to destroy my work,
> This is how I bid you all farewell.

Thésée invites direct comparisons to Racine's *Phèdre*. Racine had sought in vain a collaboration with Lully (Isherwood 204), and the great success of the first three *tragédies en musique* undoubtedly prompted him to author *Phèdre* on related subject matter just two years after the first performance of *Thésée*. The tremendous popularity of *la tragédie en musique* and its penchant for *le merveilleux* are a clear influence on Racine:

> *Théramène*
> Parmi des flots d'écume, un monstre furieux.
> Son front large est armé de cornes menaçantes;
> Tout son corps est couvert d'écailles jaunissantes,
> Indomptable taureau, dragon impétueux,
> Sa croupe se recourbe en replis tortueux.
> Ses longs mugissements font trembler le rivage.
> Le ciel avec horreur voit ce monstre sauvage;
> La terre s'en émeut, l'air en est infecté;
> Le flot, qui l'apporta, recule épouvanté.
>
> *Theramenes*
> Before our eyes spews forth a furious beast,
> A monster armed with terrifying horns,
> And all its body clothed with yellow scales:
> A thing at once indomitable bull
> And darting dragon whose hind-quarters lashed
> And twisted down in hideous slimy coils.
> Its long-drawn bellowings shake the shore: the sky
> Seems watching horror-struck at such a sight;
> The earth quakes and the air is poisoned. Then
> The wave that brought it ebbs away in fear. (Rawlings 161)

Racine's references to the four elements and supernatural forces associated with the monster find their echo in the monstrous character of the sorceress Medea in *Thésée*, who has power over earth, wind, fire, and water. Racine's monster is comparable to any of the supernatural and diabolical creatures that are ubiquitous in Lully and Quinault's *tragédies en musique*. William Brooks has noted that

> Racinian tragedy often depends largely on the juxtaposition of mythological themes with characters who are all too human. The supernatural depends on what you cannot see, whereas the operas of Lully and Quinault derive strength from what you can see. Hostile critics such as Boileau, Racine himself, Saint-Evremond, La Fontaine, assume that the spoken theatre is a pinnacle to which opera aspires but cannot reach. ("Lully and Quinault" 104–05)

After having examined the component parts of *la tragédie en musique* and the influence of Italian opera, Brooks concludes that Quinault's libretto and "its relationship with music and music itself" account for its extraordinary success ("Lully and Quinault" 111).

The dénouement of the fourth example, *Atys*, is quite tragic, as Cybèle, the Goddess from the East (i.e., Phrygia), becomes so consumed with jealousy that she has her beloved Atys killed. In a moment of regret, shown here in act 5, scene 6, she immortalizes him by turning his mutilated body into a pine tree. No wonder that this was Louis XIV's favorite opera, for he surely appreciated the absolute power of the sovereign goddess.

> *Cybèle*
> Malgré le destin implacable
> Qui rend de ton trépas l'arrest irrevocable,
> Atys, sois à jamais l'objet de mes amours:
> Reprends un sort nouveau, deviens un arbre aimable
> Que Cybele aimera toujours.

> *Cybele*
> In spite of implacable Fate,
> Whose law that you must die is irrevocable,
> Atys, be forever the object of my love:
> Take on a new form, become a beloved tree
> That Cybele will always adore.

Having provided the students with all the necessary tools to understand the rich history, music, poetry, dance, politics, staging, and aesthetic of Lully and Quinault's *tragédie en musique*, the next essential question to answer is the following: Which operas should one study within the class or a class segment on *la tragédie en musique*? Although we have put forth and developed a model for a stand-alone class on *la tragédie en musique*, we recommend using any of the CDs or DVDs in the appendix to introduce even one *tragédie en musique* into any class on neoclassical French tragedy or world literature, even in a class taught entirely in English. And, if one can only find time to include one *tragédie en musique* in the class, then it is hard to argue with the personal preference of the Sun King for *Atys*. When William Christie and Les Arts Florissants performed *Atys* in 1987, it launched a revival of the genre that continues to this day. Moreover, the 2011 DVD and its staging by renowned director Jean-Marie Villégier invites fruitful comparisons on the part of students and instructors to Racinian theater. Villégier's stage production of *Atys* resembles a somberly lit chessboard on which the main characters move about, strategize, and encounter their preordained and tragic fate. The comparisons to intrigues at Louis XIV's court are richly reflected in this exquisite staging and production. The companion disc includes interviews with the director, the conductor, and costume designer.

For a stand-alone course on Lully and Quinault's *tragédies en musique*, two approaches are possible. If the instructor wants to emphasize the experience of seeing and hearing the *tragédies en musique* in the original French and with English translation, one could adopt *Cadmus et Hermione*, *Atys*, *Persée*, and *Armide*, as DVDs with multilingual subtitles exist for all of these operas. We, however, decided in favor of a chronological selection by adopting the first four *tragédies en musique*: *Cadmus et Hermione*, *Alceste*, *Thésée*, and *Atys*. Although *Alceste* and *Thésée* are currently available only in audio versions, the adoption of the first four *tragédies en musique* truly allows students and instructors to explore the immediate evolution of the genre from the joyous first composition, *Cadmus et Hermione*, to the more somber *Atys*. As previously noted, the inclusion of *Thésée* makes it possible to see its clear influence on Racine's *Phèdre*. More important, this approach allows instructors and students to explore *la tragédie en musique* not in contrast to theatrical neoclassical French tragedy, but rather as a complex and elusive dichotomy of the neoclassical and baroque aesthetics in the *querelle des anciens et des modernes*.

The instructor can also develop discussion questions to guide the students in their reading and to foster in-class discussion and analysis. We have increasingly opted to distribute discussion questions only in class, and only after students have read the libretto, listened to the CD, or seen the DVD on their own, in order to encourage them to formulate their own interpretations of the readings and performances.

The *tragédies en musique* are so rich and beautiful that each act of each work, including the prologue, should occupy an entire class meeting. This makes it impossible to cover more than four *tragédies en musique* in an undergraduate class if there are three hours of class meetings per week in a fifteen-week semester. A graduate class could include a reading of the entirety of Norman's book, and all of Lully and Quinault's *tragédies en musique*. The undergraduate class should most probably adopt Norman's original book in English and supplement it with additional context from the instructor. A term project could require students to complete an interpretative paper on one of the *tragédies en musique* not covered in the class, assisted by the Norman book and the available recordings. The project could include an in-class lecture providing a concise summary of the plot and presenting a favorite scene, explaining its background and then showing or playing the scene to the class with the French libretto and English subtitles. In this way the class could be exposed to all the operas composed and written by Lully and Quinault. In the written report, students could provide a summary of the opera before going on to analyze and interpret its musical poetry, staging, costumes, dance sequences, and music, making references to *tragédies en musique* covered in the class. Throughout the semester, the instructor should model this interdisciplinary approach to analyzing the *tragédies en musique* under study so that students can complete their own analysis. For *tragédies en musique* not available on DVD, students should scrutinize *didascalies* (stage directions) and images carefully.

La tragédie en musique exerted an enormous influence on neoclassical tragedies and is a constituent part of what is known as the French neoclassical era. The diversity of theatrical genres and performances that took place during this time period points to a rich and diverse conception of French neoclassicism, including *le ballet de cour* (courtly ballet), *la comédie-ballet* (a genre of dialogue, dance, pantomime, and music), machine plays, tragedies, tragicomedies, and *la tragédie en musique*. The exclusion of the baroque from the notion of neoclassicism has been a significant critical oversight, for how can instructors and students understand just one constituent component (i.e, theatrical tragedy) without examining the others? And finally, this performing art deserves a listing in course catalogs because of the delightful beauty of its aesthetic. When undergraduates see, hear, and read the prologue to *Cadmus et Hermione*, they are captivated by the spectacle in the same way that seventeenth-century French audiences were; the uniquely French operatic spectacle, with its sumptuous music, superb dancing, elaborate staging, and raw emotions, becomes intoxicating. Few if any undergraduate students today have actually seen an operatic performance, yet the four times that the course has been offered at Chapman University as a stand-alone course focused on just the first four *tragédies en musique*, it has surpassed enrollment expectations. It has led to the creation of an equally successful class on nineteenth-century French opera, which is also part of the French major and minor, and a course on the great operas of the Western world, which is taught in English and offered in the university's honors program. This essay and the ressources below will hopefully provide colleagues with an inventory and analysis of the basic tools necessary to create similar course offerings or course segments in French or English translation.

Note

1. Unless otherwise attributed, example texts and translations are taken from the titles or liner notes accompanying the recorded performances in Works Cited.

Works Cited

Brooks, William. "Lully and Quinault at Court and on the Public Stage." *Seventeenth-Century French Studies*, vol. 10, no. 1, 1992, pp. 45–53.

———. *Philippe Quinault, Dramatist.* Peter Lang AG, 2009. Medieval and Early Modern French Studies 6.

Isherwood, Robert M. *Music in the Service of the King: France in the Seventeenth Century.* Cornell UP, 1973.

Kintzler, Catherine. *Poétique de l'opéra français de Corneille à Rousseau.* 1991. 2nd ed., Minerve, 2006.

Lully, Jean-Baptiste. *Alceste.* 1675. Directed by Christophe Rousset, performed by Les Talens Lyriques and le Choeur de Chambre de Namur, Aparté B076D68MH4, 2017. 2 CDs.

———. *Armide.* 1686. Directed by William Christie, performed by Les Arts Florissants, FRA Musica B004T6ABVE, 2011. DVD.

———. *Atys.* 1676. Directed by William Christie, performed by Les Arts Florissants, libretto translated by Almut Lenz and Derek Yeld, Harmonia Mundi 401257.59, 1987. 3 CDs.

———. *Cadmus et Hermione.* 1673. Directed by Vincent Dumestre, performed by Le Poème Harmonique, Alpha 701, 2008. DVD.

———. *Persée.* 1682. Directed by Marc Stone, EuroArts, 2005. DVD.

———. *Thésée.* 1675. Directed by Paul O'Dette and Stephen Stubbs, performed by the Boston Early Music Festival Orchestra and Chorus, CPO 777 240–2, 2007. 3 CDs.

Norman, Buford. *Quinault, librettiste de Lully: Le poète des Grâces.* Translated by Thomas Vernet and Jean Duron, Edition Mardaga, 2009.

———. "Remaking a Cultural Icon: *Phèdre* and the Operatic Stage." *Cambridge Opera Journal*, vol. 10, no. 3, Nov. 1998, pp. 225–45.

———. *Touched by the Graces: The Libretti of Philippe Quinault in the Context of French Classicism.* Summa Publications, 2001.

Racine, Jean. *Phèdre.* Translated by Margaret Rawlings, Penguin Classics, 1992. Dual-language edition.

Appendix: Resources

Recordings of Lully's Works

Alceste. 1675. La Grande Écurie et la Chambre du Roy et l'Ensemble Vocal Sagittarius, directed by Jean-Claude Malgoire, Disques Montaigne 782012, 1992. Astrée-Auvidis, 1994. 3 CDs.

Alceste. Les Talens Lyriques et le Choeur de Chambre de Namur, directed by Christophe Rousset, Aparté B076D68MH4, 2017. 2 CDs. Guide with French libretto and English translation.

Amadis. 1684. Les Talens Lyriques et le Choeur de Chambre de Namur, directed by Christophe Rousset, Aparté AP094, 2014. 3 CDs. Guide with French libretto and English translation.

Armide. 1686. Les Arts Florissants, directed by William Christie, FRA Musica B004T6A-BVE, 2011. DVD. Subtitles in French and English.

Armide. Choeur et Orchestre du Collegium Vocale et de la Chapelle Royale, directed by Philippe Herreweghe, Harmonia Mundi 901456.57, 1993. 2 CDs.

Atys. 1676. Les Arts Florissants, directed by William Christie, Harmonia Mundi 401257.59, 1987. 3 CDs.

Atys. Les Arts Florissants, directed by William Christie, FRA Musica FRA006, 2011. 2 DVDs. Subtitles in French, English, German, Spanish, and Italian.

Cadmus et Hermione. 1673. Le Poème Harmonique, directed by Vincent Dumestre, Alpha 701, 2008. DVD. Subtitles in French, English, Spanish, Italian, German, Dutch, and Japanese.

Isis. 1677. La Simphonie du Marais, directed by Hugo Reyne, Accord 476 8048, 2005. 3 CDs. Guide with French libretto and English translation.

Persée. 1682. EuroArts, directed by Marc Stone, 2005. DVD. Subtitles in French, English, and German.

Phaéton. 1683. Ensemble Vocal Sagittarius et les Musiciens du Louvre, directed by Marc Minkowski, Erato 4509–91737–2, 1994. 2 CDs.

Phaéton. Les Talens Lyriques et le Choeur de Chambre de Namur, directed by Christophe Rousset, Aparté B00#YFRWPI, 2014. 2 CDs. Guide with French libretto with English translation.

Proserpine. 1680. Le Concert Spiritual, directed by Hervé Niquet, Glossa GES 921615-F, 2008. 2 CDs. Guide with French libretto and English and Spanish translations.

Psyché. 1678. Boston Early Music Festival Chorus and Orchestra, directed by Paul O'Dette et Stephen Stubbs, CPO 777 367–2, 2008. 2 CDs. Guide with French libretto and English and German translations.

Roland. 1685. Les Talens Lyriques et le Choeur de l'Opéra de Lyon, directed by Christophe Rousset, Ambroisie AMB 9949, 2004. 3 CDs. Guide with French libretto and English and German translations.

Thésée. 1675. Boston Early Music Festival Orchestra and Chorus, directed by Paul O'Dette and Stephen Stubbs, CPO 777 240–2, 2007. 3 CDs. Guide with French libretto and English and German translations.

Motion Pictures

Louis, enfant roi. Directed by Roger Planchon, Les Films du Losange, 1993.

La prise de pouvoir par Louis XIV. Directed by Roberto Rossellini, Office de Radiodiffusion Télévision Française, 1966.

Le roi danse. Directed by Gérard Corbiau, K-Star / France 2 Cinéma, 2000.

Tous les matins du monde. Directed by Alain Corneau, Film Par Film, 1991.

Vatel. Directed by Roland Joffé, Légende Films, 2000.

Further Reading

Anthony, James R. "Lully." *The New Grove Dictionary of Music and Musicians*, edited by Stanley Sadie, vol. 11, Macmillan, 1980, pp. 314–29.

———. *The New Grove French Baroque Masters: Lully, Charpentier, Lalande, Couperin, Rameau.* W. W. Norton, 1986, pp. 1–70.

Apostolides, Jean-Marie. *Le roi-machine: Spectacle et politique au temps de Louis XIV.* Editions de Minuit, 1981.

Barthélemy, Maurice. "L'opéra français et la querelle des anciens et des modernes." *Lettres Romanes*, vol. 10, 1956, pp. 379–91.

Beaussant, Philippe. *Lully ou le musicien du soleil.* Gallimard / Théâtre des Champs-Elysées, 1992.

Boileau, Nicolas. *Œuvres.* Edited by Georges Montgrédien, Classique Garnier, 1961.

Brody, Jules. "What Was French Classicism?" *Continuum*, vol. 1, 1989, pp. 51–77.

DeJean, Joan. *Ancients against Moderns: Culture Wars and the Making of a Fin de Siècle.* U of Chicago P, 1997.

Félibien, André. *Les fêtes de Versailles: Chroniques de 1668 et 1674.* Edited by Martin Meade, Maisonneuve et Larosse, 1994.

Gethner, Perry. "La fonction des sentences dans les livrets de Quinault." *C.A.I.E.F.*, no. 41, 1989, pp. 129–44.

———. "The Roles of the Chorus in Late Seventeenth-Century Opera." *Ars Lyrica*, no. 91, 1998, pp. 41–49.

Grout, Donald J. *A Short History of Opera.* 2nd ed., Columbia UP, 1965.

Kintzler, Catherine. *La France classique et l'opera.* Harmonia Mundi, 1998.

Lully, Jean-Baptiste. *Œuvres complètes.* 1930–39. Edited by Henry Prunières, Broude Brothers Limited, 1966–74. 11 vols.

Norman, Buford. "Ancients and Moderns, Tragedy and Opera: The Quarrel over Alceste." *French Musical Thought, 1600–1800*, edited by Georgia Cowart, U of Rochester P, 1989, pp. 177–96.

———. *Quinault, librettiste de Lully: Le poète des Grâces.* Translated by Thomas Vernet and Jean Duron, Edition Mardaga, 2009.

———. *Touched by the Graces: The Libretti of Philippe Quinault in the Context of French Classicism.* Summa Publications, 2001.

Quinault, Philippe. *Livrets d'opéra.* Edited by Buford Norman, Littératures Classiques, 1999. 2 vols.

———. *Livrets, éditions françaises. Philippe Quinault,* quinault.info/Home/l-oeuvre/livrets/livrets-d-opera.

Tobin, Ronald W. *Racine et/ou le classicisme: Actes du colloque conjointement organisé par la North American Society for Seventeenth-Century Literature et la Société Racine.* Gunter Narr Verlag, 2001. Biblio 17, 129.

Walton, Guy. *Louis XIV's Versailles.* U of Chicago P, 1986.

Hélène Visentin

Turning to Seventeenth-Century Machine Theater to Teach Tragedy

"Machine theater" refers to multimedia performances, mainly based on mythological stories that feature scene changes and special effects—such as flying machines, metamorphoses, supernatural appearances and disappearances from above and below the stage, and spectacular lighting and sound effects—all achieved through early modern technology. Even though these performances often involved other nonverbal elements, such as dance, music, and lavish costumes, the machines were considered the most striking aspect, arousing both admiration and astonishment through advanced, even secret, mechanisms (*ingenium*). As demonstrations of technological advancement, stage technologies were used for political propaganda, just as today's Olympic Games ceremonies and ritual performances organized for an official state visit by a government figure would be used to affirm a country's political supremacy through persuasive visual imagery where technology meets art.[1] Originating in court entertainments (royal entries, ballets, operas, etc.), machine plays became increasingly successful in Parisian playhouses to the point that the most popular ones were staged across Europe, especially in London, where, during the Restoration period (1660–88), the genre of so-called Restoration spectaculars was in vogue. In that regard, machine plays were like Broadway musicals on tour!

As recent scholarship has shown, machine plays more or less obey the same set of poetic rules of neoclassical tragedy attributed to Aristotle—*nécessité*, *propriété*, and *vraisemblance* (necessity, decorum, and plausibility; see Kintzler). For that reason, teaching tragedies presented as machine plays (*tragédies à machines*) offers instructors an opportunity to present a nuanced and diverse view of neoclassical tragedy to students interested in broad questions regarding developments in literature and culture or science and technology in early modern Europe. Machine theater stretches and challenges the rules of neoclassical tragedy, in particular the theory of *vraisemblance*, as it relies on the *merveilleux* (marvelous) with mythological plots, apparitions of gods and other supernatural creatures, revealing on stage what neoclassical tragedy sought to hide. It also allows instructors to tackle the broader context of the staging and the production of a play—the scenic space with its mechanical devices and stage machinery—and thus to present the art of the theater as a whole, a total performance involving science, technology, and art. Ultimately, the study of seventeenth-century *tragédies à machines* allows students to understand that neoclassical tragedy is not just about speech and the dramatic text—a theater of discourse well represented by Jean Racine's tragedies—and that stage design and machinery should not be overlooked. Indeed, the approach enables students to realize to what extent theater is part of the visual culture of the early modern period.

I offer an overview of how to teach machine plays from two complementary perspectives: the development of science and technology in the sixteenth and seventeenth centuries, and the aesthetics and practice of the theater from the 1640s to the 1670s. Then I provide the general outline of two lesson plans: a comparative analysis of two tragedies based on the mythological story of Iphigenia, by Jean de Rotrou and Jean Racine, and a study of *Andromède*, by Pierre Corneille. Both approaches and lesson plans could be applied to a graduate seminar or to survey courses on either French culture and civilization or science and technology in early modern France or Europe (especially if the institution offers a program in the history of science). They could also be part of a larger course on tragedy, or on French or European theater, since innovative technologies spread from Italy across western and central Europe through the migration of engineers, hydraulic technicians, and architects who created their own network, which allowed for the circulation of shared knowledge and practices. To that end, the audience could be French majors or non–French majors, graduates or undergraduates.

Teaching *Tragédies à Machines* within a Scientific and Technological Context

To teach the history of technologies related to stagecraft knowledge, the instructor can direct students' attention to the vogue of and fascination with automatons and other engineering designs that can be found in the literature of *theatrum machinarum*, or machine books, that started to flourish at the end of the sixteenth century with the translation of Aristotle's *Quaestiones Mechanicae* (*Mechanical Questions*) and Heron of Alexandria's *Automata*, among others. *Theatrum machinarum* described and depicted machines that created spectacle for an audience. Instructors can find striking illustrations and assign selected passages in *Théâtre des instruments mathématiques et méchaniques* (*Theater of Mathematical and Mechanical Instruments*), by Jacques Besson, or *Les raisons des forces mouvantes, avec diverses machines tant utiles que plaisantes* (*The Reasons of Moving Forces, with Various Machines Both Useful and Pleasant*), by Salomon de Caus. For a graduate seminar, the instructor can assign secondary sources, such as Wolfgang Lefèvre, Luisa Dolza and Hélène Vérin ("Figurer la mécanique" and "Les théâtres de machines"), and Jan Lazardzig. Another point of entry is the development of optics, and more precisely the formulation of the laws of linear perspective through the circulation of architectural treatises, such as Sebastiano Serlio's *Il primo libro di prospettiva* (*Second Book of Perspective*) and Ignatio Danti Vignola's *Le due regole della prospettiva pratica* (*Two Rules of Practical Perspective*), inspired by the rediscovery of Vitruvius's *De architectura* (*On Architecture*).[2] The art of perspective revolutionized stage design by bringing coherence to the organization of the scenic space in its relationship to the auditorium—the best seat, *l'œil du Prince* ("the eye of the Prince"), being the one facing the vanishing point on the stage, dictating the scenic space around a single point of view.

To demonstrate this idea, the instructor can pair a few relevant illustrations from Vignola's *Le due regole della prospettiva pratica* (*The Two Rules of Practical Perspective*) or Jean Dubreuil's *La perspective pratique* (*Practical Perspective*) with carefully selected chapters of the first book of Nicola Sabbattini's *Pratica di fabricar scene e machine ne' teatri* (*Manual for Con-*

structing Scenes and Machines in the Theater) devoted to perspective scenery techniques, especially chapter 34, titled "Come si deve accomodare il luogo peril Principe" ("How to Accommodate the Seat of the Prince"). The six well-executed engravings by François Chauveau included in the first quarto edition of Corneille's *Andromède*, depicting the elaborate sets of the prologue and each of the five acts, can serve as an excellent example of the use of perspective on of what was known as the Italian stage. The engravings beautifully show how the illusionistic stage is governed by the laws of perspective and operated by a *scena ductilis*—sliding flat side wings allowing rapid scene changes after the prologue and each act. The engravings also illustrate both the continuity and the contiguity of decors from one scene to another, in keeping with the rules of the unity of place and time. It is worth drawing students' attention to Corneille's very detailed description of each of the six sets preceding the prologue and each act, as it finds an exact correspondence in the six engravings displaying a unified stage apparatus; students can appreciate as well the playwright's admiration for the "merveilleux artifice" 'marvelous device' of the stage and "l'égalité et les justesses de la Perspective" 'the equality and accuracy of the Perspective'[3] as stated in the description of act 1's decoration.

Students should understand that the most influential machinists were transalpine engineers or hydraulic technicians such as Tomaso Francini, Giacomo Torelli, and Gaspare Vigarini, who brought to France the most innovative technologies and skills of their time. This point enables instructors to raise the subject of the cross-border transfers of technology and science between Italy and France during this period. I recommend focusing on the Venetian stage designer Torelli, as he staged *Andromède*, among other plays, and his scenographic work is well documented (see Bjurström; Milesi). Torelli is known to have invented a chariot-and-pole system that brought both efficiency and speed to scene changes such as the one Corneille describes between acts 1 and 2 of *Andromède*: "Cette Place publique dont la Reine et Persée viennent de sortir, *s'évanouit en un instant*, pour faire place à un Jardin délicieux" 'This public plaza, which the Queen and Perseus just left, *disappears in an instant* to give way to a lovely garden' (475; emphasis added). At the peak of his career, he was called "il gran stregone" 'the great wizard,' which underlines the connection between science and magic in the early modern period, a topic that needs to be addressed in a course on science and technology.[4] Moreover, instructors can emphasize that stagecraft knowledge and practices were surrounded by a strong culture of secrecy as both "a protection of invention and control of reception," which explains why printed material and treatises are sparse (Lazardzig and Rößler 277). One of the few extant treatises is Sabbattini's, mentioned above, which explains stagecraft machinery in great detail and provides accompanying illustrations. To complement this class unit, instructors could also draw students' attention to the forty-nine "Machines de Théâtre" plates included in the tenth volume of plates of the *Encyclopédie* (*Encyclopedia*) by Denis Diderot and Jean le Rond d'Alembert and easily accessible thanks to the *ARTFL Encyclopédie* (encyclopedie.uchicago.edu). The series offers a complete view of state-of-the-art machines, showing the inventory of the fly loft over and above the stage, such as pulley systems, ropes, cables, winches, wooden beams, and drums.

Finally, instructors can bring this history into the present by explaining that in western and central Europe several theater buildings have survived, along with their authentic scene sets and stage machinery, and are used today for their original purposes. One of the most documented and best preserved is the Drottningholms Slottsteater, located on an island near Stockholm, Sweden, and built in 1766 at the request of Queen Lovisa Ulrika, the wife of King Adolf Fredrick and the sister of Frederick the Great (see Hidemark). For visual documentation, the instructor can refer students to the European Theatre Architecture (EUTA) database (theatre-architecture.eu/en/), which provides detailed information on European theater buildings and stage machinery, including photographic archives; and the Web site *Development of Scenic Spectacle* (spectacle.appstate.edu), created by the scholar Frank Mohler.

Teaching *Tragédies à Machines* within a Cultural and Literary Context

Experimentation with mechanical devices and the use of perspective scenery significantly changed stage practices the same way digital technologies (computer animation, 3D projection, virtual reality, etc.) are now transforming theater on and off stage, creating new experiences for audiences in which they are actively engaged and entertained. Instructors can teach *tragédies à machines* within this context to help students grasp the dual nature of theater—text and representation—and the relation between these two aspects. If machine plays are subordinated to some extent to the visual, what is the status of the dramatic text? To what extent is the staging of a particular play initially inscribed in the text? Do playwrights break or comply with the dramatic rules and the important principle of verisimilitude? How can playwrights both seduce the audience and please the critics?

These questions are all the more relevant when addressed in a course that deals with neoclassical tragedy, based on an Aristotelian model of theater in which spectacle is marginalized. Instructors can assign a series of readings starting with the first chapters of Aristotle's *Poetics*, with an emphasis on the part devoted to the basic elements of tragedy, in which Aristotle states, "Staging can be emotionally attractive, but is not a matter of art and is not integral to poetry. The power of tragedy can be exercised without actors and without a performance. Staging belongs more to the scene-painter's art than to that of the poets" (25–26). This initial text can be paired with selected chapters of seventeenth-century texts on the poetics of theater, such as chapter 11 of Hippolyte-Jules Pilet de La Mesnardière's *La poétique* (*Poetics*; 471–78) and book 4, chapter 9, of *La pratique du théâtre* (*The Practice of Theater*; 483–92), by François Hédelin, abbé d'Aubignac,[5] that framed the so-called doctrine classique (see René Bray), along with contemporary critical works, such as the first chapter of Anne Ubersfeld's *Lire le théâtre* and an article by Christian Delmas, "L'unité du genre tragique au XVIIe siècle" ("The Unity of the Tragic Genre in the Seventeenth Century"). For a graduate seminar, students can also be assigned Guy Spielmann's article "Pour une syntaxe du spectaculaire au XVIIe et au XVIIIe siècles" ("For a Syntax of the Spectacular in the Seventeenth and Eighteenth Centuries"). From the perspective of the *doctes*, visual spectacle was what Hélène Merlin calls "un plaisir populaire" 'a popular pleasure' (171). For instance, if d'Aubignac acknowledges that courtly performances based on the use of theatrical machines constitute "un échantillon des nouveaux miracles que la Paix nous prépare" 'a sample of the new miracles that Peace has in store for us' (485), he formulates his strongest critique of machine plays on the stage of Parisian playhouses by stating that actors simply cannot do anything right when it comes to machine technology and that they are too cheap to spend money on proper mechanical devices. This kind of statement explains why machine theater was quickly associated with a form of commercial theater that competed with the neoclassical vein regarded by learned scholars as the aesthetically "legitimate" theater, drama based exclusively on the quality of the text and its dramatic structure. Finally, the instructor can discuss the tensions between the verbal and nonverbal aspects of performance and conclude this unit by highlighting the fact that even though *tragédies régulières* and *tragédies à machines* seem at first glance to belong to two different aesthetics, their commonalities form a unity within the tragic genre aimed at pleasing, moving, and instructing the audience.

Two Lesson Plans

A first lesson plan for the graduate or undergraduate seminar compares the denouement of two versions of the tragedy *Iphigénie*, by Rotrou and Racine. As a first step, students read Racine's play. To accompany the play, students are asked to read chapters 4 and 5 of *La poétique de la tragédie classique* (*The Poetics of Classical Tragedy*), by Bénédicte Louvat, which focus on the construction of a tragic plot and its message (55–76), and *La tragédie de l'âge classique* (*The Tragedy of the Classical Age*), by Delmas (112–62 and 188–207). These chapters are concise, clear, and ideal for undergraduate students enrolled in a high intermediate course in French. For a course taught in English, I recommend selected chapters of John D. Lyons's *Kingdom of Disorder*, and for a graduate seminar, excerpts from Georges Forestier's *La tragédie française*. A reading guide supports students in their understanding and interpretation of the play, with questions on the development of the plot, the functions of tragedy in the light of Racine's statement, "La principale règle est de plaire et de toucher" 'The principal rule is to please and to move,' the unity of space (*l'unité de lieu*) and action (*l'unité d'action*), and the analysis of the main characters.

In this unit, I discuss with students why the story of Iphigenia is, in many ways, an exemplar of a perfect tragedy according to Aristotle (the conflict between filial love and the reason of state, the sacrifice of an innocent victim, etc.); then I focus on the character of Iphigenia and her virtuous conduct, analyzing how Racine changed the mythological source in order to save such a virtuous character in the name of the *bienséances* (propriety) by inventing another character (Ériphile), "cette autre Iphigénie" 'this other Iphigenia' (Préface). When we turn our attention to the play's denouement, students read the Préface of *Iphigénie* for Racine's comments on machine theater and on his construction of the tragic plot *à rebours* (backwards) with the intent to rationalize the supernatural aspects of the mythological fable related to Iphigenia's sacrifice. As students had previously been asked to note all the passages throughout the play that evoke the sacrifice, we then discuss how this sacrifice is conveyed through the rhetorical figure of hypotyposis, and to what extent this visual image is contained in the dramatic text.

Then students juxtapose the denouement of Racine's *Iphigénie* to that of Rotrou's *Iphigénie*, which heavily relies on stage machinery to perform the supernatural sacrifice of the heroine. In addition to assigning act 5 of Rotrou's *Iphigénie*, which can stand alone, I assign Pierre Pasquier's article on the architecture of the stage of the Hôtel de Bourgogne, Paris's first public theater, where Rotrou's *Iphigénie* was performed by the Troupe Royale ("L'hôtel de Bourgogne"), and "La scénographie et le décor" ("Scenography and Décor") by Pasquier and Anne Surgers. I draw attention to Rotrou's stage directions and passages of the dramatic text that explicitly refer to the use of machinery, and mentions of sound and light effects contained in the characters' dialogue in order to emphasize how the plot is dictated by the constraints of the stage and a willingness to create a spectacle to seduce the audience. I also briefly introduce students to the idea of the neoclassical so-called *palais à volonté* ("unlimited palace"), as used by Racine, to be contrasted with the multiple spaces staged at once—the mansions of the so-called *décor simultané* ("simultaneous decor")—in the public theater of the Hôtel de Bourgogne.[6] If time allows, I ask students to watch selected passages of the performance of Racine's *Iphigénie* in 1991 at the Comédie-Française, staged by Yannis Kokkos, in which the conception of the scenic space captures the idea of a *palais à volonté* and is in accord with the Racinian aesthetics.

We then turn our attention to a close study of the stage design and machinery of the Hôtel de Bourgogne. I ask students to make a list of all the special effects used in act 5, and we discuss how the machinist could have staged the appearance of the goddess Diana and rendered the lightning, thunder, and other effects. This part of the course can be supported by readings in the French translation of Sabbattini's *Pratica di fabricar scene e machine*. I also refer to a manuscript known as the *Mémoire de Mahelot* (*Memoir of Mahelot*), edited by Pasquier—an illustrated repertory of stage sets for plays performed in the 1630s and 1640s that includes over forty sketches to explain features related to French playhouses, such as the simultaneous setting, compartments, and the upper stage (also called the theater of Jupiter), a reminiscence of the theologeion of the Greek theater. The stage design for Rotrou's *Iphigénie* can clearly be compared to the decor drawing for plays such as *L'Amaranthe*, by Jean Ogier de Gombauld, *Les travaux d'Ulysse* (*The Travails of Ulysses*), by Jean-Gilbert Durval, and *La filis de scire* (*The Filis of Scire*), by Pichou, all included in the *Mémoire de Mahelot*. In these sketches we observe how the small upper-stage theater is used for the apparitions of gods in the machine. Students formulate observations about machine theater's emphasis on the visual, as opposed to neoclassical tragedy's focus on theatrical speech.

If time allows, to approach representation through an interdisciplinary lens, we look at the painting *Le sacrifice d'Iphigénie* by François Perrier, an artist inspired by Simon Vouet (other seventeenth-century French paintings based on the myth of Iphigenia include works by Sébastien Bourdon and Jean Jouvenet). The painting, contemporary to Rotrou's tragedy, depicts Iphigenia standing next to the altar, ready to be sacrificed by Calchas, while Agamemnon commands the execution to proceed and Clytemnestra implores Diana to intercede; at the top of the image, the goddess appears on a cloud holding a deer to replace Iphigenia. The composition of the image appears to be a perfect illustration of Rotrou's denouement. The instructor can ask students to "read" the painting by Perrier and discuss how the artist chose a specific scene to condense the tragic crisis of the mythological fable, and then have students compare it to Rotrou's play. It is an opportunity to reflect on how playwrights and painters differently represent a tragic moment. Second, this comparison fosters a discussion around the concept of *bienséances* in seventeenth-century theater and art, and how they differ.

As a final pedagogical activity, students can be assigned to imagine and draw the stage setting for both Rotrou and Racine's plays or encouraged to search for other pictorial works of the sacrifice of Iphigenia. They can then collaboratively create either a *PowerPoint* presentation or a digital timeline displaying these images using new technologies such as *TimelineJS*.

The second lesson plan entails a close study of *Andromède*, by Corneille.[7] In this unit, I first ask my students to read the prologue, in which Melpomene, the muse of tragedy, appears in a flying machine and asks the Sun (who rides "un char tout lumineux, tiré par quatre chevaux" 'a bright chariot, pulled by four horses') to stop his course in order to celebrate the heroic virtues of the young Louis XIV and his future exploits (459). Together, Melpomene and the Sun sing the praises of the twelve-year-old monarch, repeating the refrain that "Louis est le plus jeune et le plus grand des Rois" 'Louis is the youngest and the greatest of all Kings' (line 79). I draw students' attention to the rhyme *gloire/victoire*, which is used no fewer than three times in the prologue to praise the king (34–36, 61–62, 85–87). This precise rhyme is also used in a song in act 3, scene 3, when Perseus bravely fights the monster to rescue Andromeda (946–48 and 986–89). I introduce students to the "mirror for princes" (*speculum principum*) genre and the didactic function of literature, emphasizing the use of theatrical machines as a political tool. This approach prepares students to read the rest of the play through an allegorical interpretation, as Perseus offers an idealized image of the young Louis XIV. Students understand that the play seeks not only to entertain through the use of special effects, but also to teach the audience about cardinal virtues and social decorum by displaying royal power and prestige. This is particularly true of *Andromède*, as Cardinal Mazarin, the king's chief minister, had asked Corneille—newly elected to the Académie Française and named official poet of the king—to create a play that would reuse the decors and machines of the recent Italian opera *Orfeo*, the cost of which had previously been heavily criticized. Mazarin's goal was to appease public opinion during the turmoil of the Fronde and to enhance the prestige of France abroad. To support this idea, I direct student attention to two performance accounts: the "Argument" of *Andromède*, a brochure written by Corneille, summarizing the plot and extensively describing the decor and the machines, and the "Extraordinaire" of the *Gazette de France* devoted to an encomiastic review of the performance. If the main function of the "Argument" is to advertise the play prior to the performance and help spectators better follow the plot, the *Gazette de France* clearly served to promote royal propaganda among courtly audiences across Europe (see Welch).

I complement this unit by explaining to students that the myth of the rescue of Andromeda by Perseus was widely used in courtly performances, ceremonial entries, and paintings as a political allegory during the Counter-Reformation (in France, Spain, Italy), with Andromeda embodying the kingdom under attack, the monster representing Protestantism, and Perseus the Catholic ruler saving the heroine from the dangerous heresy (see Laframboise and Siguret; Bolduc). One striking example is "La délivrance de la France par le Persée françois" ("The Deliverance of France by the French Perseus"), a poem and engraving in which one can easily recognize through the image of Perseus the figure of Henri IV, the French king who restored peace after the Wars of Religion (El Kenz 9).

Then, over the course of four or five class sessions, I ask students to read the entire play. I teach *Andromède* by pointing out that this mythological tale possesses all the ingredients of a tragic plot: noble characters (the royal family of Ethiopia), a conflict between close family members, a dilemma between the duty of a king and his love for his daughter, a rivalry between Perseus and Phineus (the antihero to whom Andromeda is already engaged) and, at last, a heroine who has to confront impending death. And yet the subject seemed ideally suited to using machines to create a *grand spectacle*. In the "Argument" of the play, Corneille states somewhat peremptorily that he found a perfect subject to fulfill Cardinal Mazarin's order: "Pour moi, je confesse ingénument que quelque effort d'imagination que j'aie fait depuis, je n'ai pu découvrir encore un sujet capable de tant d'ornements extérieurs et où les machines pussent être distribuées avec tant de justesse" 'As for me, I confess candidly that for any effort of imagination that I have made since, I have not yet discovered a subject fit for so many adornments and where the machines could be used with such accuracy' (448). As I have noted elsewhere, Corneille "wrote a play that showed the importance of verbal expression through a unified and coherent storyline on the model of the spoken tragedy while integrating *avec justesse* nonverbal cues, such as the music and the machines" (Visentin, "Machine Plays" [U of Toronto P]).

I focus students' attention on the roles of gods in the machine by engaging them to analyze the instances of their appearances on stage, through a close reading of the dramatic text and attention to Corneille's detailed stage directions. Through a series of guided questions, students understand that gods in the machines actively participate in the tragic plot, either by delivering an oracle's message that will later play a role in the recognition scene (as when Venus predicts, at the end of act 1, the union of Andromeda with a "parfait époux" 'perfect spouse' of an as yet unknown identity) or by interfering in human affairs to join forces or create division (the divine interventions of Juno and Neptune to protect Phineus from the threat of Perseus, the son of Jupiter). The instructor might also encourage students to define the passions of the tragedy and to recognize how the machines visually express the characters' feelings (for instance, in act 3, the flight of Perseus through the air represents, literally, his impulse to love Andromeda), helping them to consider the genre of *tragédie à machines* as an investigation of human passions.

The paroxysm of the play at act 3, scene 3—Perseus flying overhead to fight the sea monster ready to attack Andromeda, chained to a rock as a sacrifice—constitutes both an exemplifying and performative image. Through his heroic action, Perseus proves to be the perfect spouse for Andromeda, confirming Venus's oracle. The composition of this tragic scene can be juxtaposed to the engraving by François Chauveau of act 3, affording the opportunity for the instructor to explain a few stage technologies (with the support of Sabbattini's treatise) and for the students to explore further the relation between a dramatic text and its visual representation. In addition, I specify that when the Comédie-Française performed Corneille's *Andromède* in 1682 to compete with the opera *Persée* by Quinault and Lully, a live horse appeared on stage for the climax of the tragedy—the rescue of Andromeda by Perseus riding Pegasus! This activity leads to an analysis of images depicting the myth of Andromeda and Perseus across time periods (by Giorgio Vasari, Piero di Cosimo, Peter Paul Rubens, Titian, Gustave Doré, Pablo Picasso, etc.). As the majority of these paintings represent the Ethiopian Andromeda with white skin, I make sure that at least one student is working on the engraving by Cornelis Bloemaert after Abraham van Diepenbeeck (Marolles), as it is one of the rare images of a Black Andromeda. Students can conduct preliminary research in order to pick an image of their choice and write an essay about the representation of the myth of Andromeda on stage and in pictorial art.

In sum, teaching *tragédies à machines* allows the instructor to open students' perspective on neoclassical tragedy by taking into account not only the dramatic text, but also aspects of the performance related to audience expectations, and early modern stage design and technology. It also allows instructors to tackle neoclassical aesthetics in relation to the poetics of spectacle to better understand the tensions inherent to the art of theater, as well as the specific visual culture in which the performing arts were developed.

Notes

To Françoise Siguret (1936–2020), who allowed me to discover seventeenth-century machine theater and, more broadly, the early modern era, launching me into an exciting academic career.

1. For a broad overview of machine theater during the baroque age, see Visentin, "Machine Plays" (Oxford), where a few ideas mentioned in this article are developed more fully.

2. These works can be consulted on *Architectura*, a database (in English and French) of manuscripts and printed architectural treatises published in France, written in French, or translated into French in the sixteenth and seventeenth centuries (architectura.cesr.univ-tours.fr/Traite/index.asp?param=en).

3. All translations from French are mine.

4. Luigi Riccoboni states, "Les machines sont les effets de la magie et du merveilleux" 'Machines are the effects of magic and wonder' (45).

5. The original editions of La Mesnardière and d'Aubignac's treatises are accessible on *Gallica* (gallica.bnf.fr); for recent critical editions, see Works Cited.

6. In Racine's *Iphigénie*, the action of the tragedy takes place in a military

camp—precisely, in Agamemnon's tent, which can be considered as the equivalent of the king's cabinet.

7. References to Corneille's *Andromède* and the paratexts of the play are from my forthcoming critical edition in Corneille's *Théâtre complet*, vol. 4, which includes a substantial introduction (see also the 1651 text available on *Gallica* and the 1974 edition by Delmas).

Works Cited

Aristotle. *Poetics*. Translated by Anthony Kenny, Oxford UP, 2013.

Besson, Jacques. *Théâtre des instruments mathématiques et méchaniques*. Barthélémy Vincent, 1578. *Gallica*, gallica.bnf.fr/ark:/12148/btv1b8609508c/f1.image.r=Th%C3%A9%C3%A2tre%20des%20instruments%20besson.

Bjurström, Per. *Giacomo Torelli and Baroque Stage Design*. Almqvist and Wiksell, 1962.

Bolduc, Benoît. *Andromède au rocher: Fortune théâtrale d'une image en France et en Italie (1587–1712)*. Leo Olschki, 2002.

Bray, René. *La formation de la doctrine classique en France*. Librairie Nizet, 1966.

Caus, Salomon de. *Les raisons des forces mouvantes, avec diverses machines tant utiles que plaisantes*. Charles Sevestre, 1624. *Gallica*, gallica.bnf.fr/ark:/12148/btv1b8626569p?rk=42918;4.

Corneille, Pierre. *Andromède*. Charles de Sercy, 1651. *Gallica*, gallica.bnf.fr/ark:/12148/bpt6k70397f.image.

———. *Andromède*. Edited by Christian Delmas, Société des Textes Français Modernes, 1974.

———. *Andromède*. Edited by Hélène Visentin, forthcoming. *Théâtre complet*, general editor, Liliane Picciola, vol. 4, Classiques Garnier, 2015–.

d'Aubignac, François Hédelin, abbé. *La pratique du théâtre*. Antoine de Sommaville, 1657. Edited by Hélène Baby, Honoré Champion, 2001.

Delmas, Christian. *La tragédie de l'âge classique, 1553–1770*. Seuil, 1994.

———. "L'unité du genre tragique au XVIIe siècle." *Mythe et histoire dans le théâtre classique: Hommage à Christian Delmas*, edited by Fanny Népote-Desmarres, Société de Littératures Classiques, 2002, pp. 33–54. Originally published in *Littératures classiques*, vol. 16, 1992, pp. 103–23.

Dolza, Luisa, and Hélène Vérin. "Figurer la mécanique: L'énigme des théâtres de machines de la Renaissance." *Revue d'histoire moderne et contemporaine*, vol. 51, no. 2, 2004, pp. 7–37.

———. "Les théâtres de machines." *Alliage*, vol. 50, no. 5, 2000, pp. 8–20.

Dubreuil, Jean. *La perspective pratique: Nécessaire à tous peintres, graveurs, sculpteurs, architectes, orfèvres, brodeurs, tapissiers, & autres se servans du dessein*. Melchior Tavernier, 1642.

El Kenz, David. "Du temps de Dieu au temps du Roi: L'avenir dans les placards ligueurs et anti-ligueurs (1589–1595)." *L'avenir dans l'affiche politique*, special issue of *Matériaux pour l'histoire de notre temps*, nos. 21–22, 1990, pp. 3–11. *Persée*, persee.fr/doc/mat_0769-3206_1990_num_21_1_410696.

Forestier, Georges. *La tragédie française: Règles classiques, passions tragiques*. 2003. Armand Colin, 2016.

Hidemark, Ove, et al., editors. *Drottningholm Court Theatre: Its Advent, Fate, and Preservation.* Byggförlaget, 1993.

Kintzler, Catherine. *Poétique de l'opéra français de Corneille à Rousseau.* Éditions Minerve, 1991.

Laframboise, Alain, and Françoise Siguret, editors. *Andromède ou le héros à l'épreuve de la beauté.* Klincksieck, 1996.

La Mesnardière, Hippolyte-Jules Pilet de. *La poétique.* 1639. Edited by Jean-Marc Civardi, Honoré Champion, 2015.

Lazardzig, Jan. "The Machine as Spectacle." *Instruments in Art and Science: On the Architectonics of Cultural Boundaries in the Seventeenth Century*, edited by Helmar Schramm et al., Walter de Gruyter, 2008, pp. 152–75.

Lazardzig, Jan, and Hole Rößler. "Joseph Furttenbach and the Transfer of Mechanical Knowledge." *Technologies of Theatre: Joseph Furttenbach and the Transfer of Mechanical Knowledge in Early Modern Theatre Cultures*, edited by Lazardzig and Rößler, Klostermann, 2016, pp. 271–309.

Lefèvre, Wolfgang, editor. *Picturing Machines, 1400–1700.* MIT Press, 2004.

Louvat, Bénédicte. *La poétique de la tragédie classique.* Sedes, 1997.

Lyons, John D. *Kingdom of Disorder: The Theory of Tragedy in Classical France.* Purdue UP, 1999.

Marolles, Michel de. *Les tableaux du temple des muses.* Antoine de Sommaville, 1655.

Merlin, Hélène. *Public et littérature en France au XVIIe siècle.* Les Belles Lettres, 1994.

Milesi, Francesco, editor. *Giacomo Torelli: L'invenzione scenica nell'Europa barocca.* Fondazione Cassa di Risparmio di Fano, 2000.

Pasquier, Pierre. "L'Hôtel de Bourgogne et son évolution architecturale." *Les lieux du spectacle dans l'Europe du XVIIe siècle*, edited by Charles Mazouer, G. Narr, Biblio 17, 2006, pp. 47–71.

———, editor. *Le mémoire de Mahelot.* Honoré Champion, 2005.

Pasquier, Pierre, and Anne Surgers. "La scénographie et le décor." *La représentation théâtrale en France au XVIIe siècle*, edited by Pasquier and Surgers, Armand Colin, 2011, pp. 79–118.

Perrier, François. *Le sacrifice d'Iphigénie.* 1632–33, Musée des Beaux-Arts de Dijon, Dijon, France.

Racine, Jean. *Iphigénie.* Edited by Georges Forestier, Gallimard, Folio Théâtre, 1999.

Riccoboni, Luigi. *Réflexions historiques et critiques sur les différents théâtres de l'Europe.* Jacques Guerrin, 1738.

Rotrou, Jean de. *Iphigénie.* Edited by Alain Riffaud. *Théâtre complet*, Georges Forestier, general editor, vol. 2, Société des Textes Français Modernes, 1999.

Sabbattini, Nicola. *Practica di fabricar scene e machine ne' teatri.* Stampatori Camerali, 1638. *Gallica*, gallica.bnf.fr/ark:/12148/bpt6k1520158g/f1.image.r=pratica%20di%20fabricare.

Serlio, Sebastiano. *Il primo libro d'architettura / Le premier livre d'architecture.* Translated by Jean Martin, Jean Barbé, 1545.

Siguret, Françoise. *L'œil surpris: Perception et représentation dans la 1ère moitié du XVIIe siècle.* Klincksieck, 1993.

Spielmann, Guy. "Pour une syntaxe du spectaculaire au XVIIe et au XVIIIe siècles." *Les arts du spectacle au théâtre (1550–1700)*, edited by Claire Lebrun-Gouanvic et al., Honoré Champion, 2001, pp. 219–60.

Ubersfeld, Anne. *Lire le théâtre.* Editions sociales, 1982.

———. *Reading Theatre.* Translated by Paul Perron and Patrick Debbèche, U of Toronto P, 2000.

Vignola, Ignatio Danti. *Le due regole della prospettiva pratica.* F. Zanetti, 1583.

Visentin, Hélène. "Machine Plays." *The Oxford Handbook of the Baroque*, edited by John D. Lyons, Oxford UP, 2019, pp. 386–408. *Oxford Handbooks Online*, February 2019, oxfordhandbooks.com/view/10.1093/oxfordhb/9780190678449.001.0001/oxfordhb-9780190678449-e-36.

———. "Machine Plays in France: Between Italian Opera and French Tragedy in Music." *Opera and Tragedy: From Absolutism to Enlightenment*, edited by Blair Hoxby, U of Toronto P, forthcoming.

Welch, Ellen R. *A Theater of Diplomacy: International Relations and the Performing Arts in Early Modern France.* U of Pennsylvania P, 2017.

Part III

The Performance of Tragedy: New Geographies, New Temporalities

Julia Prest

Neoclassical Theater in the Colonial Context: The Public Theater of Saint-Domingue

In the late eighteenth century, the former French slave colony of Saint-Domingue (in present-day Haiti) boasted the most vibrant theatrical tradition of the Caribbean region. Local newspapers featured regular notices announcing upcoming performances in several different public playhouses. From these, we learn that hundreds of spoken and musical dramas were performed in different towns before mixed audiences, gathered in the same space but segregated, between the establishment of the first public theater in the colony in the 1760s and the slave revolts of 1791. The theatrical repertoire was predominantly French, but these French works were adapted to local conditions, and a small number of new works were written locally, some of them featuring dialogue in an early form of Haitian Creole. The most popular genre by a wide margin was opéra comique, followed by other forms of comedy. However, tragedy was not unknown to the Saint-Dominguan audience: some works by Pierre Corneille and Jean Racine were performed in the colony, but by far the most widely performed author of neoclassical tragedies was Voltaire. We have evidence of performances of ten of Voltaire's tragedies in Saint-Domingue, and the actual number may have been higher. Neoclassical tragedy also reached the Saint-Dominguan audience in the form of three of Christoph Willibald Gluck's Paris operas. The relatively little-known public theater tradition in Saint-Domingue offers some rich opportunities for teachers and students wishing to explore early modern theater in new ways that reframe the centrality of the canonical playwrights, supported by some key digital resources—all of which will be outlined here.

I have recently designed a new advanced undergraduate course, entitled Saint-Domingue: Theatre and Society in a Caribbean Slave Colony, which derives from—and draws on—my ongoing research into the field. The course is open to all undergraduate students taking junior or senior honors French, and typically attracts students with an interest in theater, colonialism and postcolonialism, or social issues rather than those who are devoted to the mechanics of literary analysis. I would like to say that it attracts students interested in learning about new research methods, but I am not sure that this is the case. However, most students report afterward that they enjoyed this aspect of the course. In an expanded version, the syllabus that I have devised would also lend itself well to a graduate course in which the same texts and issues could be explored in greater depth. Our first- and second-level undergraduate courses in French feature one or two francophone texts, usually modern novels from the Caribbean or West Africa, and an overview of the French Revolution in which the so-called Haitian Revolution is mentioned only briefly. Essentially, however, students elect to take my course knowing little or nothing about the subject. Indeed, most of them encounter "Saint-Domingue" for the first time when scrutinizing the course catalog in order to choose their optional modules for the following year. This situation creates both opportunities and challenges for the teacher: the opportunities lie primarily in the fact that the students have not been overexposed to colonial or metropolitan views on the former French colony and are more open to the deliberately nonmetropolitan or "Creole" viewpoint that I encourage them to adopt; the challenges, of course, lie in the need to strike a balance between cultivating an understanding of this complex society and its vibrant theater tradition and providing the opportunity to undertake independent research in a field that is new to students. It is in the context of the independent research projects that some students choose to focus on tragic theatrical genres or what we are calling in the present volume "neoclassical" tragedy. All our students will have already studied at least one or two classically influenced plays from the seventeenth and eighteenth centuries in the

French context; in my course, they have the opportunity to study some of those plays from a very different perspective and in a new context.

Readings and lectures about Saint-Dominguan society are complemented by discussion seminars in which students can ask questions and I can assess how well they have understood the material and choose to adjust the program or format if necessary. We begin with the colonizing of Saint-Domingue in the wider context of the Caribbean region (many students have studied British colonialism in history courses at school, so this can be a useful way in to the related topic of French colonial expansion). In our seminar, we discuss, among other things, the chapter "Plantation Peoples 1630–1770" in B. W. Higman's *A Concise History of the Caribbean* (97–140), which provides a good introduction to the topic and takes us up to the period on which the module focuses: the 1770s and 1780s and up to the slave revolts of 1791. In the same week, I deliver a lecture outlining some of the theoretical and terminological challenges that the course poses, notably that of studying the colonial era in a supposedly postcolonial age and the need to be aware of colonial prejudices in our sources, and some of the ways that these can be challenged. In particular, I clarify our usage of the term *Creole*, which for the purposes of the module is used primarily to mean "local" and is opposed to the terms *French* and especially *metropolitan*.

In the following two weeks, we focus first on the transatlantic slave trade and its representation (or not) in literature, discussing the chapter "The Slave Trade in the Enlightenment" in Christopher Miller's *The French Atlantic Triangle: Literature and Culture of the Slave Trade* (62–82), together with a lecture that I deliver on the particular challenges of uncovering the voices and experiences of enslaved people from contemporary sources. We then study the free people of color (either born free or manumitted), who were a rapidly expanding and influential group in the second half of the eighteenth century in Saint-Domingue. For this we read two chapters from John Garrigus, *Before Haiti: Race and Citizenship in French Saint-Domingue*: "Race and Class in Creole Society: Saint-Domingue in the 1760s" (51–82) and "Citizenship and Racism in the New Public Sphere" (141–170). I also introduce students to a flawed but rich primary source in the form of Médéric Louis Elie Moreau de Saint-Méry's three-volume *Description topographique, physique, civile, politique et historique de la partie française de l'isle Saint-Domingue* (*Topographical, Physical, Civil, Political, and Historical Description of French*

Saint-Domingue), which includes valuable information about several of the theaters that were set up in the colony and detailed observations about Saint-Dominguan society in the 1780s.

This background information is essential to students' understanding of the theater as a social institution in the colony: although enslaved people were supposedly excluded from the public playhouse in Saint-Domingue, many must have accompanied their masters there, and it is likely therefore that some were exposed to the works that were performed; furthermore, we know that enslaved people and formerly enslaved people sometimes performed in the theater orchestra. Free people of color in Saint-Domingue were admitted to the playhouse in disproportionately small but ever-increasing numbers, and sat in designated seats. Students are sometimes shocked to learn that the public theater in Saint-Domingue was segregated by skin color, although they are not surprised to learn that the audience was predominantly, and disproportionately, white. In addition to the composition of the audience (performers are explored later in the module in the context of repertoire), we study the notion of the theater as a useful institution (not so much a didactic one, although contemporary sources occasionally describe it as one that supposedly distracts people from more dangerous pursuits and helps maintain the "purity" of their French language and identity) and, above all, with particular reference to Lauren Clay's chapter "The Production of Theater in the Colonies" (195–224), as a business. The emphasis on money-making opportunities chimes neatly with what students have already learned about French colonization of the Caribbean. The common colonial claim of saving souls is almost entirely absent from our sources, in which we detect little embarrassment about the widespread goal of making money as quickly as possible and at any (human) cost.

Students are assessed on their understanding of the core composition of Saint-Dominguan society and the function of the theater in their first assignment, which features a two-thousand-word essay using a selection of primary and secondary sources. We then undertake an analysis of theater-making in the colony, proceeding not by theatrical genre as might be standard in a course focusing on French theater, but by geographical origin and language: first, French (or, rather, francophone) repertoire, then Creole francophone repertoire, and finally Creole-language repertoire. By giving these three elements equal emphasis in the course, I make it clear to students that I am deliberately seeking to redress a contemporary imbalance that emphasized things French over things Creole.

It is at this point in the module that I introduce the crucial digital resources that enable us to assess the scope and nature of theater production in Saint-Domingue: the trilingual English-French-Creole database of named theatrical works performed in Saint-Domingue, as announced in the local newspapers between 1764 and 1791, that I have put together on the Web site *Theatre in Saint-Domingue, 1764–1791* (theatreinsaint domingue.org), and the digital copies of the newspapers from which the data are drawn, available at the *Digital Library of the Caribbean* (dloc .com) and the George A. Smathers Libraries at the University of Florida (ufdc.ufl.edu). A quick search of the database soon makes it clear that repertoire imported from France made up the majority of theatrical works performed in Saint-Domingue, and several of the announcements in the local papers allude to similarities between an upcoming performance in Saint-Domingue and previous performances in France. While it is important for students to acknowledge that the primary direction of travel for these works was east to west across the Atlantic Ocean (or from north to south, if that approach is preferred), and that many residents of Saint-Domingue did seek to reproduce metropolitan French life in the colony, I try to emphasize that theater-making in Saint-Domingue was not a matter of creating, as common prejudice would have it, a necessarily inferior copy of the metropolitan model. Rather, I encourage students to be open to the idea that local input into works that originated in metropolitan France might be considered positive creative contributions and that a performance in Saint-Domingue by people living in Saint-Domingue of a work that originated in France might result in something that we can consider on its own terms. Current interest in transnational theater can also be drawn on to support this point.

As a quick search of the database demonstrates, there is no shortage of examples of French works on which to draw for this portion of the module, though it can be useful to begin with something that is already familiar to students. It is perhaps even more useful to examine works that can be complemented with some secondary material on the Saint-Dominguan context. The corpus of such secondary material on theater in Saint-Domingue is small but expanding. I regularly update the bibliography on *Theatre in Saint-Domingue* as items are published, and it currently includes articles that address Gluck's Paris operas (Prest, "*Iphigénie en Haïti*"), Voltaire's tragedy *Zaïre* (Camier and Dubois), and Benoît-Joseph Marsollier and Nicolas-Marie Dalayrac's opéra comique, *Nina* (Prest, "Parisian Palimpsests").[1] My article on *Nina* explicitly addresses the relationship between performances in Paris and in two towns in Saint-Domingue at the same time that it explores the theatrical careers in Saint-Domingue of one white French performer and one Creole performer of mixed racial ancestry.

My database provides us with the titles of a dozen or so Caribbean-composed works from the period under consideration (the precise number is difficult to ascertain, as some works that claim to be local turn out to be or may have been French works with a local twist or a new title) of which the texts of only three are known to be extant: the first is an anonymous three-act francophone comedy called *Les veuves créoles* (*The Creole Widows*), set in the neighboring colony of Martinique but performed at least twice in Saint-Domingue, and the second is a Creole-language parody (with a French title and French-language stage directions) by a man named Clément of a patois parody of Rousseau's *Le devin du village* (*The Village Soothsayer*), called *Jeannot et Thérèse* and set in Saint-Domingue. These two works are the focus of our sessions on locally composed repertoire (see below for more information about the third, *La répétition interrompue* [*The Interrupted Rehearsal*]). *Les veuves créoles* is available in a modern critical edition that also features a detailed introduction to its context and performance history, while the text of *Jeannot et Thérèse* is reproduced in a published article by Bernard Camier and Marie-Christine Hazaël-Massieux.[2] I find that students of French can gain some sense of the text of *Jeannot et Thérèse* thanks to the stage directions, their knowledge of French combined with some very basic modern Haitian Creole that we look at together, and an examination of the source texts (*Le devin du village* and its patois parody, *Les amours de Bastien et Bastienne* [*The Love Stories of Bastien and Bastienne*]). The principal purpose of the sessions on locally composed works is to demonstrate that theater was not only imported from Europe to Saint-Domingue: *Les veuves créoles* was published in Paris, while manuscript versions of *Jeannot et Thérèse* found their way by boat to the United States and to England.

We then spend one week looking at a selection of works from a thematic perspective, focusing on African characters and characters of African ancestry. The primary objective of these sessions is to consider the tricky but important question of if and how the same work might be received in different ways in different social contexts. The database reveals that a number of plays featuring African characters were performed in Saint-Domingue, but we focus on Jean-Baptiste Radet and Pierre-Yvon Barré's *La Négresse ou le pouvoir de la reconnaissance* (*The Black Woman; or, The Power of Gratitude*) which seems, interestingly, to have been performed in

Saint-Domingue under the new title *Les Créoles africaines ou les effets de l'amour* (*The African Creoles; or, The Effects of Love*) and which is less racist than most contemporary works and even culminates in the marriage of a white Frenchman with his black African lover. *La Négresse* also plays on the theme of blackface performance, something that has particular resonance in the social context of Saint-Domingue and found its own peculiar form of expression in the colony in a series of Creole parodies featuring black characters, of which *Jeannot et Thérèse* is one. Our exploration of blackface performance in Saint-Domingue helps students gain a more nuanced perspective on one of theater's most notorious and longstanding practices.[3]

Finally, we turn our attention back to the social conditions that led to the end of Saint-Domingue and the creation of the Haitian Republic in 1804. Drawing heavily on Dubois and Garrigus's useful collection, *Slave Revolution in the Caribbean, 1789–1804*, which we complement with the original French-language versions of their chosen texts, we examine first how news of the French Revolution reached Saint-Domingue partly by way of the theater, in such works as a metatheatrical play by a local journalist, Charles Mozard, called *La répétition interrompue*, which stages the bringing of news from revolutionary France and includes Saint-Domingue's most famous performer of color, Minette, appearing as herself and celebrating the unification of the three orders of the Estates General in June 1789. Finally, we look briefly at the significance of Saint-Domingue in the French Revolution and at what became known as the "Haitian Revolution"—a period that brought an end to the regular public theater tradition in the colony.

Whereas for their first assignment all students on the module are given the same essay question and are assessed primarily on their understanding of some core, if also complex, information discussed in class, their second assignment is an independent research project on a person, work, or other topic of their choice. I meet with students individually in my office hours to discuss and approve their choices in order to ensure their viability as a three-thousand-word piece. Students are advised that they must select their topic on the basis of individual research undertaken using our two main digital resources: the *Theatre in Saint-Domingue* database and the information provided in the local French-language newspapers, which were printed and published in the two main towns of the colony, Port-au-Prince and Cap-Français (now Cap-Haïtien), several times per week: the *Affiches américaines* (*American Notices*) and the *Supplément aux affiches américaines* (*Supplement to American Notices*). I explain that the newspapers as a source of facts about theater production in Saint-Domingue are flawed in two main ways: first, because they announce upcoming performances that may or may not have taken place, and taken place as described, and, second, because they mostly announce special benefit performances put on by individuals and do not mention all the subscription performances that we know were also scheduled. In other words, the picture is incomplete. Students are encouraged to think about how these caveats should be incorporated into their final essays.

In order to promote new research, however modest, I require students to focus on a work or person about which or whom extensive research has not been undertaken and published, although for teachers wishing to focus more narrowly on neoclassical theater, this caveat could be eliminated and the work of Corneille, Racine, Voltaire, and Gluck prioritized. As the body of secondary material expands, the list of exclusions will lengthen, and I anticipate adjusting the instructions for this assignment accordingly, perhaps by promoting more detailed work that draws on a wider range of primary and secondary sources. I promote the use and importance of genuine research methods by making the process of identifying a viable topic part of the actual assessment: students are asked to write the first portion of their essay in the first person, outlining in some detail how they used the database and the newspapers to pin down a topic. In their essays, all students are required to present a minimum of two topics that they researched before making their final decision. Students thus have no choice but to familiarize themselves with the designated digital resources, and those who struggle to find a viable topic are still rewarded for their efforts. In the opening section of these essays, cogent reflections on thinner topics are rewarded as much as cogent reflections on meatier topics. In the body of the essay, written in the third person, in which students present and analyze their findings, students with thinner topics must look at these in more depth and detail than students who have more material to work with and who must be more selective. In this way, I am also able to put research into "minor" figures and contributions on much the same footing as research into "major" figures or contributions.

A good research essay in the context of this course will typically begin by presenting a series of database searches followed by, and then combined with, a series of newspaper searches. The database has two primary search modes: the simple search and the advanced search. Students tend to begin with the simple search function, which can provide basic information in a single click: Which, if any, works by Pierre Corneille were performed in Saint-Domingue? A search for "Corneille" brings up six hits, featuring four works by Pierre Corneille (two tragedies, one tragicomedy, and one comedy) and two by his brother, Thomas. A search for "Racine" brings up three tragedies and his one comedy, *Les plaideurs* (*The Litigants*). As indicated above, the principal representative of neoclassical tragedy in Saint-Domingue was Voltaire: a simple search for his name brings up fifteen different titles. The quickest way to separate these by genre is to switch to an advanced search, whose results can be displayed by work or by performance date and which features a series of headings that can be cross-referenced: title, location, performance date, genre, author, composer, beneficiary, and participant. Drop-down lists are provided for genre, author, composer, beneficiary, and participant, which facilitates the discovery of unfamiliar names and works and helps avoid wild goose chases at this early stage. An advanced search set to "works" brings up a list of works, each of them with a hyperlink to a list of performances, of that work, organized by date and location, together with details of the newspaper references from which the information was taken. Each performance date is hyperlinked to further information about that day's performance, including information about what other work or works were given that day (most performances were double bills). Similarly, an advanced search set to "performances" leads to a list of dates and locations with hyperlinks to detailed information about that day's performance and its supporting references. This use of hyperlinks aims to avoid an excess of information being displayed on the computer screen at any given time (including an excess of open windows) and "return to results" and "new search" options are provided each time. Hyperlinks are also provided from the names of authors, participants, and beneficiaries, which is particularly useful for researchers interested in the contributions of local people whose names are otherwise entirely unfamiliar. Students are encouraged to consult the database in French or even Creole.

A basic search quickly informs students of the presence or absence of an author or participant of interest to them, and a more prolonged search of either kind exposes students to names that are unfamiliar to them. Often students report that a recurring name has piqued their curiosity, and this is how many of our research projects begin. I stress to students that identifying their project is not a matter simply of finding a name that turns up in more than a handful of entries on the database; after noting down the references provided in the database, often identified in a matter of minutes, they should spend several hours reading the relevant newspaper entries online. Students can find it hard to settle into this more intense and lengthy form of research, but almost all of them report later on that they found the process rewarding.

Students quickly discover that the nature and usefulness of these newspaper articles vary enormously. Sometimes only the most basic information, the same information that is already given in the database, is provided: the works to be performed, on which day, and in which town. Occasionally the information in the newspapers is incomplete or inaccurate, and students learn that obvious mistakes had to be corrected in the database and missing information (e.g., the name of the playwright or librettist) added, while ongoing ambiguities have been acknowledged but left unresolved (this process is outlined in more detail in the notes section on the Web site that is home to the database). These efforts provide a good lesson about the nature of primary sources, which do contain mistakes. Most important, the process of searching the newspapers across a number of years and seeing other entries and articles along the way familiarizes students with what is arguably the richest and most valuable source of information about theater and society in colonial Saint-Domingue. There are no real shortcuts to this process, which has the distinct benefit of rewarding genuine hard work. Students tend to find the process of organizing and writing their research essays less challenging—or at least more familiar—than the process of researching them. The primary assessment criteria for this portion of the essay are the presentation and then the analysis of the materials in the context of what students can reasonably be expected to find out about theater and society in colonial Saint-Domingue.

Saint-Domingue: Theatre and Society in a Caribbean Slave Colony offers an all too brief introduction into an area of research and study that is deserving of more time. But it does achieve its primary goal of bringing an unknown area of theater history into the undergraduate curriculum and of introducing students to a topic that some of them choose to explore in more depth later on, in undergraduate dissertations or graduate work. It promotes the use of new digital resources in the study of the early modern period at the same time that it suggests some ways in which we can approach the colonial era from a postcolonial or, more precisely, Creole perspective. With regard specifically to neoclassical tragedy, it tells the story of how these works reached new audiences in new contexts that have been largely overlooked until now.

Notes

1. See list of works cited for full bibliographical details for these and other sources mentioned. Among future publications that I expect to use in the course are Pedro Memelsdorff's fascinating "*L'amant statue*: Staging Slavery in Pre-Revolutionary Haiti," several essays relating to theater in Saint-Domingue in the edited collection *Colonialism and Slavery in Performance: Theatre and the Eighteenth-Century French Caribbean* (Leichman and Bénac), and an essay that I have written on performances in Saint-Domingue of Voltaire's tragedy *Sémiramis* and its Creole parody, *Harpiminis.*

2. We look forward to the publication of a scholarly edition of the work, complete with its musical score, edited by Bernard Camier.

3. For this we use Julia Prest, "The Familiar Other."

Works Cited

Camier, Bernard, and Laurent Dubois. "Voltaire et *Zaïre*, ou le théâtre des Lumières dans l'aire atlantique française." *Revue d'histoire moderne et contemporaine*, vol. 54, nos. 3–4, 2007, pp. 41–69.

Camier, Bernard, and Marie-Christine Hazaël-Massieux. "*Jeannot et Thérèse*: un opéra-comique en créole au milieu du XVIIIe siècle." *Revue de la société haïtienne d'histoire et de géographie*, no. 215, 2003, pp. 135–66.

Clay, Lauren. *Stagestruck: The Business of Theater in Eighteenth-Century France and Its Colonies.* Cornell UP, 2013.

Dubois, Laurent, and John Garrigus. *Slave Revolution in the Caribbean, 1789–1804.* Bedford/St. Martin's, 2006.

Garrigus, John. *Before Haiti: Race and Citizenship in French Saint-Domingue.* Palgrave, 2006.

Higman, B. W. *A Concise History of the Caribbean.* Cambridge UP, 2011.

Leichman, Jeffrey, and Karine Bénac, editors. *Colonialism and Slavery in Performance: Theatre and the Eighteenth-Century French Caribbean.* OUSE/Liverpool UP, 2021.

Memelsdorff, Pedro. "*L'amant statue*: Staging Slavery in Pre-Revolutionary Haiti." *Music in the Mediterranean Diaspora*, edited by Kate van Orden, Harvard UP, forthcoming. I Tatti Studies in Italian Renaissance History.

Miller, Christopher. *The French Atlantic Triangle: Literature and Culture of the Slave Trade.* Duke UP, 2008.

Moreau de Saint-Méry, Médéric Louis Elie. *Description topographique, physique, civile, politique et historique de la partie française de l'isle Saint-Domingue.* Edited by Etienne Taillemite and Marcel Dorigny, Société Française d'Histoire d'Outre-Mer, 2004. 3 vols.

Mozard, Charles. *La répétition interrompue.* Imprimerie de l'auteur, 1789.

Prest, Julia. "The Familiar Other: Blackface Performance in Creole Works from 1780s Saint-Domingue." Leichman and Bénac, pp. 41–63.

———. "*Iphigénie en Haïti*: Performing Gluck's Paris Operas in the French Colonial Caribbean." *Eighteenth-Century Music*, vol. 14, no. 1, Mar. 2017, pp. 13–29.

———. "Parisian Palimpsests and Creole Creations: Mme Marsan and Mlle Minette perform *Nina* on the Caribbean Stage." *Early Modern French Studies*, vol. 41, no. 2, 2019, pp. 170–88.

———, editor. *Les veuves créoles, comédie*. Modern Humanities Research Association, 2017.

———. "Voltaire's *Sémiramis*: From French Tragedy to Creole Parody." *The Allure of the Ancient*, edited by John Steele and Margaret Geoga, Brill, forthcoming.

Radet, Jean-Baptiste, and Pierre-Yvon Barré. *La Négresse ou le pouvoir de la reconnaissance*. Brunet, 1787.

Ellen R. Welch

Ancient Stories, Modern Audiences: Neoclassical Tragedy in Multicultural France

When teaching seventeenth-century tragedy to my mostly North American undergraduate students, I approach the term *neoclassical* with some hesitation and a great deal of ambivalence. Why not let students read and appreciate these plays free from the impulse to measure them against supposedly restrictive classical "rules"? Wouldn't it be preferable to unburden these works of the weighty reception history that enshrines them as a pinnacle of French literary achievement? Might adopting the "neoclassical" category for pedagogical purposes inadvertently reproduce a nineteenth- and early-twentieth-century critical tradition that emphasized the repertoire's universal appeal to link it to notions of French cultural universalism that were complicit in the era's colonial projects?[1] With my students, I address these doubts in part by highlighting the ambivalent attitudes displayed by so-called neoclassical writers themselves—pointing out, for example, how Pierre Corneille and Jean Racine take liberties in reworking Greek and Roman sources or push back against Aristotelian poetic norms even as they profess admiration for the ancients.[2] Appreciating the complex, nuanced ways in which early modern writers negotiated their relationship to the literature of the antique past can be a point of departure for considering, in turn, the role of early modern literary traditions in today's culture.

The dramatic mode offers another natural approach to these issues, inviting students to think about plays as living texts designed to be perpetually reinterpreted for new audiences in performance. Recent productions are an obvious, effective resource for giving students a sense of the renewable appeal of neoclassical plays and for exposing them to the array of interpretations that can be brought to classic texts. Modernized productions in particular can illustrate resonances between a neoclassical play and our contemporary culture, or spark discussion about the relative success or failure of an attempt to bring an ancient story up to date. Meanwhile, stripped-down, abstracted performances can start conversations about the link between aesthetic simplicity and belief in the immutable significance of a text. Exploring how neoclassical drama is revisited in theater cultures of the French-speaking world today can therefore also be a way to study contemporary French and francophone societies' approach to this literary heritage—how they reinforce or challenge the meanings attributed to these abiding works. In what follows, I sketch the outlines of a type of assignment that uses recent productions to engage students in a meta-reflection on the making and remaking of literary value. To illustrate the kinds of discussions that can arise from this activity, I discuss one example of a production that opens up debate of the more problematic aspects of the neoclassical canon; namely, its associations with an idea of "universality" increasingly recognized as exclusionary in postcolonial France.

Overview of the Assignment

Beyond showing video clips in class to illustrate scenes under analysis, I engage students in sustained critical examinations of contemporary productions, including research and writing assignments. Using interviews with performers and directors, videos, still images, and press reviews, students reconstruct and assess a production's dramaturgical choices with respect to the original text and the context of the performance. For students unfamiliar with theater, it may be useful to provide a checklist of production elements to consider, such as casting, costumes, set design, abridgements or additions to the text, and music (see appendix).[3] Observations can build toward a critical analysis of the most striking aspect of the performance. Students might evaluate, for example, the effectiveness of video technology in Paolo Correia's staging of Corneille's *Médée*.[4] They could discuss how a radio that plays a key role in the set design of Michael Marmarinos's version of *Phèdre* highlights the political dimension of the play by representing news from the outside world.[5] They could debate the implicit premise of Stéphane Braunsweig's *Britannicus*, which sets that drama of power in a stark, modern boardroom evocative of contemporary seats of government.[6] While judging the interpretations implied by a director's choices, noticing which aspects of the play prevail in a given production and what gets left out, students also grow more confident in their own command of the source text.

I feature variations on this activity in two types of courses. For an introductory undergraduate survey of early modern French literature organized around the theme of "ancients and moderns," I include it as a whole-class discussion. Following three or four seventy-five-minute class sessions devoted to analyzing the text of an assigned play, we spend one period discussing a chosen production—or a contrasting pair of productions—in depth. In this case, I provide the primary documents to students in advance and ask them to write short response essays or to post their thoughts on an online forum in preparation for class discussion. Their task is to compare their own sense of the play based on their reading of the text with the interpretation proposed in the mise-en-scène, focusing on whatever elements of the production strike them the most. In class, students compare their analyses in small groups before coming together for a broader discussion tying the evaluation of the production back to larger issues of adaptation and notions of literary universality or "timelessness."

For an upper-level undergraduate or graduate seminar on theater, I reframe the activity as a research assignment. Over the course of the semester, each student is responsible for researching and presenting to the class one modern production of a play on the syllabus. Generally, I provide a menu of notable productions from the past ten to fifteen years, often including English-language adaptations, from which students can choose, though I also encourage students to propose a staging they have discovered for themselves, whether from their own theatergoing experiences or through initial searching. Before students commit to a particular play or production, we spend a portion of a class period working with a librarian to review helpful resources for this kind of research, including

the periodicals database *LexisNexis*, available through library subscription, which allows students to locate theater reviews in major French- and English-language publications;

Drama Criticism, edited by Lawrence J. Trudeau and distributed electronically to libraries as part of the *Gale Literature Resource Center*, a clearinghouse of reprinted critical essays on productions as well as important scholarly articles on plays;

the Bibliothèque Nationale's digital collection *Gallica*, in particular its convenient rubric devoted to theater photography, searchable by photographer, theater, or festival (gallica.bnf.fr/html/und/images/la-photographie-de-spectacle); and

the Comédie-Française's own Web site, a rich archive of programs and photographs, best accessed by using the site's search function to call up results for a particular play (comedie-francaise.fr/fr/ressources-numeriques).

The assignment can be framed to suit the specific topic of an advanced course. For example, in my advanced seminar course Theater and the Past: History as Repertoire, students analyze the productions in conjunction with theoretical reading assignments that explore how plays represent historical events and how theatrical temporality works with and against conceptions of historical time: for example, Rebecca Schneider on theater's "inter(in)animation" of past and present, Marvin Carlson on the "haunted stage," or Joseph Roach on performance as a practice of cultural memory. The assignment would work as well in a straightforward theater course, a course on neoclassicism, or a seminar on literary adaptation.

Andromaque for a New Generation

Exploring how recent productions adapt early modern plays for contemporary audiences can also open up discussions about the role of the neoclassical corpus in today's cultural debates. A particularly rich recent production that invites discussion of the relevance of neoclassical drama to a young, diverse generation is Collectif La Palmera's version of Racine's *Andromaque*. Conceived by its performers, Nelson Rafaell-Madel and Paul Nguyen, in collaboration with director Néry Catineau, this textually faithful version reconceives the play as a two-hander, showcasing its actors' virtuosity as they slip between multiple roles. La Palmera's production began as a series of "underground" performances in private apartments followed by an extended run at Le Montfort Théâtre in Paris in 2013. It has since been performed in a variety of venues, including regional theaters, high schools, the Festival OFF d'Avignon in 2014, and the Théâtre Aimé Césaire in Martinique in 2016 (see "Oreste Aime Hermione Qui Aime . . . / OFF"). A video recording of an entire performance is currently available on *YouTube* ("Oreste aime Hermione"), and student researchers will find a wealth of reviews, interviews, and promotional materials on the Internet.[7] Finally, the production works well with students because its creators designed it for an audience not yet in the habit of attending neoclassical tragedies. As Nguyen stated in an interview during the 2014 Avignon Festival, "Notre réflexion partait alors d'un questionnement simple: comment rendre 'accessible' un texte aussi puissant sans en trahir la portée?" 'Our reflection began with a simple question: how to make such a powerful text "accessible" without betraying its significance' (Géhin).[8]

The artists' self-professed intention to illuminate *Andromaque* for a new audience provides a clear starting place for analyzing the production with students. What choices do the actors and directors make to render the play meaningful to contemporary viewers? La Palmera's production incorporates several small but obvious changes and additions to the text. It renames Racine's play *Oreste aime Hermione qui aime Pyrrhus qui aime Andromaque qui aime Hector . . . qui est mort*, a handy plot summary that gives audiences unfamiliar with the play a firm grasp on its central dramatic conflict. Further demystifying the canonical tragedy, the production studs the first two acts with playful or spectacular interludes. For example, Andromaque's first speech is sung as a torch song. The actors camp it up as Hermione and Cléone in act 2, scene 1. In between scenes, they pause to review in plain language the exposition just revealed in alexandrines. These embellishments, however, largely fall away by the start of act 3. They exist to help audiences become acquainted with the major characters and their histories; thereafter, the tragic plot and Racine's verses suffice to rivet the public's attention.

In interviews, the actors and director explain their production choices as efforts to draw in spectators who might otherwise be intimidated by a versified tragedy set in ancient Greece. Inevitably, the elements that contextualize and translate *Andromaque* for modern audiences also influence the way viewers interpret the play. If students have already worked with explicitly modernized productions (such as Braunsweig's *Britannicus*), they will have seen how set design and costumes can steer audiences toward a particular interpretation of the contemporary relevance of a historical play. La Palmera's *Andromaque*, by contrast, employs a minimalist staging that is in many ways consistent with neoclassicism even if motivated by consideration for cost and portability rather than aesthetic doctrine (Gayot).

Students can appreciate how the lack of cultural specificity in the wraps and scarves that make up the characters' outfits, for example, facilitates broad reflection on the translatability of the play's central issues to times and places other than ancient Greece even as it avoids insisting on a single resonance between the play and another particular historical moment. In fact, despite the plethora of media interviews and promotional materials surrounding the production, the actors and director have scrupulously avoided interpreting their mise-en-scène for the audience. In a promotional video entitled "Pourquoi jouer *Andromaque* aujourd'hui?" ("Why Perform *Andromaque* Today?") Nguyen and Rafaell-Madel appear visibly uncomfortable with the question. Their response—about the modern relevance of themes of single motherhood and absent or dead fathers—will strike most viewers as inadequate, relatively marginal to both the play and La Palmera's production of it. The video can nonetheless serve as a point of departure for discussion with students. What do they see as the production's key themes? How can they relate them to contemporary issues?

Discussion of these questions might center on La Palmera's most substantive departure from Racine's text: an original prologue that explains the prehistory of the drama. As the play begins, the actors stroll casually onto an open stage strewn with balloons. Addressing the audience directly, they begin to tell the story of the Trojan War, reenacting events by manipulating the balloons that stand in for key figures. Hector and Achilles are "killed" with sharp pins. At last, when the Greeks ambush Troy with the infamous horse, the actors perform the massacre by stabbing all the balloons, biting them, ripping them apart with their bare hands until not a single one remains inflated. The playful tone turns quickly somber as the two actors sweep the latex carnage from the stage: "Troye est rasée de la carte" 'Troy is wiped off the map.'

This prologue clearly serves the pedagogical intentions of the production, giving necessary context for audiences who may well be unfamiliar with Greek legends. It also provides an interpretative frame for the tragedy that follows. As such, discussion of the prologue can help focus students' minds on the particular reading La Palmera gives to Racine's play. How do students react to the staging and props in these opening moments of the performance? What themes do the performers emphasize in their explanation of the war? Beyond recounting backstory, what does this prelude add to students' understanding of the play? When transitioning into examination of the rest of the drama, it would be worth reminding students that, with the first line of act 1, the stage space transforms from the site of the

Trojan massacre to Epirus. How does that metamorphosis influence their perspective on the site in which Racine's drama takes place? Having very likely already discussed themes of historical trauma and the pain experienced by its survivors during their work with the text of *Andromaque*, students tend to appreciate how the prologue highlights these aspects of the play. Even as the action shifts to Pyrrhus's palace, the stage remains haunted by Troy and the powerful image of its destruction.

Indeed, the production returns again and again to the persistent legacy of war. The explanatory asides interspersed throughout the first two acts directly remind spectators that Andromaque and Hermione are captives, forced to live under the rule of those who destroyed their families and their homes. In more oblique fashion, the simple staging keeps the eradication of Troy at the forefront of the audience's mind. A discussion of the costumes should help students notice that the characters' color-coded garb refers back to the hues of the balloons that represented them in the prologue. The denouement makes especially powerful, poignant use of that continuity, as the robes of the dead remain on the stage. Through close analysis of the staging of grief in the play's last two scenes, students can appreciate how the abandoned garments function as objects of mourning, stand-ins for corpses, but also as a visual echo of the colorful shards that littered the stage at the start of the evening. These deaths, the mise-en-scène implies, are a prolongation of that earlier massacre. The play as whole, in La Palmera's production, coheres around this idea about the lasting legacy of geopolitical violence. In reflecting on the significance of this theme, students might draw comparisons to other wars and genocides whose historical and psychological consequences continue to play out in different parts of the world.

The Question of Casting

In this context, the actors' identities—Rafaell-Madel hails from Martinique; Nguyen is of Southeast Asian heritage—may enter into dialogue with the content of the play. In the many interviews the actors have given with the media or published on La Palmera's Web site, they have not raised issues of identity. Nonetheless, casting influences interpretation. As Marvin Carlson observes, actors are never neutral amanuenses for their characters but "haunt" their roles with the associations accreted on their bodies: the memory of other roles they have famously played, their physical and personality type (52–95). In discussing La Palmera's *Andromaque*, students might consider: What is the significance of casting male actors to play both male and female roles? Does it matter that the bodies playing these characters differ from the traditional depictions in European representations, or from the actors who incarnated these roles in seventeenth-century France?

In teaching this production or others with diverse casting, it may be useful to introduce some key terms to analyze role distribution. In French the terms *le casting non-traditionnel* ("nontraditional casting") and sometimes *le casting inclusif* ("inclusive casting") cover a range of approaches differentiated in Anglo-American theater culture as "colorblind casting" ("actors are cast without regard to their race or ethnicity; the best actor is cast in the role" [Pao 4]) versus what is often called "color-conscious casting" or "purposeful casting," whereby the perceived ethnicity (or, in some cases, gender) of actors contributes something to the interpretation of the play. Angela Pao proposes further distinctions within the category of purposeful casting: "Societal casting: ethnic and female actors are cast in roles they perform in society as a whole. Conceptual casting: an ethnic actor is cast in a role to give the play greater resonance. Cross-cultural casting: the entire world of the play is translated to a different culture" (4). These terms are useful not only for their descriptive potential. As a launchpad for discussion, Pao's classification system also shows how casting's effect on interpretation can exceed a director's intentions. The distinction between colorblind and purposeful casting breaks down in the presence of strong cultural expectations for the performance of a particular repertoire. Classicist Kevin Wetmore, for example, observes that any nontraditional casting of Greek drama necessarily adds meaning to the play: "Is 'colorblind' Greek tragedy possible in contemporary production? The short answer, of course, is no. . . . [C]asting against perceived type or employing what has come to be known as colorblind casting still creates resonances on stage with historic referents" (488). He concludes, "[C]olorblind casting can be read as the imposition of a universalized and universalizing European culture on actors of color . . . [or] the Greek mask can become a form of resistance, to recolonize Greek culture in order to make a statement about race, ethnicity, politics and power in contemporary culture" (493). For the classical canon, colorblind casting automatically appears as "conceptual casting," affecting the way audiences interpret the play's significance.

Much the same can be said about the neoclassical canon in France. In fact, France has been slow to embrace inclusive casting practices, especially when it comes to the prestigious mainstays of the neoclassical repertoire. As of this writing, the Comédie-Française troupe of fifty-seven actors includes four artists of color: one *sociétaire*, or senior member of the company (Bakary Sangaré, a company member since 2002), and three *pensionnaires*, or junior members (Gaël Kamilindi, who joined in 2017, and Birane Ba and Élissa Alloula, both recruited in 2019). All have performed in productions of Molière plays at the theater. Yet Sangaré has been cast in only one neoclassical tragic role to date (as Titus in Faustin Linyekula's 2008 production of *Bérénice*), while the *pensionnaires* have not yet had a part in a tragedy by Corneille or Racine.[9] To a greater degree than productions of Shakespeare in the United States or the United Kingdom, for example, performances of neoclassical drama in France remain quite racially homogeneous (see also Catanese 10–17 and Schechner 9). In this context, it is fair to consider how diverse casting might resonate with the themes of a neoclassical tragedy.

How and to what extent does the casting of La Palmera's version of *Andromaque* influence interpretation of this play? Students will of course have different answers to this question. Some may find that the casting has little effect or that they even forget about the actors while watching the performance. Others may want to explore how *Andromaque*'s themes of exile, captivity, and geopolitical trauma resonate with France's colonial and postcolonial histories. Documents of the play's run at the Théâtre Martinique may enrich this line of inquiry—for example, an interview with theater staff in which Rafaell-Madel refers to this performance as an "aboutissement" (culmination) of the production's aims ("Oreste"). Finally, others may echo Wetmore and see the production as a "recolonizing" of the neoclassical repertoire by actors who tend to be excluded from it. Indeed, both of the production's actors have pursued other professional activities that demonstrate a commitment to ethnic and racial diversity in French theater. Nguyen is associated with the theater group La Tribu based in Pantin, a northeastern suburb of Paris. This activist troupe's expressed mission is to construct and celebrate a more culturally diverse citizenry through art. Rafaell-Madel, for his part, has participated in several productions explicitly engaged with issues of racial difference, including his own adaptation of the South African writer André Brink's novel *Looking on Darkness*, *Au plus noir de la nuit*, at the Plateaux Sauvages in Paris in 2018. Both actors have devoted a significant part of their careers to advocating for increased diversity and equity in French theater.

Rethinking Universality in French Theater Culture

In fact, like the film industry in the United States, the French theater scene has been called over the past few years to address its exclusion of racial and ethnic-minority artists. A debate about the lack of diversity in French theater broke out during the Avignon Festival in summer 2015. A few months later, a group of actors and directors created the collective Décoloniser les Arts, which articulated its mission in an open letter to theater directors published in February 2016. Media attention followed in May 2016, when the group took advantage of the recent public outcry over lack of diversity in Hollywood's Academy Awards to shine a light on the extreme racial homogeneity of France's premier theater prizes, the Molières. With the *Twitter* hashtag #MolieresSoWhite, the collective protested a slate of nominees that included just one nonwhite artist out of a total of eighty-six. Décoloniser les Arts has published a series of texts and interviews on their blog and in media outlets, which can be incorporated into classroom discussion (e.g., Cukierman; Décoloniser les Arts). The most important of these is the open letter to theater directors published in February as a kind of mission statement. The key objective is to demand greater visibility for nonwhite performers, playwrights, and directors:

> Vous savez mieux que personne la triste corrélation entre les origines de ceux qui sont sur les plateaux et de ceux que l'on espère dans les salles. Où sont les Noirs, les Arabes, les Asiatiques, les Latins, les Français des cultures minorées dans les Théâtres de France? Dans la Culture de France?
>
> You know better than anyone the unfortunate correlation between the origins of those on the stage and of those we expect to see in the audience. Where are the Blacks, the Arabs, the Asians, the Latinos, the French of minority cultures in the Theaters of France? In the Culture of France?

The document goes on to frame the lack of diversity in theater as a direct result and continuation of France's colonial past: "Ces enjeux sociétaux majeurs . . . ont à voir avec l'Histoire de France, avec la difficulté à instituer une mémoire partagée entre ceux qui se sont un jour affrontés, et l'on sait que la culpabilité occidentale est un obstacle difficile à dépasser" 'These major societal issues . . . have to do with the History of France, with the difficulty in instituting a shared memory among those who were once violently opposed to one another, and we know that Western guilt is a difficult obstacle to overcome' (Décoloniser les Arts). To redress these historical wrongs, the group calls for the collection of statistics on the presence of racial and ethnic minorities in the theater industry, as a baseline from which to work to improve representation.

This, of course, is a controversial demand in France, where laws rooted in universalist principles prevent the state from gathering data on racial or ethnic identity. Anticipating objections, several artists associated with Décoloniser les Arts have framed the effort to diversify the theater as a project to realize the ideal of universalism, to renew the image of France to conform to its current demographic profile. The collective's open letter warns, "Si la Culture est le moyen de lutter contre les replis identitaires, une Culture qui exclut et ne considère pas prend le risque de contribuer à l'apparition de certains identitarismes, nationalismes ou extrémismes religieux de tous crins" 'If Culture is the way to fight against identitarian segregation, a Culture that excludes and ignores runs the risk of contributing to the appearance of certain identity politics, nationalisms, or religious extremisms of all kinds.' Theater has thus become another cultural touchstone in an ongoing debate about the limits of universalism or about how universalism can adapt to the realities of a diverse population (see also Cukierman).

Of course, if the language of universalism has a particular resonance in France, issues of equitable representation are not unique to French theater culture. Décoloniser les Arts' first interventions on *Twitter* invite students to draw parallels to similar struggles in American cultural institutions (the problems identified by #OscarsSoWhite being far from resolved). Students might also compare the cultural status of the French neoclassical canon with that of Shakespeare's works in the Anglo-American context, where claims that the Bard represents *humanity* and *human nature* often replace a discourse of universal aesthetic value, with equally problematic implications. The status afforded to "classic" drama makes it a key site in struggles for access and equity in cultural life. Bringing these broader debates into the classroom encourages students to see the works they study not as static masterpieces but as battlegrounds on which they—as readers and spectators—also have a role to play.

Early modern French drama's relevance to contemporary audiences—including our students—resides precisely in the way that theater as a performative art and as an art of memory is always actively grappling with the renewal of the past. For the neoclassical repertory this also entails a constant questioning of the category of the "universal." Engaged theater artists offer rich resources for teaching neoclassical tragedy in a way that not only attends to the historical contexts of its production but also to these plays' role in mediating the relationship between France's literary and cultural traditions and today's society.

Notes

1. For brief discussions of the place of neoclassical playwrights in colonial school materials, see Albanese, *Corneille* 130 and *Racine* 18.

2. I frequently assign the first chapter of Norman (11–33) to drive home the ambivalence toward classical literature already present in seventeenth-century writing.

3. Instructors will also find useful resources online, such as the questionnaire developed by Catherine Duhtérian in conjunction with France's national education ministry and the Scène Nationale d'Albi.

4. The production was a collaboration between the Théâtre National de Nice and Correia's company, Collectif 8. Still photos and a video trailer are available on the Collectif 8 Web site, and a playlist of filmed scenes of the play is available on *YouTube*.

5. For a program and press pack for this production, see "*Phèdre* de Jean Racine," especially Marmarinos's own production notes.

6. For a program and dossier of still photos of this production, see "*Britannicus* de Jean Racine." A live-filmed performance was distributed in cinemas in July 2018 through Pathé Live and may be available on DVD in the future. The Web site *Pathé Live* freely offers an excerpt of the film as well as accompanying pedagogical materials on its home page (pathelive.com/education).

7. The collective's Web site (collectifpalmera.com) is a good starting place for information about the company and their *Andromaque* project. I have pieced together the production history outlined here from the Web site as well as from interviews (Gayot; Géhin; "Oreste"; "Pourquoi").

8. All translations are mine.

9. Kamilindi appeared in Ivo van Hove's *Electre/Oreste*, an adaptation of Euripides's two plays, at the Comédie-Française in winter 2019–2020. See Sylvaine Guyot's essay in this volume on Linyekula's production of *Bérénice*.

Works Cited

Albanese, Ralph. *Corneille à l'Ecole républicaine: Du mythe héroïque à l'imaginaire politique en France, 1800–1950*. L'Harmattan, 2008.

———. *Racine à l'école républicaine, ou les enjeux sociopolitique de la tragédie classique (1800–1950)*. L'Harmattan, 2013.

"*Britannicus* de Jean Racine, mise en scène Stéphane Braunsweig." *Comédie Française*, comedie-francaise.fr/www/comedie/media/document/piece-en-images-britannicus-06112018-.pdf.

Carlson, Marvin. *The Haunted Stage: The Theatre as Memory Machine*. U of Michigan P, 2001.

Catanese, Brandi Wilkings. *The Problem of the Color(blind): Racial Transgression and the Politics of Black Performance.* U of Michigan P, 2011.

Cukierman, Leila. "'Questionner l'universel,' intervention prononcée à Rouen le 13 octobre 2016. Les 11, 12 et 13 octobre 2016, les journées de la diversité." *Décoloniser les Arts Blog*, 8 Nov. 2016, blogs.mediapart.fr/decoloniser-les-arts/blog/081116/questionner-luniversel-un-texte-de-leila-cukierman.

Décoloniser les Arts. "Lettre aux directeurs et directrices de théâtres, ou de festivals, lettre aux responsables culturels." *Décoloniser les Arts Blog*, 24 Feb. 2016, blogs.mediapart.fr/decoloniser-les-arts/blog/240216/lettre-aux-directeurs-et-directrices-de-theatres-ou-de-festivals-lettre-aux-responsables-c.

Duhtérian, Catherine. "Exemple de grille d'analyse de spectacles." Scène Nationale d'Albi, Sept. 2013, sn-albi.fr/CONTENUS/medias/fichiers/grilledanalysedespectacles.pdf.

Gayot, Joëlle. "*Oreste aime Hermione qui aime Pyrrhus qui aime Andromaque qui aime Hector . . . qui est mort:* Le choix de Joëlle Gayot." *France Culture*, 17 July 2014, www.franceculture.fr/emissions/le-choix-de-joelle-gayot/oreste-aime-hermione-qui-aime-pyrrhus-qui-aime-andromaque-qui.

Géhin, Walter. "Paul Nguyen: 'Une ligne artistique qui questionne à la fois la place que tient le public dans une représentation et l'écriture contemporaine.'" *PlusDeOff*, 17 Sept. 2014, plusdeoff.com/2014/09/17/interview-paul-nguyen-theatre/.

Médée playlist. *YouTube*, uploaded by sustainthetrip, 17 Apr. 2013, youtube.com/playlist?list=PLxaEahgB7G5_vJUdOhe0XS5jSxrPZvkru.

Médée trailer. *Collectif 8*, collectif8.com/medee.

Norman, Larry F. *The Shock of the Ancient: Literature and History in Early Modern France.* U of Chicago P, 2011.

"Oreste aime Hermione qui aime Pyrrhus qui aime Andromaque qui aime Hector qui est mort." *YouTube*, uploaded by Alexis Clerget, 13 May 2017, youtube.com/watch?v=rtdWfURMHTs.

"Oreste Aime Hermione Qui Aime . . . / OFF / 18 Mai 2016." *YouTube*, uploaded by Théâtre Martinique, 19 May 2016, youtube.com/watch?v=2EC2PNJQLoA.

Pao, Angela. *No Safe Spaces: Recasting Race, Ethnicity, and Nationality in American Theater.* U of Michigan P, 2010.

"*Phèdre* de Jean Racine, mis en scène de Michael Marmarinos." Comédie-Française press dossier, 12 Feb. 2013, comedie-francaise.fr/www/comedie/media/document/presse-phedre1213.pdf.

"Pourquoi jouer *Andromaque* aujourd'hui?" *YouTube*, uploaded by Collectif-Palmera, 3 Dec. 2011, youtube.com/watch?v=gH-Ay6J2Qgg.

Roach, Joseph. *Cities of the Dead: Circum-Atlantic Performance.* Columbia UP, 1996.

Schechner, Richard. "Race Free, Gender Free, Body-Type Free, Age-Free Casting." *TDR / The Drama Review*, vol. 33, no. 1, 1989, pp. 4–12.

Schneider, Rebecca. *Performing Remains: Art and War in in Times of Theatrical Reenactment.* Routledge, 2011.

Wetmore, Jr., Kevin J. "Black Skin, Greek Masks: Classical Receptions, Race Reception, and African-American Identity on the Tragic Stage." *Revue de littérature comparée*, no. 344, 2012, pp. 487–93.

Appendix: Analysis of a Production

Lexique de mots utiles	Selected Useful Terms
L'espace théâtral	Theatrical space
Le placement des spectateurs (frontal, bi-frontal, tri-frontal, circulaire)	Stage and seating type (proscenium, traverse, thrust, in-the-round)
Le rideau	Curtain
La fosse d'orchestre	Orchestra pit
L'espace scénique (carré, rectangulaire, circulaire)	Stage shape (square, rectangular, round)
La scénographie (l'ensemble des éléments qu'on voit sur scène)	Set design
Le décor	Set
Le changement de scène / le changement de décor	Scene change
Les objets scéniques	Props
La trappe	Trapdoor
Les effets scéniques aériens	Aerial effects
L'éclairage	Lighting
La vidéo / la projection	Video projection
La musique de scène	Scene music
Les sons / le bruitage	Sound design
Les costumes	Costumes
Le maquillage	Makeup
Le casting / la distribution des rôles / la répartition des rôles	Casting
Le jeu des acteurs	Acting
La gestuelle (le langage corporel dont un acteur/une actrice se sert en incarnant un personnage)	Gesture, body language

Sylvaine Guyot

Staging the Neoclassical Canon as Intercultural Repertoire: Faustin Linyekula's *Bérénice* Diptych

"I do not know if it is possible to perform Racine today. Perhaps, on stage, this theater is three-fourths dead." So proclaimed Roland Barthes with an air of disenchantment in 1963 (149). The democratization and decentralization effort that was initiated by the French government in the 1950s, sustained by the actor and director Jean Vilar's call for, and implementation of, a *théâtre populaire*, promoted a vision of theater that should aim to reach a wider and more diverse audience than the cultural elite of the capital. In this context, the relevance of Racine was in question: Was it necessary, still, to stage such "aristocratic" theater? What could Racine, that great symbol of French neoclassicism, mean to modern audiences?

Such questions reemerged in the early 1990s in the wake of a crisis surrounding the legitimacy of the literary and dramatic canon, both within academia and within the world of performance, especially in the United States.[1] Some scholars thought that the canon had become decidedly irrelevant vis-à-vis new waves of feminist studies, cultural studies, and postcolonial studies. Others accused it of having been, and continuing to be, the instrument of a power structure aimed at preserving and disseminating dominant Western and imperialist values. In such a context, how could one possibly justify teaching and staging Racine's *Bérénice*, a play long considered the epitome of both the neoclassical sublime and the seventeenth century's universalizing aesthetic?

This essay intends to answer this question by exploring two stagings of Racine's text by the Congolese choreographer Faustin Linyekula, which provide ample material for two sessions of a college-level course: the first is a staging of *Bérénice* at the Comédie-Française in 2009; the second, a transcultural performance at the 2010 Avignon Festival entitled *Pour en finir avec Bérénice* (*To Put an End to Bérénice*). In very different ways, these two productions confront the same challenges: Does staging the seventeenth-century canon entail more than the transmission of elite values and national patrimony? Or can such a staging serve as a means to reappropriate the canon and, in so doing, generate a critique of its perpetuation? Is it possible for *Bérénice*—which deeply incarnates the theory of the king's "two bodies" that grounded seventeenth-century absolutism—to speak to, and for, a postcolonial moment? How can you speak the language of a play when that language excludes you?

Here the objective is not an analysis of Racine's text itself, but rather a reflection on the politics of the text's uses on stage with three interlocking pedagogical aims:[2] first, to encourage students to interrogate both universalizing and patrimonial readings of seventeenth-century tragedy in order to show that the early modern canon is composed of texts open to reappropriation and hybridizations, and that it can be made relevant to a number of historical temporalities; second, to invite students to think about the ideological uses of seventeenth-century tragedy for nationalistic purposes, and in so doing, to show them the ways in which theater is deeply enmeshed in social structures and power relations; and, third, to train students to analyze the mise-en-scène of a dramatic text, bringing to light the inherent ambiguity of theatrical signs on stage, and the fact that these signs are always open to interpretation—that is, when they are not irreducibly opaque.

Linyekula's *Bérénice* diptych provides material for two modules, one for each of the two productions that this essay focuses on. Taking texts and images available online as our starting point, we will first introduce students to some of the basic choices that comprise Linyekula's stagings of Racine: set design, costumes, historical references, casting, acting, and textual modifications. Next, we will frame a set of questions to ground classroom discussion, which will highlight the political importance and sociohistorical relevance that Linyekula invests in *Bérénice*. Finally, we will provide an analysis of the critical reception of Linyekula's productions in order to push students to examine the persistence of universal values—especially when those values are linked to neoclassical tragedy—within contemporary French culture.

Before plunging into specific analyses of the production, it is necessary to provide some historical context (see O'Toole). A dancer, choreographer, and theater-maker, Faustin Linyekula was born in Zaire in 1974, under the rule of the president-dictator Joseph-Désiré Mobutu. After more than a half-century as a Belgian colony (1908–60), in 1997, Zaire became the Democratic Republic of Congo (DRC). Linyekula studied literature and theater at the University of Kisangani, but in 1993 the government closed the country's universities and Linyekula went into exile and settled in Nairobi. There, in 1997, with the mime Opiyo Okach and the dancer Afrah Tenambergen, he created Gàara, the first contemporary dance company in Kenya. In 2001, Linyekula returned to the DRC and founded the Studios Kabako, a collaborative arts platform dedicated to dance, music, and video, in the rural community of Lubunga. The platform serves as a site for both artistic and technical training, cultural events, and residences for artists from the DRC and from abroad.

Linyekula's approach hinges on the conviction that culture can rehabilitate broken communities. His multidisciplinary works combine autobiography, historical references, popular music, and urban culture in order to explore the effects of Congolese history on the body and to affirm the need for collective action in the face of political chaos. Since the early 2000s, Linyekula has undertaken residencies in choreography in France. In 2007, he produced *Dinozord: The Dialogue Series III* and *Le festival des mensonges* (*The Festival of Lies*) at the Avignon Festival and directed *La fratrie errante* (*Siblings Adrift*), by Marie-Louise Bibish Mumbu, at the Théâtre du Vieux-Colombier. That same year, Linyekula received the Grand Prix from the Prince Claus Foundation for Culture and Development. In 2009, he produced *more more more . . . future* at the Kunstenfestival in Brussels and the Festival d'Automne in Paris, which was composed of an all-male ensemble of dancers and centered on Congolese *ndombolo* music. When Linyekula undertook his interpretation of Racine's *Bérénice*, he was at once locally anchored in Congolese culture and globally renowned, especially in European theatrical circles.

Bérénice, Comédie-Française, March 2009

In 2009, as part of a decade-long campaign to generate hitherto unseen encounters between the French repertoire, artists from different cultural and artistic horizons, and the company's actors, the director of the Comédie-Française, Murielle Mayette, invited Linyekula to stage a neoclassical text. By choosing *Bérénice*, Linyekula became the first African artist to stage Racine's play (see Program).

What most interested Linyekula in *Bérénice* were the changes undergone by the titular character, the queen of Palestine, who is banned from Rome because of her "oriental" origins: "Le personnage principal de la pièce *Bérénice* incarne l'exclusion même, du fait de son identité étrangère. . . . *Bérénice* raconte une expulsion. Cette question me paraît essentielle, elle seule donne un sens à ma présence aujourd'hui à la Comédie-Française" 'The main character of *Bérénice* incarnates exclusion itself, due to her identity as a foreigner. . . . *Bérénice* tells the story of an expulsion. This theme seems to me to be essential—expulsion alone gives meaning to my presence at the Comédie-Française today.'[3] For Linyekula, the tragic destiny of Bérénice resonates with his compatriots' exodus from the African continent and their often precarious situations: "Je ne peux travailler ici sans penser à mes amis congolais, arrivés sur le territoire français pour tenter leur chance, et qui se trouvent aujourd'hui dans des situations irrégulières, sans papier . . . expulsé[s]" 'I cannot work here without thinking of my Congolese friends, who come to France to try their luck, and find themselves today struggling, without papers . . . expelled" (Linyekula, "*Bérénice*: Un quartet improbable"). The parallel with contemporary European politics of migration has a second—local—parallel with the current Congolese political situation:

> La question d'étrangeté est également pertinente au Congo, où l'on se déchire depuis plusieurs années autour du concept de la "congolité." L'appartenance se réduit partout à une question de sang, alors qu'elle devrait être à mon sens une question d'histoire partagée. Qu'est-ce qui fait que l'on reste ou non un étranger? (Linyekula, "Faustin Linyekula")
>
> The question of foreignness is equally pertinent to Congo, where we have been tearing each other apart for years over the concept of "Congo-ness." Belonging is always reduced to a question of blood, when, the way I see it, it should be a question of shared history. What should determine whether one remains a foreigner or not?

Bérénice's story also resonates with the feeling of foreignness felt by Linyekula upon his arrival at the Comédie-Française, which he responded to by adopting the distant attitude of an ethnologist:

> For me it was as if I were visiting a pygmy village. In a way, I turned ethnography on its head. At the end of the nineteenth century the Europeans came to study us as wild, strange animals. At the beginning of the twenty-first century I decided to study the strange behavior of a French tribe . . . in the heart of Paris . . . called the Comédie-Française. (Rollhäuser 36)

Thus, it was neither the characters' psychology nor the weight of transcendental destiny that interested Linyekula in Racinian tragedy. Rather, his approach had a twofold aim: to render relatable the history of exclusion (of the foreigner, of difference, of the body) and to make space for a history that has more to tell.

Description of the Performance

A number of specific dramaturgical choices characterize Linyekula's mise-en-scène (see Tonelli). "Il s'agit en effet d'une distribution inattendue tant les acteurs semblent à première vue entretenir des liens peu naturels avec leurs rôles" 'The casting has an unexpected quality, such that the actors seem to have a particularly unnatural relationship to their roles,' the director has said ("*Bérénice*: Un quartet improbable"). A man of Iranian origin, Shahrokh Moskhin Ghalam, plays the role of Bérénice; a woman, Céline Samie, plays Antiochus; Bakary Sangaré, the first actor of African origin to be part of the Comédie-Française, plays Titus; and every confidant, Arsace, Phénice, and Paulin, is played by the same actor, Bruno Raffaelli.

The set is almost entirely bare. Eleven costumes belonging to the Comédie-Française's collection hang from a clothing rack at stage right. Among these costumes are two sets of armor fit for a Roman emperor. At the beginning of act 2, Titus puts one of them on, and then discards it at the end of act 3. The program indicates that the armor was worn by Richard Fontana, who played Titus in Klaus Mikaël Grüber's staging of *Bérénice* in 1984, one of the most striking productions of the last fifty years at the Comédie-Française. At stage left, there is a leather armchair. And toward the back of the stage, there is a white tarpaulin rolled into a ball, into which Titus plunges headfirst after the long hypotyposis in which Bérénice recounts the spectacular splendor of his coronation.

The actors are present on stage for the entirety of the show. A number of scenes are acted almost without any movement at all, facing the audience. When they move, the actors walk slowly, tracing rectilinear trajectories; in act 5, they follow the line of a circle that they have traced with chalk on the ground. The majority of movements are composed of facial twitches, faint gestures, slight choking, and sudden breath. Concerning this aesthetic of "trembling," Linyekula has said:

> Mais parmi les mots mêmes, un terme revient, régulièrement, souvent: le verbe trembler. . . . Qu'est-ce qui tremble à ce point dans le corps de Bérénice? . . . La dimension chorégraphique de mon travail se situe dans ce mouvement simple, parfois imperceptible; cet état physique qui affecte la manière de dire, les émotions, les décisions, les mots eux-mêmes. C'est le tremblement. ("*Bérénice*: Un quartet improbable")

> Among the words themselves [in the play], one, in particular, recurs, routinely: the verb "to tremble." . . . What does it mean to tremble like this in Bérénice's body? . . . The choreographic dimension of my work lies in the simplicity of this movement, which is so often hardly perceptible—and yet, such a physical state affects ways of speaking, emotions, decisions, words themselves. Trembling.

Once more, the combination of minimalist gestures with speech at once intense and muffled recalls—at least for those members of the audience attuned to such lineages—Grüber's previous mise-en-scène.

Racine's text is performed in its entirety, with the exception of act 3, of which only the first scene is retained: Titus reads his part from a piece of paper into a microphone. It is also important to note that scenes 1–4 of act 5, during which Bérénice decides to leave, take place in total darkness; the light returns gradually at the beginning of scene 5, at which point the queen declares, "Me voilà résolue" 'Here I stand, determined' (5.1.1315), before plunging headfirst into the white tarpaulin at the back of the stage, echoing Titus's similar collapse at the end of act 1.

Toward the end of the performance, the white tarpaulin is hung at the back of the stage. Once the last words are spoken, and Titus is alone on stage, photographs of Senegalese *tirailleurs* are projected onto the tarpaulin—after they fought for France and were repatriated to Dakar in 1944, these soldiers were shot by French forces at the Thiaroye transit camp when they mutinied against discrimination and the revocation of their military pension.

Discussion Questions

Based on this descriptive presentation of the most remarkable elements of the production, the class discussion will attempt to grasp the ways in which Linyekula invests Racine's tragedy with a striking array of meanings. To move beyond the descriptive to the interpretative stage, we suggest three interrelated avenues of questioning: What are the effects produced by the "unexpected casting"? What is the place given to the body in the mise-en-scène of the play? Does Linyekula update *Bérénice*, or does he historicize it? The paragraphs to follow do not exhaust the possible answers to these questions, but they outline a number of relevant directions in which the discussion can be led.

The transcultural and transgender casting prompts an intersectional reading that exhibits the entanglement of race, gender, and ethnicity in the mechanisms of exclusion dramatized in Racine's text. Importantly, it is the actors portraying the two characters from the "Orient," Bérénice and Antiochus, who are playing against gender. This inversion also underscores the shaking up of the patriarchal order embodied by Bérénice. Linyekula describes her as "masculine, presque virile dans ses décisions" 'masculine, almost virile in her decisions' as she stands before a trembling emperor, who himself is at once wordless and tearful; "c'est elle qui, alors même que les sentiments et les apparences se décomposent au fil de l'action, semble décider de la progression de la tragédie et de son dénouement même" 'even as feelings and appearances dissolve over the course of the action, it is [Bérénice] who seems to decide the direction, even the outcome, of the tragedy' ("*Bérénice*: Un quartet improbable").

More generally, each actor is faced with a fundamental foreignness with regard to the role that he or she is tasked with performing. Thus, it is not only the foundational exclusion of an absolutist-imperialist order that is emphasized (as reflected by the queer Bérénice), but also the internal division that comes with incorporation into a system of domination (as reflected by the transcultural Titus). "Le fait d'être étranger, aux autres et à soi, est au cœur de mon propos . . . C'est cette tension du déplacement, celui des codes et des perceptions, que je recherche comme point de départ d'une exploration" 'The fact of being foreign, both to others and to oneself, is at the heart of my project. . . . I look for the tension of displacement, that of codes and perceptions, as my point of departure' (Linyekula, "*Bérénice*: Un quartet improbable"). The dramaturgy of "displacement" allows Linyekula to consider the function of his own exteriority, as both an African and a choreographer, within the Parisian theatrical institution that has invited him to be a part of it. The choice of the Black actor Bakary Sangaré to play Titus, the Roman emperor who is reluctant to assume the persona that his title demands, is particularly striking in this regard. Indeed, such a choice provides an image of the challenges of a Congolese choreographer working within the Comédie-Française and reappropriating a French neoclassical tragedy that the critical tradition has long associated with pure textuality.

This comment offers the opportunity to direct students to the second question for discussion: In what ways does the mise-en-scène work to emphasize the tensions between body and speech? Titus's collapse, after the description of his coronation, and Bérénice's, after her decision to leave, onto the white tarpaulin offer a striking visual transposition of the crushing weight of normative discourse. The restraint produced by the aesthetic of "trembling" renders especially palpable the cries and moans that escape a body painfully subjugated by the law. Titus's donning and then removal of the armor, as well as the scripted reading of his soliloquy in act 3 from a microphone, signals his reluctance to take on the behavioral and discursive traits of his social position. In turn, the mise-en-scène of act 4, in which Bérénice's words resonate in a set steeped in darkness as she is making the decision to leave the man she loves, suggests the erasure of the body demanded by the absolutist order.

Moreover, the geometrization of the actors' displacements translates on stage the conventions imposed by alexandrine verse on the body, as well a visual realization of the border that is about to separate the two lovers and cultures. The tragic destiny of Racine's characters does not follow a thread (*Bérénice*, we should remember, is a tragedy with no peril of death), but a line. The circle traced in chalk at the beginning of act 5 materializes a space in which the margins are strictly separated from the center. Linyekula's production elicits a ceremonial tragedy in which everything seems to obey strict constraints; gestures can only be hinted at; and speech only ever emerges from within a heavy silence, trembling.

Still, Linyekula does not offer a dehistoricized reading of neoclassical tragedy. The third question for discussion concerns the heterogeneous temporalities assembled on stage. As we have noted, the director makes a discreet yet direct reference to Grüber's 1984 mise-en-scène, which had been a key event in the twentieth-century history of the Comédie-Française. The subtle memory pervading the spectacle suggests that staging Racine always requires an engagement with the "great" productions of the past. And just as the character of Titus can hardly bear the role of emperor imposed on him by his illustrious ascent, so, too, the actor playing Titus must confront the phantasm of Richard Fontana (incarnate in the armor):

> Il ne s'agit pas d'enfiler ces costumes, mais de les observer comme des objets témoins de l'histoire: comment le comédien qui incarne Titus peut-il négocier avec le costume de Richard Fontana? La question de la succession est alors posée; question prégnante dans la pièce alors que Titus succède à Vespasien. ("*Bérénice*: Un quartet improbable")
>
> The task is not to put on these costumes, but to regard them as testimonial historical objects. How can an actor playing Titus navigate the fact of Richard Fontana's costume? Thus, the question of succession emerges—a question very much alive, too, in the text, as Titus succeeds Vespasian.

Linyekula relates the sedimentation of theatrical tradition to a practice of conservation that he sees at work in French culture more generally:

> Je suis . . . frappé par le caractère muséal de la Comédie-Française, qui conserve ses archives, ses costumes, les détails des costumes, ses accessoires, certains de ses décors ou de ses toiles. On garde ici les traces du passé, on les liste, on les archive. J'ai grandi dans un pays où le passé s'efface systématiquement.
>
> I am . . . struck by the museum-like quality of the Comédie-Française, which preserves its archives, its costumes, the details of its costumes, its props, its sets. Here, we conserve traces of the past, we make lists out of them, we archive them. I grew up in a country in which the past was systematically erased.

In place of the "traces" of an artistic past, the spectator will be made to substitute another past: that of the West African soldiers who served France in World War II and were massacred by the French army at the Thiaroye camp. How should we interpret this sudden anachronism? The passage from one history (of a theatrical patrimony) to another (of colonialism) seems to point to the amnesia built into French national mythology. By projecting the portraits of slain Senegalese soldiers, the director confronts the audience with the faces of those whose existence has been denied by the dominant powers and written out by official historiographies.

The students will be prompted to comment on how these final images invite the spectator to reread *Bérénice* through the prism of both colonial history and present-day discrimination: "[Bérénice] est en quelque sorte le tirailleur sénégalais avant la lettre; elle est l'ancêtre des jeunes Africains qu'on expulse à coups de charters" 'In a sense, [Bérénice] is the Senegalese soldier avant la lettre. She's the cousin of the young Africans that we regularly kick out on cheap flights' (Linyekula, "Faustin Linyekula"). While juxtaposing two experiences of oppression—the foreign queen banned from imperial Rome and the African soldiers oppressed by colonial powers—the denouement of the play nonetheless does not say anything explicit about the link between the two. The students' attention should thus be drawn to the fact that the spectator is left to determine the relationship between the Roman Empire and modern colonialism.

What kind of history is Linyekula pointing us toward? Is such a history ongoing, or discontinuous, or both? Bérénice and the colonized would seem, here, to be victims of two systems of domination, absolutism and colonialism, which are parallel, but linked by forces other than historical causality. Or is Linyekula suggesting a genealogy of colonial practices and discourses? We need only remember that *Bérénice* was written at a moment in which the kingdom of Louis XIV was beginning to lay the foundations of French imperialism. In any case, Linyekula makes theater into a site of militant reflection, in which the canon is made to "tremble" in order to resurrect the memory of those that history has forgotten.

Reflections on the Reception

We conclude the unit by asking the students to analyze several reviews and interviews published on the occasion of the play's opening. I suggest assigning the readings without providing the political or institutional affiliations of the comments' authors, and inviting the students to identify the ideological and cultural biases in each piece by focusing on what components of the production are privileged, and what dramaturgical choices are ignored or criticized. By doing so, students can better appreciate the nature of theater criticism as an evaluative discourse that is not just a discussion of aesthetics, but is also shaped by ideological filters.

Three commentaries are worth considering. First, that of Murielle Mayette, the director of the Comédie-Française:

> La mise en scène de Faustin Linyekula, sans les grands costumes historiques, sans même le recours spectaculaire à son savoir-faire de chorégraphe, rend l'universalité de la pièce. D'un seul coup, elle nous raconte que les grands orages à l'intérieur du corps, les ravages de la passion, peuvent tomber dans chaque cœur, quels que soient le sexe ou l'époque.

> Faustin Linyekula's mise-en-scène, which refuses the grand costumes and postures of the past, which refuses, even, the artist's own choreographic practice, renders palpable the universality of Racine's text. With great force, the play teaches us that the body's interior torments, the ravages of passion, can befall any human heart, regardless of sex or epoch.

Second, that of a journalist for *Le Nouvel Observateur*, a left-leaning weekly magazine:

> [C]ette *Bérénice* est enfin une métaphore de l'expulsion. La pièce se conclut par un hommage aux tirailleurs sénégalais, renvoyés chez eux sans remerciement ni demande de pardon. Toute la question étant de savoir, si pour cette ultime provocation, Linyekula ne connaîtra pas le même sort. ("*Bérénice*: Un alien au Français")
>
> [I]n the end, this *Bérénice* is a metaphor for expulsion. The piece concludes with an homage to Senegalese soldiers, who were sent home without ever being thanked or asked for forgiveness. We might wonder whether Linyekula will suffer the same fate for making such a provocation.

Finally, that of a theater critic for *Figaro*, a daily conservative publication:

> La troupe de la Comédie-Française interprète la fameuse pièce de Racine dans une mise en scène absconse. . . . Pourquoi un micro et une mélodie, trop forte d'ailleurs, pour accompagner la tirade de Titus (Bakary Sangaré, non crédible)? Que comprendre quand les protagonistes se jettent sur la bâche qui servira d'écran à la fin pour projeter des images de tirailleurs africains? Quel symbole ce cercle tracé à la craie sur la scène par les protagonistes?
>
> Ni le talent indéniable des comédiens, ni l'histoire intemporelle d'un dilemme entre l'amour et le devoir ne réussissent à toucher le cœur du public. Ce dernier reste comme en retrait du drame qui se déroule sous ses yeux. Indifférent, vaguement curieux. Reste, par bonheur, un texte fabuleux sur les égarements d'une âme tiraillée par des désirs d'honneur et de gloire.
>
> The Comédie-Française's troupe offers an abstruse interpretation of Racine's famous text. . . . What is the need for a microphone and a song to accompany Titus's soliloquy (played, not so credibly, by Bakary Sangaré)? What are we meant to understand when the protagonists throw themselves onto the tarp that later serves as a screen onto which photographs of African soldiers are projected? What does the circle traced in chalk on the ground symbolize?
>
> Neither the undeniable talent of the actors, nor the timelessness

> of the dilemma between love and duty, are able to touch the heart of the audience. We remain at a distance from the drama that unfolds before our eyes. Indifferent, half curious. Nonetheless, the text happily remains a powerful depiction of a soul driven mad by the desires for glory and honor. (Simon)

By celebrating the universality of Linyekula's *Bérénice*, Mayette's praise—it is worth remembering that Mayette commissioned the show—generates a surprising kinship with the biting criticism of the *Figaro* journalist: both reproduce the myth of a "timeless" Racine, and in so doing, both refuse to engage with Linyekula's militant updating of the play. Mayette covers over Linyekula's contemporary stakes entirely, while the *Figaro* journalist denounces it. Both reactions, above all, reveal the immovability of audience expectations when an artist aims at the monuments of cultural patrimony: to "update" Racine, as the article in *Le Nouvel Observateur* suggests, remains a "provocation."

We can begin, then, to see why, the following year, Linyekula conceived *Pour en finir avec Bérénice*, which explores the ways in which the image of French neoclassical tragedy as a universal cultural object has been historically constructed.

Pour en finir avec Bérénice, Avignon Festival, July 2010

Initially, Linyekula's project had been to stage two parallel productions, one with the actors of the Comédie-Française, the other with his own actors from Kisangani. But in response to the lukewarm reception of his first *Bérénice* in Paris, and in the wake of the fiftieth anniversary of Congo's independence, he chose instead to create an adaptation of Racine's text entitled *Pour en finir avec Bérénice*. This adaptation was staged in Angers, and then in Kisangani, before it was accepted in July 2010 for the sixty-fourth Avignon Festival, where Linyekula was the sole sub-Saharan African artist invited (Press dossier [Festival d'Avignon]; "Faustin Linyekula pour *Pour en finir*").

> Je me suis . . . rendu compte que mon travail sur le théâtre classique ne pouvait pas s'arrêter là. Pour le finir, il fallait emmener Racine dans mon monde, le faire entrer en résonance avec les questions linguistiques, culturelles, politiques qui se posent aujourd'hui au Congo. D'autant que cette pièce, où se joue le destin d'une princesse amoureuse d'un empereur romain qui va la rejeter car Rome ne veut pas d'elle à cause

> du sang oriental qui coule dans ses veines, se prête à une lecture actualisée. (Linyekula, "Faustin Linyekula")
>
> I realized . . . that my work on neoclassical theater could not stop there. In order to finish it, I had to bring Racine into my world, I had to make him resonate with the linguistic, political, and cultural questions that define Congo today. Indeed, the play—in which a princess is in love with a Roman emperor who ultimately rejects her because of the "Oriental" blood running through her veins—lends itself to a contemporary reading.

In order to "update" *Bérénice*, Linyekula deterritorializes Racine and stages the text with Congolese actors:

> Plonger ce texte, comme un espace clos, avec ses propres règles, ses propres logiques, dans la réalité du Congo aujourd'hui, et observer comment cette réalité peut infiltrer, contaminer *Bérénice*. . . . Comment le français résistera-t-il à des bouches qui ne le maîtrisent pas? Comment la tragédie pourra-t-elle ou non se transformer, prise en charge par des corps et des histoires différentes? (Press dossier [Theatre National de Chaillot])
>
> The goal is to immerse [Racine's] text—with its own rules, its own logics—into the reality of Congo today and to see how this reality can infiltrate and contaminate *Bérénice*. . . . How will the French language resist tongues that have not mastered it? How will the tragedy change, or not, when occupied by different bodies and different histories?

By approaching the tragedy from within the African territory, and by putting it into contact with dance and Congolese music, Linyekula returns us to the question of the universality of Racine's text. *Pour en finir avec Bérénice* deconstructs the notion of cultural community by introducing the idea of alterity, and in so doing, it reveals both the processes of literary canonization and the role that canonization has played in colonial domination.

Description of the Performance

The stage setup is simple: a long table; six wooden chairs; clumps of earth and stones scattered across the floor; stage right, a suspended ladder, which does not touch the ground, and leads nowhere, beneath which a circle is drawn in red earth; and stage left, a white tarpaulin rolled up in a ball, with a microphone and a bowl of water in front of it (see Zeizig). It is worth noting that the show was performed outdoors at Avignon, in the Cloître des Carmes, a venue that that is at once open and simultaneously a symbol of enclosure, both a patrimonial monument and a site of appropriation, where theatre occupies a religious space.

In a prologue, an actor facing the audience introduces the world of the play, taking a real story as inspiration. In the 1950s, a Belgian professor of French, André van Keulmans, founded the first theater troupe in Stanleyville (the colonial name of Kisangani), which was composed of students from the Athénée Royal, a school for European children. On the night before Congolese independence, van Keulmans decided to stage *Bérénice*. Racine's queen, exiled to Rome, and then expelled, was meant to serve as an image of the colonist, anguished because he was about to be forced to leave the country he considered his own. "Comment peut-on se sentir étranger dans son propre pays?" 'How can one feel like a foreigner in one's own country?' the prologue comments ("Pour en finir" [*YouTube*] 00:24–00:33; "*Pour en finir*" [*Théâtre Contemporain*] 00:46–00:51). The declaration of independence prevented van Keulmans from finishing his production. This, the prologue declares, is the work that the actors of Linyekula's production wish to take up: "Nous avons retrouvé les traces de cette production. C'est notre point de départ" 'We've come upon traces of this production. It's our starting point' ("*Pour en finir*" [*Théâtre Contemporain*] 01:12–01:23). The show introduces itself, thus, as the "trace" of an interrupted project, which it intends not to reconstruct, but to reappropriate for the present moment—a group of Congolese actors will perform a show once conceived by a Belgian colonist for European actors.

By way of a second introduction, the spectator is made to witness a kind of ritual sacrifice. Linyekula lies on the ground facedown within the circle of red earth beneath the ladder. The six actors—three men, three women—are dressed in contemporary clothing (T-shirts, dresses, trousers) and their faces are painted white; they begin to circle Linyekula, gazes fixed on his trembling body, rhythmically tapping stones together before hurling them at him (see "Pour en finir" [*YouTube*] 00:57–01:12).

As a whole, the show takes place in a heteroglossic mode, with a plurality of languages, discourses, registers, and systems of signs functioning at multiple levels. Taking "le livre abandonné auquel il manque des pages" 'the abandoned book with missing pages' that they have found as their starting point, the actors, their faces covered in white, and wearing Versailles-style wigs fashioned out of cotton, declaim excerpts from *Bérénice*:

some excerpts are read at the table; others are acted; others are danced. The actors change parts over the course of the play, and at certain moments two passages are superimposed on each other (see "Pour en finir" [*YouTube*] 01:13–01:34).

In one scene, young Congolese students attend a class in which *Bérénice* is translated into Lingala, one of the four Bantu languages spoken in the DRC; in another, a student recites *Le corbeau et le renard* (*The Crow and the Fox*), by Jean de La Fontaine, in a French so mechanical that one gets the impression the student understands nothing of what she is saying. "La langue française a tué le pays" 'The French language killed this country,' one actor says at some point (*Pour en finir*). A constellation of heterogenous discourses alternates with Racine's verses. First, we hear the speech given by Patrice Lumumba, the inaugural president of an independent Congo, on 30 June 1960:

> La République du Congo a été proclamée et notre cher pays est maintenant entre les mains de ses propres enfants. Ensemble, mes frères, mes sœurs, nous allons commencer une nouvelle lutte, une lutte sublime qui va mener notre pays à la paix, à la prospérité et à la grandeur. Nous allons établir ensemble la justice sociale et assurer que chacun reçoive la juste rémunération de son travail. ("Discours" 199)
>
> The Republic of Congo has been proclaimed and our beloved country's future is now in the hands of its own people. Brothers, let us commence together a new struggle, a sublime struggle that will lead our country to peace, prosperity and greatness. Together we shall establish social justice and ensure for every man a fair remuneration for his labor. ("Speech" 45)

Further on, we hear an assortment of news reports and radio advertisements. The actors routinely step out of their roles to comment on the play, on the foreignness of its language, and on its meaning, and to evoke the conditions of Congolese nationals. The recent history of war in Congo is evoked: "2,5 millions . . . Non 3. —Mais non il y a eu cinq millions de morts. Je vous dis qu'il y en a eu quatre, cinq!" '2.5 million . . . No, three. —No, no, five; five million dead. I'm telling you, there were four, five million!' And, in turn, the question of what it means to engage in theater in the current context of their country is asked: "Peut-on jouer une tragédie dans un pays qui *est* une tragédie? . . . Est-il seulement possible de faire du théâtre dans un pays où la parole sur la place publique ne circule pas?" 'Can one perform a tragedy in a country which *is* a tragedy? . . . Is it even possible to do theater in a country where public speech has no life?' (*Pour en finir*).

Throughout the entire performance, Linyekula, bare-chested, in shorts, dances to the music of the guitarist Flamme Kapaya within the circle of red earth drawn beneath the ladder. His body convulses improvisationally, alive with fluids and tremblings, which suggest a stabbing pain. At one moment, an actor performs Titus's speech from the second scene of act 2, "Hélas! à quel amour veut-on que je renonce!" 'Alas! how ardent is the love that they want me to deny!' by way of a dance on the ground directly parallel to Linyekula.

In the last part of the performance, the actress who has been playing Bérénice washes the white makeup off her face with water from the bowl on the ground, and then proceeds to wash the face of each of the other actors as they circle around her, banging rocks together (see "*Pour en finir*" [*Théâtre Contemporain*] 02:32–03:17). In the performance's final moments, a slow, moving circle forms around Bérénice (played by a new actress), who lies, lifeless, on the floor: a new sacrificial victim. The piece ends with a quote from the sociologist Stuart Hall, whose work on the connections between power, identity, and culture assailed the amnesia induced by colonial power: "On m'a demandé ce que je venais faire quand je suis arrivé en 1951 en Angleterre" 'The first time I came to England in 1951, someone asked me, 'Why are you here?'' Hall said. "Et j'ai répondu: je viens terminer le voyage colonial. . . . Vous avez façonné ma vie et je suis venu vous regarder dans les yeux" 'I answered: I am here to complete the colonial journey. . . . You shaped my life, I came to look you in the eyes" (*Pour en finir*).

Discussion Questions

This performance clearly opens multiple avenues for discussion with students. In particular, it paves the way for an introduction to the postcolonial politics of contemporary theater, which will be sketched out in the following paragraphs.

Pour en finir avec Bérénice takes up the "canonical counter-discourse" that Helen Tiffin identifies as a recurrent trait of postcolonial literature. This discourse works to reinvest texts from the European canon "from the cross-cultural standpoint of the imperially subjectified 'local'" in order to reveal the canon's ideological biases and usages and, in turn, to question both its authority and its aesthetic value (Tiffin 23; see also Gilbert and

Tompkins). Linyekula shows the ways in which supposedly universal cultural values were imposed by the colonial education system through the teaching of French neoclassical tragedy; in so doing, he makes theater into a counter-hegemonic device that reveals the extent to which the dramatic canon is a historicized construct that serves European hegemony. In order to achieve this, Linyekula creates what M. Jacqui Alexander calls "palimpsestic time" (190). The time on stage (the story of Bérénice), the time of the text's creation (the Versailles-style wigs), the time of its later reception (education during the colonial period), and the present, unfolding time of Euro-Africans (the play's performance both in Congo and in Avignon) are all juxtaposed within the same dramatic frame in order to generate postcolonial interrogation.

The diglossic dimension of Linyekula's production makes the current uses of the French language in Congo one of the main questions raised for reflection. French was imposed as an official language at the end of the nineteenth century by the Belgian king Leopold II, and was maintained throughout the colonial period; it continues to dominate education, journalism, politics, business, and cinema, even though the vast majority of the population has not mastered it: "Comment parler de démocratie dans un pays où toute la vie publique est en français, des médias au gouvernement, une langue que maîtrise seulement 10% de la population?" 'How can we speak of democracy when all of public life—the media, the government—is in French, and only ten percent of the population speak it fluently?' ("Portrait").[4] Racine's text becomes the embodiment of the linguistic power exercised by colonial culture. The two school scenes described above, as well as the differences in the six actors' abilities to grasp the form of the alexandrine, show that the French of "high" culture has functioned as a tool of marginalization. French, that is, has been the site of a communication breakdown, the source of a fracture between the masses, the ruling classes, and Western elites.

What to make, then, of the two ritual sacrifices—the dancer at the beginning, Bérénice at the end—that frame the play? The opening stoning that Linyekula stages emblematizes the silenced Black body, which is at once an object of the colonial gaze and violently subjected by white power. This ritual, further, points to the experience of abjection that colonialism instills in the colonized (thus the "white masks" that encircle Linyekula). As for the ritual sacrifice of Bérénice, is it simply a mirroring of the opening sacrifice, suggesting that the banishment of a foreign queen from imperial Rome provides a historical analogy for the effects of colonialism on its subjects? Or could it be a postcolonial invitation to sacrifice *Bérénice*—the neoclassical French tragedy par excellence—and, thus, to root out the colonial heritage from Congolese culture? Would such extirpation resonate with the manner in which Bérénice cleans the white makeup off the other actors' faces at the performance's end?

Such an emancipation, perhaps, would provide a space for the colonized to find their own language with which to speak the experience of exclusion, and to free themselves from the dramaturgic forms of "high" (i.e., French) theatrical culture. The two ritual sacrifices frame Linyekula's production with a double erasure: first, of Congolese culture, which invalidates the notion that it would be possible to return to a precolonial identity; second, of the colonizing culture incarnate in Racine, which provides the conditions for the Congolese people to take "[their] beloved country's future" "into [their] [own] hands," as the projection of Lumumba's 1960 speech suggests.

At this point, it would make sense to turn the discussion to the meaning of the ladder suspended at the back of the stage, which nobody climbs, as if the weight of the past were too great to overcome. Is the ladder, perhaps, the image of a Congolese people caught between the abyss of stolen history and the search for a path—yet unfound—of their own? The adaptation of a seventeenth-century tragedy becomes the occasion for a reflection on the tragic instability of postcolonial identity, or, an occasion to uncover what Frantz Fanon called "zones of occult instability," wherein the oppressed can forge meaning of their own (Fanon 182).[5] A national Congolese culture independent of its colonial ties does not yet exist, and so a new local identity remains to be invented: "C'est mon sentiment. L'impression que nous n'avons pas de fondation et qu'on ne sait pas où on va. Mais les corps résistent" 'This is what I feel. We have no ground to stand on, and we do not know where we are headed. But bodies resist' ("*Pour en finir*" [AFP]).

How does the resistance of the body manifest itself? Here, Linyekula's unceasing dance provides a key element for reflection. Within the context of a performance focused on the residues of colonialism, the dance introduces the subjective perspective of embodied experience and shows the ways in which collective memory lives within the body. Could we say, then, that the dance constitutes a ritual of countermemory aimed at official amnesia? Does it work to exhume the local—sacrificed—history that lives on in the Congolese body? "Ma danse pourrait être une tentative pour me souvenir de mon nom" 'My dance could be an attempt to remind myself of my own name,' Linyekula says ("Entretien"). Does his tormented body express the pain of a colonized body subject to a foreign language? Or are its many contortions rather the expression of the freedom of a body that refuses to be submitted to the symbolic system of colonial culture? The circle drawn in earth within which Linyekula's dance takes place traditionally functions as the sacred site in which the living meet the dead and the yet to be born, but here it may also signal the vestigial cultural power of the colonizer and the paradoxical suffering that the colonized undergo in order to free themselves from the colonial past that constitutes them. Through this intercultural unsettling and unresolved traffic, Bérénice and *Bérénice* become figures of the schizophrenic divide between colonial heritage and freedom.

But it is worth noting, still, that Linyekula's dance does not only contain a message; it seeks to create an image. In so doing, Linyekula distances himself from the long-standing cliché of neoclassical tragedy in which meaning is founded on the musicality of the verses only. More generally, he troubles the Western model of representation, which is founded on the preeminence of the text.

> [L]e territoire mental, mais aussi le territoire géographique, physique, historique que j'essaie de partager, sont éminemment instables. C'est comme si je me trouvais en face d'un tas de ruines, et il me faut construire un abri avec ces ruines. . . . Les acteurs prennent la parole pour évoquer le quotidien congolais qui se mêle aux vers raciniens. J'ai jeté mon corps de danseur au milieu de ce brouhaha et de ces ruines. Pour moi, le théâtre est toujours une question de corps: un corps qui parle, qui chante, qui danse, qui crie. (Linyekula, "Faustin Linyekula")
>
> [T]he mental territory, but also the geographic, physical, and historical territories, which I am trying to share, are eminently unstable. It is as if I found myself before a pile of ruins, and I had to construct a shelter out of them. . . . The actors speak about Congolese daily life and mix it with Racine's verses. I threw my dancer's body into the middle of this mess and these ruins. For me, theater is always a question of the body: a body that speaks, sings, dances, cries out.

The "cry" of the body imposes the "non-signifying presence" that Paul Rae identifies as the surplus of insoluble difference that characterizes contemporary cosmopolitan theater (21). Such presence does not entirely undo the discursive system: the moment in which the actor playing Titus dances with Linyekula as he delivers the soliloquy in act 2 shows that the performance stages both the disjunctions and the possible conjunctions between the physicality of modern performance and the textuality of neoclassical tragedy.

The stakes of Linyekula's production, then, are the revitalization of that which has been sacrificed and tossed away—both the culture of the colonized and the corporeal matter of French seventeenth-century tragedy. The performance works against the erasures of official historiography and the conformism of critical tradition, which flow from the same gesture of concealment: the concealment of the material determinations of history and culture.

The remaining question concerns the effect of Linyekula's production in a context such as the Avignon Festival, which is emblematic of the cultural institutions of the Global North. The following year, the production was performed in two of the greatest theaters of the French language: the Théâtre de Chaillot, in Paris, and the KVS Theater, in Brussels. *Pour en finir avec Bérénice* participates in "intercultural theater" as it has recently been redefined.[6] The new interculturalism is "no longer dominated by charismatic white men," but consists in "performance-from-below" by non-Western minority voices (Knowles 59). By combining various modes of performance, including theater, dance, and music, as well as the performance of everyday life, interculturalism "creates representations that are unbound and open, and potentially resistant to forms of imperialist culture" (Lo and Gilbert 47; see also Fischer-Lichte). Far from reproducing cultural hierarchies or feeding the fantasy of an euphoric synthesis of cultures, it works to transform modes of contact, rendering visible frictions, power relations, and intercultural blockages. The citation from Stuart Hall that closes Linyekula's play embodies its force in nuce: Like Stuart Hall in Great Britain in 1951, Linyekula came to Avignon in 2010 to "look in the eyes" of its white majority, to interrogate the ownership of colonial memories, and to trouble fixed narratives of identity. In other words, *Pour en finir avec Bérénice* turns the Avignon Festival into a site for a collective (re)negotiation between local and global relations, between different historical temporalities, and between different cultural forms.

We can return, then, to the production's title: Is "the end of Bérénice" the end of the debate? Does Linyekula's version sever ties with its neoclassical precedents? Does it mark the close of (neo)colonialism?

Reflections on Reception

It should be of no surprise that the reception of *Pour en finir avec Bérénice* was mixed. Below are three possible articles for students to read and to reflect on the ways in which increasing emphasis was given to Linyekula's race and ethnicity in the reviews of the time. Most of the journalists praised the postcolonial politics of the production:

> Pourtant, ce que propose Faustin Linyekula dans la paix du Cloître des Carmes n'est pas une mise en pièces du chef-d'oeuvre de Racine, mais une interrogation profonde sur le rapport entre la culture, le colonisé, le colonisateur. Sur la manière dont une oeuvre peut être interprétée par un Africain, fruit de sa tradition et de sa langue originelles mais nourri des lettres françaises, de Baudelaire, de Rimbaud. (Mereuze)

> What Linyekula offers amidst the peace of the Cloître des Carmes is not an ode to Racine's masterpiece, but a profound interrogation of the relations between culture, colonizer, and colonized. He shows the ways in which such a work can be interpreted by an African, nourished by his traditions and original languages, but also nourished by French literature, by Baudelaire, Rimbaud.

The magazine *Les Inrockuptibles* similarly praised Linyekula's politics, with a review entitled "Festival d'Avignon: Congo, pour en finir avec l'amnésie" ("The Avignon Festival: Congo, to Put an End to Amnesia"), in which they celebrate his production as a "trop rare" 'truly rare' event in French culture (Arvers).

However, when the production was performed at the Théâtre de Chaillot, an article attacking the production, entitled "Pour en finir avec la complaisance" ("To Put an End to Overindulgence"), was published on the Web site of the *Nouvel Observateur*.

> Il est assurément de notre devoir d'Européen de tendre la main et d'aider avec vigueur des artistes issus de pays comme le Congo qui ont traversé une guerre effroyable du fait de leurs propres tyrans, sans doute soutenus en sous-main par des intérêts occidentaux . . . Mais fallait-il faire venir en Europe ce spectacle conçu par Faustin Linyekula et donné par des "comédiens" qui ne sont jamais que de piètres amateurs ou alors des débutants sans talent particulier? N'y a-t-il pas une frontière à maintenir entre travail social, aussi remarquable soit-il, et travail artistique présenté dans de hauts lieux du théâtre? . . . [L]es quelques vers de Racine qui subsistent sont massacrés, ânonnés de façon affligeante par des "acteurs" qui font peine à voir et dont il est proprement

> indécent d'exhiber la faiblesse en public. Cela de surcroît dans le cadre d'un festival de théâtre qui se veut le plus brillant du monde. Et aujourd'hui dans celui du Théâtre de Chaillot. (Gubernatis)
>
> It is surely our duty as Europeans to offer a helping hand to those artists fleeing from countries like Congo, which have experienced horrible war due to tyrants undoubtedly aided by Western powers. . . . But was it necessary to bring Faustin Linyekula's production to Europe, and to perform it with "actors" who are nothing more than paltry performers, or at best, talentless beginners? Is it not worth preserving some kind of border between activism, however remarkable, and the art of our greatest theaters? . . . [T]he few verses of Racine that subsist are massacred, monotonously recited in a painful manner by "actors" who hardly make themselves visible and are hardly fit for the stage. Such are the excesses of a festival that sees itself as the world's greatest festival, which, today, spill over into the Théâtre of Chaillot.

This article unleashed a lively debate. An article denouncing the offensive neocolonialism of the *Nouvel Observateur* critique soon appeared, describing the first sentence quoted above as "inacceptable," or "incredible":

> Elle sous-tend qu'un artiste congolais, africain ne peut être programmé parce qu'il est talentueux. Pourquoi toujours renvoyer les créateurs "africains" à leurs origines? . . . Si le spectacle est raté pour certains, pourquoi ne pas le considérer simplement comme tel? Certes Faustin Linyekula évoque son pays, à partir de son histoire. Mais tous les artistes le font. Il parle d'en finir avec *Bérénice*, comme symbole de la violence de la colonisation par le langage et montre la difficulté à dire cette langue imposée.
>
> It implies that a Congolese, African, artist cannot be commissioned [simply] because he is talented. Why must we always send the "African" artists back to their origins? . . . If certain critics consider the performance to be a failure, why not simply critique it as it is? Of course Faustin Linyekula evokes his country and its history. All artists do that. He speaks of the end of *Bérénice* as a symbol of the colonial violence done by language, and shows the difficulty of speaking such a violently imposed language. (Doumbia and Bély)

This polemic speaks for itself: it is clear that Linyekula is onto something when he insists on the political dimension of the dramatic canon in *Pour en finir avec Bérénice.*

I present these works within a course aimed at attuning students to theater as a social practice, in which institutional, ideological, and historical factors directly influence dramaturgical choices and aesthetic judgment. It is therefore valuable to add a final perspective to the discussion by pointing out to students that Linyekula's Racinian productions were presented a year apart at the Comédie-Française and the Avignon Festival, the two institutions that most function as makers and markers of value in the fields of theater and performance in France.

Founded in the seventeenth century by Louis XIV, the Comédie-Française is the largest national stage in France, and the only one to have a resident troupe; historically, it has functioned as the protector of theatrical patrimony, staging (if not exclusively) canonical authors, well-known actors, and established directors. On the other side, the Avignon Festival was founded in 1947 by Jean Vilar in order to encourage young theater-makers and the creation of popular theater, and has since served as the site of legitimation for emerging artists and forms. Do the Comédie-Française's commissioning of Linyekula and the Avignon Festival's programming of his work point to a recognition on the part of France's cultural institutions that the country's colonial past is integral to its national history?

Regardless, the diversity of the reception that Linyekula received in France demonstrates that certain sectors of the public continue to resist such a recognition—and that this resistance is linked to the persistence of a sacred image of Racine's tragic oeuvre. At the same time, the movement, paradoxical in some ways, that led Linyekula from the French national repertory theater to the more innovative Avignon Festival invites us to recognize the fundamental vitality of the neoclassical canon, which is ever susceptible to serving as a political theatrical laboratory that features, questions, and reconfigures cultural value.

Notes

This article benefited from a EURIAS fellowship at the Paris Institute for Advanced Study (France), cofunded by Marie Skłodowska-Curie Actions, under the European Union's Seventh Framework Programme for research, and from funding from the French state, Programme Investissements d'Avenir, managed by the Agence Nationale de la Recherche (ANR-11-LABX-0027-01 Labex RFIEA+).

1. See Francois Cusset, who discusses the *querelle du canon* (also known as the "canon wars" for the frequent virulence that marred the debates) that shook up not only the humanities but the American university as a whole (15).

2. For an overview of the main trends in the contemporary stagings of Racine, see Guyot.

3. All translations from French are my own.

4. Out of forty-two million inhabitants, the RDC has four million French speakers.

5. On the relation between postcolonial theater and "zones of occult instability," see Hutchison.

6. The notion of intercultural performance is an umbrella term, and slippery, and therefore one of the most notoriously debated concepts in theater and performance studies. This is not the place to enter into the details of the historiographical critique of the category.

Works Cited

Alexander, M. Jacqui. *Pedagogies of Crossing: Meditations on Feminism, Sexual Politics, Memory, and the Sacred*. Duke UP, 2005.

Arvers, Fabienne. "Festival d'Avignon: Congo, pour en finir avec l'amnésie." *Les Inrockuptibles*, 19 July 2010, lesinrocks.com/2010/07/19/scenes/scenes/festival-davignon-congo-pour-en-finir-avec-lamnesie/.

Barthes, Roland. *On Racine*. Translated by Richard Howard, U of California P, 1992.

Bérénice. Written by Jean Racine, directed by Faustin Linyekula, produced by Comédie-Française / Théâtre de Gennevilliers / Studios Kabako, 26 Mar.–7 May 2009, Studio-Théâtre of the Comédie-Française, Paris.

"*Bérénice*: Un alien au Français." *Le Nouvel Observateur*, 15 Apr. 2009.

Cusset, François. *French Theory: Foucault, Derrida, Deleuze et Cie et les mutations de la vie intellectuelle aux États-Unis*. La Découverte, 2005.

Doumbia, Eva, and Pascal Bély. "L'article inacceptable de Raphaël de Gubernatis dans le *Nouvel Observateur*." *Le Festivalier*, 14 Apr. 2011, festivalier.net/2011/04/raphael-de-gubernatis/.

Fanon, Frantz. *The Wretched of the Earth*. Translated by Constance Ferrington, Penguin Books, 1990.

"Faustin Linyekula pour *Pour en finir avec Bérénice*." Press conference. *Théâtre Contemporain*, 16 July 2010, theatre-contemporain.net/video/Conference-de-presse-du-16-juillet-1828.

Fischer-Lichte, Erika. "Interweaving Cultures in Performance: Different States of Being In-Between." *New Theater Quarterly*, vol. 25, no. 4, 2009, pp. 391–401.

Gilbert, Helen, and Joanne Tompkins, editors. *Post-colonial Drama: Theory, Practice, Politics*. Routledge, 1996.

Gubernatis, Raphaël de. "Pour en finir avec la complaisance." *Le Nouvel Observateur*, 31 Mar. 2011, nouvelobs.com/culture/20110330.OBS0532/spectacle-pour-en-finir-avec-la-complaisance.html.

Guyot, Sylvaine. "Les mises en scène modernes de Racine." *Théâtre complet*, by Jean Racine, edited by Sylvaine Guyot and Alain Viala, Classiques Garnier, 2013, pp. 1143–72.

Hutchison, Yvette. "'Zones of Occult Instability': A South African Perspective on Negotiating Colonial Afterlives through Intercultural Performance."

Interculturalism and Performance Now: New Directions?, edited by Charlotte McIvor and Jason King, Palgrave Macmillan, 2019, pp. 153–79.

Knowles, Richard Paul. *Theatre and Interculturalism*. Palgrave Macmillan, 2010.

Linyekula, Faustin. "*Bérénice*: Un quartet improbable." Interview by Piette Notte. *Studios Kabako*, kabako.org/txt-entretiens/berenicequartet.html.

———. "Entretien avec Faustin Linyekula." Interview by Irène Filiberti. *Studios Kabako*, kabako.org/txt-entretiens/entretien.html.

———. "Faustin Linyekula: 'La congolité n'est pas une question de sang.'" Interview. *Jeune Afrique*, 13 July 2010, jeuneafrique.com/196000/culture/faustin-linyekula-la-congolit-n-est-pas-une-question-de-sang.

Lo, Jacqueline, and Helen Gilbert. "Toward a Topography of Cross-Cultural Theatre Praxis." *TDR / The Drama Review*, vol. 46, no. 3, 2002, pp. 31–53.

Lumumba, Patrice. "Discours prononcé lors de la cérémonie de l'indépendance à Léopoldville le 30 juin 1960." *La pensée politique de Patrice Lumumba*, edited by Jean Van Lierde, Présence Africaine, 1963, pp. 198–201.

———. "Speech at the Ceremony of the Proclamation of the Congo's Independence." *The Truth about a Monstrous Crime of the Colonialists*, Foreign Languages Publishing House, 1961, pp. 44–47.

Mayette, Murielle. "*Bérénice*, l'étrangère universelle." *Magazine du Conseil général des Hauts de Seine*, May-June 2009.

Mereuze, Didier. "*Bérénice*, une tragédie africaine." *La Croix*, 21 July 2010, la-croix.com/Culture/ActualiteBerenice-une-tragedie-africaine-_NG_-2010-07-20-554557.

O'Toole, Sean. "My True Country Is My Body." *Frieze*, 23 Nov. 2016, frieze.com/article/my-true-country-my-body.

"Portrait. Faustin Linyekula. L'échappée belle." *Les Inrockuptibles*, 14–20 Apr. 2009.

Pour en finir avec Bérénice. Written and directed by Faustin Linyekula, Avignon Festival, 17–24 July 2010, Cloître des Carmes.

"Pour en finir avec Bérénice." *YouTube*, uploaded by QuaiTV, 4 Dec. 2012, youtube.com/watch?v=5_5Qe5tedsk.

"*Pour en finir avec Bérénice*: Extraits Vidéo." *Théâtre Contemporain*, uploaded 16 July 2010, theatre-contemporain.net/video/Pour-en-finir-avec-Berenice-extraits-video.

"*Pour en finir avec Bérénice*: Spectacle sur la douleur identitaire au Congo." AFP Agence France-Presse, Angers, 13 May 2010.

Press dossier for *Pour en finir avec Bérénice*. Festival d'Avignon, 2010, Cloître des Carmes, studylibfr.com/doc/8750331/faustin-linyekula-pour-en-finir-avec-Bérénice.

Press dossier for *Pour en finir avec Bérénice*. Théâtre National de Chaillot, 2011.

Program for *Bérénice* at the Studio-Théâtre of the Comédie-Française, Paris. 2009, comedie-francaise.fr/www/comedie/media/document/programme-berenice0809.pdf.

Rae, Paul. "Where Is the Cosmopolitan Stage?" *Contemporary Theatre Review*, vol. 16, no. 1, 2006, pp. 8–22.

Rollhäuser, Lorenz. “The Studios Kabako.” Radio playscript. *Presence of the Colonial Past—Afrika auf Europas Bühnen: A Reader on the Focus of the Theaterformen Festival Braunschweig 2010*, Festival Theaterformen, 2010, pp. 36–42, www.academia.edu/5455464.

Simon, Nathalie. “Une Bérénice déchue.” *Le Figaro*, 31 Mar. 2009, lefigaro.fr/theatre/2009/03/31/03003-20090331ARTFIG00337-une-berenice-dechue-.php.

Tiffin, Helen. “Post-colonial Literatures and Counter-discourse.” *Kunapipi*, vol. 9, no. 3, 1987, pp. 17–39.

Tonelli, Victor. “*Bérénice*. F. Linyekula 2009.” Photographs. 10 Nov. 2016, www.victor-tonelli.com/-/galleries/berenice-flinyekula-2009.

Zeizig, Émile. “Pour en finir avec Bérénice.” Photographs. *Mascarille—Portail des photographes du spectacle vivant*, mascarille.com/galerie/index.php?/category/941.

Part IV

Tragic Politics: Between the Ancien Régime and the Present

Marc Bizer

Reflections on Free Will and (Self-)Governance in Racine and Contemporary Politics

Those who teach subject matter pertaining to the early modern must try to make the unfamiliar less strange and the foreign intelligible to their students. Increasingly, instructors are urged to make the cultural productions we study "relevant"—advice that is often offensive to specialists schooled in the necessity of understanding periods on their own terms and keenly aware of the current pressures to make the liberal arts increasingly vocational. Yet in teaching seventeenth-century French tragedy to undergraduates, it does seem wise to attempt to strike a middle ground between historicizing and modernizing. One can convincingly demonstrate both how Racine's tragedy was clearly grounded in concerns of the time and how those questions are surprisingly pertinent in the very different context of today. Indeed, in the sixteenth and seventeenth centuries in France, there was an intense focus on establishing parallels between governing a people and governing oneself. Perhaps less explicitly raised today, this topic is nonetheless truly apt. By focusing on problems of governance, we can help students not only grasp the genre of tragedy, but also learn both to discern the historical specificity of Racine's play and to reflect on problems of self-governance among governmental leaders in our own time.

In France, the rebirth of tragedy coincides more or less with the outbreak of the sixteenth-century Wars of Religion; this was no coincidence, for theatrical tragedy seemed extremely appropriate for giving expression to experiences that were felt to be tragic; prefaces to tragedies often stressed the parallels between the tragic subjects represented on the stage and historical events. Since these traumatic wars left deep scars, inscribed in the Edict of Nantes itself, which mandated *oubliance* ("forgetting"), seventeenth-century playwrights observed in their approaches to subject matter, as the critic Thomas Pavel argued, an "art of distancing" with respect to recent history (see Pavel; Frisch). In terms of governance, the reinforcement of monarchical power in the seventeenth century reflected the will to avoid the strife that had pitted powerful aristocratic families against one another in the sixteenth century. This political evolution was accompanied by important aesthetic and stylistic transformations in which the seventeenth century often repudiated the excesses of the sixteenth (as in François de Malherbe's rejection of the Pléiade's poetry), preparing the way for neoclassicism. Nevertheless, it would be simplistic to divide these two centuries into walled gardens and ignore the threads of continuity across imposed, even artificial divisions. It is also the purpose of this essay to pursue some of these threads up to the present.

Without assuming any direct influence, it is very instructive, both in terms of having students compare contrasting worldviews and in highlighting the evolution of the theme of governance across two centuries, to use the treatment of free will and self-governance in Rabelais's comic novel to illustrate similar aspects of Jean Racine's late tragedy *Phèdre*. At the beginning of act 3, near the climax of the play, Phèdre is in disarray, having disastrously revealed to Hippolyte her feelings for him with the encouragement of her governess, Œnone, who had come to see Phèdre's passion in a more favorable light after receiving news of the death of Phèdre's husband, Thésée. I go over this scene slowly and carefully, choosing two students to play the roles of Phèdre and Œnone, and asking the class to listen and analyze Phèdre's laments and Œnone's responses to them. It is important to remind students that Thésée's absence has left a power vacuum that a successor, necessarily male, must fill: Will it be Hippolyte, Thésée's first son by another marriage, or one of Phèdre's sons? As we shall see, ensuring the political success of Phèdre's son is Œnone's main concern throughout most of the play. Phèdre, both in thrall to her passion and filled with despair over her rejection at the end of act 2 by Hippolyte (whose sword she seized to kill herself upon experiencing his reaction to her declaration), she blames Œnone for giving her hope (just as Œnone had used guilt to get Phèdre to reveal her secret in the previous act). Œnone recognizes Phèdre's dejection and urges her to move past her predicament by focusing her attention on taking the reins of power (3.1.755–58). Then Phèdre replies straightforwardly that she cannot govern a country given that she is incapable of governing herself:

> Moi, régner! Moi, ranger un État sous ma loi,
> Quand ma faible raison ne règne plus sur moi?
> Lorsque j'ai de mes sens abandonné l'empire?
> Quand sous un joug honteux à peine je respire?
> Quand je me meurs? (3.1.759–63)

> I reign? Shall I, shall I make laws of state
> When my poor reason reigns no more on me?
> When I have lost the empire of my senses?
> When I, so yoked by shame, can scarcely breathe?
> When I am dying?[1]

In François Rabelais's *Gargantua*, the giant Gargantua who at the end of the Picrocholine Wars has successfully defended his father's land against the choleric aggressor-king Picrochole, proposes to reward his key knight, the monk Brother John, by putting him in charge of a monastery. Like Phèdre, Brother John refuses to govern others ("de moyne il ne voulait charge ny gouvernement" 'of monks he wanted neither the responsibility nor the governance'), yet he does so not out of a sense of despair or helplessness, but rather out of a sense of modesty, echoing Socrates: "comment . . . pourrais-je gouverner autrui, alors que je ne sais me gouverner moi-même?" 'how . . . could I govern others, when I am unable to govern myself?' Then Brother John makes a counterproposal: he would like to be allowed to build a monastery according to his own conception: the Abbey of Thélème (190).

The Abbey of Thélème (whose name comes from the ancient Greek word *θέλημα* 'thelema,' signifying "the will") is full of paradoxes, constituting an anti-abbey in many respects. Not only are the inhabitants of Thélème the opposite of typical monastic characters (being handsome, wealthy, and cohabiting with the opposite sex), but the community's most salient feature is that they face no constraints at all: their only rule is "Do what you will" 'Fay ce que voudras.' This striking motto, which conflates a passage in Paul's first epistle to the Corinthians, "Quod vult faciat" 'Let him do what he will' (*King James Bible Online*, 1 Cor. 7.36), with another from Augustine's *Homilies on the First Epistle of John*, "dilige et quod vis fac" 'Love, and do as you will,' insists on charity, love, as the precondition to all Christian action (see Duval 172–85 and Screech 187–94). It presupposes that those who observe it are intrinsically good, since freedom for them always results in virtuous action; they have the "instinct, . . . aiguillon qu'ils appellent honneur et qui les pousse toujours à agir vertueusement et les éloigne du vice" 'instinct, . . . spurs that they call honor and which always drive them to act virtuously and keep them from vice' (Rabelais 203). Indeed, the Thelemites are always miraculously of one mind and continually led to do good by their free will without threat of punishment. They are also not merely seeking forbidden fruit in confirmation of the truism that we cherish whatever is illicit, but instead enjoying precisely a freedom customarily denied monks and nuns.[2] Nevertheless, lest we think otherwise, the Thelemites do not enjoy absolute freedom; Edwin Duval's incisive commentary on this passage clarifies that the Christian context of "Do what you will" as established by the writings of Saint Paul, Augustine, and Erasmus connotes "Christian conscience concerning all things indifferent" (172–73). In other words, these good Christians do not have complete freedom with regard to the tenets of Christian teachings but rather as far as discretionary matters are concerned (eating and drinking, for example).

In the world of Racine's tragedy, Trézène represents the negation of a utopia like Thélème. While Trézène does constitute a kind of community, it is an unstable dystopia that opens in chaos. Its royal inhabitants (Phèdre and Hippolyte) are pursuing the very fruit forbidden to them. When Thésée moved Phèdre to Trézène, Hippolyte was already living there in exile, sent by Phèdre in an attempt to stave off the passion that had begun when she saw him in Athens after marrying Thésée (1.3.269–316). Aricie, whose Pallantides brothers were killed by Thésée in a struggle for the throne, also resides there under a sort of house arrest. When act 1 opens, Hippolyte declares to Théramène, his tutor, that he is leaving to search for his father, who has been gone for six months, as well as to flee Aricie, whom he loves but whom Thésée was determined to prevent from having offspring, lest she avenge her fallen brothers. Last but not least, Phèdre is apparently dying of a mysterious illness. Soon after Œnone persuades her to reveal her secret, the messenger Panope appears in scene 4, announcing Thésée's death. The king's disappearance, coinciding with the peripeteia, entails that the community of Trézène effectively finds itself living in a misreading of the situation of Thélème: literally free to do whatever they want. Although they share with the Thelemites the fact that they are presumably "libres, bien nés, bien éduqués, vivant en bonne société" 'free, well born, well bred, living in good company' (Rabelais 203), the inclination to do good is greatly challenged for the inhabitants of Trézène, many of whom suffer from the most dreadful of seventeenth-century vices, namely passion.[3]

There is so much to draw students' attention to in act 1—and it is incumbent on the instructor to help students become more comfortable with this very unfamiliar tragic universe—that I usually find myself lacking the time to insist upon what I consider to be a very important point in the light of Racine's reuse of the "do as you will" theme after the news of Thésée's death. Whereas Œnone confesses that upon learning of Phèdre's passion, she understood why Phèdre wanted to die, she affirms that in the present circumstances different laws apply ("ce nouveau malheur vous prescrit d'autres lois" 'this new calamity prescribes for you other laws' [1.5.340]). This is a wonderful opportunity for students to discuss whether they agree that Thésée's reported death has changed the rules governing Phèdre's behavior, and whether legal actions are necessarily moral actions (one could introduce the example of the film director Woody Allen's marriage to his erstwhile companion Mia Farrow's adopted daughter Soon-Yi Previn as a similar case). Unlike in Thélème, freedom in Trézène is not limited to "things indifferent," for there are none; everything matters greatly. As Racine explains in his preface to the play, it is important to create an environment in which virtue is put to the test and where "Les moindres fautes y sont sévèrement punies" 'the slightest faults are severely punished' (819). In order to woo Aricie, Hippolyte, himself under the effects of passion, dispenses with his father's edict that Aricie never be allowed to marry. Phèdre, however, is the character who undergoes the harshest trial. When she is first being questioned by Œnone about the causes of her "mal" 'suffering,' Œnone asks her, "Vos mains n'ont point trempé dans le sang innocent?" 'Your hands have been scarcely been defiled by innocent blood?' (1.3.220), to which Phèdre responds, "Grâces au ciel, mes mains ne sont point criminelles" 'Praised be heaven, my hands have committed no crimes' (1.3.221). She then adds that she wishes her heart were as innocent as her hands, which could give rise to another lively discussion about belief systems in which thoughts themselves are considered sinful, and what the ethical difference is between thinking reprehensible thoughts and committing reprehensible acts.

Yet it is precisely at the beginning of act 3, when Phèdre's disarray is complete, that her "virtue," or what we could call nowadays her personal sense of responsibility, is most severely put to the test. Phèdre's refusal to govern despite Œnone's plea, because she recognizes that she is unable to govern herself, creates a split, a standoff, between the two. Phèdre is completely consumed by the personal, yet Œnone consistently views the situation in terms of political expediency and survival. Although the question of where fate ends (Phèdre's passion for Hippolyte has been fated as a punishment visited upon her grandfather, the Sun, by Venus) and personal responsibility begins is fundamental to the play, the two opposing forces are most equally matched at this climax point. In the turmoil of the first scene of act 3, Œnone is only able to get Phèdre to turn her thoughts to state governance by paradoxically (and tragically) rekindling her hopes of a union with Hippolyte. This leads catastrophically to Phèdre's declaration, which itself foreshadows the disaster to come: "Sers ma fureur, Œnone, et non point ma raison" 'Serve my madness, Œnone, not my reason' (1.3.792). Racine has brilliantly illustrated at this point how dependent the ability to rule is on self-control: having lost any ability to govern herself, Phèdre abandons her will to Œnone. Emboldened by the tacit approval, Œnone now proposes the exact crime which she feared Phèdre had already committed in act 1—namely, defiling innocent blood—by falsely accusing Hippolyte of having attempted sexual assault on Phèdre. In a precise echo of line 220, Phèdre has a glimmer of conscience when she asks, "Moi que j'ose noircir et opprimer l'innocence!" 'Would I dare to bear false witness?' (3.1.893), to which Œnone replies, "Mon zèle n'a besoin que de votre silence" 'All you have to do is remain silent' (3.1.894). This recalls typical gangster movie scenes, where Phèdre's Œnone would have said, "Say no more. I'll take care of it!" Yet the situation deteriorates further: Phèdre goes from being keenly aware of how wrong it would be to falsely accuse to acquiescing, allowing that very act to be committed in her name by an accomplice.

Because the interactions between Phèdre and Œnone in this act are situated precisely in the zone between accepting responsibility and acquiescence, act 3 provides an excellent opportunity for students to debate the extent of Phèdre's personal responsibility. It is therefore advisable at this point to ask the students to discuss briefly whether or not Phèdre should be held responsible if Œnone commits a crime in her name and without her explicit assent. The plot of this tragedy can lead to fruitful discussions about how allowing wrongdoing to occur without protest in certain situations in everyday life may lead to a crime. Indeed, underscoring Phèdre's abandonment of her own free will, Racine, in what is surely the most uncanny recall of the Abbey of Thélème's guiding principle in the play, causes Phèdre to consciously and explicitly seal her own fate by stating at the end of the scene, "Fais ce que tu voudras, je m'abandonne à toi. / Dans le trouble où je suis, je ne puis rien pour moi" 'Do what you will, I leave myself in your hands. / In the distress where I am, I can do nothing for myself' (3.1.911–12). One cannot help but conclude that, unlike the inhabitants of Thélème (but in accordance with Erasmus's own interpretation of Saint Paul's epistle), those of Trézène will not do the right thing when left to their own devices.

Turning now to the question of the relation between the exercise of personal self-control and the ability to occupy a leadership role, we can see how it intersects with contemporary debates about politicians' private behavior and their ability to conduct themselves ethically as public figures—and possibly allow a foray into comparing and contrasting contemporary political behavior on both sides of the Atlantic. Traditionally, the French public (and the French press) have had much more tolerance for the dalliances of their political leaders—and seen from this perspective, Racine would seem, much to the chagrin of the French, to be more American than French—but a turning point may have been reached with Dominique Strauss-Kahn. While head of the International Monetary Fund (IMF), Strauss-Kahn became the subject of a criminal investigation for sexual assault, after which a trial for organizing prostitution at a hotel in Lille made fully public a life of consorting with prostitutes and engaging in orgies. Once again, as a way of highlighting cultural differences between France and the United States, students could debate under what conditions the separation between private and public life should no longer be observed, and more specifically under what circumstances private proclivities or obsessions would prevent those in a position of responsibility from devoting themselves in a serious and sustained manner to their professional duties. While one must obviously be circumspect in raising contentious contemporary political issues in any class, if appropriate, one can surely ask students to find timely examples of deep conflicts between private "passions" (in the seventeenth-century sense of the word) and public duty in presidents and their administrations in the United States. To some extent, as evidenced by the Monica Lewinsky scandal, Bill Clinton was reminiscent of Phèdre: both aware of falling short of the mark and incapable of acting otherwise. More generally, an instructor could encourage higher-order thinking by asking students to comment on contemporary politics from the philosophical stance presented in the passage by Rabelais or the one by Racine.

Since both Rabelais and Racine ask us to reflect in profound ways on the effect of external constraints (or lack thereof), whether they be fate, laws, or familial ties, on our behavior, these texts offer rich opportunities for debates about whether people will indeed do what is ethically best on their own, and what sorts of constraints are appropriate. Moving to the context of the contemporary United States, questions such as whether citizens exercising their legal right to bear arms will act in the interest of public safety in doing so come to mind. At the same time, the issue of the appropriateness of rules and prescriptions has taken on new life in our own era, not only for individuals but also for corporations: insofar as American jurisprudence has recognized that they have "rights," one can also ask whether it is wise to trust that corporations will act ethically in a relatively unconstrained regulatory environment.

Perhaps precisely because Phèdre is depicted as being in the throes of passion, but also given the influence of entrenched patriarchal attitudes, students may have difficulty thinking about her as the queen that she is, as someone who governs. Thus, another question that could be contextualized and debated is the importance of Phèdre's gender for the play's engagement with the struggle between passion and public responsibility, since the female sex was historically considered to be more emotional and hence more unstable. Furthermore, while ancien régime monarchy may appear to have little in common with modern democracy, the interview with David Frost during which Richard Nixon eventually let slip the famous phrase, "Well, if the president does it, it's not illegal" ("Transcript") brilliantly illustrates that, not unlike Phèdre and beneficiaries of royal absolutism such as Louis XIV, even recent American politicians have been seduced by the idea that they might be above the law.[4]

Teachers might invite students to examine how Phèdre's willingness to evade responsibility ebbs and flows in the play. Just as the weakening of her will is gradual, so is the strengthening of her resolve. When, moved by a sense of remorse, she endeavors in act 4, scene 4, to intercede given Thésée's impetuous threats against his son, she abruptly loses her resolve as soon as an incredulous Thésée informs her of Hippolyte's defense that he loves someone else, Aricie. Through jealousy, Phèdre's passion is rekindled, leading to the extremely poignant and tense scene where, initially, Phèdre rages to an ever-strategizing Œnone, who is fearful that Phèdre will undermine the accepted plan, by overtly asking her to "perdre Aricie" 'kill Aricie' (4.6.1259). Then, suddenly, at the moment of anagnorisis (4.6.1264), Phèdre does an about-face, realizing finally that (in contrast with line 220), she does indeed wish to plunge her hands in the blood of an innocent, and thereby becomes fully conscious of the enormity of her crimes. It is telling that it is in the mouth of the ever-justifying Œnone (and not Phèdre) that Racine places the words that one can never overcome one's destiny: "on ne peut vaincre sa destinée" 'one can't conquer one's fate' (4.6.1297), followed by what must clearly be the ultimate excuse, yet one based on hubris: that even the gods themselves have suffered from illicit loves (4.6.1304–06). Nevertheless, Phèdre's last monologue before her final acknowledgement of guilt to Thésée appears to retreat from a full sense of responsibility. In what is surely an admonishment to the originally aristocratic audience of the play, and reflecting a hatred of court culture common to many prominent writers in both sixteenth- and seventeenth-century France, she condemns those in a position to give advice to rulers and those who inevitably flatter and encourage their impulses rather than correcting them: "Tous ceux, qui . . . par de lâches adresses, / Des princes malheureux nourrissent les faiblesses" 'All those, who . . . with base craft and guile / Feed the [weaknesses] of unlucky Princes' (4.6.1321–22). Furthermore, in her dying words to Thésée, Phèdre appears to be sliding back down the slippery slope toward irresponsibility insofar as she recognizes only fate and Œnone as determining factors in her guilt: "Le ciel mit dans dans mon sein une flamme funeste; La détestable Œnone a conduit tout le reste" 'Heaven in my heart kindled the fatal flame / Detestable Œnone did the rest' (5.7.1625–6). Students could be given excerpts from these different speeches and asked whether Phèdre contradicts herself; they should also decide to what extent they themselves consider Phèdre responsible for the crimes she committed.[5]

This leaves at least one question, one contradiction to be examined through discussion. How patriarchal and misogynistic was Racine's world-view? How do Phèdre's flaws compare to Thésée's? His character Thésée also showed himself to be highly prone to losing self-control, to being impulsive, and thereby losing the ability to distinguish right from wrong; furthermore, like his wife, Phèdre, but less passively, Thésée believes that he can avoid responsibility by asking someone else to do his dirty work for him (4.4.1134). As already seen, Racine claims that the slightest mistakes are severely punished in his play. There is considerable use of the word "monster" as it applies to different characters in the play—before the actual sea monster, the incarnation of Thésée's vengeance, appears at the end. I've found it useful to give a list of the different occurrences of the word *monstre* and ask students in groups to rank the characters in terms of the degree of their monstrousness.[6] Whereas the inhabitants of Rabelais's Thélème represent the epitome of physical and moral beauty, Racine's seeming inversion of that community results in a Trézène full of monsters of varying degrees of moral hideousness. Whereas relatively early in the publication of his Gargantuan chronicles, Rabelais was at least willing to consider the potential of human beings to reach the ancient Greek ideal of being *kalos kagathos* (both beautiful and good)—at the cost of being almost completely alike and of one mind—in Racine's worldview, the omnipresence of passion makes even this seem not only impossible, but dangerously naive. Surely this is the key to the tragedy of Phèdre.

Notes

1. The English translations of *Phèdre* come from the dual-language edition translated by Margaret Rawlings. In some cases, I have identified my interpretive divergences from this translation by offering alternatives in brackets. The translations of Rabelais's *Gargantua* are my own.

2. "Quand ils [les gens libres, bien nés . . .] sont affaiblis et asservis par une vile sujétion ou une contrainte, ils utilisent ce noble penchant, par lequel ils aspiraient librement à la vertu, pour se défaire du joug de la servitude et pour lui échapper, car nous entreprenons toujours ce qui est défendu et convoitons ce qu'on nous refuse" 'When they [free, wellborn people] are weakened and enslaved by vile subjection or constraint, they use this noble penchant, by which they would aspire freely to virtue, to undo the yoke of servitude and escape it, for we always undertake what is forbidden and covet what is refused us' (203).

3. According to Furetière's *Dictionnaire universel*, the primary meaning of "passion" is "souffrance corporelle" 'bodily suffering,' as in "The Passion of Christ," but the meaning pertinent to theater is "tout desir violent, ou inclination qui nous donne de l'affection pour quelque chose" 'any violent desire, or inclination which gives us affection for something' (my trans.).

4. Consider Donald Trump's actions vis-à-vis Ukraine that led to articles of impeachment being brought against him in January 2020 (see Feldman) or the outcome of the Supreme Court decision *Trump v. Vance* from July 2020, in which the president was deemed not exempt from subpoenas of his income tax returns.

5. After all, in accordance with Aristotle's requirements for a tragic hero, Racine states in his preface that Phèdre "n'est ni tout à fait coupable, ni tout à fait innocente" 'is neither entirely guilty nor entirely innocent' and that he has made her "moins odieuse" 'less hateful' than in ancient tragedies (817). On the subject of Phèdre's guilt, Georges Forestier's discussion in his Pléiade edition is an excellent starting point. For further reading, see Guyot; Lyons; Greenberg.

6. Phèdre describes herself to Hippolyte as a monster (2.6.703), then calls Hippolyte a monster (3.3.884). Thésée calls Hippolyte a monster (4.2.1045) and Phèdre calls Œnone a monster (4.6.1317) before, speaking to Thésée, Aricie alludes to Phèdre as a monster (5.3.1445–46). Finally, the monster sent by Neptune appears (5.6.1515–16).

Works Cited

Augustine. Homily 7. *Homilies on the First Epistle of John*, ccel.org/ccel/schaff/npnf107.iv.x.html.

Duval, Edwin. *The Design of Rabelais's* Tiers Livre de Pantagruel. Droz, 1997.

Feldman, Noah. "Is Trump Above the Law?" *New York Review of Books*, 16 Jan. 2020, nybooks.com/articles/2020/01/16/is-trump-above-the-law.

Forestier, Georges. "Phèdre et Hippolyte: Notice." Racine, *Œuvres complètes*, pp. 1611–39.

Frisch, Andrea. *Forgetting Differences: Tragedy, Historiography and the French Wars of Religion*. Edinburgh UP, 2015.

Furetière, Antoine. "Passion." *Dictionnaire universel*, 1690, xn—furetire-60a.eu/index.php/science/868133681-physique/729527763.

Greenberg, Mitchell. *Baroque Bodies: Psychoanalysis and the Culture of French Absolutism*. Cornell UP, 2001.

Guyot, Sylvaine. *Racine et le corps tragique*. PU de France, 2014.

King James Bible Online, kingjamesbibleonline.org/1-Corinthians-Chapter-7/#36.

Lyons, John D. *Kingdom of Disorder: The Theory of Tragedy in Classical France*. Purdue UP, 1999.

Pavel, Thomas. *L'art de l'éloignement: Essai sur l'imagination classique*. Gallimard, 1996.

Rabelais, François. *Gargantua*. 1534. Translation, preface, and notes by Guy Demerson, Points, 1996.

Racine, Jean. *Phèdre. Œuvres complètes, tome I: Théâtre-Poésie*, edited by Georges Forestier, Gallimard-La Pléiade, 1999, pp. 817–76.

———. *Phèdre*. Translated by Margaret Rawlings, Penguin Classics, 1992. Dual-language edition.

Screech, Michael. *Rabelais*. Gallimard, 1992.

"Transcript of David Frost's Interview with Richard Nixon." 1977. *Teaching American History*, 2020, teachingamericanhistory.org/library/document/transcript-of-david-frosts-interview-with-richard-nixon.

Toby Wikström

Exploring Early Modern Globalization through Seventeenth-Century French Tragedy

The development of French tragedy from the 1550s onward coincided with what is arguably the most important historical phenomenon of early modernity: the sudden increase in cross-planetary circulation of people, goods, capital, flora, fauna, diseases, and cultural practices whose profound and often destructive repercussions remain with us today. During a period commonly considered the golden age of French tragedy, the 1600s, France became increasingly embedded in a host of global trade and diplomatic networks stretching all the way to Mughal India and China via the Ottoman Empire.[1] By the time the tragedies of Pierre Corneille and Jean Racine appeared on Parisian stages in the seventeenth century, France, though far weaker than the expansive Asian empires, had established colonial outposts in North America, the Caribbean, and the Indian Ocean and had entered the Atlantic slave trade. Despite the rise of French neoclassical tragedy in this period of increased global contacts, the most acclaimed playwrights avoided directly staging the contemporaneous early modern intercultural encounters that we find in the tragedies of William Shakespeare (*Othello*, *The Tempest*) and Miguel de Cervantes (*Los baños de Argel [The Bagnios of Algiers]*).[2] The Moors in *Le Cid* are shadowy offstage figures who only serve to emphasize the greatness of the titular hero, while the cross-cultural encounter in *Bérénice* is set in antiquity, involving a Palestinian princess and a Roman emperor instead of early modern societies. In France, what I am calling "early modern cross-cultural tragic encounters" vanished from the tragic stage after Nicolas Desfontaines's *Perside* (1644) and did not resurface until Louis Ferrier de la Martinière's 1702 *Montézume*. Instead of a focus on connection, the tragic stage shifted to the portrayal of closed foreign worlds; for example, the most famous neoclassical tragedy with an exotic subject matter, Racine's *Bajazet* (1672), only represents interactions between Ottoman characters within the seraglio.

If, however, we widen our definition of French neoclassical tragedy to include the lesser-known, pre-Cornelian tragedy of the early 1600s, which similarly drew on the models and subjects of the ancients, the seventeenth-century French theatrical engagement of the global comes sharply into focus. Virtually unknown today, especially to undergraduates, a number of early- to mid-seventeenth-century French playwrights, including Jacques du Hamel, Nicolas Chrétien des Croix, Pierre Mainfray, and Desfontaines, explored contemporaneous globalization in the tragic genre, staging early modern border crossings, slavery, religious conversion, and other highly charged instances of cross-cultural encounters where European superiority was far from guaranteed.[3]

Teaching the plays exposes students to a rich vein of the French tragic corpus that has been overshadowed by the canonical works of Corneille and Racine. The definition of what the tragic genre was, what it discussed, and what it staged has been dominated by the models Corneille and Racine provide, but this narrowing of the tragic corpus obscures the diversity of subjects and people that the tragic label actually encompassed. In addition, teaching the global tragedy does more than expand the canon; it also allows students to grasp changing early modern attitudes toward globalization. By examining seventeenth-century views of world connectedness as presented on the tragic stage, students begin to historicize the contemporary globalization that they experience daily and that they often assume is a uniquely modern phenomenon.

This essay focuses on a pair of undeservedly obscure early-seventeenth-century tragedies that in my experience have proven especially productive in allowing undergraduates to explore the important topic of early modern and contemporary global connections: Chrétien des Croix's *Les Portugais infortunés* (*The Unfortunate Portuguese*) and the anonymous *Le More cruel (The Cruel Moor)*. Each is accessible to advanced undergraduate students and readily available in a recent edition with pedagogical footnotes and modernized spelling.[4] I will give background information on both plays, discuss their representation of globalization, and suggest ways of stimulating conversation in the classroom around these texts. I will conclude by discussing final assignments that prompt students to move beyond individual plays to think more expansively about the evolution of representations of the global on the seventeenth-century French tragic stage.

Les Portugais infortunés

Taking up questions of border crossing, international law, and ethnic diversity, Chrétien des Croix's 1608 tragedy uncannily echoes many of the issues that concern the globalized world today and is suitable for third- or fourth-year courses on seventeenth-century theater or senior seminars on topics such as cultural difference or colonialism. Composed by a Breton playwright, the tragedy was published in the cosmopolitan port city of Rouen, a flourishing center of international trade, publishing, and theater closely rivaling Paris in the early seventeenth century (Bardet 187–94; Mellot 61; Louvat-Molozay 17, 77). It is possible the play was staged there, although no traces of performances have been found. Appearing at a time when European knowledge of sub-Saharan Africa was still limited, Chrétien's tragedy is the first known French play to feature a contemporary sub-Saharan African setting and characters (Cohen 1–7; Curran 42–43). Like Shakespeare's roughly contemporary *The Tempest* (1611), Chrétien des Croix's play centers on the aftermath of a shipwreck. In this case, the playwright based his plot on written accounts of historically attested events: the loss of a spice-laden Portuguese galleon off the Cape of Good Hope in 1552 and the survivors' hostile encounter with a tribe in what is today Mozambique. In Chrétien des Croix's tragedy, the starving, wandering Lusitanians happen upon the Manicain tribe in a desert landscape. The Portuguese leader, Sose Sépulvède, seeks an audience with his counterpart, Mocondez, king of the Manicains, in order to request badly needed food and drink. Suspecting that the Portuguese have designs on his territory, Mocondez grants them a meeting on the condition that they surrender their weapons, a stipulation they accept. The Manicain king promptly has his men strip the defenseless foreigners of all their remaining earthly possessions and leaves them to die naked in the wastelands. Sépulvède watches his family perish from starvation before succumbing himself.

Comprising 2741 lines of alexandrine verse written in early-seventeenth-century French, *Les Portugais infortunés* might appear daunting to undergraduates. Yet there are strategies instructors can use to illuminate the play's rich and uncannily prescient meditation on issues of burning importance in today's world: the legal and ethical dimensions of border crossing, the question of hospitality toward refugees, and the topic of cultural relativism. One method particularly suitable for classes focusing on intellectual history is to focus on the prologue to the play as an excerpt. The prologue presents a debate between two allegorical figures on the justice of the right of passage (*ius perigrinandi*), one of the major issues for theorists of the Law of Nations (*ius gentium*), the early modern precursor to modern international law (Pagden 61). Over the course of 336 lines—an ideal length for an assignment and a seventy-five-minute-class session—the anti-expansionist Génie, or "Démon du cap de Bonne-Espérance" ("Demon of the Cape of Good Hope") squares off against the Christian archangel Raphaël, the "tuteur des voyageurs," or patron saint of travelers (713). Echoing avant la lettre twentieth-century critics of colonialism, the Génie furiously criticizes the European rapine of the world ("Les barbares qu'ils sont! privés d'humanité / Ravagent nos pays par leur impiété" 'These inhumane barbarians / impiously ravage our lands' [lines 103–04]) and vows to stop their exploitation of indigenous resources, particularly gold ("J'empêcherai pour moi qu'on tire de mes veines / Le métal qui leur coûte un million de peines" 'I will never let them extract from my veins / The metal that costs them a million travails' [89–90]).[5] Raphaël, on the other hand, praises European expansion, predicting that "la foi chrétienne / Abolira du tout la folle loi païenne" 'the Christian faith / Will wipe out the mad pagan law' (176–77), and declares that the Génie will not be able to stop the inexorable movement of European expansion beyond the Cape of Good Hope and into the Indian Ocean and beyond: "Ton Cap dorénavant sera libre passage / Pour voir de l'océan l'un et l'autre rivage, / Et pour aller encor prêcher en chacun lieu / De ce rond univers l'Évangile de Dieu" '[Christians] will freely round Your Cape / To cross the ocean / and preach the Holy Gospel / everywhere on the globe' (333–36).

This dispute over the justness of globalization presents numerous teaching opportunities. One productive approach is to ask students to try to determine which of the two parties, if either, triumphs in the debate, prompting them for specific evidence, such as each figure's rhetoric, the number of lines of dialogue they receive, and the order of their interventions. Does it matter that the Génie has the first word and Raphaël the last? My classroom experience suggests that discussion of this issue usually remains inconclusive. Once the students, in their examination of the finely balanced sides, have reached an impasse, I give a twist to the proceedings by asking them what, if anything, the two sides have in common. Finally, I ask them to relate the prologue to the rest of the tragedy. If given enough time to reflect (ideally in groups), students begin to realize that the situation of the Portuguese shipwreck survivors in no way conforms to either of the lofty theoretical positions on the right of passage embodied by the prologue's dueling theoretical figures. Neither avaricious conquerors nor missionaries selflessly propagating their faith, the Portuguese are refugees, and their requests for food and water raise the issue of *hospitality*, an ethical question ignored by the dueling parties in the prologue. The lofty theoretical binary opposition announced in the prologue fails to anticipate the radically different, third possibility offered by the concrete praxis of ground-level cross-cultural contact in acts 1–5.

Another effective teaching option for students who are not advanced enough to read the entire play is to assign just the prologue and the first act, in which the Portuguese stragglers encounter the Manicains. Besides allowing students to compare the prologue to the beginning of the onstage action, this selection gives students the opportunity to examine the messy ambiguity of early modern first encounters. In contrast to contemporaneous representations of European–extra-European intercultural communication as clear and unproblematic (Greenblatt 95), the cross-cultural interactions in the tragedy are shot through with misunderstandings and a fatal lack of symbolic transparency. The first group encounter between the Portuguese and Manicains in the tragedy indicates this handily, for both sides fail to understand each other's motives and unfamiliar symbolic practices. This encounter occurs when the Manicains (referred in this passage of the text as "Éthiopiens") catch sight of the approaching Portuguese while preparing a ceremony:

> *Chœur d'ethiopiens*
> Sus, que chacun de vous d'une gaillarde danse
> Solennise ce jour en toute réjouissance.
>
> *Autre du chœur*
> Comme avez de coutume, ensemble chantez,
> Femmes, et à vos voix nos pas seront comptés.

Autre du chœur
Quels hommes sont-ce là qui ont blanche la face?
Ce sont quelques larrons, fuyons de cette place. (2.1.697–702)

Chorus of Ethiopians
Dance, all, and with great joy
Celebrate the day.

Other member of chorus
As is your custom, sing, women,
And provide the rhythm for our dance.

Other member of chorus
Who are these white men?
They are thieves, let us flee.

In the next scene, the perspective shifts to the Portuguese, who describe the approach of a group of Manicains.

Choeur
Voilà venir les Noirs de leurs longs bois armés,
Ils portent mine d'être au combat animés.

Sose
Il ne les faut tuer, mais qu'on les épouvante:
Que chacun au combat fièrement se présente. (2.2.801–04)

Chorus
Behold the approaching Blacks armed with long poles,
They seem prepared for combat.

Sose
Do not kill them, only frighten:
Prepare, all, for combat.

Sose then orders the Portuguese to fire a warning shot at the advancing Manicains, with the result that the latter disperse in fright (2.2.809–10). Similar to the Manicains in the previous scene, the Portuguese here are unsure of the motives of the opposing party. The ambiguity of the characters' lines ensures that theatrical audiences and readers are also uncertain about the tribe's intentions.

When analyzing this scene in class, I adopt a twofold pedagogical approach. First, the class acts out the highly kinetic scene, an activity that ensures the students have grasped the text and actualized it in its natural performance conditions. Next, to unpack the ambiguity of the episode, students work in pairs and compile a list of questions spurred by the encounter. They might generate questions like the following: Are the Manicains, at least those who did not flee, carrying sticks, marching—perhaps in unison—and making certain facial expressions because they are in the midst of their original ceremony? Or are they conducting a welcome ceremony for the Portuguese? Or marching to attack the intruders? Are the various signs deployed—the sticks and facial expressions—ritual indications of hospitality or hostility? Of course, there is no clear answer, neither for the characters nor for the student spectator-readers. At the very least, however, the suddenness of the encounter in the desert and the mutual unfamiliarity of each side with the other's appearance, intentions, and symbolic practices captures well the untidy nature of cross-cultural first encounters during the era of early modern globalization.

Le More cruel

Published in Rouen at roughly the same time as *Les Portugais infortunés*, the anonymous *Tragédie française d'un More cruel envers son seigneur nommé Riviery, gentilhomme espagnol, sa demoiselle et ses enfants* (*French Tragedy of a Moor's Cruelty toward His Lord, the Spanish Nobleman Riviery, and His Lady and Children*), more commonly known by the abbreviated title *Le More cruel*, offers another prime opportunity for advanced undergraduates to think through global connections and cross-cultural relations in early modernity. As deserving of attention as it is unknown, this short but ambiguous exploration of some of the most historically charged manifestations of globalization—Christian-Muslim relations, slavery, and protoracial thought—is guaranteed to stir discussion in even the most reticent of classrooms.

Reflecting a widespread fascination with violent Moors in the early modern European cultural imaginary of which Shakespeare's *Tragedy of Othello, the Moor of Venice* (1604) is the most famous iteration, the tragedy stages in ghastly detail the revenge that a wronged Moorish slave enacts upon his master, the Spanish gentleman Riviery, and his master's family (Lochert 113).[6] Feeling penitent after beating his Moorish slave, Riviery frees his bondsman but retains him as a domestic servant. When Riviery is away hunting, the Moor imprisons his master's wife and three children in the family castle and rapes the wife. Notified of his family's imprisonment, the Spaniard rushes back from the hunt, only to witness the Moor propel his oldest son to his death from the top of the castle. The Moor then offers to spare Riviery's remaining sons if the Spaniard cuts off his own nose. Shut out of the castle, the patriarch has little choice but to uphold his end of the grisly bargain, only to see the Moor go back on his word, killing the other children, the wife, and, finally, himself, thereby denying Riviery any chance of revenge.

Alongside this provocative subject matter, a concrete reason for the play's assured success in the classroom is its convenient length of just under a thousand verses, which allows instructors with already packed syllabi to assign the play in two manageable portions for third-year courses or one for weekly senior seminars. In addition to suggesting activities that draw out the ambiguity of the tragedy, I will discuss methods for teaching *Le More cruel* alongside *Othello*. This classroom-tested approach allows students to take a comparative, transnational view of cross-cultural phenomena that were global rather than national in early modernity and that continue to resonate on a planetary scale today.

My strategy when teaching *Le More cruel* is to start at the beginning of the play and lead my students through a close reading of its daring opening monologue. Here, the Moor, having received a horrific beating from his master, appeals to the Prophet Mohammed for protection and justice:

> Ô Prophète Mahon qui as sous ta conduite
> Tout le peuple qui tient ta loi qui est écrite
> Regarde par pitié et par compassion
> Celui qui est tenu en telle extorsion. (1.1.1–4)
>
> O Prophet Mohammed who protects
> All the followers of Your written law
> Behold with pity and compassion
> He who suffers this bondage

I ask students to explore the implications of a Muslim captive praying to the prophet of Islam in a French tragedy performed before a French audience at a time when the Muslim faith was commonly perceived as a constantly expanding religion threatening to wipe Christianity off the face of the planet (Poumarède 15). Why begin the tragedy in such a manner? What effect might the invocation of a different religion with a distinct sacred law (however distorted by the typical orientalist equation of Mohammed with Allah Himself) have on French audiences and readers in the cosmopolitan port city of Rouen in the early seventeenth century, shortly after the end of a forty-year religious civil war opposing Catholics and Huguenots? How might audience members have felt about being included in the very intimate circuit of communication between a believer and his Prophet? And why does the Moor get the first word and cast himself as the wronged party in a tragedy whose title emphasizes his crimes, and not those of his master? Over the course of the discussion, my objective is to prompt students to think about the intertwined concerns exhibited here: dramatic expediency (the rhetorical necessity of conquering the audience at the beginning of the performance) and the representation of cross-religious contact (the invocation of an expansive world religion). Does the very exposure of an audience to animated invocations of Islam provocatively serve to expand the faith?

A second strategy, valuable for emphasizing the ambiguities of the tragedy and exploring its representation of early modern globalization, involves comparing the original print edition's illustrated frontispiece to the stage action. One of five woodcuts adorning the first, undated edition published by the eminent Rouen printer Abraham Cousturier, the frontispiece features the title of the play and, right beneath it, a depiction of the master Riviery striking the Moor with a baton (*Tragédie française* 556).[7] A liminal, paratextual element, the frontispiece might seem an authoritative representation of the text it illustrates by virtue of its position as the very first object seen by the reader and by virtue of its copresence with the text in the same physical volume. Asking the class to compare the image of the beating in the frontispiece to the title and, more broadly, to the plot events helps students puncture this facile assumption. In small groups, they generate a list of questions prompted by the frontispiece that can in turn be molded into the following pointed queries: Why does the title of the play emphasize the crimes of the Moor, whereas the first image that conditions the readers' reception of the text shows Riviery hitting the slave? Why does the illustration depict a scene that does not feature directly in the play but is only reported in the discourse of slave and master? Both the Moor and Riviery's claims to justice in the tragedy are contingent upon their differing accounts of an original transgression that the playwright deliberately leaves shrouded in ambiguity. Who chose to disambiguate the tragedy, and why? Furthermore, what attitude would the image of the large white man beating his small black slave have elicited in readers in early modern Rouen: compassion, perhaps, or cruel amusement?

Another option that has proven fruitful in the classroom is teaching *Le More cruel* alongside *Othello*. Both the anonymous French tragedy and the vastly more famous English work feature Moorish characters who answer malevolent provocation with poignant monologues of great pathos and homicidal acts. Since *Le More cruel* is short, advanced undergraduates in a weekly seminar should be able to prepare both texts for the same class. In a class with two seventy-five-minute sessions per week, the comparative reading might take three meetings. Ahead of the first session, I ask students to compare the use of geographic setting and references in each tragedy on the class electronic discussion board. This virtual conversation sets up an in-class conversation on the marginal status of the two Moorish characters in their respective societies, and on related, wider issues arising from the increasing connectedness of the early modern world. An efficient way of conducting this classroom exchange involves comparing the final monologues of the Moor (5.1.950–63) and Othello (the famous "Soft you, a word or two before you go") before they commit suicide (5.2.398–421). Here, the Moor appeals again to the Prophet before plunging to his death from the castle walls in order to evade capture, whereas Othello, after realizing his horrendous error in killing Desdemona, pleads with the assembled Venetians to tell his story accurately: "I pray you in your letters, / When you shall these unlucky deeds relate, / Speak of me as I am." (5.2.400–02). To focus our analysis, I hand out a side-by-side printout of the two monologues and ask students to work in pairs. We sift through the similarities and differences in the two Moors' articulation of their own marginality and in the playwrights' deployment of geographical references—the neutral "vagueuse onde" 'rolling waves' of the French tragedy (5.1.960) versus the complex, exotifying tropes of *Othello* ("must you speak . . . / of one whose subdued / eyes, / Albeit unused to the melting mood, / Drops tears as fast as the Arabian trees / Their medicinable gum" [5.2.403, 408–12]). Students develop an extranational perspective on issues that concern both tragedies; namely, religion, slavery, and protoracial thought. Of course, in early modernity as well as today, these issues went beyond the narrow confines of the nation and were European and indeed global in scope.[8] My ultimate pedagogical objective here, inspired by Susan Rubin Suleiman and Christie McDonald's call for a French global literary history (ix–xxi), is to align the scale of the students' reading practices—in this case transnational reading—with the global scale of the subject matter they are considering.

Tracing the Disappearance of the Global

I hope to have shown the pedagogical effectiveness of a pair of early seventeenth-century tragedies, *Les Portugais infortunés* and *Le More cruel*, for helping students understand early modern globalization. Not only do these plays shatter students' preconceptions of neoclassical French tragedy, but they also offer rich meditations on the grand historical forces of global connectivity. I conclude class discussion of this global tragedy with a question aimed at prompting student reflection on the tragic genre and the historical context: Why did the tragedy of early modern cross-cultural encounter die out in the middle decades of the seventeenth century as the neoclassical aesthetic became increasingly stringent? By grappling with the disappearance of the global in favor of tragedies situated in closed and historically remote worlds, undergraduates are asked to consider the important matter of French tragedy's evolution. They are better equipped to think about changing attitudes toward the global over the course of the 1600s and to read the canonical Corneille and Racine from a vantage point that is attuned to the nuances and shifts in how the portrayal of intercultural exchange differs from these earlier tragic versions. These insights can in turn help students think more profoundly about the evolving perceptions of globalization in their own time.

Notes

1. For discussions of early modern globalization, including its non-Eurocentric nature, see Charles H. Parker, *Global Interactions in the Early Modern Age, 1400–1800.* For French involvement, see, most recently, Patrick Boucheron and colleagues, *Histoire mondiale de la France* (*Global History of France*), and Faith E. Beasley, *Versailles Meets the Taj Mahal: François Bernier, Marguerite de la Sablière, and Enlightening Conversations in Seventeenth-Century France.*

2. In my book manuscript "Staging and Erasing the Global in Early-Modern France," in contract with Northwestern University Press, I argue that a combination of neoclassical poetic injunctions against representing excessively alien mores and the imposing royal usage of exotic performance within courtly entertainments celebrating French empire made the substantive, tragic performance of cross-cultural encounters all but impossible to stage.

3. Relevant tragedies by authors not covered here include Jacques Du Hamel's *Acoubar*, which critiques French imperial designs on Canada; Pierre Mainfray's *La Rhodienne, ou la cruauté de Soliman* (*The Rhodienne; or, The Cruelty of Soliman*), about the Ottoman conquest of Rhodes; and Nicolas Desfontaines's rewrite of Mainfray, *Perside, ou la suitte d'Ibrahim Bassa* (*Perside; or, The Suit of Ibrahim Bassa*). Of these, Mainfray's play is the most accessible to undergraduates, due to its brevity, its rich discussion of world conquest and religious conversion, and its availability in modern French.

4. Like Mainfray's plays, both tragedies are available in *Théâtre de la cruauté et récits sanglants en France* (*Theater of Cruelty and Bloody Stories in France*), edited by Christian Biet and colleagues.

5. This and all other translations to English in this essay are mine.

6. The playwright drew his plot from a novella that François de Belleforest had published in the 1566 volume of his *Histoires tragiques* (*Tragic Histories*) and which was based on a widely circulated anecdote of a master's brutal death at the hands of his Moorish slave. See Giovanni Gioviano Pontanus's *De obedientia* (*On Obedience*), Matteo Bandello's *Novelle* (*Tales*), and Jean Bodin's *Les six livres de la République* (*The Six Books of the Republic*).

7. The image is also available on *Gallica*: gallica.bnf.fr/ark:/12148/bpt6k706769/f2.item.

8. For arguments that the concept of race slowly formed as a result of global expansion and New World plantation slavery in particular, see Boulle 59–80.

Works Cited

Bandello, Matteo. *Nouvelles.* Translated by Adelin Charles Fiorato et al., vol. 3, Imprimerie nationale, 2002.

Bardet, Jean-Pierre. *Rouen aux XVIIe et XVIIIe siècles: Les mutations d'un espace social.* SEDES, 1983.

Beasley, Faith E. *Versailles Meets the Taj Mahal: François Bernier, Marguerite de la Sablière, and Enlightening Conversations in Seventeenth-Century France.* U of Toronto P, 2018.

Belleforest, François de. *Le second tome des histoires tragiques, extraites de l'italien de Bandel, contenant encore dixhuit histoires traduites & enrichies outre l'invention de l'autheur.* Robert le Mangnier, 1566.

Biet, Christian, et al., editors. *Théâtre de la cruauté et récits sanglants en France (XVI*e*–XVII*e *siècle).* Robert Laffont, 2006.

Bodin, Jean. *Les six livres de la République.* 1576. Vol. 1, Fayard, 1986.

Boucheron, Patrick, et al., editors. *Histoire mondiale de la France.* Seuil, 2017.

Boulle, Pierre. *Race et esclavage dans la France de l'Ancien Régime.* Perrin, 2007.

Chrétien des Croix, Nicolas. *Les Portugais infortunés.* 1608. Biet et al., pp. 711–804.

Cohen, William B. *The French Encounter with Africans: White Response to Blacks, 1530–1880.* Indiana UP, 1980.

Curran, Andrew. *The Anatomy of Blackness: Science and Slavery in an Age of Enlightenment.* Johns Hopkins UP, 2011.

Desfontaines, Nicolas. *Perside ou la suitte d'Ibrahim Bassa.* Toussaint Quinet, 1644. *Gallica*, gallica.bnf.fr/ark:/12148/bpt6k717388?rk=21459;2.

Du Hamel, Jacques. *Acoubar ou la loyauté trahie: Tragédie tirée des Amours de Pistion & Fortunie, en leur voyage de Canada.* 1603. Edited by Roméo Arbour, Éditions de l'Université d'Ottawa, 1973.

Greenblatt, Stephen. *Marvelous Possessions: The Wonder of the New World.* U of Chicago P, 1991.

Lochert, Véronique. "Le Maure cruel: Représentations théâtrales de la violence orientale." *Orient baroque / Orient classique: Variations du motif oriental dans les littératu'es d'Europe (XVI*e*–XVII*e *siècle)*, edited by Anne Duprat and Hédia Khadhar, Éditions Bouchene, 2010, pp. 113–27.

Louvat-Molozay, Bénédicte. *L' "Enfance de la tragédie" (1610–1642): Pratiques tragiques françaises de Hardy à Corneille.* PU Paris-Sorbonne, 2014.

Mainfray, Pierre. *La Rhodienne ou la cruauté de Soliman.* 1621. Biet et al., pp. 660–92.

Mellot, Jean-Dominique. *L'édition rouennaise et ses marchés (vers 1600–vers 1730): Dynamisme provincial et centralisme parisien.* École des Chartes, 1998.

Pagden, Anthony. *Lords of All the World: Ideologies of Empire in Spain, Britain and France c.1500–c.1800.* Yale UP, 1995.

Parker, Charles H. *Global Interactions in the Early Modern Age, 1400–1800.* Cambridge UP, 2010.

Pontanus, Giovanni Gioviano. *Opera omnia soluta oratione composita.* Edited by Anton F. W. Sommer, Im Selbstverlag, 2004.

Poumarède, Géraud. *Pour en finir avec la croisade: Mythes et réalités de la lutte contre les Turcs aux XVIe et XVIIe siècles.* PU de France, 2009.

Shakespeare, William. *The Tragedy of Othello, the Moor of Venice.* 1622. Edited by Barbara A. Mowat and Paul Werstine, Simon and Schuster, 2009.

Suleiman, Susan Rubin, and Christie McDonald. "The National and the Global." *French Global: A New Approach to Literary History*, edited by McDonald and Suleiman, Columbia UP, 2011, pp. ix–xxi.

Tragédie française d'un More cruel envers son seigneur nommé Riviery, gentilhomme espagnol, sa damoiselle et ses enfants. c. 1610. Biet et al., pp. 555–91.

Sylvie Romanowski

Racine's *Britannicus* and the Absolutist Court of Louis XIV

In *Britannicus* the word *cour* occurs twenty-eight times, twice as frequently as in any other play by Racine (in *Bérénice*, fourteen times [Freeman 260]).[1] Word counts are useful to verify an intuition that a certain word does occur frequently, thus giving a clue to that concept's importance for the work.[2] *Britannicus* provides a basis for a course that focuses first on a royal court under the ancien régime, then studies how Enlightenment thinkers reexamined and criticized this institution and how their vision of a more democratic society based on equality eventually led to the French Revolution. The course, From Classicism to Enlightenment, meant for advanced undergraduates, starts with *Britannicus* and includes some fables of La Fontaine centered on the kingly lion and passages from Jean de La Bruyère's chapter on the court in his *Caractères* (*Characters*), continues with Jean-Jacques Rousseau's *Discours sur l'origine de l'inégalité* (*Discourse on the Origin of Inequality*) and excerpts from Montesquieu's *De l'esprit des lois* (*The Spirit of Laws*) and Voltaire's *L'ingénu*, and ends with Pierre Beaumarchais's *Le mariage de Figaro* (*The Marriage of Figaro*). These readings are accompanied by excerpts from Norbert Elias's *La société de cour* (*The Court Society*). If the course were longer than ten weeks, other readings could be added, for example, from Alexis de Tocqueville's *De la démocratie en Amérique* (*Democracy in America*).

Much has been made of neoclassical theater's universal appeal and its focus on eternal human themes; my presentation of the genre goes in another direction. I focus on a central institution of the ancien régime: government by a monarch and a surrounding court. This approach gives students a vital historical perspective on the culture that produced this literature, the reforming and transforming efforts of Enlightenment thinkers, and the workings of modern democratic societies.[3] *Britannicus* both depicts and criticizes a court and therefore functions as an introduction to the main themes of this course.[4]

Ancien régime society was hierarchical, headed by a court and a king. In a modern society in the developed world, many hierarchies—financial, corporate, judicial, governmental, religious, cultural—coexist simultaneously. In the French ancien régime, there was a basic national structure, with three estates—the church, the nobility, and the *tiers état* (the third estate; in other words, everyone else)—and above this structure there was a royal court. The court was organized as a pyramidal structure with several ranks of nobles, and the king at the top, answerable only to God. Louis Dumont explains it thus: "Nous définirons alors la hiérarchie comme *principe de gradation des éléments d'un ensemble par référence à l'ensemble*" 'So we shall define hierarchy as the *principle by which the elements of a whole are ranked in relation to the whole*' (*Homo hierarchicus* 92; *Homo Hierarchicus* 66). The court was a model of government for society, and it represented the highest level of cultural accomplishment, setting trends and tastes in diverse domains of life ranging from clothes to food to gardens. The court was idealized as a place of perfection, as Baltasar Gracián states at the beginning of *L'homme de cour* (*The Courtier's Annual Oracle*): "Tout est maintenant au point de sa perfection, et l'habile homme au plus haut" 'Everything is now at the height of perfection, and the skillful man is at the top' (7; my translation). However, there was a countertrend of court critique across various genres from the Renaissance on, to which this play contributes (see Smith).

In all ranks, the individual was defined in relation to other selves and to his or her place on the social ladder. Nowhere were individuals defined primarily in relation to their own specificity as they are in modern democratic societies. Dumont explains, "[L]es sociétés traditionnelles, qui ignorent l'égalité et la liberté comme valeurs, qui ignorent en somme l'individu, ont au fond une idée collective de l'homme" 'traditional societies, which know nothing of equality and liberty as values, which know nothing, in short, of the individual, have basically a collective concept of man' (*Homo hierarchicus* 21; *Homo Hierarchicus* 8). David Haley says that in such a world, the idea of autonomous self-fashioning is "foreign"; rather, he says, "courtiers fashion a self that conforms to the idea of the monarchical society of which they are a part" (32). Hence "the courtier regards his public image as objective, existential fact: his true self" (33). This view differs from Stephen Greenblatt's thesis in *Renaissance Self-Fashioning*, that in the sixteenth century there was a new emphasis on self-definition and individualism. Control over the court's members could be exercised not only by overt means such as demoting, imprisonment, or exile, but also by more covert means and microcontrol over people's lives and behavior through daily rituals, including rules of etiquette that regulated numerous aspects of life—for example, rising and getting dressed in the morning, knowing on what kind of chair one could sit or whether one had to remain standing—that today would seem fastidious and excessive.

Louis XIV's court was widely imitated in Europe before the Revolution as the exemplar of a successful court. Without diverging far from the model he had found in the courts of the Italian and French Renaissance,[5] the king concentrated power in his own hands, exercising a strong personal rule. This was the paradigm Racine knew when he wrote his plays, especially *Britannicus*, whose plot revolves around the acquisition, the exercise, and the retention of absolute rule.

The plot, which would have been familiar to the audience, centers on Néron's desire to acquire absolute power over those who currently hold it; namely, his mother, Agrippine, and her allies. In ancien régime France, kingship was inherited, defined by bloodlines and fixed principles of primogeniture and Salic law: succession was clear, based on birth order and gender. But in this tragedy no one comes to power by regular means: *Britannicus* portrays a counterexample to the ideal French manner of acquiring power. Adding to the play's complexity there are two power grabs, one by Agrippine in Néron's name occurring just before the play, and one by Néron for himself.

Néron was not destined by birth to be emperor; even less was Agrippine in line to be empress. Néron was put in that position by a series of actions his mother performed over many years for her own benefit. In act 1, scene 1, and in her exceptionally long speech in act 4, scene 2 (lines 1115–222), Agrippine describes how she overcame many obstacles to achieve her goals: she divorced her first husband, going through intermediaries friendly to the reigning emperor (even Pallas, whom she didn't like very much); she had to persuade the Roman senate to change the laws defining incest so she could marry her cousin, Claude, the emperor, and induce him to admit Néron into his family and adopt him; she had to persuade Claude to disinherit his own son, Britannicus; she exiled his son's supporters and placed her own supporters around Néron with bribes, gifts, and spectacles. Néron's current position results from a series of conspiratorial actions, acts of performative speech consisting of declaring, repudiating, divorcing, disinheriting, adopting, and ordering.[6] The outcome of these verbal actions seems simple: Néron becomes the emperor. But his position is constructed laboriously, and he does not rule fully yet. Albine's exclamation at the beginning of the play lays this out clearly: "Quoi? vous à qui Néron doit le jour qu'il respire, / Qui l'avez appelé de si loin à l'Empire?" 'You to whom Nero owes the life he breathes, / who called him, from so far, to the emperorship?' (1.1.15–16).[7] Both given in nature by blood ("le jour qu'il respire" 'the life he breathes') and created by human words ("appelé" 'called') against long odds ("de si loin" 'from so far'), his power seems natural but is actually constructed. When Agrippine threatens to reveal all the actions that put her son at the top of the hierarchy, Burrhus answers bluntly, "Madame, ils ne vous croiront pas" 'They'll not believe you, madam' (3.3.854), adding simply, "Madame, c'est un fils qui succède à son père" 'This, madam, is a son succeeding his father' (860), which is the natural means of succession. In reading this passage with students, we focus on the words that show Burrhus understands how Agrippine actually constructed Néron's position (emphasis added):

> En *adoptant* Néron, Claudius par son *choix*
> De son fils et du vôtre a confondu les droits.
> Rome l'a pu *choisir*. Ainsi, sans être injuste
> Elle *choisit* Tibère *adopté* par Auguste;
> Et le jeune Agrippa, de son sang descendu,
> Se vit *exclu* du rang vainement *prétendu*.
> Sur tant de *fondements* sa puissance établie
> Par vous-même aujourd'hui ne peut être affaiblie:
> Et s'il m'écoute encore, Madame, sa bonté
> Vous en fera bientôt perdre la volonté. (3.3.861–70)

> In adopting Nero, Claudius by design
> confused the rights of his son and your own.
> Rome, then, could choose him. Thus, without prejudice
> it chose Tiberius, stepson of Augustus;

and young Agrippa, descendant of his blood,
saw barred to him the vainly asserted rank.
Fixed upon such examples, Nero's power
cannot be weakened, now, by you yourself:
And if he hears me still, madam, his goodness
will soon persuade you to abandon the wish.

Yet Burrhus uses the word "fondements" 'fixed' (better translation: "founded"), which seems ironic—or perhaps he is being the good courtier flattering Agrippine. What seems and should be foundational is really constructed, and this highly abnormal situation, in which there is not one ruler, but two, Agrippine and Néron, is made to seem natural.[8]

This unstable combination can continue as long as both players are willing to play the game: Agrippine admits that she has done everything for herself. I ask students to note the repetitions of the words "moi" and "moi seule" in the speech where she describes how she has put Néron in power in the place of the rightful heir, Britannicus:

Je sais que j'ai moi seule avancé leur ruine;
Que du trône, où le sang l'a dû faire monter,
Britannicus par moi s'est vu précipiter. (1.1.60–62)

I know that it was I alone that worked their ruin,
that from the throne, which his blood claimed for him,
Britannicus saw his hopes by me cast down.

When she says that, as a result of her actions, "Néron jouit de tout" 'Nero enjoys all' (67), Agrippine is not being truthful, for he does not yet enjoy what he wants, and will get by the end of the play: undivided and absolute power. Néron has status without full power, and Agrippine has power without full status. The play centers on a second power grab by Néron, who no longer wants to share power with his mother. He pushes her away from the throne at a reception for ambassadors, thus broadcasting to the court that he wanted both status *and* power. Agrippine complains succinctly, "Je vois mes honneurs croître, et tomber mon crédit" 'I see my honors grow and my credit fall' (90). She recounts an almost comic scenario: "Sur son trône avec lui j'allais prendre ma place" 'I went to place myself beside him, on his throne' (102–03). How can two people occupy one seat? But she realizes that many ambassadors had come to Rome in order to recognize him, not her, "au nom de l'univers" 'in the world's name' (102). Néron had governed in name only, under the thumb of his mother, who boasts that "mon ordre au palais assemblait le sénat" 'my order/would bring the senate to the palace' (93–94). Now he signifies that he wants to rule alone on the throne. First he lets his anger show ("[L]aissa sur son visage éclater son dépit" '[L]et his displeasure show in his countenance' [106]) when Agrippine approaches the throne, but this is a spontaneous show of feeling that is unproductive in realizing his aims; then, more master of himself, he rushes to embrace her with "faux respect" 'sham respect' (108) to prevent her from sitting on the throne. She is lucid about Néron's intent when she mentions that day as being "triste" 'sad' (99) for her, giving her a "coup fatal" 'that unlucky stroke' (111; better translation: "fatal blow") that leaves her with a foreboding of her own downfall: "le pouvoir d'Agrippine / Vers sa chute, à grands pas, chaque jour s'achemine" 'Agrippina's power / from day to day draws quickly to its end' (112).

Thus, Néron is forced to do what Louis XIV did not have to do (nor did his father or his grandfather before him). Courtiers could easily see Racine's play as reinforcing, by a negative example, the benefit of well-established practice. As Timothy J. Reiss argues, tragedy may represent a negative situation and have another, positive effect in mind: "Tragedy encloses the ambiguities in a kind of exorcism, through and in discourse" (23). In the milieu and time in which this play was written, any other social system was simply unthinkable: indeed, it was more than a century before the system was overthrown during the French Revolution. And yet a sense of fragility lay beneath the appearance of stable and clear succession laws and made absolutist rule all the more attractive. In many domains in the second half of the century, a rhetoric of order, certitude, and regulation was actively promoted: by René Descartes in science and philosophy; by Claude Favre de Vaugelas and the Académie Française in French grammar, vocabulary, and spelling; by Louis Le Vau in architecture (e.g., the palaces of Versailles and Vaux-le-Vicomte); by André Le Nôtre in garden design; and of course by the preoccupation with rules for composing theatrical works, especially for tragedy but even comedy.[9] This was in reaction to the sixteenth century's Wars of Religion and the civil war in the seventeenth century known as the Fronde. The more recent turmoil in England, where Charles I had been deposed and beheaded, was a reminder of the dangers that could befall even kings, which was reinforced by the presence of Henriette d'Angleterre, the daughter of Charles I, who was still living at the French court when *Britannicus* was first performed (she died six months later, in 1670). The memories of the War of Devolution, involving the inheritance of the Spanish throne, were also fresh in people's minds.

Even under an unquestioned, "natural" ruler, there is an instability present in all courts—competition for recognition among the courtiers as they seek to gain whatever advantages can be had within the system. With students, it is interesting to contrast this dynamic with representative democracies, where electoral candidates officially align themselves with specific political principles or parties (e.g., conservative, liberal, centrist, socialist, Republican, Democrat, etc.). In a court society, courtiers are not organized in the name of principles, but in ad hoc groups, in French, *cabales*. Cabals are temporary alliances between persons close to the center of power, whose aim is to obtain specific advantages within the hierarchy. Their machinations might be secret, though their membership was not; nor did they seek to overturn the monarch. Emmanuel Le Roy Ladurie defines them thus:

> Une cabale est une construction provisoire, quoique pouvant durer jusqu'à deux décennies et au-delà: elle vise . . . à obtenir divers avantages tels que pouvoir, prestige, argent, nominations à des postes dans le haut clergé ou dans les commandements de l'armée, progrès d'un tel ou un tel dans les rangs ducaux, princiers, etc. (*Saint-Simon ou le système de la Cour* 222)

> A cabal was a temporary construct, though it might last for up to two decades or even longer. Its purpose was to obtain various advantages in court and government such as power, prestige, money, appointments to high clerical or military positions, and promotions within the ranks of dukes, princes, and so on. (*Saint-Simon and the Court of Louis XIV* 149–50)

Ladurie contrasts this with democratic systems, where there is an official opposition, whereas court society is "un système sans opposition officielle ni organisée, ou sans que cette opposition parvienne à accéder au pouvoir" 'a system in which there was no official opposition . . . or in which that opposition could not accede to power' (*Saint-Simon ou le système de la Cour* 222; *Saint-Simon and the Court of Louis XIV* 150).

In *Britannicus*, Racine portrays cabals at work, not between courtiers vying for power and favor, but between two would-be rulers. This particular twist opens up a most terrifying possibility: that there is no single, easily recognized ruler. The play has rightly been called a tragedy of cabals (Couton) and the stakes could not be higher. Agrippine has pushed aside her husband Claude's own son, Britannicus ("Britannicus par moi s'est vu précipiter" 'Britannicus saw his hopes by me cast down' [1.1.62]), and allowed him to love, and be loved by, Junie, to keep him quiet, so to speak. Britannicus is thus an enemy of Agrippine, but at the same time, the continued existence of Britannicus keeps Néron in check ("Il faut qu'entre eux et lui je tienne la balance / Afin que quelque jour, par une même loi, / Britannicus la tienne entre mon fils et moi" 'I must hold the balance between them [the other possible rivals] and him / so that one day Britannicus may hold it / with the same justice, between my son and me' [68–70]). After Néron's kidnapping of Junie, Britannicus and Agrippine find that they have a common enemy in the newly resolute Néron; Agrippine is the first to state this situation explicitly ("Comme vous je ressens vos injures" 'Like you I take your injuries to heart' [1.3.299]), and she suggests a new alliance that leaves Britannicus skeptical ("La croirai-je?" 'Shall I believe her?' [1.4.305]). However, Britannicus is a relatively quick learner, compelled by his desperation to retrieve his beloved Junie, and by the middle of the play he speaks like a conspirator ("Nos ennemis communs ne sont pas invincibles, / Madame," 'Our common enemies can still be opposed, / madam' [3.5.895]) and counts heads in the senate ("La moitié du sénat s'intéresse pour nous" 'Half the senate / is mindful of our interests' [904–05]). He goes too far, however, betraying how inexperienced he still is, when he starts to say that "Sylla, Pison, Plautus" are on his side, thus irritating Agrippine, who interjects vehemently, "Prince, que dites vous? / Sylla, Pison, Plautus! les chefs de la noblesse!" 'What are you saying, Prince? / the leaders of the nobility—Sulla, Piso, Plautus!' (906–07). The memories of the high aristocracy's rebellion during the Fronde are not too far off. Britannicus quickly retracts his assertion: "Non, vous avez trop bien établi ma disgrâce: / D'aucun ami pour moi ne redoutez l'audace" 'Fear nothing, madam. / You have too well established my disgrace' (911–12). Britannicus realizes that he is but a pawn in the hands of Agrippine. She is interested in her own power and in Néron's subservience to her, a choice she had earlier framed in misleadingly moral-sounding terms: "Tout, s'il est généreux, lui prescrit cette loi; / Mais tout, s'il est ingrat, lui parle contre moi" 'If he is noble-minded, all speaks for me / but if he is ungrateful, all against me' (1.1.21–22). Now she realizes that she will have to use stronger means: "J'assiégerai Néron de toutes parts" 'I will lay siege to Nero on every hand' (3.5.925).

I draw the students' attention to the ways in which all of these actions depend on human invention and the skillful use of speech. Burrhus, Narcisse, and Agrippine conjure images in order to manipulate the hesitant Néron; all three appeal to what public opinion will say about the emperor after any given action. Richard Goodkin has analyzed cogently the difference between the two speeches of Burrhus and Narcisse, and, embedded in those speeches, the short imaginary speeches that Burrhus and Narcisse put in the mouths of Romans. Goodkin explains why Narcisse's embedded speech, beginning with "*Néron*, s'ils s'en sont crus, *n'est point fait pour l'Empire*" '"Nero"—to hear them tell it—"was not born / to the emperorship"' (4.4.1468), is the more powerful of the two: Narcisse plays upon Néron's vanity and reputation as a strong man by making him imagine with horror that Romans despise him as a mere entertainer of common folk and soldiers. Burrhus (4.3.1360–64) appeals to virtue, an ideal easily undone by selfish considerations of personal power: Néron is less moved by the image of "*Partout, en ce moment, on me bénit, on m'aime*" 'At this time, everywhere, I am blessed, I am loved' (1360) than by the shame of being viewed as a pawn in Agrippine's, Seneca's, and Burrhus's hands (Goodkin 126). Images, imagined speeches, and reputations are fragile constructions that can change easily. As Barbara Woshinsky says, the play is "created out of a tension between story and image" (69). Such tensions are the very stuff of cabals at court. The most skillful use of images and the best performances win the day, but they are always capable of being outdone by another more powerful statement. Instability is inherent in a system built on shifting alliances and theatrical performances.

Who is the tragic hero in this tragedy? Of course, it is the one for whom the play is named, Britannicus, who is stripped of his legitimate inheritance. But as we saw, he is not a pure victim, since he takes part in the machinations to reclaim power. There is another victim, Junie, who has no stake in acquiring power—a moral, tragic victim of evildoers who does not participate in these cabals. Her purity is reinforced by her entry into the vestal temple at the end of the play. The contrast between Néron's sadistic capture of Junie and Junie's reciprocal love for Britannicus is central to the impact of the tragedy on the spectators: in Junie, perhaps even more than in Britannicus, the spectators have someone to pity. However, even Junie, who seems so different, is part of this world.[10]

Asking students to undertake a critical, close reading can yield interesting insights that enrich their first impressions of a seemingly uncomplicated character. Obviously, Néron's love for Junie is mediated by sadism, as he falls in love with her because he sees her suffering when she is kidnapped, and by jealousy, because she is already loved by someone else. In short, his love is not for Junie, not for her sake; rather, it arises from other emotions. René Girard explains, refuting the ideal of romantic love as illusory, that all love is mediated by one or more third terms: "Comme toutes les victimes de la médiation interne, celui-ci [le jaloux] se persuade aisément que son désir est spontané, c'est-à-dire qu'il s'enracine dans l'objet et dans cet objet seulement" 'Like all victims of internal mediation, the jealous person easily convinces himself that his desire is spontaneous, in other words, that it is deeply rooted in the object and in this object alone' (20–21; *Deceit* 12). So we ask the question: Is Junie's love pure, unmediated?

After all, Junie is given to Britannicus in an arranged marriage, normal for such echelons of royalty, because he is the last of an illustrious family, disinherited from his rightful place as heir to the emperor. Junie says that Britannicus accepted this union obediently: "Il m'aime; il obéit à l'Empereur son père" 'He loves me; he is obedient to the emperor, his father' (2.3.559). How did such an arranged marriage turn into love? When Junie is asked by Néron why she loves Britannicus, the mediation is clear when she tells the story twice in the same scene (2.3.553–61 and 643–48), ending with "La fuite d'une cour que sa chute a bannie / Sont autant de liens qui retiennent Junie" 'the flight of a court alienated by his fall, / these are so many ties to assure my love' (647–48). She loves him precisely because he is disinherited and nostalgic for "un temps plus heureux" 'a happier time' (557), now unrealizable. Junie represents a vanished world, evoking for Britannicus a lost grandeur, which, as Paul Bénichou states in his chapter on Racine, is at the heart of all Racinian tragedy: "[L]a lamentation racinienne [a] pour objet la perte d'une grandeur prestigieuse" 'Racinian lamentation has for its object the loss of a wondrous grandeur' (*Morales* 154; *Man* 165). Junie lists "ces mêmes malheurs" 'the misfortunes'—"les honneurs abolis, son palais déserté, / La fuite d'une cour que sa chute a bannie" 'his honors gone, his palace empty, the flight / of a court alienated by his fall'—as tying her to Britannicus (645–47). Goodkin notes succintly that "the love of Britannicus and Junie is far from indifferent to the world of power . . . what keeps him and Junie together is their position as have-nots" (120).

I push students to go further: Racine strongly suggests that making Néron jealous of their reciprocal love was part of their reason for loving each other. Junie asks Britannicus, while Néron is hiding behind a curtain listening to their exchange, "Qu'est devenu ce cœur qui me jurait toujours / De faire à Néron même envier nos amours?" 'Where is the heart that always swore to me / we should make even Nero envy our love?' (2.6.717–18). In a layered moment of infinite mirroring, Junie is evoking the jealousy she and Britannicus wanted to make Néron feel, reinforcing their love for each other, as Néron listens, forbidding them to see each other, and rendered explosively jealous by their reenactment of their previous show of love: "Mais je mettrai ma joie à le désespérer. / Je me fais de sa peine une image charmante" 'but I shall be delighted to dash his hopes. /

I find the image of his grief enchanting' (2.8.750–51). The appeal of inciting Néron's jealousy of their reciprocated love rears its head even in an apparently "pure" love. Indeed, a "pure" love is impossible in the world of the court, where individuals exist only in relation to other selves and have no inner identity, where instability and competition dominate, and where what seems natural is artificial and composed by human acts.

Although Junie has never lived at court, she understands it well. She even curtly admonishes Agrippine—"Le changement, Madame, est commun à la cour" 'Change, madam, is a frequent thing at court' (5.3.1581)—who, despite her long experience of court life, believes mistakenly and naively that once she has spoken, she is obeyed: "Il suffit. J'ai parlé, tout a changé de face" 'Enough. I have spoken: all is quite reversed' (1583). Junie also contrasts with Britannicus, who urges her naively to join "de sa [Néron's] cour la jeunesse" 'the youth of the court' and to enjoy "d'un festin la pompe et l'allégresse" 'the pomp and jubilance of a banquet' (5.1.1483–84)—the very banquet where Britannicus will be poisoned to death. Junie is able to save her own life by lying, feigning to visit Octavie—skillfully escaping from the palace through "des chemins écartés" 'a different course' (5.8.1725; better translation: "little-known passages"). She has been at the court only a short time, but she is singularly able to negotiate her way to the outside. Her final act in the play is to save her life and construct her future existence through a performative speech embedded in Albine's final narration: "*Mais pour lui conserver une foi toujours pure, / Prince, je me dévoue à ces Dieux immortels*" '*But to keep pure my covenant with him, / I pledge myself to those immortal Gods*' (1736–37). Her last speech is addressed to the statue of Augustus, to whom she pays homage by embracing his knees and feet, a ritualistic gesture of fealty to a greater emperor than either Néron or Britannicus could be. And it is this act that saves her, for the people, moved by this spectacle, "que ce spectacle étonne . . . la prend sous son appui" 'whom this sight astonished . . . agree to take her under their guardianship' (1739, 1742), protect her from the savage attack by Narcisse by carrying her into the safety of the temple.

The only way Junie can rescue herself and preserve her dignity is to join a religious order, one of the principal escapes from both ancient and modern courts, especially for women. Similarly, at the end of Lafayette's novel, *La princesse de Clèves*, the heroine retreats from the court, splitting her time between a convent and her home. Even in her home, Lafayette stresses, the princess spends her time in "des occupations plus saintes que celles des couvents les plus austères" 'occupations more saintly that those of the most austere houses of religion' (253; *Princesse* 156). Other alternatives are unimaginable, tragic, even in some comedies: for example, Alceste sees a bleak future at the end of *Le misanthrope*:

> Trahi de toutes parts, accablé d'injustices
> Je vais sortir d'un gouffre où triomphent les vices,
> Et chercher sur la terre un endroit écarté
> Où d'être homme d'honneur on ait la liberté. (Molière 5.4.1803–06)

> Meanwhile, betrayed and wronged in everything,
> I'll flee this bitter world where vice is king,
> And seek some spot unpeopled and apart
> Where I'll be free to have an honest heart.

To understand how difficult it was to envision another type of society, I quote one superlative observer who knew both traditional and democratic types of society. Tocqueville begins *De la démocratie en Amérique* with the sentence, "Parmi les objets nouveaux qui, pendant mon séjour aux Etats-Unis, ont attiré mon attention, aucun n'a plus vivement frappé mes regards que l'égalité des conditions" 'Among the new objects that attracted my attention during my stay in the United States, none struck me more vividly than the equality of conditions.' Such equality, he observes, "donne à l'esprit public une certaine direction, un certain tour aux lois; aux gouvernants des maximes nouvelles, et des habitudes particulières aux gouvernés" 'gives a certain dimension to the public mind, a certain turn to the laws; to those governing, new maxims, and particular habits to the governed' (37; *Democracy* 4). Tocqueville describes ancien régime society thus: "[L]e droit de commander descend alors de générations en générations avec les héritages; les hommes n'ont qu'un seul moyen d'agir les uns sur les autres, la force; on ne découvre qu'une seule origine de la puissance, la propriété foncière" '[T]he right to command is passed down with inheritances from generation to generation; men have only a single way to act on one another, force; you discover only a single source of power, landed property' (*De la démocratie* 38; *Democracy* 6). While stating that equality is "un développement providentiel" 'a providential development" (*De la démocratie* 41; my trans.) in history, to be admired and assisted, Tocqueville is nevertheless awed by the difference:

> Le livre entier qu'on va lire a été écrit sous l'impression d'une sorte de terreur religieuse produite dans l'âme de l'auteur par la vue de cette révolution irrésistible qui marche depuis tant de siècles à travers tous les obstacles, et qu'on voit encore aujourd'hui s'avancer au milieu des ruines qu'elle a faites. (*De la démocratie* 42)

> The entire book that you are about to read has been written under the impression of a sort of religious terror produced in the soul of the author by the sight of this irresistible revolution that has marched for so many centuries over all obstacles, and that we still see today advancing amid the ruins that it has made. (*Democracy* 14)

If Tocqueville, gifted with great intellectual means, could express terror at this new society, one can surmise how terrifying it must have been for others. There is a profound sense of loss in his introduction, of being between two social orders, one no longer valid, the new one not yet firmly established:

> Ainsi nous avons abandonné ce que l'état ancien pouvait présenter de bon, sans acquérir ce que l'état actuel pourrait offrir d'utile; nous avons détruit une société aristocratique, et, nous arrêtant complaisamment au milieu des débris de l'ancien édifice, nous semblons vouloir nous y fixer pour toujours. (*De la démocratie* 47)

> Thus we have abandoned what the old state could present of the good, without acquiring what the current state would be able to offer of the useful; we have destroyed an aristocratic society, and, stopping out of complacency amid the debris of the former edifice, we seem to want to settle there forever. (*Democracy* 22–23)

Encouraging students to move from Racine to Tocqueville as a means of understanding the prerevolutionary period is useful because it enables them to appreciate the boldness of Enlightenment thinkers—for example, how revolutionary are Montesquieu's concept of the separation of powers and Rousseau's passionate denunciations of inequality; how new public spaces, so-called third spaces of discourse, had to be created for new public opinions to emerge, and how eventually nothing less than the Revolution itself could overturn the courtly model.[11]

Britannicus presents a picture of a court that is supposed to be brilliant and exemplary, but is so only in appearance. It is ruled by an absolute monarch but is roiled by vicious cabals, and the transmission of power from one generation to the next is fragile. The tragedy shows a paradox: while the courtly organization of society persists, bolstered by the belief that inheritance of power is based on a foundational, natural order, in actuality power is acquired by speech acts and human decisions. The mirror that the play held up to its audience sends a negative and all too possible image that had to be conjured away. Louis XIV is said to have admired *Britannicus*, which was performed at court and thereby gained in popularity. Finally, I ask students to hypothesize what the Sun King and his entourage understood when they saw the play: perhaps an admonition to be more exemplary, or the consoling conclusion that their reign was more stable and more natural than Racine's pessimistic vision of the fragility and cruelty of courtly life.

Notes

1. That Racine became aware of the play's focus on the court is suggested by the change in his description of Narcisse; in the first preface the character is called "un très méchant homme" 'a very mean man' (385); but in the second preface he is described as "cette peste de cour" 'that court nuisance' (390). The word "cour" occurs nowhere in the first preface and three times in the second preface. (All translations are mine unless otherwise attributed.)

2. For instance, I wrote an article on living spaces in *Tartuffe* after I verified my impression that the word *céans* ("in this place") appeared there more frequently than in any other play by Molière.

3. Both Dumont and Le Roy Ladurie stress the advantages of comparative and contrastive studies of different political and social systems, even very different ones. For example, Dumont, who studied Indian castes, states, "[L]a caste a quelque chose à nous apprendre sur nous-mêmes" '[C]aste has something to teach us about ourselves' (*Homo hierarchicus* 14; *Homo Hierarchicus* 1).

4. See the appendix for supplemental sources.

5. For a history of the court's institution in the Middle Ages, see C. Stephen Jaeger.

6. "Performative" is the term used by J. L. Austin to describe speech that does something (as opposed to constative speech, which describes): "To *say* something is to *do* something" (12).

7. All translations of Racine are by George Dillon. The spelling has been modernized.

8. On the tension between the idea of a foundational nature and the contrasting principle of artificialism, see the work of Clément Rosset, who describes the resurgence of artificialist thought in the seventeenth century.

9. On science, see Stephen Toulmin; on art and literature, see Erica Harth and John Lyons. For a broader view of the ideological shift from the Renaissance to the classical age (the mid-seventeenth century to the end of the eighteenth century), see especially Michel Foucault's works describing the new episteme defined by the classification, ordering, and organizing of all fields of knowledge and human experience (*Folie, Les mots*).

10. Even Roland Barthes misreads Junie as "la Vierge Consolatrice par un rôle d'essence" 'the consoling virgin by essence' (*Sur Racine* 93; *On Racine* 88) who becomes "une Femme Vengeresse" 'a revenging woman' (*Sur Racine* 94; *On Racine* 88), but that is only because she opposes Néron. Lucien Goldmann, however, sees Junie as central to the play: "Le sujet de *Britannicus* est le conflit entre *Junie et le monde*" 'the topic of the play is the conflict between Junie and the world' (367; my trans.).

11. On the emergence of public opinion and public spaces, see particularly the work of Jürgen Habermas.

Works Cited

Austin, J. L. *How to Do Things with Words.* 2nd ed., Harvard UP, 1962.

Barthes, Roland. *On Racine.* Translated by Richard Howard, Performing Arts Journal Publications, 1983.

———. *Sur Racine.* Seuil, 1963.

Bénichou, Paul. *Man and Ethics: Studies in French Classicism.* Translated by Elizabeth Hughes, Anchor Books, 1971.

———. *Morales du grand siècle.* Gallimard, 1948.

Couton, Georges. "*Britannicus*, tragédie des cabales." *Racine/Britannicus*, edited by Pierre Ronzeaud, Klincksieck, 1995, pp. 63–70.

Dumont, Louis. *Homo hierarchicus: Le système des castes et ses implications.* Gallimard, 1966.

———. *Homo Hierarchicus: The Caste System and Its Implications.* Translated by Mark Sainsbury et al., U of Chicago P, 1980.

Elias, Norbert. *La société de cour.* Translated by Pierre Kamnitzer, Calmann-Lévy, 1974.

Foucault, Michel. *Folie et déraison: Histoire de la folie à l'âge classique.* Plon, 1961.

———. *Les mots et les choses: Une archéologie des sciences humaines.* Gallimard, 1966.

Freeman, Bryant T., and Alan Batson. *Concordance du théâtre et des poésies de Jean Racine.* Cornell UP, 1968.

Girard, René. *Deceit, Desire, and the Novel: Self and Other in Literary Structure.* Translated by Yvonne Freccero, Johns Hopkins UP, 1965.

———. *Mensonge romantique et vérité romanesque.* Grasset, 1961.

Goldmann, Lucien. *Le dieu caché: Etude sur la vision tragique dans les* Pensées *de Pascal et dans le théâtre de Racine.* Gallimard, 1955.

Goodkin, Richard E. "Racine and the Excluded Third (Person): *Britannicus*, *Bérénice*, *Bajazet* and the Tragic 'Milieu.'" *Continuum*, vol. 2, 1990, pp. 107–49.

Gracián, Baltasar. *L'homme de cour.* Translated by Amelot de La Houssaie, Editions Mille et une Nuits, 1997.

Greenblatt, Stephen. *Renaissance Self-Fashioning: From More to Shakespeare.* U of Chicago P, 1980.

Habermas, Jürgen. *The Structural Transformation of the Public Sphere: An Inquiry into a Category of Bourgeois Society.* MIT Press, 1989.

Haley, David. *Shakespeare's Courtly Mirror: Reflexivity and Prudence in* All's Well That Ends Well. U of Delaware P, 1993.

Harth, Erica. *Ideology and Culture in Seventeenth-Century France.* Cornell UP, 1983.

Jaeger, C. Stephen. *The Origins of Courtliness: Civilizing Trends and the Formation of Courtly Ideals, 939–1210.* U of Pennsylvania P, 1985.

Lafayette, Madame de. *La princesse de Clèves.* 1678. Edited by Jean Mesnard, Garnier-Flammarion, 2009.

———. *The Princesse de Clèves; The Princesse de Montpensier; The Comtesse de Tende*. Translated by Terence Cave, Oxford UP, 1992.

Le Roy Ladurie, Emmanuel, with J. F. Fitou. *Saint-Simon and the Court of Louis XIV*. Translated by Arthur Goldhammer, U of Chicago P, 2001.

———. *Saint-Simon ou le système de la Cour*. Fayard, 1997.

Lyons, John D. *Kingdom of Disorder: The Theory of Tragedy in Classical France*. Purdue UP, 1999.

Molière. *Le misanthrope. Œuvres complètes*, edited by Robert Jouanny, vol. 1, Garnier, 1962.

———. *The Misanthrope*. The Misanthrope *and* Tartuffe, translated by Richard Wilbur, Harcourt, Brace and World, 1965, pp. 1–152.

Racine, Jean. *Britannicus. Œuvres complètes, tome I: Théâtre-Poésie*, edited by Georges Forestier, Gallimard-La Pléiade, 1999, pp. 377–438.

———. *Three Plays of Racine: Phaedra; Britannicus; Andromache*. Translated by George Dillon, U of Chicago P, 1961.

Reiss, Timothy J. *Tragedy and Truth: Studies in the Development of a Renaissance and Neoclassical Discourse*. Yale UP, 1980.

Romanowski, Sylvie. "'I? Leave This House?' Space and Language in *Tartuffe*." *Approaches to Teaching Molière's* Tartuffe *and Other Plays*, edited by James F. Gaines and Michael S. Koppisch, Modern Language Association of America, 1995, pp. 33–41.

Rosset, Clément. *L'anti-nature: Éléments pour une philosophie tragique*. 1973. 2nd ed., PU de France, 1990.

Smith, Pauline M. *The Anti-Courtier Trend in Sixteenth-Century French Literature*. Droz, 1966.

Tocqueville, Alexis de. *De la démocratie en Amérique*. 1835–1840. Gallimard, 1986.

———. *Democracy in America: Historical-Critical Edition of* De la démocratie en Amérique. Edited by Eduardo Nuella, translated by James T. Schleifer, Liberty Fund, 2010.

Toulmin, Stephen. *Cosmopolis: The Hidden Agenda of Modernity*. U of Chicago P, 1990.

Woshinsky, Barbara R. *Signs of Certainty: The Linguistic Imperative in French Classical Literature*. ANMA Libri, 1991.

Appendix: Further Reading

Chambers, Ross. *Room for Maneuver: Reading (the) Oppositional (in) Narrative*. U of Chicago P, 1991.

Doubrovsky, Serge. "L'arrivée de Junie dans *Britannicus*: La tragédie d'une scène à l'autre." Ronzeaud, pp. 105–29.

Emelina, Jean. "L'espace dans les tragédies romaines de Racine." *Littératures classiques*, vol. 26, 1996, pp. 125–38.

Hale, Jane Alison. "La perspective et le pouvoir: L'échec de Néron et le triomphe du spectateur." *Papers on French Seventeenth-Century Literature*, vol. 13, no. 24, 1986, pp. 312–28.

Maskell, David. *Racine: A Theatrical Reading*. Clarendon Press, 1991.

McGowan, Margaret. "Racine's 'Lieu Théâtral.'" *Form and Meaning: Aesthetic Coherence in Seventeenth-Century French Drama*, edited by William D. Howarth et al., Avebury, 1983, pp. 166–86.

Méthivier, Hubert. *Le siècle de Louis XIV*. 14th ed., PU de France 1998. Que sais-je? 426.

Rohou, Jean. "Structure et signification dans *Britannicus, Bérénice* et *Mithridate*." *Littératures classiques*, vol. 26, 1996, pp. 51–72.

Romanowski, Sylvie. "Molière's *Le Misanthrope*: A Critique and Reluctant Defense of Courtly Life." *Contemporary Theatre Review*, vol. 6, no. 1, 1997, pp. 49–63.

Ronzeaud, Pierre, editor. *Racine/Britannicus*. Klincksieck, 1995.

Schröder, Volker. "Politique du couple: Amour réciproque et légitimité dynastique dans *Britannicus*." *Cahiers de l'Association Internationale des Etudes françaises*, vol. 49, 1997, pp. 455–91.

Serroy, Jean. "De *L'école des femmes* à *Britannicus*: Il faut qu'une porte soit ouverte ou fermée." *Littératures classiques*, vol. 27, 1996, pp. 52–63.

Tobin, Ronald W. "Néron et Junie: Fantasme et tragédie." Ronzeaud, pp. 177–88.

Venesoen, Constant. "Le dénouement de *Britannicus*: Le sens du récit d'Albine." *Papers on French Seventeenth-Century Literature*, vol. 21, 1994, pp. 113–20.

Weinberg, Bernard. *The Art of Jean Racine*. U of Chicago P, 1963.

Jeffrey M. Leichman

Of Tragedy and Kings in Corneille and Césaire

This essay presents a comparative approach to teaching early modern French tragedy, underscoring how the traditions instituted by neoclassical authors are transmitted and transformed across the centuries on the French-language stage. Articulating this class around the figure of the king allows for an engagement with political and historical developments in French and francophone societies as they are reflected and debated through innovative performance and dramaturgical practices. While this essay focuses specifically on Pierre Corneille's *Cinna* and Aimé Césaire's *La tragédie du roi Christophe* (*The Tragedy of King Christopher*), I teach these plays along with texts from the intervening centuries—notably, Marie-Joseph Chénier's *Charles IX, ou L'école des rois* (1789; *Charles IX; or, The School for Kings*) and Alfred Jarry's *Ubu Roi* (1896; *King Ubu*), a sequence that lends a greater historical coherence to the aesthetic and thematic evolution that has made this a successful unit in the past.[1] While I have taught this unit in French classes at both a small liberal arts college and a large public university, the availability of the primary-source texts in English translation makes it feasible to incorporate these plays into English-language instruction as well.

The diachronic corpus provides concrete examples of how neoclassical tragedy remains a fertile source of structural and affective tropes that can speak powerfully to the modern world, helping students to see the modernity of Corneille as well as Césaire's aesthetic homage to the Grand Siècle, whose techniques he adapts in order to confer grandeur and historical sweep on his twentieth-century parable. Situated at the confluence of the personal and the political, both *Cinna* and *La tragédie du roi Christophe* can be read as meditations on the intersection of absolutism and individual character, a tension that emerges as an important preoccupation for the French-language stage. Corneille's Auguste and Césaire's King Henry Christophe represent two poles of a centuries-long examination of what it means to rule—over oneself and one's people—while seated on a throne of unlimited power.

Perhaps the first potential obstacle that presents itself is the wide historical scope of the subject matter embraced in these works, for which the required basic knowledge (of imperial Rome, seventeenth-century France, postrevolutionary Haiti, and the twentieth-century Caribbean) cannot necessarily be assumed. This is in part what motivates my endorsement of "spoilers": I will often present a thumbnail sketch of the play's action, or even of the main plot points of a particular reading assignment, before students do the reading. Armed with an understanding of what is happening, students are free to focus on how the author doles out information—to readers, to spectators, and to characters within the play—without having to worry about misunderstandings with respect to the basic storyline. In exchange for sacrificing some of the pleasure of discovering the plot, students gain clarity that facilitates their work on stylistically difficult passages. This pedagogical strategy also aligns with modernist theoretical currents. Denis Diderot, in formulating the *drame* in the mid eighteenth century, suggested that the audience's interest is riveted by watching characters discover their entrapment in circumstances that spectators already fully understand; while in the twentieth century, Bertolt Brecht, an important influence on Césaire's dramaturgical practice, argued that full exposition of the narrative allowed the public to better understand the historical and economic forces that determine individual action.

Framing the unit in terms of the historical development of tragedy provides students with a broad framework for how to advance this argument, but the best discussions invariably arise from topics that students themselves suggest, rather than those imposed from above. Emphasizing from the beginning that student responses will drive in-class discussion confers a greater sense of ownership and investment. Electronic learning environments (*Moodle*, *Blackboard*, and others) are useful here: I divide the class into two groups that are assigned to alternate in posting responses to the reading before each class session, offering up an observation or a question, or responding to a classmate's entry. Each session sees a new student in the role of *rapporteur* (reporter), who is released from submitting written work but must open the discussion with an oral synthesis of the posted reactions. This format provides a frequent check-in with student interests, allowing the instructor to catch misunderstandings and fill in gaps in responses, all while providing a convenient forum for short, informal written assignments that can be graded on a regular basis. The *rapporteur* function provides an additional short, graded oral activity, developing skills around constructing an efficient, nonrepetitive summary of arguments.

I often begin this unit by asking students about their most common associations with the terms *tragedy* and *tragic*, as a way of establishing how casual usages ("that is a *tragic* outfit," "the *tragic* death of the sea birds," "the *tragedy* of my fall semester," etc.) differ from the classical and neoclassical understandings of these terms. Devoting time at the beginning of the unit to Aristotle's *Poetics* (read in French) and d'Aubignac's *La pratique du théâtre* (*The Practice of Theater*) can help define the object of study in contrast to the general sense of bad luck and untimely demise that this term often evokes, establishing a more precise and productive understanding.[2] In both cases, excerpts suffice to underscore important principles that structure the European mimetic tradition and the ideals of stage composition articulated in the seventeenth century, furnishing a robust set of concepts that can lend structure to student responses to dramatic works. Given the central thematic preoccupation of this class, I tend to curate these readings to emphasize their discussion of royalty. Misfortune, violence, and loss can befall anyone; but tragedy requires kings and queens.

In chapter 6 of his *Poetics*, Aristotle gives his most concise definition of tragedy's salient components, as well as introducing the concept of catharsis. This selection could serve as the entirety of the reading from this work, as Aristotle introduces key distinctions between story (*muthos*), character, thought, and language, as well as the notion, dearer to seventeenth-century theorists than to the period's playwrights, that stage action is a merely seductive accessory to tragedy, whose perfection resides in its adherence to literary precepts. The minimum Aristotelian notion of tragedy as the imitation of an action characterized by reversal and recognition, undertaken by high-status characters and recounted in poetic language, can then be compared to d'Aubignac's *La pratique du théâtre*, a summation of aesthetic prescriptions from the Richelieu-era transformation of theater into a vehicle for nation-forming and the propagation of cultural soft power for the emerging absolutist monarchy.

In his introductory chapter, d'Aubignac draws an explicitly theatrical link between the glory of classical antiquity and that of the present French state, where spectacles provide the public with moral instruction and examples of courage. This social-political framing of the stage's function is further reinforced in the discussion of acceptable subjects for the tragic stage (book 2, chapter 1), in which the author declares the king inviolable in the French dramatic tradition, a key precept that neoclassical tragedy would bear out time and again. Perhaps the most revealing theoretical insight turns on the question of the play's outcome. As articulated in d'Aubignac's chapter "Du dénouement" (book 2, chapter 9)—and as confirmed in *Cinna*—the protagonist's death is not the defining feature of tragic theater, to the great surprise of many students.

Because Césaire's *La tragédie du roi Christophe* bears the strong imprint of Bertolt Brecht's theories of politically engaged dramaturgy, I have used excerpts from Brecht's *Short Organum for the Theatre* to introduce salient characteristics of this politically engaged poetics, in conjunction with selections from Césaire's analysis of colonial subjugation in his *Discours sur le colonialisme* (*Discourse on Colonialism* [Pinkham]). While Brecht's emphasis is primarily economic, his theories of representation massively influenced postcolonial playwrights as well, for whom the techniques of denaturalizing stage action provided an important tool kit for communicating the historical and cultural stakes behind the strongly normative representational traditions inherited from neoclassical theory.[3] Emphasizing the origins of tragic theory at the beginning of the unit, and then presenting alternatives to these powerful theatrical precepts, encourages students to think genealogically about the evolution of the French-language stage, beginning with highly prescriptive, centralizing rules articulated in the seventeenth century. This critical stance with respect to the political implications of tragic theory in turn mirrors the thematic and formal reflections on staging the king, whose theatrical reign serves as a sign and symptom of evolving ideas about the relation between individual and authority in each successive age.

Numerous thematic parallels between these two plays make them apt subjects for comparison and contrast. While the plot of each revolves around male characters, women are nevertheless granted important roles—Emilie's thirst for revenge drives the conspiracy to assassinate Augustus, and in both *Cinna* and *Christophe* the figure of the queen is endowed with a kind of second sight, providing important counsel in addition to a connection to divination through proleptic dreams. Likewise, both Corneille and Césaire reflect on the meaning of freedom in a social context where its opposite, slavery, remains a social reality. Cinna's conspiracy is betrayed by the treacherous Euphorbe, an *affranchi*, or freed slave, whose name (evocative of the French word *fourbe*, or scoundrel) announces his character, while Christophe's mortal enemy is Pétion, leader of the republic in the south of Haiti, a free person of color who never experienced the humiliations of chattel slavery that constitute the king's formative experiences. When teaching these texts together, I use these thematic elements as support for a structural comparison. One effective way in to this kind of reading lies in close attention to beginnings and endings, which also helps valorize the theoretical readings, fostering comparison between prescriptions and practice in tragedy.

Communicating the backstory that sets the action of the play in motion is one of the signal challenges of theatrical writing, especially in the light of Aristotle's recommendation against long descriptive passages. For Corneille, the challenge also lies in fictionalizing events that would have already been familiar to elite viewing publics, remaining close to the historical script while allowing for the margin of invention required to create an emotionally gripping story. As such, opening scenes merit extended scrutiny: What expectations does the author set up by beginning with a monologue, as in *Cinna*? How is the past invoked, and to what ends, in establishing the present conflict? What information is omitted, sought out, or related in a biased manner, and how does this motivate the subsequent action? By inventing the character of Emilie, and positing her desire to avenge her father as the prime motivator of the plot to assassinate Auguste, Corneille's parable of clemency imbricates individual passion with political calculation. The long tirade that opens the play announces the inward focus that will remain an important feature of the drama, which culminates not in a physical battle, but in Auguste's own struggle to master the same vengeful passions that Emilie enumerates in the first scene. The opening scene thus reflects the priorities of the stage at the apogee of the Richelieu–Louis XIII administration, where the legitimation of an emerging "absolutist" government that sought to concentrate power in the hands of a single person depended on establishing the incontrovertible personal merit of whoever wore the crown.

Césaire's prologue to *La tragédie du roi Christophe* begins in a "low" register, with a parable in the form of a popular Caribbean pastime. At a cockfight in Haiti, the roosters Pétion and Christophe engage in mortal combat—although which bird lies dead at the end is deliberately left unclear. This brief scene establishes a strong sense of place and of the bloody stakes of postcolonial politics, while also serving as a mise en abyme of the tragedy that the theatrical audience has gathered to witness. Only after calling attention to the spectacle, in the theater, as well as on the stage of history, does Césaire present the historical setup of the drama, in the form of a direct address by the Présentateur-Commentateur (Presenter-Commentator), whose Brechtian monologue-cum-history-lesson makes no effort to hide its narrative and pedagogical aims, intentionally breaking the spell of illusion in order to place the audience in a more intellectual, critical frame of mind with respect to the history that underpins the plot of the play. This tonal dissonance is repeated throughout the play, as scenes of gripping drama alternate with buffoonish farce, metatheatrical commentary, and indigenous forms, including Creole songs and Vaudou traditions.

As much as these plays' opening scenes provide a key to understanding the authors' stylistic and narrative goals, their dénouements can be read as a statement on the meaning of tragedy at the time of their writing. The actual course of history restrains the inventiveness of the playwright; as related in the anecdote from Seneca, later retold by Montaigne, on which Corneille based his play, the protagonists live on after the action is finished, a conclusion that often elicits significant discussion on the formal boundaries of tragedy. I have found this to be especially true for anglophone students steeped in Shakespeare and, consciously or not, in Jan Kott's formulation of the "Grand Mechanism," in which the tyrant's murderous rise and bloody fall constitutes the essential script of history (3–56). Indeed, to the extent that Shakespeare constitutes the most universally shared experience of tragedy for American students, the comparison can be revealing. Corneille's Auguste is absolved of the crimes committed by Octave by virtue of raison d'état: the perfidies of his rise to absolute power are washed away by the stability and glory of Rome under his benevolent autocracy. The symbolic death of the scheming, treacherous striver Octave is consecrated by the emperor's new name, the inalterable adjective of majesty replacing the moniker attached to a fallible individual. Considered against the Shakespearean canon, neoclassical French theater offers up a different theory of history, and thus a different set of possibilities for the dénouement of tragic action onstage.

Césaire, the theorist of Négritude, addresses his play to a world in which the question of sovereignty—both of the state and of the political elites that would direct it—confronted the leaders of newly decolonized francophone African states that achieved independence in the early 1960s. His parable of the first Black nation in the New World issues a prophetic warning against the inadvertent reenslavement of independent peoples by the very liberators who assured their legitimate place on the world stage. Henry Christophe's ceaseless activity and indomitable energy define his success as a general, and, as self-proclaimed king of the Royaume du Nord (Northern Kingdom), he models his court after the Bourbon monarchy, building himself sumptuous palaces and deploying his ruthless African janissaries, the Royal Dahomets, to enforce the "Code Henry," a successor to Louis XIV's Code Noir, the legal document that regulated the status and punishment of slaves in French overseas possessions in the seventeenth and eighteenth centuries. Yet, for all his vigor, he ends his life in a state of humiliating debility, crippled by a stroke and hemmed in on all sides by his enemies as Baron Samedi, the Vaudou god of death, comes to lead him away. His body is immured in the monumental Citadelle fortress, the paradoxical symbol of his reign, built by the forced labor of recently freed Haitians in order to protect them from reenslavement at the hands of foreign invaders. Entombed standing up, Henry is deprived of repose in death as he was in life, forever struggling to drag his country and his people out of the mud without ever heeding the accumulated wisdom of their centuries of suffering. Reference to the trajectories of different postcolonial leaders, from Castro to Mobutu to Mugabe, can help bring home how the tragic king's transformation and fall remains relevant in today's world.

Reading the plays for their political-historical message points out how the audience's emotional engagement in the machinations of the tragic plot serves to advance arguments on subjects of broad and lasting public concern. The explicitly political stakes of each play make for engaging in-class discussions, not least in the present age of strongman autocrats and dwindling institutional checks on their power. Cinna's muscular defense of absolutist prerogatives (act 2, scene 1) outlines a theory of royal government consonant with Richelieu's vision of a strong monarchy, while his coconspirator Maxime defends, with equal passion, an argument in favor of devolving power onto consuls drawn from the aristocracy—a far cry, as students will point out, from our present understanding of democratic rule, but an important argument in early modern France, where the nobility had yet to accept the absolute authority of the crown. Corneille's rhetorical clarity in this scene makes it a fine subject for written analysis with respect to the historical arguments provided and to their applicability in the modern world. The revelation, in the following scene, of Cinna's insincerity—he only wants Auguste to remain on the throne so that he can be killed while still emperor—can in turn lead to a wholly different analysis of political doublespeak and calculated flattery. These macro-scale concerns in turn are deeply embedded in character studies, as Corneille reflects on the intersection of power and personality, developing a psychologically astute portrait of an exemplary royal figure as a metaphor for pressing questions about the limits of individual agency. In the final scene of the play, Auguste famously overcomes his desire for revenge on the protégés who would be his assassins, providing an example of the kind of affect control—"Je suis maître de moi comme de l'univers" 'I'm master of myself as of the world' (115; *Cinna* [Penguin] 189)—that fuses individual and political virtues in an exemplary moment of self-actualization, illustrating the sublimation of individual desire in service to the greater good that defines the ideal king.

La tragédie du roi Christophe is shot through with political considerations that overlap with a study of Henry's outsized ambition and implacable resolve; the subject can be construed as the tragedy of kingship as much as the tragedy of a king, which makes it an ideal companion piece to the celebration of monarchy in *Cinna*. Henry is driven by the depth and breadth of the transformation required to allow Haiti to stand as an equal with its former colonial masters; as he says to his counselor, Baron Vastey, "[L]e matériau humain lui-même est à refondre" '[T]he human material needs recasting' (50; Breslin and Ney 31). While there is no single scene that states its competing theses as clearly as in *Cinna*, Césaire provides a clear stylistic key to reading the political stakes of the historical moment, which provides a nice entry into discussing the importance of the many performance codes within the play that are integral to understanding its meaning. For example, the note prior to the first scene stipulates its "style bouffon et parodique" 'clowning and parodic style' (18; Breslin and Ney 9), setting the deliberations of the republican government under the sign of impotent aping (confirmed during scene 6, when the debate in the senate is again designated as "style parodique" 'parodic style' [46; Breslin and Ney 28]), incapable of the decisive action required to protect Haiti from Napoleonic predation and to elevate its formerly enslaved populace into a proud, free people. Henry Christophe begins the play as president of a united Haiti following the death of Dessalines, but abandons the pompous and ineffectual democracy in favor of a kingdom in the North where he will remake the Haitian people in his inflexible, indefatigable image, setting in motion a brutal regime of forced labor in order to eradicate the historical curse of slavery. Césaire frames Christophe's kingship as a moral, rather than political, quest to lead the Haitian people toward a new historical destiny by reforming their innermost selves in a reckless program that foreshadows the trajectory of certain Maoist movements in the decades following the play's publication. As king, Christophe chafes at constraints on his mission to transform the people, and does not hesitate to turn away from the traditional theological underpinnings of monarchy, when these structures and beliefs contradict his desires. He first orders the assassination of the archbishop who supported his rise but pricked his conscience, in a reminiscence of Henry II and Thomas Becket, before raising his sword to the thunder and rain in a mad defiance of heaven itself, a heroic display of the heedless determination to impose his will that will eventually lead to his downfall.[4]

One particular challenge common to the teaching of both of these plays—namely, verse, both Corneille's classical alexandrine line and the freer meter and frequent recourse to Creole song forms in Césaire—can be reframed as opportunity. The many obstacles to comprehension posed by verse, including syntactical inversions, enjambment, extended metaphors, and cultural allusions (in this case from both the neoclassical and Caribbean worlds), are well known to foreign-language instructors. Yet, given that theatrical poetry is composed for oral recitation, recourse to out-loud reading can be an effective and accessible way to help students resolve these problems for themselves. While other essays in the present volume address fully engaging in performance as a classroom strategy, even circumstances that do not allow for this kind of exercise can take advantage of an inherent, and often overlooked, truth about theater. While acting is commonly imagined as an art of speaking, listening is in fact the crucial skill that performers often find hardest to develop, just as learning to listen to students is one of the cornerstones of effective teaching.

Students are asked to identify problem passages in each reading assignment, which they will later read aloud in small groups of peers who can help extract meaning from the formal or stylistic complexities. The emphasis is less on proficient performance (although out-loud reading is also excellent for developing confidence in oral phonetics and prosody) than on trying to reconnect literary forms that can sometimes appear remote with the immediacy of a speaking body, and attending to the different meanings conveyed by voice as distinct from those that are available on the printed page. For this exercise to be most effective, the speaker—the student who has identified a problem passage—should be reminded to speak *to* a classmate, even when the dramatic situation implies an interlocutor who cannot reply, as in apostrophe or soliloquy. Often the mere fact of acknowledging the directionality of speech is enough to overcome difficulties, as students speak verse in order to effect change in an addressee, completing the emotional circuit that is a distinguishing feature of theatrical situations. Variants on this exercise include asking the interlocutor to translate the passage into casual speech after hearing it read out loud, or to generate adjectives to describe the intended effect of the utterance on those to whom it is directed—always with the emphasis on reading as a reciprocal activity in which the listener, far from being a passive receptacle, is coauthor of the meaning. In this sense, d'Aubignac's oft-cited apothegm "Parler c'est agir" 'To speak is to act' (407; my trans.) applies to neoclassical tragedy in the classroom as much as on the stage.

Theatrical techniques can be powerful classroom tools, not least for the way in which they allow for a distribution of *parole*, or speech, among the various actors in the maieutic drama of the humanities classroom. The essentially democratic ideals of this approach stand in stark contrast to the absolutism that emerged in tandem with French neoclassical stage poetics, a political shift marked in *Cinna* by Augustus's transformation from executor of the law to its embodiment (see Bilis). Three centuries later, *La tragédie du roi Christophe* returns to the fusion of the state and the sovereign in post-independence Haiti, the tragedy of Christophe's reign underscoring the dangers of the assimilation of nation with monarch that had been earlier celebrated in Corneille's play. While transporting Henry Christophe's remains to their final resting place in the Citadelle fortress, his pallbearers articulate a crucial link between kingship and theater: "Son poids, c'est sa parole. Faut savoir la comprendre" 'His weight is his words, telling us something. We have to understand what he means' (150; Breslin and Ney 95). Speech emerges as a common source of power in both politics and theater, the linchpin of representing sovereignty on stage. In turn, neoclassical tragedy and its modern descendants afford an excellent opportunity to equip students with a firsthand experience of both powerful language and the language of power, appropriating the structures and discourses of theatrical kingship in the context of modern liberal arts education.

Notes

1. The flexibility of this theme allows instructors to make a wide variety of choices with respect to their individual goals and preferences. For example, Voltaire's exoticized theatrical despots in *Zaïre* and *L'orphelin de la Chine* (*The Orphan of China*) open up discussions of tragedy's formal and political destiny on the prerevolutionary eighteenth-century stage, Hugo's *Le roi s'amuse* (*The King Amuses Himself*) and *Marie Tudor* provide a context to discuss the impact of Romanticism on French theater, and Ionesco's absurdist meditation on individual mortality, *Le roi se meurt* (*Exit the King*), reframes the question of individual and political sovereignty for an age of existential angst.

2. Since the course uses a French translation of Aristotle, critical terms are employed in French throughout the unit. The R. Dupont-Roc and J. Lallot edition is out of print but remains available in many research libraries; in addition to providing a clear translation, this edition explains lexical choices with respect to key concepts that have acquired significant philological baggage. In English, Malcolm Heath's edition of the *Poetics* includes a thorough introduction and a complete set of lexical and conceptual notes. Hélène Baby's edition of *La pratique du théâtre* provides a reliable modern text; a 1684 English translation, *The Whole Art of the Stage*, is available online through the EEBO portal at the University of Michigan (name.umdl.umich.edu/A26187.0001.001).

3. Brecht coined the term *Verfremdungseffekt* to describe the deliberate distancing and denaturalization of the acting style appropriate to his theory of politically engaged theater. While contemporary scholars will refer to "V-effekt," Willett translates this as "alienation effect" or "A-effect;" see Brecht, *Short Organum* §42–68, pp. 191–202.

4. Jean Anouilh's retelling of this story in *Becket, ou L'honneur de dieu* (*Becket; or, The Honor of God*) could also be used for another perspective on modern French-language tragedies of kingship.

Works Cited

Anouilh, Jean. *Becket ou L'honneur de Dieu.* Edited by Bernard Beugnot, Folio, 2010.

Aristotle. *Poetics.* Translated by Malcolm Heath, Penguin Classics, 1997.

———. *La poétique.* Translated by R. Dupont-Roc and J. Lallot, Seuil, 1980.

Bilis, Hélène E. *Passing Judgment: The Politics and Poetics of Sovereignty in French Tragedy from Hardy to Racine.* U of Toronto P, 2016.

Brecht, Bertolt. *A Short Organum for the Theatre. Brecht on Theatre: The Development of an Esthetic*, edited and translated by John Willett, Farrar, Straus and Giroux, 1964, pp. 179–205.

Breslin, Paul, and Rachel Ney, translators. *The Tragedy of King Christophe*, by Aimé Césaire, Northwestern UP, 2015.

Césaire, Aimé. *Discourse on Colonialism.* Translated by Joan Pinkham, Monthly Review Press, 1972, abahlali.org/files/_Discourse_on_Colonialism.pdf.

———. *Discours sur le colonialisme.* 1950. Présence Africaine, 2000.

———. *La tragédie du roi Christophe.* 1963. Présence Africaine, 2000.

Corneille, Pierre. *Cinna.* 1641. Edited by Georges Forestier, Gallimard, 1994.

———. *Cinna. The Cid; Cinna; The Theatrical Illusion,* translated by John Cairncross, Penguin Books, 1975, pp. 113–94.

d'Aubignac, François Hédelin, abbé. *La pratique du théâtre.* Edited by Hélène Baby, Champion, 2001.

———. *The Whole Art of the Stage.* William Cadman, 1684, name.umdl.umich.edu/A26187.0001.001.

Hugo, Victor. *Théâtre 1: Hernani; Le roi s'amuse; Amy Robsart; Marion de Lorme.* GF-Flammarion, 1999.

———. *Théâtre 2: Ruy Blas; Lucrèce Borgia; Marie Tudor; Angelo, tyran de Padoue.* GF-Flammarion, 1999.

Ionesco, Eugène. *Le roi se meurt.* Folio, 1973.

Kott, Jan. *Shakespeare Our Contemporary.* Anchor Books, 1966.

Voltaire. *L'orphelin de la Chine. Œuvres de 1753–57*, edited by Basil Guy et al. *Œuvres complètes de Voltaire*, vol. 45A, Voltaire Foundation, 2009.

———. *Zaïre.* Edited by Pierre Frantz, Folio, 2016.

Part V

Explorations in Theory and Technology

Jennifer Row

A Queer Eye on Racine and Corneille

Teaching neoclassical tragedy through queer theory is a twofold endeavor. On the one hand, neoclassical tragedy, carefully contextualized, can help students think about the history of sexuality and, more broadly, the place of literature as evidence in regard to the historiography of minority identities of the past. On the other hand, neoclassical tragedy can illuminate certain qualities of queer theory and critique, and show that early modern drama can itself contribute to theorizing queer sexuality.

One of the challenges of designing lessons pairing queer theory and neoclassical tragedy is the anachronism of bringing contemporary critical theory to early modern literature. In my classrooms, I endeavor to preserve the alienness of queerness—that is, the familiar-yet-unfamiliar nature of early modern sexuality—and to explore what the friction of this particular strangeness, in tension with our contemporary understanding of sexuality, desire, and erotics, can itself accomplish. One of my teaching objectives is to show that even a genre often thought of as stodgy, such as seventeenth-century tragedy, can inform and enrich our understanding of titillating sexuality and nonnormative desires. I hope that students will gain the critical and analytical skills to read these neoclassical texts against the grain, to revisit what they know about sexuality and about tragedy as a whole, and thus to expand their horizons of possibility of what "counts" as queer. A second objective is for the students to grasp the political and historical importance of queerness and to understand the stakes of the expansiveness of queer analysis and queer critique. Finally, students should be able to think metacritically about atemporal or anachronistic uses of categories from the present (such as the cross-application of queer paradigms) and to see anachronism itself as both an obstacle and an illuminating perspective. In this essay, I take up Racine's *Esther* and Corneille's *Polyeucte* as two key texts to illustrate these objectives and approaches.

The term *queer* as it is used today responds to late-twentieth-century concerns that the fixed categories *lesbian* and *gay* were too strongly anchored in biography or identity. Queerness, in contrast, "can never define an identity; it can only ever disturb one" (Edelman 17); it signals the "open mesh of possibilities, gaps, overlaps, dissonances and resonances, lapses and excesses of meaning when the constituent elements of anyone's gender, of anyone's sexuality aren't made (or can't be made) to signify monolithically" (Sedgwick, *Tendencies* 8). In short, queerness, for the theorists of the late nineties and early aughts, highlights a disruptive sense of sexuality that challenges the heteroreproductive norm and destabilizes the evidences, experiences, and identity categories that shore up the monolithic sense of "normative" (monogamous, straight, reproductive) sexuality. This broad definition serves to highlight how sexuality resides in myriad acts, tendencies, affinities, and intimacies, not necessarily cleaving to a fixed sense of "homosexuality" or "heterosexuality." Furthermore, the "antinormative" aspect of queerness also serves to critically intervene in regimes that privilege sexual norms and ideals tied to the nuclear family and heteroreproductivity.

Such an expansive sense of queerness mirrors many of the complexities of seventeenth-century *sodomie*. "De la sodomie" ("Of Sodomy") in Claude Le Brun de La Rochette's *Les procès civils et criminels* (*Civil and Criminal Proceedings*) can shed light on the historical sense of *sodomie* for a graduate or upper-level undergraduate class. In these five pages, La Rochette describes the act as a sexual crime between two men or between men and women "contre usage naturel" 'against natural usage' (41), implying anal sex; when two women "se corrompent l'une l'autre" 'corrupt one another' (43); or even sex with a "beste brute" 'beastly animal' (42). Other components include masturbation, "chose viliane & odieuse" 'a villainous and odious thing' (40), and sodomy between women, called "tribadisme."[1] Certainly, this is not the only text concerning *sodomie*, but it does concisely list the confusion of definitions and is therefore a useful point of departure for students. This French jurist's vision of *sodomie* here also echoes early modern English concerns and documents, as Jonathan Goldberg, Jeffrey Masten, Mario diGangi, and others have analyzed, as "a void" of socially ordered meaning—that is to say, a negation of the "socially constructed hierarchies that are taken to be natural, that social ordering that is thought to participate in and replicate the order of being (Goldberg 122). Graduate or advanced undergraduate students in comparative literature could be asked to analyze the French and English perspectives on sexual transgression. Graduate students might compare the wealth of analysis on the queer English renaissance/ Shakespeare/ tragedy and the relative paucity of research on queerness in neoclassical French tragedy.

Prior to the discussion of the historicity of sexual acts in the classroom, I suggest that the debates around the *bienséances* (the neoclassical rules of propriety) may share an ideological root with the trigger warnings of today. The *bienséances* may be considered, roughly, a set of guidelines proscribing action that might be too shocking to stage before the public. This meant that careful attention was paid to what kinds of acts, visibilities, and gestures (such as murder, suicide, sex, or pregnancy) might be considered too vulgar or too disturbing for a public audience to see. Similarly, in the classroom, trigger warnings, as advanced signaling of potentially shocking material, may be thought of as primarily concerned with calibrating the disclosure of exceptionally violent, traumatic, or even sexually explicit content in order to help students approach difficult topics while minimizing the risk of being retraumatized or shocked. As when seventeenth-century theater critics and playwrights deliberated over whether shocking material might hamper the audience's enjoyment and engagement, trigger warnings are used to set the grounds for students to be optimally receptive to learning and discussion (and not "closed off" by unsettling content). Trigger warnings have been dismissed as being patronizing (and similar complaints were leveraged against the "handholding" of the *bienséances* in the theater [Row 75]) but they can be a powerful way to open the conversation around difficult topics. Instructors must take into account the institutional climate in which they teach, the backgrounds of their student population, and the impact of current events, from the #MeToo movement against sexual assault to the harrowing pervasiveness of rape and assault on campuses. In the specific context of queering neoclassical tragedy, instructors should set strong guidelines for respectful disagreement and engagement. How might one, for example, deal with a student who adamantly believes that homosexuality is sinful and wrong while another student may be struggling with nascent bisexual desires? How does one calibrate class discussion if a student is openly transgender and another student makes a dismissive joke?

In my own classroom, my students and I develop "rules of engagement" that remain up for debate and adjustment throughout the semester. I ask students to discuss and design rules that address gender identity, disability needs, and general classroom respect. Often, students have asked for protocols that I did not realize might be needed; they have responded with proposals to establish a funny and unique hand sign to ask classmates or myself to repeat what has been said, guidelines for what to do in case of accidentally misgendering a student, and so on. Discussing possible trigger warnings for the reading material and collaborating on the "rules of engagement" can allow students to more deeply and freely interact with this new material and with each other.

Sexual Evidence: *Iphis et Iante*

While Isaac de Benserade's *Iphis et Iante* is not traditionally read as a neoclassical tragedy (and might be more precisely classified as a tragicomedy), elements from its gender-bending plot appear within a tragic register. Moreover, the play's treatment of gender offers a valuable window into early modern perspectives of same-sex love that complement the other approaches and historical contextualizations that I highlight in this essay. Finally, as Jeffrey Masten has argued, the genre of tragicomedy itself is a queer, "interbred" admixture of two genres or species that should not normally be mixed (201). Masten's proposition could invite metareflection at the graduate level on the subgenres of tragedy and the possibilities of expression within tragedy itself.

The play, taking inspiration from Ovid's *Metamorphoses*, tells the tale of Iphis, biologically female but disguised as male since birth because Iphis's father has vowed to kill off any female progeny. Iphis falls in love with a woman, Iante, who believes Iphis is a man. Their wedding night is written in such a way that it could be staged with poignancy or with humor, insofar as Iphis must finally reveal the truth of her gender to Iante. The two must legally consummate their marriage, but with the added twist of Iphis's secret, their nuptial sex would have been considered a moral-legal violation (akin to Rochette's *sodomie*) in the seventeenth-century context. Two plot twists complicate the situation: the bride, Iante, is not actually disappointed in the revelation of Iphis's body; rather, she expresses concern over the legal implications of their marriage:

> Ce mariage est doux, j'y trouve assez d'appâts
> Et si l'on n'en riait, je ne m'en plaindrais pas:
> Je n'aurais pas regret qu'on nous joignît ensemble,
> Si l'on ne profanait le nœud qui nous assemble. (105)
>
> This marriage is sweet: in it I find plenty of delight
> And if people didn't mock it, I wouldn't complain:
> I would have no regrets that we have been joined together
> If the matrimonial knot that binds us were not so profaned.

Iphis uses the conditional tense to "glimpse the relativity of her society's codes and to envisage a hypothetical alternative reality" (Harris, "Disruptive Desires" 159). She expresses a type of erotic desire that oscillates between pleasure-filled acceptance and anxiety over deviant transgression.

The other plot twist concerns the fact that Iphis's male neighbor Ergaste is certain that Iphis is a woman in male disguise, and continually professes his love to Iphis. This has the comedic and poignant effect of one male character proclaiming his desire for another character who appears on stage as male, effectively staging love between men. The gender confusion is finally resolved when the goddess Isis descends in a deus-ex-machina moment to change Iphis's gender, and the whole play ends with a bit of a joke about the baby the male Iphis and his wife, Iante, will have.

Notwithstanding the happy ending, there are tragic elements apparent in the yearnings and longings that Iphis, Iante, and Ergaste express. They seem to grasp for a language that can adequately encompass the complicated desires that thread through layered gender categories (both social and biological) as well as the rules—in flux—that govern acceptable and unacceptable bodies, from the nonscandal of lesbian sex to male desire for a male-appearing body. The play thus illustrates and enriches the early modern world that Michel Foucault describes in *The History of Sexuality*: "Homosexuality appeared as one of the forms of sexuality when it was transposed from the practice of sodomy onto a kind of interior androgyny, a hermaphrodism of the soul. The sodomite had been a temporary aberration; the homosexual was now a species" (43). That is to say, the acts described by La Rochette do not necessarily produce an identity (such as gay, straight, or queer) under what Foucault calls a "species." Such acts do not "name" an identity, but they do disturb the social order of things.

Reading Foucault's *History of Sexuality* is crucial in courses that embark on this queer analysis through the lens of biopolitics. To regard the history of sexuality biopolitically is to see it as the capillary management of many minute affects, behaviors, and tendencies that produce sex as their consequence. Reading *Iphis et Iante* in the light of Foucault's theories and primary texts such as La Rochette allows students to leverage an early modern understanding of a range of sexual acts and transgressions in order to destabilize our contemporary notion of the regime of identities, and to think about the degree to which the regimes of sexual "normalcy" are represented and coalesce on stage.

Tragedy allows us to explore this early modern worldview of sexuality. What does neoclassical tragedy highlight about the ways that queerness has to negotiate, hijack, or contend with some of the structures, forms, and limitations of representation? Is it possible to theorize the relation between the formal qualities of neoclassical tragedy, the *bienséances* and the *règles classiques* (the neoclassical rules limiting tragedy to one place, one day, and one plot), and the historic and aesthetic conditions of possibility for queerness? Queering neoclassical tragedy prompts students to ask questions about the place of literature and other aesthetic cultural productions as evidence of queer desire when thinking about the past. This brings us to the larger question, What counts as evidence of sexuality, or of queerness? One could, for example, challenge students to brainstorm factors that could count as evidence of sexuality as it is defined today. To assist them in this endeavor, I would assign the section "Christmas Effects" from Eve Kosofsky Sedgwick's *Tendencies* (5–9). By using a list of imagined constitutive components of sexuality, Sedgwick destabilizes the monolithic notion of sexuality as the "common sense of [Sedgwick's] time presents as a unitary category" (6). Sedgwick demonstrates that sexuality does not necessarily cohere under umbrella terms such as "gay" or "straight." She lists

> the gender assignment of your preferred partner (supposed to be the same as her/his biological sex);
> the masculinity or femininity of your preferred partner (supposed to be the opposite of your own);
> your self-perception as gay or straight (supposed to correspond to whether your preferred partner is your sex or the opposite);
> your preferred partner's self-perception as gay or straight (supposed to be the same as yours);
> your procreative choice (supposed to be yes if straight, no if gay);

> your preferred sexual act(s) (supposed to be insertive if you are male or masculine, receptive if you are female or feminine);
> your most eroticized sexual organs (supposed to correspond to the procreative capabilities of your sex, and to your insertive/receptive assignment);
> your sexual fantasies (supposed to be highly congruent with your sexual practice, but stronger in intensity);
> your main locus of emotional bonds (supposed to reside in your preferred sexual partner) (6–7)

Sedgwick's list shows that we commonly understand all these components to be valid and validating factors of sexuality. Similarly, I assign students to work in pairs to construct their own lists in response to two questions: What factors (such as fantasies, sexual partners, etc.) count as evidence of sexuality today, and what did or did not count as sex in the seventeenth century? How can such evidence of sexuality be preserved, recorded, or archived, and how would this have been done in the seventeenth century?

In response to the first question, students might point out that components of Sedgwick's list do not necessarily seem to fit the seventeenth-century context neatly (for example, Iante's desire for the female Iphis may count as a "sexual fantasy" but does not necessarily mean that she claims a lesbian identity). As students respond to the second question, I push them to understand that reading for sexualities in the past is complicated. I highlight that in today's society we think of evidence of sexuality as existing in both officially and unofficially recorded domains (e.g., court documents and medical reports, or journals and photographs). In the group discussion that follows, I point out that many official archiving techniques do not allow for the complex multiplicity of partial or contradictorily overlapping desires that Sedgwick outlines. I introduce José Esteban Muñoz's observation that "instead of being clearly available as visible evidence, queerness has instead existed as innuendo, gossip, fleeting moments, and performances that are meant to be interacted with by those within its epistemological sphere—while evaporating at the touch of those who would eliminate queer possibility" (6). Advanced undergraduate students might read the Muñoz article in addition to "Evidence of Experience," in which Joan W. Scott challenges the masculine, empiricist investment in observation and reliance on fixed ontologies in favor of feminist (and queer) belief in experience and other affective, ephemeral moments. In this light, we might also brainstorm a third list that responds to a third question: What kinds of ephemera might not immediately appear as evidence, but need to be considered as evidence for the purposes of thinking about queer histories?

At this point in the course, I ask students about the relation of neoclassical tragedy to the status of "evidence" that we crafted in the second list. It would be ideal to introduce this discussion once they have already thought about the sociopolitical culture of the seventeenth century, taking into account that tragedy could be considered both official and ephemeral: a phenomenon concrete enough to be state-sanctioned as a genre, meeting the conditions and approval of the king and institutions such as the Académie Française, but nevertheless fleeting, only creating its "meaning" in the moment of performance. From the viewpoint of the historian, theater might also have a secondary status as evidence of queer desire; although literature lacks the legal authority of court documents or calendars, its relative license makes it more hospitable to imaginative and unexpected eroticism. From the viewpoint of the literary scholar, tragedy's powerful affective impact (through catharsis and through ideological representation of absolutist, sovereign power) had wide-reaching implications for the sociocultural sphere as well as the political sphere. Overall, the readings and the brainstorm exercise sequences serve to prime students to think expansively and imaginatively about what can and cannot count as evidence of queer desire. The classroom discussion could then be guided by a few questions: What does the epistemological hunger for such evidence say about the ways that sexuality is organized and ordered in our society today? Or, more simply, why is sexuality associated so strongly with evidence (or sexuality and surveillance) when other types of more visible identities (such as disability, race, or gender) do not necessarily need proof or invite such scrutiny? Is tragedy a fertile site for thinking about queerness?

The Closet as Metaphor and Method: *Polyeucte* and *Esther*

Pierre Corneille's *Polyeucte* and Jean Racine's *Esther* illustrates the theory of what Sedgwick calls the "epistemology of the closet." Students should read Sedgwick's introduction (*Epistemology of the Closet* 1–66) and first chapter (67–90), which argue that the closet is the "defining structure for gay oppression in this century" (71), not only because the structure of the closet invites excavatory readings (to unearth the "truth" or the "secret" hidden behind the closet door) and therefore legitimizes surveillance practices, but also because of the binarisms that the closet produces. The closet itself perpetuates a monolithic and dualistic understanding of sexuality, that there can be such a thing as a coherent "inside" and "outside" to sexuality, and it also perpetuates the so-called homo-hetero divide.

Many queer theorists, rooted in the anglophone or American Studies tradition, have tended to rely on texts from the American nineteenth century to the present, overlooking the rich possibilities of French seventeenth-century literature. Sedgwick's analysis shows that we can bring theory to tragedy, but we can also, conversely, let neoclassical tragedy show us how to theorize. Racine's play closely follows the biblical tale in which the queen Esther, secretly a Jew, must self-identify as Jewish in order to save her people from destruction. Her husband, King Assuérus, has been convinced by a conniving vizier to have all the Jewish people in the kingdom slaughtered. Outing herself as Jewish puts Esther in a precarious—and possibly deadly—position, but it is an act of courage, undertaken to elicit the king's empathy toward her people.

Racine's text deeply resonates with the emotions of fear and anticipation that one might experience when one is considering revealing a secret part of one's identity. Esther, for example, prays, "Accompagne mes pas / Devant ce fier lion, qui ne te connaît pas. / Commande en me voyant que son courroux s'apaise / Et prête à mes discours un charme qui lui plaise" 'Accompany my steps / before this proud lion, who does not know you. / Command that his wrath dissipate upon seeing me / and lend to me and my words a charm that pleases him' (1.4.357–60). The text uses the doubled sense of *pas* ("steps" or "negation") to highlight how fraught the first "step" out of the closet can be, especially when that step is into a terrain that wishes to negate one's very existence.

And yet, the equivalences between coming out of a Jewish closet and coming out of a homosexual closet are not perfect. Sedgwick uses the affective richness of the play to explore the tensions around disclosure, teasing out seven ways in which the presumed concreteness of Jewish identity serves as a specific counterpoint to the tenuousness of the binaristic identity categories fomented by the epistemology of the closet. For example, she writes regarding Esther's Jewish identity, "[T]here is no suggestion that that identity might be a debatable, a porous or mutable fact about her," insofar as Esther invokes her family and her bloodline as part of, as evidence of, and as origin of her identity. In contrast, queer identities are often questioned or challenged when coming out of the closet (the infamous "it's just a phase" assumption). The reason for this, Sedgwick points out, is that our views on sexuality are organized around a "radical and irreducible incoherence" (85) that holds that sexuality can be both “minoritiz[ed],” by maintaining that “there is a distinct population who ‘really are’ gay,” and “universaliz[ed],” by suggesting that “sexual desire is an unpredictably powerful solvent of stable identities.” We can see this rhetoric play out today. In the minoritizing category, some hold that LGBTQ people are “born that way” and can no more dictate their own sexual identity than they can choose their adult height. A universalizing approach could range from the thought that “everyone is a little bit gay” to the fears that inclusive sex education in the classroom could “turn students gay.” This universalizing viewpoint could lead to homophobic fears that homosexuality could be transmitted or taught. Overall, both the minoritizing and universalizing approaches can serve as bids for the validity of lesbian or gay identities, but they can also be wielded to stigmatize and denigrate. Sexuality is fluid and fungible, Sedgwick reminds us, and the force of the “epistemology of the closet” changes not just the social perception of the person coming out but also the “erotic identity of the person who received the disclosure,” which is “apt also to be implicated in, hence perturbed by it” (Sedgwick 81).

Students, in small-group discussions, should point out connections and dissimilarities, as Sedgwick does, between Esther’s moment of self-disclosure as a disenfranchised identity and the contemporary notion of the closet. They can then build on this conversation to theorize the cross-applicability of the closet to different minoritized identities, and the problems and advantages of coalition-building between different forms of denigrated, hidden identities (across various cultures, time periods, and more). Discussion of the Wars of Religion and French political sentiments regarding Huguenot and Catholic identities and beliefs can illuminate fears surrounding secret conversion, the fungibility of identity, and the relationship between bloodline (family) and faith with regards to the articulation of religious identity. Sedgwick’s analysis of the fungibility and interminability of identity offers a useful counterpoint discussion to the early modern anxieties around Protestant and Catholic conversion and the visibility or hiddenness of such proclaimed affinities. Theories of equivocation in the early modern period (see Ferguson 265–332) might further enrich the student debate.

In this light, I might also ask the students to reflect on the differences and similarities between the disclosure of a converted identity—with its political and personal valences—and the disclosure of a sexual identity (with its own political and personal impacts).

Corneille's *Polyeucte* is another tragedy that features a plot around "closeting." In the play, set in ancient Armenia (c. 250 CE) under the rule of the Roman Empire, the Armenian Polyeucte decides to convert to Christianity, a crime against both the Roman government and the state-sponsored pagan religion. He dismisses the pleas of his wife, Pauline, and his father-in-law, the governor Félix, in favor of following his dear friend Néarque to his martyred death. Pauline, meanwhile, is shaken by the reappearance of her former lover, Sévère, while she tries to convince Polyeucte to retract his conversion in order to avoid death. The "minoritizing" and "universalizing" views of sexuality and identity are both held, though each view is incongruous with the other: the position of Christian martyr can be read as a metaphor for a minoritized, hidden religious identity in addition to the rich and complicated tender ties that queer the friendship between Polyeucte and Néarque. Students should also understand that, while in the play Christianity is depicted as a minoritarian religion, in the French seventeenth century and even contemporary cultural tradition, Christianity (Catholicism) is the majoritarian identity that requires protection. The 2017 staging at the Théâtre des Abbesses highlights the radical-political nature of Polyeucte's fanaticism by depicting his conversion as one to Islam—this particular staging offers a resonant link for students who have grown up in a world where religious terrorism and charges of fanaticism are the stuff of everyday news.

I ask students to read from John Boswell's *Same-Sex Unions in Pre-modern Europe* and reflect on what it means for Polyeucte and Néarque to be treated as a queer couple. For Boswell, one of the founding theorists and writers of gay history, Polyeuct and Nearchos stand as one of three key early Christian queer martyr pairs. Drawing upon B. Aubé's account in *Polyeucte dans l'histoire*, Boswell reminds us that "St. Polyeuct and Nearchos . . . were described in their fourth-century biography as 'brothers, not by birth, but by affection.' They enjoyed 'the closest possible friendship, being both comrades and fellow-soldiers'" (141). Describing more than merely a fraternal affection, however, Boswell (citing Aubé) recounts an episode in which Nearchos and Polyeuct learn that all Christians are to be executed for their faith. In it Nearchos says, "But this, dearest [φίλτατε], is precisely what weighs on my soul. There is something worse than the death of humans: the separation that I fear might take place [. . .] for I had feared that I would lose you from my love [φιλίας] and that we would lose the unity of our soul [συνειδήσεως]" (143). Aubé's account continues, “Polyeucte then roused within himself the organ of his soul, and reaching for Nearchos with his bodily eyes, took his hand and asked, ‘Is this then what you feared, Nearchos, and was this your suspicion about us from the beginning? Did you realize this about the bodily part of our love?’” (143).

According to Aubé, it is the strength of this love and the fear of being separated from one another that propels Polyeucte to convert. Corneille’s version of the story foregrounds this notion of fear of separation. After Félix has Néarque executed, he asks, “Et notre Polyeucte a vu trancher sa vie?” ‘And our Polyeucte saw his life cut short?’ confirming that, per his orders, Polyeucte has been forced to watch his friend die. Albin responds, “Il l’a vu, mais hélas! Avec un œil d’envie. / Il brûle de le suivre au lieu de reculer” ‘He saw the execution, but alas! with an envious eye / He was burning to follow him instead of retreating’ (3.4.958–59). An undergraduate class might be able to find moments in the play where the language of desire, amorous burning, and passion (e.g., “brûle” ‘burn’) is used. The class could then compare Polyeucte’s cold rejection of heterosexual marriage to the ardent intimacy he shares with Néarque.

Following the Boswell text, I ask the class to trace moments where the text emphasizes *suivre* (“to follow”) and other terms indicating following, closeness, or sameness between the men. Then we could debate if *champ lexical* (lexical field) of sameness echoes this love between friends (between men), as emphasized by Boswell, or points to a minoritized identity (of being on the same page, on the same team). For example, when Stratonice (Pauline’s friend) describes Polyeucte’s conversion to her, she says, “Voici de leur vieille amitié l’indigne fruit” ‘Behold what unworthy fruit is borne from their old friendship’ (3.2.808), a comparison that underscores that the conversion is wrought from a closeness, an intimacy, as well as implicitly comparing the “fruits” of a too-close same-gender friendship with reproductive fruits from a heterosexual relationship (children).

On one level, Néarque and Polyeucte themselves paint the moment of disclosing their identity as almost a coming out. Néarque says,

> Allons, cher Polyeucte, allons aux yeux des hommes
> Braver l’idolâtrie, et montrer qui nous sommes;
> Puissai-je vous donner l’exemple de souffrir,
> Comme vous me donnez celui de vous offrir!
> . . . .
> Ne perdons plus de temps: le sacrifice est prêt;
> Allons-y du vrai Dieu soutenir l’intérêt;

Allons fouler aux pieds ce foudre ridicule
Dont arme un bois pourri ce peuple trop crédule;
Allons en éclairer l'aveuglement fatal;
Allons briser ces dieux de pierre et de métal:
Abandonnons nos jours à cette ardeur céleste;
Faisons triompher Dieu: qu'il dispose du reste! (2.4.645–48, 711–18)

Let us go, dear Polyeucte, let us go and under the gaze of all
Stand up to idolatry, and reveal who we are;
If only I could set the example of suffering,
as you set the example of offering yourself up!
. . . .
Let us waste no more time: the sacrifice is ready;
Let us go there to sustain the interest of the true God;
Let us go and dash to the ground this ridiculous thundering
With which a too-naïve people arm themselves;
Let us go shatter these gods of stone and metal:
Yield our days to this celestial ardor;
Let us make God triumph; may he deal with the rest!

As an exercise, students can compare the militant-revolutionary tone of Polyeucte and Néarque's "coming out" to the anxieties present in Esther's mulling over her own disclosure of identity. Certainly, a closer reading of the affective language reveals both similarities and differences.

For a second exercise, students can examine moments in the text where the *secte* ("sect") of Christianity can be read as an allegory of queer identity. Pauline's friend Stratonice describes the Christians at the beginning of the play: "Leur secte est insensée, impie, et sacrilège, / Et dans son sacrifice use de sortilège" 'Their sect is insane, impious and sacrilegious / and uses sorcery in its sacrifice'(1.3.257–58). Similarly, the ever-compassionate Sévère, despite the fact that his rival Polyecute's death means that he himself could marry Pauline, tries to defend Christianity to his friend, saying, "La secte des chrétiens n'est pas ce que l'on pense, / On les hait, la raison je ne la connais point . . . / Par curiosité, j'ai voulu les connaître" 'The sect of the Christians is not what one thinks, / We hate them, but I do not understand the reason for it . . . / Out of curiosity, I wanted to know them' (4.6.1412–13, 1415). In the language around the *secte* as a group, we see that the play presents Christianity as a metaphor for a denigrated minority.

Yet Christianity is also depicted as "universalizing," insofar as Néarque "turns" Polyeucte (act I, scene 2) and Polyeucte's martyred blood "turns" Pauline:

Son sang, dont tes bourreaux viennent de me couvrir,
M'a dessillé les yeux, et me les vient d'ouvrir.
Je vois, je sais, je crois, je suis désabusée:
De ce bienheureux sang tu me vois baptisée (5.5.1725–28)

His blood, which his executioners covered me with,
Washed out my eyes, opened them for me.
I see, I know, I believe, I am disabused:
In this blessed blood you see me now baptized

Christianity is shown here as something that can be transmitted not through the traditional, diachronic pathways of blood-as-genealogy (as was the case with Judaism in *Esther*) but through the synchronic spattering of blood-as-contagion. In class discussion we might reflect on whether Christianity is painted in minoritizing and universalizing rhetoric. Since queerness is imagined to be transmittable by homophobic rhetoric, Christianity's fluidity therefore operates as a more similar allegory of queerness in *Polyeucte* than *Esther*'s presentation of Jewish identity.

Following these exercises, I bring the class back to the discussion of the role of literature and history, and the previously discussed ways that *sodomie* was viewed as contrary to the order of things, not necessarily a sexual identity, but rather as a category of disruptive erotic/sexual acts. We could review the terms surrounding *sodomie* and compare them to the varying ranges of identity presented in *Polyeucte*. The queer identity is present in both allegorized and literal guises, from Polyeucte and Néarque's aberrant friendship to the rhetoric of Christianity as a minoritized sect to fears of universalized transmission to a divergent coming-out narrative.

Other neoclassical tragedies that might be discussed in class include Racine's *Phèdre*, which could be presented in the context of incest and illicit desires, and Œnone's devotion to Phèdre read as a type of queer attachment. We might also think of queer undertones in Catherine Bernard's *Laodamie*, which depicts sisterly love as a force set in equal, structural opposition to the politics of heterosexual, royal love. In *Laodamie*, the love between sisters is not equivalent to same-sex desire, but its interruptive force carries a queer effect by undermining the primacy of heterosexuality.

Approached with careful historical and methodological planning, neoclassical tragedy can illuminate how theater both models and mirrors changing notions of sexuality in the seventeenth century. Without this structuring, one could risk teaching queerness as a "freakish" aberrancy, instead of as part and parcel of a changing culture that was grappling with different ideas about sexuality. Although the traditional genre of neoclassical tragedy eliminated "bodily" representation, both in terms of corporeal violence and sexuality, there is still eroticism present in the texts: an occasion for students to learn to reconsider the various ways that sexuality is evidenced. Neoclassical tragedies also offer a window into the ways that minoritized, denigrated identities might have been affectively experienced or expressed, and thus provide an occasion for students to reflect on the epistemologies of identity today. Finally, early modern notions of *sodomie*, both present and implicit in tragedies, shed new light on the possibilities of queerness and queer theory today.

Note

1. All translations are my own unless otherwise attributed.

Works Cited

Benserade, Isaac de. *Iphis et Iante.* 1634. Lampsaque, 2000.

Bernard, Catherine. *Laodamie.* 1688. *Théâtre des femmes de l'Ancien Régime: XVIIe–XVIIIe siècle*, edited by Henriette Goldwyn et al., Classiques Garnier, 2014.

Boswell, John. *Same-Sex Unions in Premodern Europe.* Vintage, 1995.

Corneille, Pierre. *Polyeucte: Tragédie.* 1643. Larousse, 1965.

Edelman, Lee. *No Future: Queer Theory and the Death Drive.* Duke UP, 2004.

Ferguson, Margaret. *Dido's Daughters: Literacy, Gender and Empire in Early Modern England and France.* U of Chicago P, 2003.

Foucault, Michel. *The History of Sexuality, Volume 1: An Introduction.* Translated by Robert Hurley, reissue edition, Vintage Books, 1978.

Goldberg, Jonathan. *Sodometries: Renaissance Texts, Modern Sexualities.* Fordham UP, 2010.

Harris, Joseph. "Disruptive Desires: Lesbian Sexuality in Isaac de Benserade's *Iphis et Iante* (1634)." *Seventeenth-Century French Studies*, vol. 24, no. 1, 2002, pp. 151–63, doi:10.1179/c17.2002.24.1.151.

La Rochette, Claude Le Brun de. *Civil and Criminal Proceedings. Homosexuality in Early Modern France: A Documentary Collection*, edited by Jeffrey Merrick and Bryant Ragan, Oxford UP, 2000, pp. 15–16.

———. *Les procès civils et criminels.* Pierre Calles, 1611.

Masten, Jeffrey. *Queer Philologies: Sex, Language, and Affect in Shakespeare's Time.* U of Pennsylvania P, 2016.

Muñoz, José Esteban. "Ephemera as Evidence: Introductory Notes to Queer Acts." *Women and Performance: A Journal of Feminist Theory*, vol. 8, no. 2, 1996, pp. 5–16. *Taylor and Francis Online*, doi:10.1080/07407709608571228.

Polyeucte. By Pierre Corneille, directed by Brigitte Jacques-Wajeman, 10 Jan. 2017, Théâtre des Abbesses, Paris.

Racine, Jean. *Esther*. 1689. *Théâtre complet*, pp. 905–81.
———. *Phèdre*. 1677. *Théâtre complet*, pp. 819–904.
———. *Théâtre complet*. Edited by Alain Viala and Sylvaine Guyot, Editions Classiques Garnier, 2014.
Row, Jennifer. "Queer Time on the Early Modern Stage: France and the Drama of Biopower." *Exemplaria*, vol. 29, no. 1, Winter 2017, pp. 58–81.
Scott, Joan W. "The Evidence of Experience. (Questions of Evidence)." *Critical Inquiry*, vol. 17, no. 4, 1991, p. 773, doi:10.1086/448612.
Sedgwick, Eve Kosofsky. *Epistemology of the Closet, Updated with a New Preface*. U of California P, 2008.
———. *Tendencies*. Routledge, 1994.

Anna Rosensweig

An Affective Approach to Teaching Neoclassical Tragedy

The teaching of French neoclassical tragedy tends to emphasize the genre's aesthetic principles more than its preoccupation with the passions. As a result, neoclassical tragedy risks appearing to students as passionless, ruled by reason and structure rather than flights of feeling. Yet the passions are central to neoclassical tragedy and tragic theory on a number of levels. For one, debates about the aesthetic principles of tragedy—*bienséance* (decorum), *vraisemblance* (verisimilitude), and the unities—often centered during the seventeenth century on how to maximize the genre's emotional effects (see, e.g., Forestier; Goodkin; Lyons, *Kingdom* [43–82], *Tragedy*). For another, the passions drive much of the action on the tragic stage itself. Many French tragedies feature at least one character who cannot control his or her passions. Kings are overcome with rage. Sisters cannot stop mourning their brothers. Love leads both men and women to violate codes of propriety. Neoclassical tragedy presents the passions as volatile forces that often cannot be contained.

Recent scholarship on neoclassical tragedy has stressed how important the passions are to understanding the genre's social and political force (see, e.g., Guyot; Hoxby; Ibbett [60–97]; Koch; Lyons, *Tragedy*). Together, this scholarship challenges the long-standing idealist view of tragedy (neoclassical and otherwise), which has overemphasized rules and reason. In this essay, I propose an approach to teaching neoclassical tragedy that incorporates this recent scholarship into the classroom. The passions—and the struggles to contain them—provide those who teach neoclassical tragedy with a powerful means of engaging twenty-first-century students in the genre. Contemporary students are certainly no strangers to the power of emotions. What is more, many of them are acutely aware that definitions of emotional excess are shaped by social and political circumstances. Emphasizing the complex role of the passions allows us to immerse students in a genre that might otherwise (falsely) appear abstract and feel too far removed from their experience.

In the pages that follow, I detail an affective approach that cultivates students' engagement in the emotional stakes of neoclassical tragedy. Central to this approach is a classroom environment that encourages students to reflect on their own emotional responses to tragedy and validates these emotional responses as part of critical inquiry. As a result, my approach to teaching neoclassical tragedy departs from modes of instruction that ask students to think without considering how they feel. In order to elucidate how this affective approach works in practice, I focus on a pedagogical experiment I conducted while teaching a course on neoclassical tragedy, titled Crimes of Passion: Love and Death on the French Classical Stage, for advanced undergraduates at the University of Rochester.

My desire to experiment with affective pedagogy derived in large part from a previous experience teaching Crimes of Passion, during which I had largely failed to get students to grasp how crucial the passions are to understanding the political, social, and personal stakes of neoclassical tragedy. I had designed this first iteration of Crimes of Passion around the idea that tragedy is a genre of tensions between passion, emotional excess, and control. I was focused on making sure that students learned how the passions operate in these dramas and theoretical texts. The students who took this version of the course were bright, attentive, and hardworking, but they struggled to understand the passions' centrality in neoclassical tragedy and their role in shaping tragedy's place in seventeenth-century society. The problem, I realized, was that as an instructor I had approached the class in a way that was at odds with the material: while asking the students to engage with the emotional stakes of tragedy, I had addressed their reason without attending to their emotions. In other words, I had inadvertently stripped our collective inquiry of its emotional charge by approaching the passions thematically as a subject to be examined rather than as a force to be reckoned with.

After this initial experience with Crimes of Passion, I tried another approach, one that was informed by research in critical pedagogy. Emboldened by Paulo Freire's critique of the traditional "banking concept of education," which positions students as empty vessels waiting to be filled with information by the teacher (72), and bell hooks's call for "engaged pedagogy," which "necessarily values student expression" (20), I decided to explicitly elicit students' emotional responses to tragedy in the second iteration of the course.[1] Throughout the semester, I asked students in regard to the readings, "How does that make you feel?" I was uneasy at first about employing such a question, which did not fit into my sense of how to teach literature or how to run a classroom. I was used to thinking of students' emotional reactions as preanalytical, unreflective, and beside the point. This discomfort arose despite my training in performance studies, a field that places the body, corporeality, and lived experience at the forefront of our understanding of how knowledge and power are produced (and reproduced). I am committed to this kind of analysis but nevertheless had to push myself to incorporate these intellectual convictions and commitments into the classroom.

I was also wary of asking students how they felt about the readings for several other reasons. For one, "How does this make you feel?" seemed like a very personal question, and I did not want to infringe on students' privacy. For another, it seemed like a therapist's question rather than an educator's. I distinctly remembered one of my graduate school professors stating that the literature classroom should under no circumstances come to resemble group therapy. And, finally, I had no idea how I would assess students' responses. Would I grade their feelings? If so, how? And to what end? At the beginning of the semester, with these concerns in mind, I decided that I would solicit students' emotional responses to the tragedies we were reading together, but I would not ask them to share these emotional responses. After all, my primary goal was to encourage students to attend to their own emotional responses, rather than to require that they confess their feelings.

Most sessions of the second iteration of Crimes of Passion began with a writing prompt. Sometimes the prompt was, "How did today's reading make you feel?" Other times, I asked students to write about their reading experience and suggested they consider questions such as, Where were you when you read? Was it a quiet, private space or a loud, public space? What was the weather like? How were you feeling then and there? Given that students were responding to these prompts in French, I encouraged them to practice circumlocution if they didn't have the precise vocabulary to describe a particular mood or scene.[2] At the start of each writing session, I made it clear that their responses to these prompts were for their eyes only; they would not be asked to share their responses with me or with their classmates. The first five to seven minutes of each class session were devoted to writing that I never saw or graded. I often participated in these writing activities, responding to the prompts and reflecting on how I felt. I adopted this practice of not sharing as a way of respecting students' privacy and allowing them some freedom from pedagogical surveillance. What transpired was unexpected: the practice of writing alone, together, made students more comfortable with one another and fostered a sense of community.

As the semester progressed, I began to use multipart writing prompts in order to help students connect their emotional responses to neoclassical tragedies with the emotional landscapes of the tragedies themselves. At the beginning of our discussion of Jean Racine's *Andromaque*, for example, I gave students a three-part prompt, explaining that they would keep their responses to questions 1 and 2 to themselves but that we would use their responses to question 3 to guide our discussion of the play:

1. How are you feeling today?
2. How did the first act of *Andromaque* make you feel?
3. Pick a character from *Andromaque*. What is this character feeling?

Variations I have used for question 3 include asking students to compare and contrast the feelings of two characters in a scene or asking them to focus on the mood or tone of a scene as a whole. Asking students a series of questions such as the ones I've just outlined—in which they move from an accounting of their own feelings to an accounting of their feelings about the play, then to an accounting of how the emotions or passions are at work in the play—encouraged them to make personal, embodied connections to neoclassical tragedies, which cultivated their interest in engaging with this genre in a sustained way.[3]

What accounts for the success of these writing prompts? Telling students that they will not be asked to share the most personal parts of their writing makes them more eager to share their responses and reactions to the questions that are under discussion. What is more, asking students to account for how they feel—and how they feel about the play under discussion—authorizes them to express their personal feelings about the play. When teaching the first iteration of this course, I was concerned with helping students distinguish between an opinion and an argument. I did not abandon that distinction during the experiment with affective pedagogy; students in the second iteration of this course were given several traditional assignments, such as composing papers that made well-developed arguments supported by textual evidence. However, what this group of students and I explored together was how, very often, one's personal opinion or one's feeling about a text shapes the arguments that one is able to make. In other words, feelings and opinions can shape which arguments are intelligible. Acknowledging our emotional responses to texts helps us move beyond, through, or around the limitations that these responses impose on our critique.

A scene from Crimes of Passion illustrates the critically generative effect of authorizing students to express their feelings. At the beginning of the semester, the class read excerpts from Plato's *Republic* (books 7 and 10) and Aristotle's *Poetics* (chapters 4 through 6). We also read Richard Goodkin's "Neoclassical Dramatic Theory in Seventeenth-Century France." These readings helped establish the group's collective understanding of the passions' importance to the poetics of tragedy as a genre, as well as to receptions of tragedy in both ancient Greece and seventeenth-century France. The first seventeenth-century tragedy that we read together was Pierre Corneille's *Le Cid*, and the students' experience with *Le Cid* remained a touchstone throughout the semester, a reference point as we moved on to other texts. I was thus not surprised that a student brought up *Le Cid* during our discussion of *Andromaque*. We had begun to explore the chain of romantic relationships that links Racine's characters when a student pointed to a moment in the third act where Hermione speaks to Oreste about her engagement to Pyrrhus:

> Mais que puis-je, Seigneur? On a promis ma foi.
> Lui ravirai-je un bien qu'il ne tient pas de moi?
> L'amour ne règle pas le sort d'une princesse.
> La gloire d'obéir est tout ce qu'on nous laisse.
> Cependant je partais, et vous avez pu voir
> Combien je relâchais pour vous de mon devoir. (*Andromaque* 3.3.819–24)

> What can I do, sir? I was pledged to him.
> Shall I take back from him what others gave?
> Can love decide a princess' destiny?
> All we are left with is obedience' crown.
> Yet I was ready to depart. You saw
> How far I could make light of duty's laws. (*Andromache* 3.3.819–24)

After reading this passage out loud, the student made the following comment: "Ce passage m'a fait penser à Chimène" 'This passage made me think of Chimène [from *Le Cid*].' Thrilled that a student had begun to make a connection between the two plays, I began nodding and asked her to elaborate. She continued, "Elle parle du devoir et de la gloire et du conflit avec l'amour" 'She speaks about duty and glory and about the conflict with love.' As I continued to nod enthusiastically, she added, "Mais Hermione ne croit pas au devoir" 'But Hermione doesn't believe in duty.' At this last statement, my nodding got slower. I was unsure of what the student meant, but I noticed other students begin to signal their agreement. One of these other students chimed in, "Oui, je n'aime pas Chimène, mais j'aime Hermione" 'Yeah, I don't like Chimène, but I like Hermione.' I was perplexed, but the students all seemed to be on the same page.

In a previous semester, I likely would have felt that our discussion had taken an unproductive turn and that I needed to regain control and move the students toward more appropriate, more academic reactions to and questions about the text. I was in fact a bit annoyed by the direction the conversation had taken, in part because we had spent so much time earlier in the semester talking about Chimène, about the conflict between her love and duty, about *bienséance* and the *querelle du* Cid, that I was surprised to hear "Je n'aime pas Chimène" 'I don't like Chimène.' Given my experiments with affect and opinion, however, I decided that I would let the class talk about their preferences for a while. I would listen and try to determine what their dislike of Chimène and preference for Hermione was all about. In the end, I was glad to have curbed my annoyance enough to hear more.

What emerged from our conversation was that, while the students had previously understood why Chimène was duty bound and why she loved Rodrigue but experienced her love for him to be abhorrent, they now found Chimène's repeated expressions of her duty and her resulting emotional state completely alienating. Hermione, in contrast, cut a more compelling figure to the students because her expression of duty seemed strategic. As the student who started the conversation noted, Hermione does not really seem to believe in or care about her duty. She speaks the language of duty, but duty is not the emotional force that animates the play. The students explained that they could relate to Hermione but not to Chimène. Chimène seemed foreign, whereas Hermione seemed familiar. The students' account of their reactions led to a discussion about how these reactions were shaped in part by their own cultural context. For these students, familial duty and honor were not necessarily primary modes of emotional attachment or affiliation. As a result, Hermione's ability to speak the language of duty without necessarily subscribing to it was more emotionally intelligible to them. They had all had the experience of fulfilling an obligation that they did not particularly enjoy or find meaningful. They had not, however, experienced the inner turmoil of having two deeply felt obligations conflict with each other.

After the students recognized how their personal reactions were bound up with their cultural context, I was able to move the conversation from the characters' relative likeability to the differences between the affective landscape of *Le Cid* and that of *Andromaque*, and more broadly between Corneille's dramaturgy and Racine's. By "affective landscape," I mean the ways that the passions figure and give meaning in each tragedy. At the point in the semester when the students expressed their dislike for Chimène, we had already talked about some of the differences between Cornelian and Racinian tragedy. We had discussed, for example, Jean de La Bruyère's articulation in his *Caractères* (*Characters*) of the two dramatists' respective relationships to the passions and their visions of human nature:

> Corneille nous assujettit à ses caractères et à ses idées, Racine se conforme aux nôtres; celui-là peint les hommes comme ils devraient être, celui-ci les peint tels qu'ils sont. Il y a plus dans le premier de ce que l'on admire, et de ce qu'on doit même imiter; il y a plus dans le second de ce que l'on reconnaît dans les autres, ou de ce que l'on éprouve dans soi-même. L'un élève, étonne, maîtrise, instruit; l'autre plaît, remue, touche, pénètre. (84)
>
> Corneille subjects us to his Characters and Ideas; Racine's are more comfortable to our own: the one paints Men as they ought to be; the other describes 'em as they are. There is in the first more of what we admire, and ought to imitate; and in the second more of what we discover in others, and approve in ourselves. Corneille elevates, surprises,

> triumphs, and instructs; Racine pleases, affects, moves, and penetrates. (*Characters* 23–24)

Whereas Racine provides a stirring account of the human condition, Corneille offers an admirable ideal of human potential. Whereas Racine models his characters on fallible humans, Corneille's characters are models of what humans should be. While my students had appreciated these distinctions intellectually, they did not fully understand these distinctions until they felt them in their respective reactions to Chimène and Hermione.

Another demonstration of affective pedagogy's potential occurred during our discussion of Corneille's *Suréna*. In our opening writing session, I had prompted students first to identify the emotions expressed in a particular scene and then to identify the verbs that were used in relation to or surrounding these emotions. Together, the students generated a list of verbs that included *dissimuler* ("to dissimulate"), *cacher* ("to hide"), and *feindre* ("to pretend"). They observed that many of the verbs associated with emotions in *Suréna* had to do with the careful management of their expression. Emotions could be shared in some settings but had to be concealed in others. The students' observations generated a robust discussion of the dynamics of secrecy in *Suréna*, as well as of the play's delineation of public and private space. The students also reflected on how the felt experience of emotions that one can publicize and share differs from the felt experience of emotions that one must endeavor to keep hidden.

Affective pedagogy means addressing students as embodied subjects who feel. The breakthrough moment the students had in class about why they preferred Hermione over Chimène was the result of a pedagogy that appealed to their emotions as well as their reason. We had read Plato and Aristotle; we had read seventeenth-century dramatic theory; we had carefully analyzed linguistic and poetic elements of the plays; and we had also reflected in journal entries on our emotional states in general, on our emotional reactions to the plays, and on the affective landscape of each play. Throughout the semester, our affective work occurred alongside our more traditionally critical or academic endeavors. Given neoclassical tragedy's preoccupation with the passions, and given that performances were seen and felt by embodied spectators, this genre is an ideal site through which to reclaim the importance of affective work in the classroom.

My experiment with Crimes of Passion pushed me to recognize how deeply thought and feeling are coimplicated, even if I cannot always determine precisely why or how. Further, my experiment meant relinquishing control over the classroom in ways that did not always feel comfortable. Assuring students that they would not have to report on (nor would I collect) certain writing prompts, and allowing students to express personal opinions about characters, scenes, and plays, were not part of my usual pedagogical repertoire. Despite my own discomfort, I found that the most productive moments in my tragedy course that semester—the moments when the students seemed to be listening most attentively to the plays, to one another, and to me—were those during which the students were most attuned to their emotional reactions and able to incorporate these reactions into their analysis.

I would be remiss if I did not acknowledge a factor that contributed to the success of my initial experiment with affective pedagogy: a very small class size. I had only four students in this second iteration of Crimes of Passion. The small number of students greatly facilitated my ability to launch such an experiment in the first place because it was possible for me continually to take the measure of each student's interest and engagement. This is not to suggest that an affective approach must be limited to small seminars. The approach could be scaled up in a larger class through small discussion groups in which students share their feelings, observations, and insights.

Another way to incorporate affective pedagogy into a larger class would be to make some of the journal-writing prompts more guided. I gave my students the relatively open-ended task of identifying the emotions at work in a particular tragedy and specifying a passage that illustrated one or more of these emotions. Logan J. Connors provides a different model in his "Increasing Engagement in French and Francophone Studies: Structured Journaling on the Emotions with La Fayette's *La princesse de Clèves.*" Connors uses structured journaling in his survey course on French literature from the Middle Ages to the Revolution, which he reports usually varies in enrollment from twelve to twenty-four students. Before he asks students to begin reading the assigned novel, he devotes some class time to identifying terms from the text related to emotion and social interaction. He then asks students to generate definitions for these words based on their own experiences as twenty-first-century college students. Connors writes,

> Then I assign a journal exercise in conjunction with the reading for the next class, inviting students to write about some of the emotion words that we had studied together in class. I ask them to contextualize, in the

> first part of the story, words like *inclination*, *trouble*, *passion*, *rougeur*, *froideur*, *modestie*, *respect*, and *intelligence*—words that La Fayette uses to describe the emotional events of the novel and that sometimes have radically different definitions today. (1477)

Connors reports that this structured journaling exercise helps students mark the differences between their contemporary emotional vocabulary and the emotional vocabulary of *La princesse de Clèves* and of the French seventeenth century more broadly. The exercise yields similar results to the sequence of questions I asked in my course on neoclassical tragedy. In both cases, helping students attend to the differences between premodern emotional landscapes and their contemporary experiences sparked their curiosity and intellectual engagement.

Instructors often assume that students are simply uninterested in genres such as neoclassical tragedy, which are different and distant from those they regularly engage with in our contemporary moment. We also assume that we can only capture their interest once they have acquired a certain level of linguistic, cultural, or historical competence. In other words, we assume that reason must precede passion. What I have found instead is that we often have too little information about students' emotional responses to or interest in the material—whether positive or negative—because we have not asked them.[4] Encouraging students to attend to their emotional states and to account for their emotional responses to genres such as neoclassical tragedy lowers potential barriers to sparking and sustaining their interest. Asking students to account for these reactions increases their overall engagement with the material and heightens their desire to improve their linguistic, cultural, and historical competencies. Finally, affective pedagogy does not entail abandoning critical inquiry but instead involves recognizing the role that emotions play in shaping our inquiry.

Notes

1. My desire to develop an affective approach to teaching neoclassical tragedy was shaped by several (often overlapping) teaching and research interests in performance studies, affect theory, the history of the emotions, and critical pedagogy. Key references in addition to Freire and hooks include Sarah Rose Cavanagh, Jill Dolan, Jacques Rancière, Barbara H. Rosenwein, and Margaret Werry and Róisín O'Gorman.

2. Other ways to help students navigate the linguistic challenge of expressing a variety of feelings in French include having students anonymously submit vocabulary questions that came up during the writing prompt and then having the group

work through some of these questions together as a warm-up during the following session; and providing a *tableau d'humeur*, or mood chart, from which students can match different facial expressions with the corresponding vocabulary.

3. In the course syllabus, I explained that students were to bring a journal to class each day in which they would record their responses to these writing prompts. I did not read or grade their journals but instead counted students' participation in these writing exercises as part of their overall participation grade.

4. Hélène Merlin-Kajman writes persuasively about the dangers of failing to take seriously what might be considered naive or untrained responses to literature in *Lire dans la gueule du loup: Essai sur une zone à défendre, la littérature* (*Reading in the Mouth of the Wolf: Essay on Literature, a Zone to Defend*).

Works Cited

Aristotle. *Poetics*. Translated by Malcolm Heath, Penguin Classics, 1996.

Cavanagh, Sarah Rose. *The Spark of Learning: Energizing the College Classroom with the Science of Emotion*. West Virginia UP, 2016.

Connors, Logan J. "Increasing Engagement in French and Francophone Studies: Structured Journaling on the Emotions with La Fayette's *La princesse de Clèves*." *PMLA*, vol. 130, no. 5, Oct. 2016, pp. 1476–80. *MLA Journals*, doi:10.1632/pmla.2015.130.5.1476.

Corneille, Pierre. *Le Cid*. 1637. Edited by Boris Donné, Flammarion, 2009.

———. *Suréna*. 1674. Edited by Jean-Pierre Chauveau, Gallimard, 1999.

Dolan, Jill. *Geographies of Learning: Theory and Practice, Activism and Performance*. Wesleyan UP, 2001.

Forestier, Georges. *Passions tragiques et règles classiques: Essai sur la tragédie française*. PU de France, 2003.

Freire, Paulo. *Pedagogy of the Oppressed*. 1968. Translated by Myra Bergman Ramos, 30th anniversary ed., Continuum, 2000.

Goodkin, Richard E. "Neoclassical Dramatic Theory in Seventeenth-Century France." *A Companion to Tragedy*, edited by Rebecca Bushnell, Wiley-Blackwell, 2009, pp. 373–92.

Guyot, Sylvaine. *Racine et le corps tragique*. PU de France, 2014.

hooks, bell. *Teaching to Transgress: Education as the Practice of Freedom*. Routledge, 1994.

Hoxby, Blair. *What Was Tragedy? Theory and the Early Modern Canon*. Oxford UP, 2015.

Ibbett, Katherine. *Compassion's Edge: Fellow-Feeling and Its Limits in Early Modern France*, U of Pennsylvania P, 2018.

Koch, Erec R. *The Aesthetic Body: Passion, Sensibility, and Corporeality in Seventeenth-Century France*. U of Delaware P, 2008.

La Bruyère, Jean de. *Les caractères ou les mœurs de ce siècle*. 1694. *Œuvres complètes*, edited by Julien Benda, Gallimard, 1951. *The ARTFL Project*, lib.uchicago.edu/efts/ARTFL.

———. *The Characters, or Manners of the Present Age*. *The Works of Monsieur de La Bruyere*, 6th ed., vol. 2, London, 1713. *Google Books*, books.google.com/books?id=2GCQcxD7AUcC.

Lyons, John D. *Kingdom of Disorder: The Theory of Tragedy in Classical France*, Purdue UP, 1999.

———. *Tragedy and the Return of the Dead*. Northwestern UP, 2018.

Merlin-Kajman, Hélène. *Lire dans la gueule du loup: Essai sur une zone à défendre, la littérature*. Gallimard, 2016.

Plato. *The Republic*. Edited by G. R. F. Ferrari, translated by Tom Griffith, Cambridge UP, 2000.

Racine, Jean. *Andromache. Andromache; Britannicus; Berenice*, translated by John Cairncross, Penguin Books, 1967.

———. *Andromaque*. 1667. Edited by Jean-Pierre Collinet, Gallimard, 1994.

Rancière, Jacques. *The Emancipated Spectator*. Translated by Gregory Elliott, Verso, 2011.

Rosenwein, Barbara H. *Generations of Feeling: A History of the Emotions, 600–1700*. Cambridge UP, 2016.

Werry, Margaret, and Róisín O'Gorman. "Shamefaced: Performing Pedagogy, Outing Affect." *Text and Performance Quarterly*, vol. 27, no. 3, July 2007, pp. 213–30. *Taylor and Francis Online*, doi:10.1080/10462930701412353.

Theresa Varney Kennedy and David Jortner

Corneille versus the Académie Française: Teaching *Le Cid* through Courtroom Drama

Although first published as a tragicomedy, Pierre Corneille's *Le Cid* significantly contributes to students' understanding of French tragedy, since the quarrel that surrounded *Le Cid* determined the evaluative criteria for future tragedies. That said, students often struggle to balance historical content with an appreciation of the play itself. Some students find fault with the play once they are exposed to the criticisms that the Académie Française launched against Corneille. Other students—especially those in the dramatic arts—stand suspicious of censorship in any form and ultimately side with the playwright. Students generally fail to appreciate the complexity of the issues that the quarrel (and the play) inspired. As such, their interpretations tend to be one-sided. This knowledge gap inspired us to craft a student-centered role-playing exercise that encourages robust engagement with this centuries-old masterpiece. We incorporated aspects that engaged more active learning: information sharing, collaborative work, student-to-student dialogue, and referential questions.

Interdisciplinary collaboration also enables students, and instructors, to see *Le Cid* from a better-informed perspective.[1] The way the play is understood often depends on the students' academic backgrounds. For instance, French majors tend to study these plays as works of literature, neglecting the performance aspects. In contrast, theater majors often miss French historical and cultural references.

Regular guest lecturing and team teaching in each other's courses led us to develop a large-scale role-play simulation project involving both graduate theater students and undergraduates studying French.[2] Borrowing from other disciplines' use of mock trials and Mark C. Carnes's Reacting to the Past series, our role-playing simulation pits the Académie Française against Corneille in a contemporary American court of law.[3] Carnes's model is the most immediately applicable to our simulation since it involves historical figures and classical texts. Carnes pioneered the Reacting to the Past curriculum in the late 1990s. Reacting to the Past is an innovative curriculum in which students adopt roles and play out scenarios based on primary documents. The method promotes game playing rather than reenactment. Players take on roles that "include objectives to achieve and ideas to advance; they require players to promote various interpretations of the texts that accompany every game" (Proctor 10). Students essentially run the class while instructors serve as guides. The goal of Reacting to the Past is to allow students, by role-playing historical figures, to come away with a greater understanding of the actions, opinions, and ideals of those persons. Moreover, the games require that students "engage the texts on several levels. First, they must read them. Then, they must create persuasive speeches, films, cartoons, broadsides or essays about them. Finally they must use them as a foundation for their spoken attempts to persuade other players to adopt their interpretations of the texts" (Proctor 11). By taking on roles that may be inimical to their own thinking, students are forced to reevaluate previously held ideas.[4]

While inspired by Reacting to the Past, our pedagogical exercise deviates significantly from it in several ways. Reacting to the Past games can run anywhere from one class period to a week or more.[5] For our simulation activity we wanted to stay within the framework of a single three-hour class. We also needed to find a structure suited to both a graduate theater class and an undergraduate French class. The idea of an American courtroom scenario allowed us to find roles for all participants that played to the pedagogical needs of both classes. Moreover, we could expect all the students to be familiar with courtroom proceedings, especially the nature of testimony and cross-examination.

Our courtroom drama simulation activity achieves a threefold objective. First, it deepens students' understanding of the issues debated by seventeenth-century theorists and playwrights. There can be no doubt that taking on the role of a historical figure compels students to spend more time reading and reflecting on primary sources. Second, the simulation engages other disciplines (e.g., literature and history) by dramatizing conflicts such as Chimène's struggle to be heard in a male-dominated society, or the call in transitional times to incorporate old and new forms of government, language, and art. Finally, the exercise incites students to confront their own twenty-first-century mindsets regarding artistic freedom and censorship, and to reconsider the positive and negative impact that rules have on the creative process. The simulation provides a unique, participatory, and engaging mechanism for thinking about censorship and creative freedom in the modern world.

Introducing *Le Cid* to an Undergraduate French Class

In preparation for serving as jurors in a mock-trial case between Corneille and the Académie Française, our undergraduates spend a few classes discussing *Le Cid* as well as the historical *querelle* ("quarrel"). We recommend the Petits Classiques Larousse edition of the play, which is geared toward French high school students. The *fiches d'identité* introducing the author and the play are informative without giving too many details, and the extensive vocabulary explanations in the footnotes makes reading in verse more approachable for beginning-level literature students.

Reading in verse is not the only hindrance to student engagement. The tendency to perceive the instructor as the authority on the text and the expert in matters of interpretation is a great obstacle to a student-centered approach. It thus becomes crucial to find innovative ways to adopt student-centered language activities when teaching literature in the target language (Katz 155). As Kramsch states, the teaching and exploration of literature should be a "social event" in which students experience multiple interpretations of the reading (364). Active learning prevents students from viewing the instructor as the only source of information and encourages an exchange of personal expression and interpretation.

To encourage active learning, Theresa Kennedy starts the unit on *Le Cid* with a clue-gathering discussion activity. After hearing a fifteen- to twenty-minute lecture on the history of seventeenth-century France and the development of the Académie Française, students make a list on the chalkboard of characters in *Le Cid* and brainstorm cultural values or personality traits revealed by the characters' words, actions, or thoughts. For instance, they may note that honor and duty require Rodrigue to be courageous and valiant while they require Chimène to be submissive and obedient. It is important that students understand that decorum (*bienséance*) prohibits Chimène from making a public display of her feelings for Rodrigue. Later, students should be able to recognize the ways in which Chimène violates decorum when we discuss the *querelle*. Students may also compare Don Diègue with the Count. To fully understand the political implications of *Le Cid*, students need to recognize the opposing orders that each of these characters respectively represents: the old order, in which an individual may hold power over his own fiefdom, and the new order, in which the king has absolute authority over all of his subjects. This tension between the old and the new drives the plot. The character sketches serve as an opportunity to guide students toward important observations regarding the play as the action unfolds. This open discussion also sets the tone for the rest of the unit, with students aware that they must give their opinion and actively participate.

Kennedy begins familiarizing students with the *querelle* and the literary debates surrounding tragicomedy early in the unit on *Le Cid*. She invites students to make predictions as they progress through the play about which aspects the Académie Française might have criticized. For instance, she asks them to explain why the Académie would not have approved of the scene in which Rodrigue visits Chimène after killing her father in a duel. This kind of discussion helps students review the rules of seventeenth-century theater and encourages them to critically engage with the text. Students may refer to quotes by seventeenth-century theorists to support their ideas. They may also refer to passages in Corneille's *Examen du Cid* to see how the playwright defends this particular scene.

To familiarize students with the *querelle*, Kennedy distributes selected passages from Georges de Scudéry's *Observations sur* Le Cid and Jean Chapelain's *Sentiments de l'Académie*.[6] On the last day of the unit, students participate in a small-scale in-class debate. Half the students defend Corneille, accused of writing a defective, immoral play, while the other students defend the Académie Française's attacks on *Le Cid*. Prior to the debate, students work in small groups to brainstorm and discuss possible arguments based on the quotes distributed to them in class. Those defending Corneille may want to refer to passages or quotes taken from the author's *Examen* or his *Trois discours sur le poème dramatique*. Sometimes a guest professor decides which team has made the more convincing arguments. At the end of the in-class activity, the instructor discusses with students their upcoming role as jurors in the role-playing simulation with the graduate students.

Teaching *Le Cid* to Graduate Theater Students

In contrast to the undergraduate French theater course, David Jortner's graduate course in theater theory is a broad overview of theoretical ideas from Plato to Ibsen. In addition to reading *Le Cid* in translation, students read documents from the *querelle* (translated and collected in Dukore) and are invited to determine how the arguments therein may be applicable to their own artistic work on stage. They explore the aesthetic and theoretical ideas endorsed by Corneille and his contemporaries by reading Scudéry's "Observations on *Le Cid*," Chapelain's "Sentiments of the Academy on *Le Cid*," and Corneille's *Three Discourses on Dramatic Poetry*. To bridge the gap between late-seventeenth-century and eighteenth-century conceptualizations of theory and practice, they read extracts from Racine's prefaces to *Andromaque*, *Britannicus*, *Bérénice*, and *Phèdre*, Voltaire's "Discourse on Tragedy," and Diderot's "On Dramatic Poetry." Students also have a strong background in earlier theoretical work such as Aristotle's *Poetics*, Senecan tragedy, and Elizabethan dramaturgy. Prior to the seminar on Corneille and *Le Cid*, students write a three-page interrogative that summarizes the *Cid* controversy and how it relates to dramatic works they have previously read. These written responses are then distributed to the class for other students to read and comment upon.

There are three main prompt questions that guide the presimulation graduate-student discussion on *Le Cid* and French neoclassicism: What is the relation between form and function and between genre and its intended purpose? Why do the theorists base their dramatic rules on those of the ancients? How does censorship affect creativity? Students are initially exposed to the prefaces and the literary or theatrical debates going on in seventeenth-century France. The discussion questions used to elicit student responses focus on the question of genre and the rules for the theater:

> Which kinds of questions or discussions come up over and over in the prefaces? Why? Students will want to discuss concepts such as verisimilitude, the unities, decorum, and catharsis, and may refer to *The Whole Art of the Stage*, by François Hédelin, abbé d'Aubignac, or to Corneille's *Three Discourses*.

What are the rules (verisimilitude, decorum, etc.), and where do they come from? Students may refer to Aristotle's *Poetics*, but others may point out that Aristotle does not specifically mention the unity of place at all.

Why do theorists attempt to follow the ancient Greeks and Romans? (Theater students may need to be reminded that France was in the process of transitioning from a decentralized to a centralized government, and that order, clarity, good taste, and moral purpose—all notions associated with the recently rediscovered works of Aristotle, Horace, and other Greek and Roman writers—were values the budding centralized government sought to instill in seventeenth-century French aristocracy. The Greek tragic writers Sophocles and Euripides became more important toward the mid seventeenth century as tragedy began to replace tragicomedy.)

Why are these rules being advanced, and by whom? How are seventeenth-century French politics directly connected to seventeenth-century French theater? Students may discuss the important role that the Académie Française played in reinforcing the monarchy's control over literary and theatrical production. Since the French monarchy sought to centralize its power, the theater could be used as a propagandist tool.

What are the characteristics of tragicomedy, and why is it dismissed in the middle of the seventeenth century? How does tragicomedy differ from tragedy? Students should be able to define the basic characteristics of tragicomedy based on *Le Cid* or other tragicomedies they have read. Students who have carefully read Aristotle's *Poetics* will remember that for Aristotle, tragedy, as opposed to other genres (e.g., comedy and epic), inspired the tragic pleasure of pity and fear in the spectator. And if catharsis (purgation of emotion) was a desired outcome of a theatrical performance, then tragedy was an ideal genre for a society concerned with reinforcing the values of seventeenth-century nobility (e.g., glory and grandeur) and discouraging negative conduct (e.g., the desire for revenge, jealousy).

During the first part of the discussion, led by both Jortner and Kennedy, students are exposed to the underlying paradoxes upon which the *querelle* is based. French Academicians modeled their "new" theatrical rules on "old" ideas previously conceived of by the Greeks—a civilization that France perceived as one of the greatest ever. This is one reason that tragicomedy, a genre more associated with imaginative fiction than with Greek or Roman history, was written off mid century. Paradoxically, French writers looked backward in order to move forward. At the same time, seventeenth-century French writers could not agree on how to interpret and implement the rules, and students are encouraged to compare theory and practice. The discussion questions force students to think about what made *Le Cid* problematic in the seventeenth century, why it was censored, and why it would be challenging to stage it today for a contemporary American audience:

Why was *Le Cid* attacked? By whom? How does Corneille defend himself? Do you think he is right? (Students will refer to Corneille's *Three Discourses* to discuss how the playwright justifies his modifications to the rules for the theater. Some theater students are highly critical of the playwright's attempt to include so many events in such a short span of time and will side with Georges de Scudéry in his "Observations on *The Cid*." Students may also point to Scudéry's criticism of Chimène.)

Has *Le Cid* stood the test of time? Why or why not? Why may it be difficult for a twenty-first-century audience to relate to the work? Which values are emphasized in the play? Students may discuss their understanding of seventeenth-century French honor as it is presented in the play—a concept that is at odds with the emphasis that contemporary American society places on individuality.

How do you interpret the ending of the play? Is there a political purpose for this kind of message in the seventeenth century? (Corneille's use of a deus ex machina, in which the king resolves a debt of honor and approves a controversial marriage, is not the most esteemed plot device, but it is intentional on Corneille's part. Students may point out that the king's goodness and mercy are what allow a return to order.)

What makes Rodrigue the quintessential Cornelian hero? Rodrigue places duty above romantic interests. Students may allude to Corneille's discussion of the hero in *Three Discourses*.

How are women gendered in this play? How are they constructed as women? Why is it so difficult to relate to them today? How does the Infanta compare with Chimène? It is difficult for twenty-first-century American students to understand how duty (and honor) influenced female conduct in early modern France. Women from powerful political families were often required to stifle romantic interests in the name of duty. While the Académie Française viewed the role of the Infanta as superfluous, students may point out that she is the ideal Cornelian heroine who successfully extinguishes her feelings for Rodrigue in the name of duty. Students may refer to Scudéry's "Observations on *The Cid*" in Dukore.

What makes this pre-neoclassical period attractive to us today? Are rules bad for creative artists? How does censorship affect or effect creative thought? Theater students may discuss the fact that constraints often serve as a source of innovation.

What did theater audiences expect in the seventeenth century? How did audiences change in the eighteenth century? It is important for students to realize that theater audiences would undergo a transformation throughout the early modern period. For instance, students may refer to eighteenth-century writers such as Diderot and Beaumarchais, who insisted that all of the ranks of society be represented in plays. (A good reference for theater students is Jeffrey Ravel's *The Contested Parterre: Public Theater and French Political Culture, 1680–1791.*)

The discussion questions also allow students to situate the play and the *querelle*'s complex debates within their historical and social context. For instance, the Académie Française viewed Chimène's betrothal to the murderer of her father as improper. Issues of censorship in seventeenth-century France had recently become more concerned with the illicit portrayal of female desire (DeJean 17, 20). As such, the Académie Française viewed Chimène's continued passion for the murderer of her father in particular as a threat to public morality. Moreover, Chimène's claim to an honor (mainly vengeance) that was traditionally identified as "male" also violated rules of decorum. While the Académie Française endeavored to reinforce moral and ethical standards with regard to female conduct, Corneille justified his choices on the authority of historical sources.

Mock Trial

The mock trial gives students an opportunity to role-play both sides of the issues that the members of the Académie debated: Does Corneille respect the unity of time by having the action take place in a twenty-four-hour period, the unity of place by representing events within a logical geographic space, and the unity of action by ridding the plot of superfluous elements? Moreover, do the characters respect decorum: Do they conduct themselves according to the norms of their status and gender, and does the play reflect the world as it should be? Finally, is the play verisimilar; are the events plausible?

The structure of the mock trial forms the basis of this activity. With Kennedy serving as judge and the undergraduate students as jury, the graduate students play litigants: one side representing the academy and the other representing Corneille. Our mock trial is based on civil rather than criminal litigation; the goal is for the graduate students to convince the undergraduates to vote for their side at the end of the trial. The addition of the undergraduate jury raises the stakes for our graduate students and supplies the undergraduates with an important role to play. Judge Kennedy ensures that the students keep their arguments within the realm of historical documents and sources.

Graduate students on each side prepare a list of witnesses pulled from the authors of documents on the *querelle* and later sources. Students take on the roles of Corneille, Scudéry, Chapelain, and Aristotle, among others (for a full cast of characters and representative texts, see appendix). A graduate student performs as a witness (for example, Scudéry) while another member of the team asks questions and elicits testimony, allowing the witness's words to construct their argument. In turn, the opposing side is offered the chance to cross-examine the witness. As before, we ask that the students use direct quotations from material as the basis for questions or answers. The cross-examination format also allows students to ask for clarification and to deconstruct the opponents' arguments. In this scenario, we encourage students to ask questions based on texts written by historical authors and theoreticians; it is interesting, for example, to hear what the student playing the role of Corneille has to say in response to quotations or ideas from Shakespeare, Plato, or the Académie Française launched at him by the opposition.

After the last student on the Académie side gives testimony, the opposing side places Corneille on the stand. Again, both testimony and cross-examination allow for in-depth exploration of Corneille's aesthetic choices in the process of writing *Le Cid* as well as his responses to the concerns raised by the Académie Française. For instance, following Scudéry's testimony, the cross-examiner may ask Corneille why he decided to violate the unity of time by packing so many events into a twenty-four-hour period. The student operating as Corneille may want to refer to his *Three Discourses on Dramatic Poetry*, in which he argues that the Aristotelian dramatic guidelines were not meant to be subject to a strict literal reading. Students then call a second round of witnesses who include theorists such as the secretary of the Académie Française, Jean Chapelain, and Aristotle. One student on each side is then tasked with delivering a closing argument that summarizes his or her main views and addresses the issues brought up by the opposition. Finally, the undergraduate students are instructed to deliberate for a few moments and then deliver a verdict. This allows students to discuss which arguments they find to be most influential and why.

Assessment

Assessment and follow-up differs for each class. The role of censorship in theater is discussed throughout the graduate course, beginning with the Platonic objections to theater. By joining the debate over *Le Cid*, students will undoubtedly arrive at a greater understanding of how "regular" academicians exploited the rules to censor and regulate not only literary production but also society. In the seventeenth century, political authorities believed that theater had an obligation to raise society's moral standards. While many students assume that censorship is a vestige of the past and always deleterious, by physically inhabiting the roles of Scudéry, Chapelain, and others, they are forced to consider the political, social, and aesthetic arguments for censorship and control. The theorists' motivations become clearer, even if students disagree with their opinions. In addition, it is interesting for theater students to examine the idea that aesthetic and political restrictions, rather than quashing innovation, may instead be a source of inspiration and creativity.[7] In short, a result of this exercise is that students gain a more nuanced and complex understanding of the interrelation between censorial control and artistic innovation.

As a follow-up in the undergraduate French class, students discuss what they learned about seventeenth-century theater as a result of their participation in the mock trial. They are often divided as to whether or not they agree with the Académie's criticisms based on seventeenth- and twenty-first-century standards. Students can easily memorize the rules for the tragic genre, but the mock trial helps them internalize the complexity of their origins and implications.

In sum, the controversy over *Le Cid* can seem distant to twenty-first-century students. Activities such as the exercise described above allow students to embody the critical discourses and arguments argued by Corneille and the Académie Française. When given the opportunity to take on the roles as adjudicators and advocates, students become active learners engaged with the materials and ideas. Moreover, the Reacting to the Past curriculum is flexible enough to allow for adaptation and evolution. For instance, students in graduate French courses should read texts in the original French and may want to include other members of the Académie Française. Instructors of undergraduate French courses may adapt the Reacting to the Past method to emphasize literature, rather than history, by having students take on characters from the play, such as Chimène or the Infanta, who could serve as witnesses. These modifications would expand the cast of characters, encourage improvisation in the target language, and provide more roles for larger classes. It would also provide a more diverse cast of characters, since members of the Académie Française in the early modern period were all men.

In the case mentioned above, graduate students in theater studies and undergraduate students of French successfully collaborated on the court-case simulation. Collaboration benefits all. The presence of the undergraduate audience, not accustomed to the presumptive artistic freedom associated with twenty-first-century theater, requires the graduate students to reflect upon the pedagogical effects of their arguments. For undergraduate students, participating in theater as a site of advanced scholarship, cultural importance, and reflection, instead of mere entertainment, deepens their learning experience. As for the instructors, collaboration strengthens collegiality and offers new opportunities for creative scholarship.

Notes

1. For a study that discusses the benefits of interdisciplinary teaching and learning at institutions of higher learning, see Lattuca 145–56.

2. Once per academic year, the theater professor David Jortner teaches a graduate seminar on dramatic theory that includes a unit on neoclassical French theater. Meanwhile, Theresa Kennedy offers a survey course of French theater every two years that alternates with a survey course of French literature. Corneille's *Le Cid* figures on all three syllabi.

3. Many mock trials teach jurisprudence by placing students in the roles of litigators or judges, from which positions they grapple with issues of criminal or constitutional law.

4. We are not the first instructors to be inspired to apply the Reacting to the Past curriculum to the *Cid* controversy. Jane Barnette, in personal communication with David Jortner, has noted that she has used it in her theater history classroom,

and Amy Hughes refers to her model for a similar exercise in *The Teaching Portfolio: A Practical Guide to Improved Performance and Promotion/Tenure Decisions.* Andrew Kircher is working on a written version of a game in which student teams attempt to persuade undecided individuals to agree with their side's position while a student portraying Cardinal Richelieu serves as facilitator.

5. Proctor suggests six game sessions for most typical reacting games: these would be preceded by two to three setup sessions and a debriefing session. Clearly, we did not have that much time in our respective courses; however, Proctor does suggest "micro games," which can be played in a single session, although he emphasizes the need for setup and debriefing. For more on setup, see Proctor 105–14.

6. These works, along with all of the other documents related to the *querelle*, may be found in Armand Gasté's invaluable collection, *La querelle du* Cid*: Pièces et pamphlets publiés d'après les originaux* (*The Quarrel of* Le Cid*: Plays and Pamphlets Based on the Original*). For a more recent and accessible edition, readers should refer to Civardi. For translations of key passages from the *querelle*, see Beasley in this volume.

7. The noted American contemporary theater director Anne Bogart is in agreement with this as well. The MFA students also read Bogart's work *A Director Prepares: Seven Essays on Art and Theater*, where she writes, "Paradoxically, it is the restrictions, the precision, the exactitude that allows for the possibility for freedom. The form becomes a container in which the actor can find endless variations and interpretive freedom" (46).

Works Cited

Aristotle, *Poetics.* Translated by Malcolm Heath, Penguin Classics, 1997.

Bogart, Anne. *A Director Prepares: Seven Essays on Art and Theater.* Routledge, 2001.

Carnes, Mark C. *Reacting to the Past.* 2018, reacting.barnard.edu.

Civardi, J.-M., editor. *La querelle du* Cid *(1637–1638): Édition critique intégrale.* Champion, 2004.

Corneille, Pierre. *Le Cid.* Larousse Editions, 2012.

———. Le Cid *and* The Liar. Translated and edited by Richard P. Wilbur, Mariner Books/Houghton Mifflin Harcourt, 2009.

———. *Examen du Cid.* Louisiana State UP, 1978, pp. 159–64.

———. *Trois discours sur le poème dramatique.* Flammarion, 1999.

DeJean, Joan. *The Reinvention of Obscenity: Sex, Lies, and Tabloids in Early Modern France.* University of Chicago Press, 2002.

Dukore, Bernard F., editor. *Dramatic Theory and Criticism: Greeks to Grotowski.* Thomson/Heinle, 1985.

Gasté, Armand. *La querelle du* Cid*: Pièces et pamphlets publiés d'après les originaux.* H. Welter, 1898.

Hughes, Amy. "Theater." *The Teaching Portfolio: A Practical Guide to Improved Performance and Promotion / Tenure Decisions*, edited by Peter J. Seldin et al., Jossey-Bass, 2010, pp. 363–71.

Katz, Stacey. "Teaching Literary Texts at the Intermediate Level: A Structured Input Approach." *SLA and the Literature Classroom: Fostering Dialogues. Issues in Language Program Direction: A Series of Annual Volumes*, edited by V. M. Scott et al., Heinle, 2001, pp. 154–71.
Kramsch, Claire. "Literary Texts in the Classroom: A Discourse." *Modern Language Journal*, vol. 69, 1985, pp. 356–66.
Lattuca, Lisa R. *Creating Interdisciplinarity: Interdisciplinary Research and Teaching among College and University Faculty*. Vanderbilt UP, 2001.
Proctor, Nicholas W. *Reacting to the Past Game Designers Handbook*. 4th ed., CreateSpace, 2018.
Ravel, Jeffrey, *The Contested Parterre: Public Theater and French Political Culture, 1680–1791*. Cornell UP, 1999.

Appendix

Cast of Characters	**Texts in Dukore**
Aristotle	*Poetics* (31–55)
Georges de Scudéry	"Observations on *The Cid*" (211–17)
Pierre Corneille	"Apologetic Letter" (217–20) "Three Discourses on Dramatic Poetry" (226–37)
Jean Chapelain	"The Opinions of the French Academy" (220–26)
François Hédelin, abbé d'Aubignac	*The Whole Art of the Stage* (238–49)
Jean Racine	"First Preface to *Andromache*" (253) "First Preface to *Britannicus*" (253–54) "Preface to *Bérénice*" (254–55) "Preface to *Phaedra*" (255)
Charles de Marguetel de Saint-Denis, seigneur de Saint-Évremond	"On the Characters of Tragedies" (269–70) "Of Ancient and Modern Tragedy" (271–76) "To an Author Who Asked My Opinion of a Play Where the Heroine Does Nothing but Lament Herself" (277)
Voltaire	"Preface to *Oedipus*" (278–79) "A Discourse on Tragedy" (280–85)
Denis Diderot	*Encyclopedia* "Comedy" (287–89) "Tragedy" (290–91) "On Dramatic Poetry" (292–93)
Pierre Augustin Caron de Beaumarchais	"An Essay on Serious Drama" (297–304)

Hélène E. Bilis

Neoclassical Tragedy, Distant Reading, and the Digital Sphere

This essay offers strategies for drawing on digital platforms to introduce undergraduate students both to the genre of French neoclassical tragedy and to the field of the digital humanities (DH). The goal is to integrate the teaching of literature with DH approaches by assigning projects that use digital resources to study French tragedy and by encouraging students to reflect on how digital tools shape their understanding of tragedy and their learning experience more generally. As an outcome of the approach, I see three intertwined goals: students will discover and evaluate a Franco-American collaborative DH project related to neoclassical theater; they will learn how to approach a database from a humanities perspective as they manipulate and analyze large quantities of data; and they will deepen their understanding of the material history of theater, specifically with regard to the defining French theatrical institution that is the Comédie-Française.

The assignments I describe could be applied to a semester-long course dedicated either to French theater or to DH approaches, or adapted to French culture, history, or literature courses as part of a unit focused on neoclassical theater. No technological expertise is required to implement the activities I propose, only interest in bringing digital media into the classroom. The Comédie-Française Registers Project (CFRP) will stand out as the primary resource discussed in this essay, but the framework, steps, and assignments I describe are meant to be transferable to other digital platforms focused on theater.[1]

The Promise and Pitfalls of the Digital Sphere

When turning to digital approaches to teach tragedy, I always devote the first session of class to reflecting with students on how the reader of texts and the user of digital materials perform distinct roles with important differences. I aim to sensitize students from the start to the ways in which a specific medium shapes their impression of the materials they are considering and to alert them to the possibilities and constraints of digital and nondigital resources.[2] We brainstorm how going online to consult materials or viewing a digital archive differs from opening a book in a dorm room, visiting the college stacks, or making a trip to a special collection to consult a first edition of a text. Students consult the Web site of the Bibliothèque Nationale de France (BnF.fr) to look up the conditions and fees for in-person access and list the pros and cons of consulting *Gallica* (Gallica.fr) instead (this provides a good opportunity to introduce them to the site and its contents, of which most undergraduates have no prior knowledge). Unsurprisingly, students first mention the elimination of time constraints: digital tools make texts and images previously consultable only by traveling to France accessible in a matter of seconds. They emphasize the ease of consulting a digital text at any time of day, including in the middle of the night and on national holidays. After browsing the BnF calendar, they see this as an especially positive aspect. Some students use the term "democratization of access" to signify that professional credentials and scholarly expertise—the BnF's infamous *justificatifs de recherche*—are no longer required for those wishing to consult heralded texts: on *Gallica*, first-year college students can now view digitized manuscripts and private correspondence by authors on their syllabi from their own dorm rooms.

Notwithstanding their enthusiasm for the massive time-saving opportunities of digitization, students never fail to mention that without going in person to a library they lose the benefits of browsing the shelves and discovering an unexpected book in the process. Some will note that it's difficult to read digital materials under a tree, on a park bench, or while taking a bath, where many print books are read. If time allows, they read chapter 3 of N. Katherine Hayles's *Writing Machines* (35–45), which is focused on media specificity and refers to Mark Bernstein's "bathtub theory of literature" (if you can't read it while bathing, then it's not literature [36]), or we read Robert Coover on the promise of interactive and polyvocal hypertexts (see also Brown). Students often express their preference for underlining passages by hand, writing notes in margins, and reading linearly—practices that the digital discourages or does not render in the same way as the printed text.

Over the course of our introductory browsing of *Gallica*, we discuss the transformations in research brought by *Google Books*, automated data retrieval, and Google Ngram searches. I offer a brief demonstration of the Project for American and French Research on the Treasury of the French Language's *ARTFL Project* Web site, focusing especially on the *Dictionnaires d'autrefois* (*Dictionaries of the Past*; artfl-project.uchicago.edu/content/dictionnaires-dautrefois). In smaller seminar classes, I bring in a Petit Robert or Larousse dictionary and ask a couple of students to use them to look up the terms *théâtre*, *tragédie*, and *dramaturge* while I project the *ARTFL* search boxes on the classroom screen. The *ARTFL* search retrieves definitions from the 1606 *Thresor de la langue françoyse tant ancienne que moderne* (*Treasure of the French Language Both Old and Modern*), eight editions of the *Dictionnaire de l'Académie Française* (*Dictionary of the French Academy*; 1690–1932), and other sources within seconds, before the students using the hard copy have even located the letter *T*. We discuss how the affordances of the digital text allow students to do research on a new scale, and we reflect on the knowledge sharing that becomes possible when students are no longer dependent on the holdings of their own academic institution alone. The ARTFL Project, based at the University of Chicago, has created a common platform for readers all around the world, albeit those with access to a subscription.

From speed, access, and convenience, the conversation usually moves to funding. Students marvel that with digital access, they need not spend money to buy dictionaries, visit museums, or consult archives; they foresee never needing to pay fines at the university library for late returns of their books. In turn, instructors may task students with investigating the economics that brought these tools to their fingertips. Depending on how much time they have to dedicate to the issue, and in particular on whether they are teaching a DH-centered course or a shorter unit, instructors may draw students' attention to the funding agencies, university partnerships, and private sponsors or public donors listed on the digital platforms. In laying the ground for my students' work on French neoclassical tragedy, I ask them to seek examples (based on the interesting contrasts they raise and their relevance to the theater) from the platforms they will consult, such as *Google Books*; *ARTFL*; *Gallica*; *The Comédie-Française Registers Project*; *Molière 21*; *Naissance de la critique dramatique* (*Birth of Dramatic Criticism*); *Theatre in Saint-Domingue (1764–1791)*; *Château de Versailles*; and *JSTOR*.

For French courses, students should undertake all this *navigation* (browsing) in French, which will expose them to the jargon of *les humanités numériques* (the digital humanities) in context. Students should note how funding policies are worded and how user agreements are framed. An accompanying homework assignment may ask students to do the following in comparing two of the suggested platforms:

identify and analyze the mission statements and the stated protocols for downloading data or making reference to the site: compare fair-use policies between platforms and discuss eventual paywalls and subscription rules;

describe the intended users and primary audiences targeted (e.g., professional scholars, undergraduates, theater aficionados, tourists);

note how the members of the team that created, constructed, and currently maintains the platform are credited;

offer an initial assessment and critique of how navigable the site is, taking into consideration the user interface as well as the functionalities, affordances, and constraints of the platforms under investigation.

At this point students are primed to consider the labor involved in digitizing the texts and images, capturing and cleaning the data stored on the platforms, and constructing the databases. I ask them to read Paige Morgan's essay about the emotional labor of digital work, "Not Your DH Teddy-Bear," and introduce them to the *Student Collaborators' Bill of Rights* (Di Pressi et al.) in order to foreground the idea of invisible and precarious labor in relation to archival and digital projects, which typically entail a separation of duties and unequal professional recognition of team members' contributions (see also Graban et al.; Elerding and Risam). Students reflect on how "democratized access" is often the result of complex financial agreements, the unheralded labor of library workers and graduate students, and the privilege of attending a North American university.

While the unit outlined above may seem to have strayed from the central subject of this volume—neoclassical tragedy—I must emphasize the importance of attuning students to the benefits and costs of working with digital tools so they will use those tools with an informed critical perspective. While most of the first and second sessions of the unit are devoted to discussions of materiality, access, form, and vocabulary (e.g., *faire défiler un texte* ["scroll through a text"], *parcourir un site* ["search a Web site"], *la lisibilité ou disposition d'un texte* ["the readability or layout of a text"]) related to the digital realm, students simultaneously begin reading a tragedy from our syllabus. I assign Racine's *Bérénice* as an introduction to French neoclassical tragedy because, on the one hand, it seems to conform to the Aristotelian rules of tragic regularity, which I am able to explain to students as we read the tragedy's stripped-down plot. On the other hand, in paying close attention to Racine's famous preface, in which he insists that blood and death are not defining features of tragedy, we can see the innovation the playwright proposes and his departure from Aristotelian precepts, especially with regard to the notion of catharsis. Racine proposes instead that the genre hinges on provoking a feeling of "tristesse majestueuse" 'majestic sadness' (450) in the spectators. Students are able to gauge how Racine innovates while working within the neoclassical precepts. In framing our readings of *Bérénice*, I draw parallels with our digital discussions by reflecting on the differences between reading a tragedy in a classroom and going to see one at the Comédie-Française. Pointing to particularly theatrical moments in the tragedy, such as when Titus grabs the letter from Bérénice's hand in act 4 or when, overcome with emotion and fatigue, the eponymous queen sits down in act 5, I ask students to reflect on the effect Racine hoped to create with the gestures and how their interpretation could vary in reception from a crowd of spectators or a reader in an armchair. Echoing our discussions of the digital realm, our close readings serve to heighten students' awareness of materiality and form, and of the specificities of theatrical performance.[3]

At this juncture, class sessions are divided between close readings of the tragedy and discussion of pedagogically useful DH readings. Students read Stephen Ramsay's polemical essay "Who's In and Who's Out," which argues that to do DH work is to build: "Digital Humanities is about building things. . . . if you aren't building, you are not engaged in the 'methodologization' of the humanities. . . ."[4] Mark Sample's reply, "The Digital Humanities Is Not about Building, It's about Sharing," is a strong rejoinder that engages students in the debate around how DH practitioners define the field and its applications.[5] We contrast Ramsay's willingness to delimit DH work and Sample's cheerful optimism that the methods will erase disciplinary and economic barriers. The accessible tenor of the discussion is a good model of academic debate for undergraduates and gives them a clear opening to articulate their thoughts on the question.

In trying to understand what Ramsay means by "building things," we list the various skills that have been put to use in designing a digital platform. At this point we begin to pay sustained attention to the CFRP. Students list the participants who were involved in building the platform: the principal investigators (professors); the data verification team (graduate students); the software team of coders, programmers, and media design specialists; and the documentarians and associate researchers, a mix of scholars involved at different levels. We discuss the skills each group offers and how the collaboration among the numerous partners listed differs from traditional humanistic research. As we enter into this discussion, I assign students important scholarship on *Bérénice*, usually Georges Forestier's introduction to the play in the Pléïade edition and Sylvaine Guyot's study of the royal body in Racine. We ask whether the important arguments advanced in those scholarly analyses are or are not evidence of "building something"; if we decide they are not building, we reflect on how else we might describe their function or contribution.

Once students have focused on a close reading of the play and a selection of secondary texts that will help them historically contextualize the tragedy, we turn to an introduction of "distant reading." I usually assign Franco Moretti's essay "The Slaughterhouse of Literature" and the chapter on graphs of his *Graphs, Maps and Trees* (3–31).[6] These selections allow us to grasp the concepts of *lecture à échelle mondiale* ("reading on a world scale") and *lecture à distance* ("distant reading"), and they serve to showcase Moretti's enthusiasm for the promise of automated data: "In the last few years, literary studies have experienced what we could call the rise of quantitative evidence. This had happened before, of course, without producing lasting effects, but this time it is probably going to be different, because this time we have digital databases and automated data retrieval . . ." ("Network Theory" 1). In considering Moretti's enthusiasm for automated data retrieval alongside the CFRP platform, the crucial point to make is the difference between distant reading of fictional texts and distant reading of archives.

First Experience with Distant Reading of Registers

To illustrate the different approaches entailed by different kinds of texts, I demonstrate the digitized facsimile of registers found on the CFRP platform (cfregisters.org/en). To keep the unit focused, I frame the early searches around *Bérénice* and Racine, the tragedy and playwright with which the students are familiar. As always, in conjunction with their digital explorations, we continue our close reading of the tragic genre. I assign Corneille's *Le Cid* as a good contrast, in terms of the tragic characters, language, and denouement, to *Bérénice*.

Students use the CFRP Discovery Tool located on the "Database" page to identify the registers that relate to Racine's tragedy. They enter "Bérénice," and with the click of a button they discover that from 1680 to 1791, the tragedy was staged 135 times, and that its longest run was eight performances in the 1742–43 season. I split the class into groups of three, with one focused on Racine's corpus, another on Corneille's (I hand out a list of his most famous plays, including comedies), and a third on Molière's (again, I provide a list of his major plays). I ask each group to prepare a report on the assigned playwright's most successful works, according to the registers. I find this is an excellent exercise to introduce useful expressions that students do not always encounter in literature classes, such as *une baisse* ("a decrease"), *une augmentation* ("an increase"), *par rapport à* ("in comparison"), *on observe ceci ou cela* ("one can observe this or that"), and *au fur et à mesure* ("progressively"), to name a few. Students are generally amazed to learn that the most successful play by Racine, France's foremost tragedian, was his now rarely read comedy, *Les plaideurs* (*The Litigants*), staged 685 times. They are surprised to learn that the longest run of his masterpiece *Phèdre* was only eleven performances (staged 542 times, it was his most successful tragedy; *Iphigénie*, second in popularity, was staged 482 times). The Corneille group is dumbfounded to discover that the canonical playwright's masterpiece, *Le Cid*, tallied only 475 performances, placing its author well behind his rival Racine and in a different class altogether (twenty-sixth overall) from the most successful playwright of all, Molière. While his *Tartuffe ou l'imposteur* (*Tartuffe; or, The Imposter*) takes first place in number of performances (956), Molière has no fewer than six plays in the top ten and occupies the top three spots on the pedestal with *Le médecin malgré lui* (*The Doctor in Spite of Himself*), at 892 performances, and *L'école des femmes* (*The School for Wives*), at 744. *Le Cid* is the only play by Corneille to appear in the top thirty, and his second-most-performed play, a comedy, *Le menteur* (*The Liar*), occupies the forty-first rank (381 performances). *Horace*, a canonical masterpiece, thought to have been a key influence for Jacques-Louis David's *The Oath of the Horatii* and often read in French classrooms, does not figure in the top fifty and at only 267 performances is behind *Rodogune* (318) and *Cinna* (286).

In the light of these discoveries and the useful *classement* ("ranking") provided by the CFRP, which I project on the classroom screen and ask students to discuss, the obvious first question is the status of the tragic genre in comparison to comedy. Although my introduction to tragedy through *Bérénice* and Racine highlights the primacy of tragedy as the most elevated genre in early modern France because of the prestige of its rules derived from the ancients and the honors bestowed on its playwrights in the seventeenth century and today in the French canon, students quickly grasp that comedy was the preeminent genre in terms of performances and receipts at the Comédie-Française. They understand why the institution to this day is nicknamed "la maison de Molière." This revelation allows them to advance hypotheses and ask follow-up questions about the seeming discrepancy between reputation and financial success. It is useful here to let students ask questions and create a list of the considerations that allow platform users to interpret the data on the rankings. At this point, we return to close reading in two different directions: we discuss *Le Cid* along with its *querelle* and begin reading Racine's *Phèdre*, and we examine the registers carefully.[7]

General Exploration of the Registers

In moving from the rankings (i.e., distant reading) to a careful consideration of the registers themselves, students will understand how the registers were written, what they looked like, what they covered, and how they evolved over the course of the eighteenth century (including changing vocabulary and records). On the "Registers" page (cfregisters.org/en/registers/receipt-registers), students click on date ranges to see examples of the registers from different time periods. I assign one group to research the early years of the troupe in the 1680s, another to explore the 1730–40s era, and a third to search toward the end of the chronology, from 1775 into the 1790s. Sliding the cursor across the screen allows users to scroll through the register book; thus students gain a good sense of the material presentation of the registers by trying to decipher the handwritten documents and the notes in their margins. The earlier exercise comparing print and online dictionaries gives them a good point of comparison in imagining the time and labor involved in searching through this archive without digital tools.

In their firsthand consideration of the registers, students grasp the choices the data entry team had to make in extracting data and fitting it into a spreadsheet. We read Johanna Drucker's articulation of "data vs. capta," a useful concept for all quantitative approaches. Reexamining the intellectual foundations of digital humanities, putting techniques of graphical display on a foundation that is humanistic at its base,

> requires first and foremost that we reconceive all data as capta. . . . *Capta* is "taken" actively while *data* is assumed to be a "given" able to be recorded and observed. From this distinction, a world of differences arises. Humanistic inquiry acknowledges the situated, partial, and constitutive character of knowledge production, the recognition that knowledge is constructed, *taken*, not simply given as a natural representation of pre-existing fact.

The notion that "data" is neither an objective fact nor an unproblematic "given" is particularly intuitive for students of French, who have learned that the word for *data* is literally "given" (*donnée*). In considering the registers closely, students realize the extent to which the data of the registers is "capta," based on a process of selection, construction, and interpretation that vividly underscores the status of the archive as neither stable nor transparent.

Since the course is centered on tragedy, an activity on the lexicon of the stage (such terms as, for example, *amphithéâtre* [amphitheater], *balcon* [balcony], *les feux* [lights], *une part* [a share], and *la recette* [box office intake]) should be included. I assign one or two key terms from the registers to each student to post to a collaborative online dictionary for the class, allowing peers to "build" something together and consult one another's work. Each entry should include

- a definition based on research in the *Dictionnaires d'autrefois* or using *Lexilogos* tools;[8]
- two or three images of what the word refers to, taken either from the CFRP or from another online source;
- an explanation of the word's occurrence in the registers. Is it consistently listed throughout the length of the registers' chronology, or does it disappear, and how does the student account for its evolution? Is it the result of a change in the vocabulary used to identify it, a change in the theater's architecture that no longer warrants its use, or another development?
- student commentary on the term. Are these discoveries surprising? What uncertainties remain about the word's meaning?

Beyond the specifics of the definitions, which foster an understanding of the changing architecture of ancien régime theater, the overarching question students must answer, based on their analysis of the registers, is: What are the reasons the Comédie-Française troupe kept such detailed receipts of the plays performed?

Other materials offered on the CFRP platform, such as high-resolution images of the different theaters the Comédie-Française occupied, and the maps of Paris where they were located, inform the class's research. Students learn that the Comédie-Française existed at four different locations between 1680 and 1792, and that each venue's situation and capacity influenced the gross number of tickets sold and must be accounted for in a comparison across time. Economic inflation and the changing price of tickets also become topics of discussion as students understand that some of the pricier seats located on or near the stage were eliminated to make room for the actors: all these changes disappear in the database's merely quantitative rendering of the registers. Students learn that *la part des pauvres*, a portion of the box-office receipts, was given to the Catholic Church as a gesture of goodwill toward an institution that frowned upon the prominence of the theater, again influencing the numerical bottom line. Firsthand consultation of the registers also uncovers that the practice was to perform two works per night. Knowing this, students must contemplate whether the receipts for a particular date reflect the popularity of the headlining play alone or represent the combined popularity of the two performances and playwrights listed.

These discussions help students evaluate how the data extracted from the registers in the browser complements other scholarly methodologies, including close readings and historical and visual studies. Students are able to undertake research using the basics of the different methods and to articulate a perspective on these methods' respective merits and drawbacks. In contrast to a DH approach that would minimize the materiality of the texts, this approach heightens students' awareness of the medium they are using and encourages them to reflect on how it shapes their thoughts and arguments regarding the success of French tragedies.

Distant Reading: Theater History versus Literature

By now, students have a firm grasp of the CFRP platform and its potential to facilitate research in theater history. We are ready to pivot back to the plays themselves, framing our return as an exercise both in literary close reading and, eventually, in literary distant reading, in contrast to the historical documents we have been considering. In analyzing the fluctuations in the popularity of Corneille and Racine's tragic works, our investigations addressed success in terms of the economics reflected in the CFRP registers; however, in our return to the tragedies we evaluate their success in terms of plot and character construction, dramatic action, and poetry.

Students are often struck by the tragedies' *huis clos* ("no exit") atmosphere, where only a limited number of characters, confined to one location, speak to each other over the course of five acts. These exchanges constitute the main action of the play, since the rules of neoclassical decorum discourage overtly physical interactions among characters on stage. The plot is advanced almost entirely through the dialogue, monologues, or longer speeches of the tragic characters. For twenty-first-century undergraduates, usually more versed in the plays of Shakespeare than Racine, this drama of "talking heads" can seem downright odd, and its structure can seem mystifyingly rigid. Students hypothesize that these kinds of interactions and the nuances of tragedy's poetry were likely hard to grasp within the walls of the boisterous and crowded theaters where the farcical and more physical gestures of comedy were valuable assets for the public stage, explaining, perhaps, the genre's popularity over tragedy at the Comédie-Française.

I present the students with Moretti's distant reading of *Phèdre*, in which he draws from Alex Woloch's concept of "character space" to quantify the presence of the various characters in Racine's play and in Shakespeare's *Hamlet* ("Operationalizing").[9] Dramatic works lend themselves particularly well to the "operationalization" process and to conducting network analyses since, in contrast to novels, there are no ambiguities in how words are distributed among the various speakers: in theater, character-space turns into word-space. This insight is especially relevant to French neoclassical tragedy, a genre where, as Roland Barthes has noted with regard to Jean Racine's corpus, "Parler c'est faire" 'To speak is to do' (60; my trans.). In analyzing *Phèdre*, Moretti counts the number of words and the number of interlocutors allocated to each character as a measure of centrality to the drama. In *Phèdre*, although the eponymous heroine speaks the most (twenty-nine percent of the play's total words, compared to Hippolyte's twenty-one percent and Thésée's fourteen percent), she addresses herself most often to her confidante, Œnone, in a relationship that is markedly decentered from the exchanges of the other characters in the play. Thus, although Thésée speaks significantly less than his wife, he is the play's most central character in that he is most connected to all the other characters. These two criteria, the number of words spoken by a character and the number of their interactions, lead us to evaluate character dynamics from a new angle: the quantified relationship between characters. In my experience, doing a distant reading of the play mostly serves to confirm insights about the characters that students had already noted; nonetheless, observing how much Phèdre speaks to Œnone in contrast to how little Œnone speaks to Phèdre strikes students as warranting further discussion of the dynamic of power between the two women. The quantification of their exchanges also prompts discussion of the role of confession versus action in the play and underscores the importance of silence within the plot, a phenomenon that cannot be represented by the quantification of character space.[10]

In Pamphlet 6, Moretti reserves the bulk of his commentary for an "operationalization" of *Hamlet*, including an experiment in which he erases the eponymous character entirely from the character map of the tragedy to see what dynamics remain when Hamlet is no longer at center of the character network (Moretti argues that Horatio becomes an unexpectedly central character who deserves renewed attention). Moretti's focus on *Hamlet* leaves much space for students to model their interpretation of *Phèdre* after the Shakespeare example. Having established the basics of mapping character relations and quantifying tragic exchanges as a static snapshot of the overall work (indeed, as a map) in contrast to a linear and teleological assessment of the plot, I offer students additional models of distant reading in the following exercises. I pose the following questions regarding a network map of *Bérénice* (fig. 1):

According to your interpretations, what does the network map "view" reveal about character interactions within the tragedy? Provide a narrative description of what we can learn from the visualization.

Are there character dynamics reflected in the character map that had gone unnoticed in your close reading of the tragedy?

What are important aspects of the tragedy that the visualization occludes? Give specific examples.

In a perspective that echoes but ultimately differs from the data-gathering critique related to the CFRP, students reflect on the nature of humanities data and how the quantification of fictional texts differs from the quantification of historical documents. Students understand how this data extracted from a literary text can be captured, created, and visualized

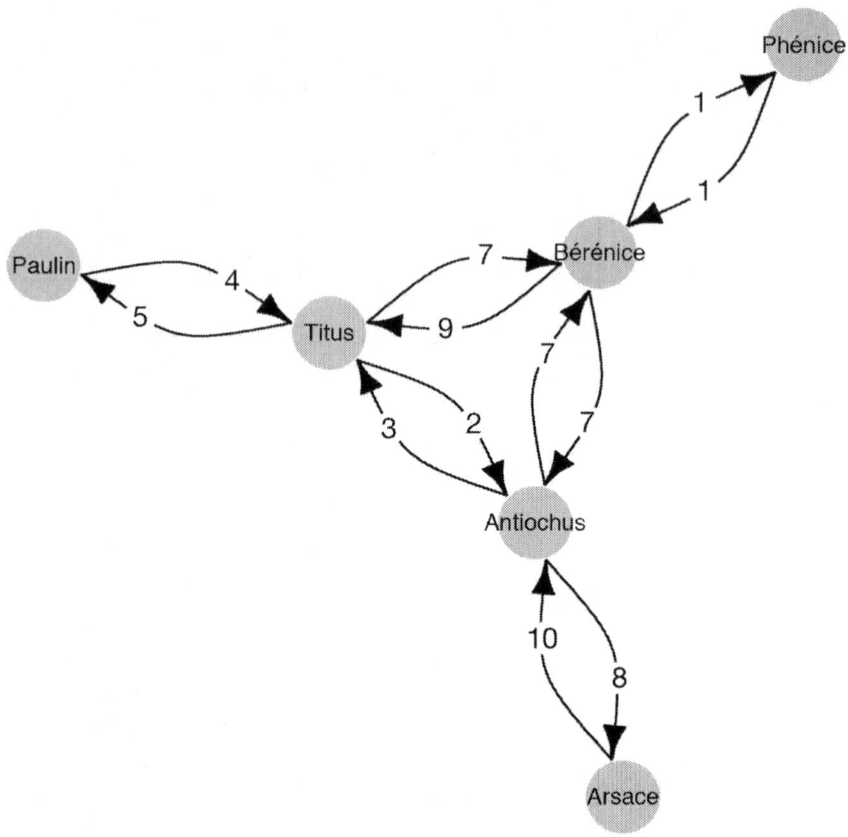

Fig. 1. *Bérénice* character network map. Each character is a node, and the edges represent all interactions longer than five verses between characters.

in order to make an argument, and they are able to formulate questions that apply the data when seeking to advance an interpretation of the play. They are capable of evaluating the method and articulating a perspective on the merits and drawbacks of such a distant reading approach.

Figure 1 includes an element of directionality by noting how many exchanges of more than five verses one character has with another. Students remark on the balance in the quantity of speech between characters, which they see as a reflection of the balance of characters' prominence in the plot: they are all very equal despite Titus's status as the Roman emperor. For a short follow-up assignment, I find it pedagogically useful to ask students to analyze a character map of a tragedy they have not read. They can compare the visualizations of character dynamics in *Andromaque*, *Bérénice*, and *Phèdre*, noticing how the relationships are broader in *Andromaque*, where some of the main characters never communicate directly with each other, in contrast to *Bérénice*, where the three main characters have extended interactions within the claustrophobic love triangle. Students come to realize the degree to which *Bérénice* is a tragedy of the tête-à-tête, whereas the other plays have only one (Thésée) or two characters (Hermione and Pyrrhus) with high degrees of centrality who communicate with all the other characters in what we might call, after Moretti, different "regions" ("Network Theory" 5) of the plot. It can be revealingly productive to try to label these different regions. When students eventually read *Andromaque*, their first reaction is to point out that by excluding the older Trojan War generation—the one of Achilles, Hector, and Hélène, who weigh so heavily on the onstage characters—a network map based on word space (fig. 2)

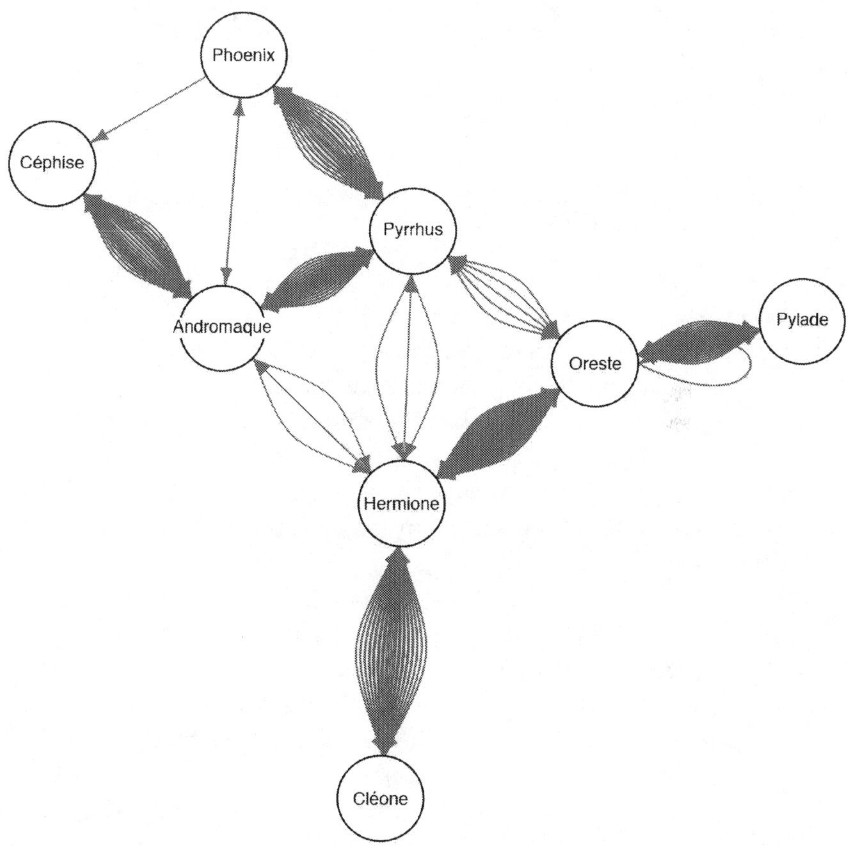

Fig. 2. *Andromaque* character network map. Each character is a node, and the edges represent all interactions longer than five verses between characters.

fails to capture the nuanced generational dynamic that is so determining of the tragic characters' actions.

To close out this section on distant reading and literary interpretation, I introduce the concept of word mining of tragedy (*la fouille des textes*), including word clouds produced using the digital tool Voyant (voyant-tools.org). By following the directions on the platform, students learn that they can enter a tragic text found on the *Théâtre Classique* Web site (theatre-classique.fr/), which includes 1,220 digitized plays from the seventeenth and eighteenth centuries, and determine word frequency occurrences and authorial vocabulary preferences, additional facets of distant reading. In these exercises and discussions, students focus on the tragedies and playwrights we have read in class, comparing the lexicon of Corneille to Racine and the favorite expressions of both playwrights as a means of interpreting their works. We do not fail to ponder whether a distant reading of theatrical texts is legitimate, or how it differs from applying the same methods to a novel, given the importance of performance and staging in defining the meaning of a dramatic text.

Final Assignment: Asking More Complex Questions of the CFRP Database

For the last assignment dedicated to distant reading, we return to the CFRP using its most advanced search function, the cross-tab browser. If students had begun using this search function right away, I believe they would not have questioned the process—the choices, fluctuations, and erasures—such a function entails in assembling data. Now they encounter this data critically and knowledgeably. For the final project, each student creates three separate data visualizations based on the evidence provided by the CFRP, focusing on Racine and his tragedies in some capacity. I leave the particulars of the approach broad so students may define their searches according to what most intrigues them. They choose the plays, time periods, and comparisons they wish to explore—many end up comparing Molière to Racine in an interesting departure from the age-old practice of comparing Racine to Corneille. Students provide the resulting visualizations created by the CFRP, including explanatory titles and legends to render the visuals decipherable. They supply a two- to three-page narrative and interpretation of the visualization, including a reflection on the choices, problems, and omissions the data presentation creates. I have found it beneficial for students to present their visualizations orally to the rest of the class, because it forces them to articulate clearly the questions that spurred their visualizations and allows them to practice their French language skills.

By the end of this unit, students have come to understand that distant reading has little value without the careful close reading that spurs an intriguing question beforehand and will give meaning to the visualization afterward. Students understand why neoclassical tragedy, because of its codified plot structure, recurring character types (the sovereign, the love interest, the confidants, etc.), and small number of characters, is a particularly promising genre for conducting distant reading analyses, but they also come away with a healthy skepticism toward the notion that the quantified version of the play can reveal dynamics unrecognizable to the naked eye. Nonetheless, they grasp the promise of reading and interpreting on a new scale. In working with the CFRP, students understand the value of historical contextualization in DH methods and recognize the partialness of the database. The exercises we have undertaken have fostered renewed respect for qualitative analysis alongside quantitative methods. Finally, students have acquired familiarity with the vocabulary and concepts of neoclassical French tragedy and the language of digital humanities, including the skills necessary to analyze the graphs they have created based on these works. Students walk away surprised at the variety of skills they can learn in their French class.

Notes

The approaches I outline here were developed in a team-taught course designed with Hélène Visentin, with the support of Laura M. O'Brien, both of whom I wish to acknowledge and thank since, without them, none of these projects could have been undertaken.

1. See in particular the Saint-Domingue theater project (theatreinsaint-domingue.org); *Naissance de la critique dramatique* (www.ncd17.fr), and *Theatre Classique* (theatre-classique.fr). See also Schöch.

2. See Schuwey for helpful ways of addressing these questions and the French vocabulary that comes with them.

3. The essays in this volume by Sylvaine Guyot, Blair Hoxby, Laurence Marie, Jennifer Tamas, and Ellen Welch address the important questions of performance.

4. Ramsay's articulation originally appeared in an MLA panel on DH and was later refined in "Developing Things: Notes toward an Epistemology of Building in the Digital Humanities" (with Geoffrey Rockwell). If time allows, I assign chapter 1 of his *Reading Machines: Towards an Algorithmic Criticism.*

5. For a semester-long course that goes beyond the theater unit, instructors might add readings from Gold.

6. For instructors wishing to teach DH in French, the Dobenesque translation, *Graphes, cartes et arbres*, can be used to engage discussion in the target language. Depending on how far instructors wish to go in distant reading examples, they can easily draw from Stanford Literary Lab pamphlets, especially "Quantitative Formalism: An Experiment" and "Network Theory, Plot Analysis."

7. For more on teaching *Le Cid* and its quarrel, see Beasley and Kennedy and Jortner in this volume.

8. *Lexilogos* includes Furetière's *Dictionnaire universel* (*Universal Dictionary*; lexilogos.com/francais_classique.htm), which the *Dictionnaires d'autrefois* does not include.

9. Alex Woloch defined character space in these terms: "The amount of narrative space allocated to a particular character . . . the space of the character within the narrative structure . . . the space that he or she occupies within the narrative totality . . . the narrative's continual apportioning of attention to different characters who jostle for limited space within the narrative totality" (13–14).

10. I find it useful to pair these discussions of word space and character space with excerpts from Tamas, which emphasizes the role of silence and the unsaid in the plot.

Works Cited

Barthes, Roland. *Sur Racine*. Editions du Seuil, 1963.

Brown, Bill. "Materiality." *Critical Terms for Media Studies*, edited by W. J. T. Mitchell and Mark B. N. Hansen, U of Chicago P, 2010.

Coover, Robert. "The End of Books." *The New York Times Review of Books*, 22 June 1992.

Di Pressi, Haley, et al. *A Student Collaborators' Bill of Rights*. *HumTech*, University of California, 8 June 2015, humtech.ucla.edu/news/a-studentç-collaborators-bill-of-rights/.

Drucker, Johanna. "Humanities Approaches to Graphical Display." *Digital Humanities Quarterly*, vol. 5, no. 1, 2011, digitalhumanities.org/dhq/vol/5/1/000091/000091.html.

Elerding, Carolyn, and Roopika Risam, editors. *Gender and Digital Labor*. Special issue of *First Monday*, vol. 23, nos. 3–5, Mar. 2018, firstmonday.org/ojs/index.php/fm/issue/view/590.

Gold, Matthew K., editor. *Debates in the Digital Humanities*. U of Minnesota P, 2012.

Graban, Tarez Samra, et al., editors. "Invisible Work in Digital Humanities." *Digital Humanities Quarterly*, vol. 13, no. 2, 2019, www.digitalhumanities.org/dhq/vol/13/2/000421/000421.html.

Guyot, Sylvaine. *Racine et le corps tragique*. PU de France, 2014.

Hayles, N. Katherine. *Writing Machines*. Media Work, MIT Press, 2002.

Moretti, Franco. *Graphes, cartes et arbres*. Translated by Etienne Dobenesque, Broche, 2008.

———. *Graphs, Maps, Trees: Abstract Models for a Literary History*. Verso, 2005.

———. "Network Theory, Network Analysis." Pamphlet 2, Stanford Literary Lab, May 2011.

———. "'Operationalizing'; or, the Function of Measurement in Modern Literary Theory." Pamphlet 6, Stanford Literary Lab, Dec. 2013.

———. "Quantitative Formalism: An Experiment." Pamphlet 1, Stanford Literary Lab, Jan. 2011.

———. "The Slaughterhouse of Literature" *MLQ: Modern Language Quarterly*, vol. 61, no. 1, Mar. 2000, pp. 207–27.

Morgan, Paige. "Not Your DH Teddy-Bear; or, Emotional Labor is Not Going Away." *Digital Humanities in the Library / of the Library: A DH+LIB Special Issue*, edited by Caitlin Christian-Lamb et al., 29 July 2016, acrl.ala.org/dh/2016/07/29/not-your-dh-teddy-bear.

Racine, Jean. *Andromaque. Œuvres complètes*, pp. 199–256.

———. *Bérénice. Œuvres complètes*, pp. 450–509.

———. *Œuvres complètes, tome I: Théâtre-Poésie*. Edited by Georges Forestier, Gallimard-La Pleiade, 1999.

———. *Phèdre. Œuvres complètes*, pp. 821–76.

Ramsay, Stephen. *Reading Machines: Toward an Algorithmic Criticism.* U of Illinois P, 2017.

Ramsay, Stephen, and Geoffrey Rockwell. "Developing Things: Notes toward an Epistemology of Building in the Digital Humanities." *Debates in the Digital Humanities*, U of Minnesota P, 2012, pp. 75–84.

Sample, Mark. "The Digital Humanities Is Not about Building, It's about Sharing." *@samplereality*, 25 May 2011, samplereality.com/2011/05/25/the-digital-humanities-is-not-about-building-its-about-sharing.

Schöch, Christophe. "Topic Modeling Genre: An Exploration of French Classical and Enlightenment Drama," *Digital Humanities Quarterly*, vol. 11, no. 2, 2017, digitalhumanities.org/dhq/vol/11/2/000291/000291.html.

Schuwey, Christophe. *Interfaces: L'apport des humanités numériques à la littérature.* Alphil, PU Suisses, 2019.

Tamas, Jennifer. *Le silence trahi: Racine ou la déclaration tragique.* Droz, 2018.

Woloch, Alex. *The One vs. the Many: Minor Characters and the Space of the Protagonist in the Novel.* Princeton UP, 2003.

Notes on Contributors

Faith E. Beasley is professor of French and women's and gender studies at Dartmouth College. She is the author of *Revising Memory: Women's Fiction and Memoirs in Seventeenth-Century France* (1990), *Salons, History, and the Creation of Seventeenth-Century France: Mastering Memory* (2006), and *Versailles Meets the Taj Mahal: François Bernier, Marguerite de La Sablière, and Enlightening Conversations in Seventeenth-Century France* (2018), which explores the encounter between France and India during France's Grand Siècle. Beasley edited the collection *Teaching Seventeenth- and Eighteenth-Century French Women Writers* (2011) and, with Katherine Ann Jensen, *Approaches to Teaching* The Princess of Clèves (1998). She was a Guggenheim Fellow in 2012–13.

Hélène E. Bilis, associate professor of French at Wellesley College, is the author of *Passing Judgment: The Politics and Poetics of Sovereignty in French Tragedy from Hardy to Racine* (2016) and coeditor (with Jennifer Tamas) of *L'éloquence du silence: Dramaturgie du non-dit sur la scène théâtrale des 17e et 18e siècles* (2014). She is developing a digital pedagogical edition and translation of Lafayette's *La princesse de Clèves.* With students and library partners at Wellesley she designed an open-source digital exhibit, *Between Hairstyle and History*, on an almanac that belonged to Marie-Antoinette.

Marc Bizer is professor of French literature at the University of Texas at Austin. He has published three books: *La poésie au miroir: imitation et conscience de soi dans la poésie latine de la Pléiade*; *Lettres de Rome:* Les Regrets *et la tradition épistolaire*; and *Homer and the Politics of Authority in Renaissance France.* He is currently working on a study of the relation between early modern French tragedy and the history of emotions.

John Boitano received his PhD in French and Romance philology from Columbia University. He is the chair of the Department of World Languages and Cultures and associate professor of French and peace studies at Chapman University. He has published a book on Blaise Pascal with Biblio 17 and articles on Pascal, Gabriel Naudé, and seventeenth-century missionaries to China.

Juliette Cherbuliez is professor at the University of Minnesota and director of its Consortium for the Study of the Premodern World, promoting innovative research and teaching in global premodern studies across disciplines and institutions. Author of *In the Wake of Medea: Neoclassical Theater and the Arts of Destruction* (2020) and *The Place of Exile: Leisure Literature and the Limits of Absolutism* (2005), she coedited (with Andrew Billing) *L'esprit* *créateur*'s issue on Paris as an economic center of modernity and has published on premodern tragedy, women's literature, spectatorship in history and theory, and material culture.

Andrea Frisch, professor of French at the University of Maryland, College Park, is the author of *The Invention of the Eyewitness: Witnessing and Testimony in Early Modern France* (2004) and *Forgetting Differences: Tragedy, Historiography, and the French Wars of Religion* (2015).

Sylvaine Guyot is professor of Romance languages and literatures, and of theater, dance and media at Harvard University. She is the author of *Racine et le corps tragique* (2014), *Racine ou l'alchimie du tragique* (2010), and *Les scénographies de l'éblouissement* (forthcoming), and coeditor of a critical edition of Racine's *Théâtre complet* (2014). She has coedited *L'oeil classique,* a special issue of *Littératures classiques* on early modern vision and visuality (2013); *Littéraire*, a Festschrift for Alain Viala (2018); and the online volume *Databases, Revenues, and Repertory: The French Stage Online, 1680–1793* (2020). She is a principal researcher of the Comédie-Française Registers Project and the founding director of the theater company La Troupe at Harvard. In 2018–19, she was a EURIAS fellow at the Paris Institute for Advanced Study.

Blair Hoxby is professor of English at Stanford University. He is the author of *What Was Tragedy? Theory and the Early Modern Canon* (2015), which received Honorable Mention from the Renaissance Society of America's Gordon Book Prize, and articles on early modern French drama in journals such as *Comparative Literature*, *ELR*, and the *Cambridge Opera Journal* and in collections such as *The Oxford Handbook on the Baroque* (2018), *A Cultural History of Theatre* (2017), *Politics and Aesthetics in European Baroque and Classicist Tragedy* (2017), and *Early Modern Theatricality* (2013). He is currently editing two collections of essays that treat French neoclassical tragedy: *Tragedy in the Enlightenment: Affect, Philosophy, and the Historical Turn* and *Opera and Tragedy: From Absolutism to Enlightenment.*

David Jortner is associate professor and graduate program director of theater at Baylor University. His primary research areas include modern Japanese theater, the intersections of Japanese and American culture, and theater historiography. He has published numerous articles and book chapters and has edited numerous volumes as well. An active director, Dr. Jortner has staged a wide variety of plays.

Theresa Varney Kennedy is professor of French at Baylor University. Her primary research interests are in early modern French theater, female playwrights, and the representation of women in neoclassical French theater and beyond. She has published articles in such journals as *Yale French Studies*, *The French Review*, *Papers on French Seventeenth-Century Literature*, and *Women in French*. She is coauthor of a critical edition of Madame de Maintenon's *Proverbes Dramatiques* (2014) and author of *Women's Deliberation: The Heroine in Early Modern French Women's Theater, 1650–1750* (2018).

Jeffrey M. Leichman is Jacques Arnaud Associate Professor in the Department of French Studies at Louisiana State University, where he has received three Tiger Athletic Foundation teaching awards as well as the Robert Udick award for undergraduate instruction from the College of Humanities and Social Sciences. He is project director of the National Endowment for the Humanities–funded Interactive VR Simulation of an Eighteenth-Century Paris Fair Theatre and coeditor of the volume *Colonialism and Slavery in Performance: Theatre and the Eighteenth-Century French Caribbean* (2021). In 2018–19, he was a fellow at the Institut d'Etudes Avancées de Nantes.

John D. Lyons is Commonwealth Professor of French at the University of Virginia and Chevalier de la Légion d'Honneur. He is the author of *The Tragedy of Origins* (1996), *The Kingdom of Disorder* (1999), *The Phantom of Chance* (2011), and *Tragedy and the Return of the Dead* (2018). He is the editor of the *Cambridge Companion to French Literature* (2015), the *Oxford Handbook of the Baroque* (2019), and *The Dark Thread: From Tragical Histories to Gothic Tales* (2019).

Laurence Marie is a lecturer at Columbia University and the author of *Inventer l'acteur: Émotions et spectacle dans l'Europe des Lumières* (2019). She has written on performance and the visual arts, the reception of Shakespeare, and the history of aesthetic ideas in eighteenth-century Europe. More recently, her research has focused on colonial theater.

Ellen McClure is associate professor of French and history at the University of Illinois at Chicago, where she also directs the Mellon-funded Engaged Humanities Initiative. She works on the intersection of early modern French literature, religion, and politics and is the author of *The Logic of Idolatry in Seventeenth-Century Literature* (2020) and *Sunspots and the Sun King: Sovereignty and Mediation in Seventeenth-Century France* (2006), as well as several articles on Corneille, Racine, Lafayette, and La Fontaine.

Larry F. Norman is the Frank L. Sulzberger Distinguished Service Professor of Romance languages and literatures and theater and performance studies at the University of Chicago. He is the author of *The Shock of the Ancient: Literature and History in Early Modern France* (2011), which was awarded the Aldo and Jeanne Scaglione Prize for French and Francophone Studies by the Modern Language Association of America; and *The Public Mirror: Molière and the Social Commerce of Depiction* (1999).

Jeffrey N. Peters is professor of French at the University of Kentucky. His most recent book is *The Written World: Space, Literature, and the*

Chorological Imagination in Early Modern France (2018). He is also the author of *Mapping Discord: Allegorical Cartography in Early Modern French Writing* (2004), which was awarded the 2005 Aldo and Jeanne Scaglione Prize for French and Francophone Studies by the Modern Language Association of America.

Julia Prest is professor of French and Caribbean studies at the University of St Andrews, Scotland. Her research interests focus on early modern French, francophone, and Creole theater, including ballet and opera. She is the author of two monographs, three coedited volumes, and three critical editions, as well as numerous scholarly articles. She is also the creator of the *Theatre in Saint-Domingue* performance database.

Sylvie Romanowski, professor emerita of French at Northwestern University, specializes in the literature of the seventeenth and eighteenth centuries, particularly novels and theater. She is the author of *L'illusion chez Descartes: La structure du discours cartésien* (1974) and *Through Strangers' Eyes: Fictional Foreigners in Old Regime France* (2005). She has written articles on Malraux, Cyrano de Bergerac, Molière, Racine, Rousseau, Colette, Ernaux, and Maryse Condé. She also translated Alexander von Humboldt's *Essai sur la géographie des plantes* and wrote an essay on a plate accompanying that work (2009).

Anna Rosensweig is the James P. Wilmot Distinguished Assistant Professor of French at the University of Rochester. Her research and teaching focus on early modern literature and culture, the intersections of literature and political theory, and performance studies. Her work has appeared in journals such as *L'esprit créateur*, *The French Review*, and *Renaissance Drama*, and she is currently completing a book manuscript on the endurance of early modern resistance theory in French tragedy.

Jennifer Row is assistant professor of French at the University of Minnesota and is the 2020–22 Imagine Fund cochair of Arts, Design, and Humanities. Her publications in *ASAP/Journal* and *Exemplaria* focus on French and English early modern theater, queer and feminist theory, dance studies, and affect theory. In 2016–17 she was awarded the Solmsen Fellowship in pre-1700 studies at the University of Wisconsin-Madison. She is the author of two monograph manuscripts: *Queer Velocities: Time, Sex, and Biopower on the Early Modern Stage*, and *The Body Perfect: The Aesthetics of Ableism in the Early Francophone World.*

Jennifer Tamas, agrégée de lettres modernes, is associate professor of French at Rutgers University. She coedited a book on Madame de Sévigné (2012) and a volume (with Hélène Bilis) on the tension between the said and the unsaid onstage in seventeenth- and eighteenth-century French theater (2014). Her monograph, *Le silence trahi: Racine ou la déclaration tragique* (2018), focuses on theater, and she has published several articles on early modern passions. Her book in progress about the relation between mourning and ghosts is titled "Spectral Companions: Widows, Agency and the Power of Tears, 1555–1791."

Louise Thomas has concertized as a pianist extensively throughout Europe, North America, and Asia at such venues as the Tchaikovsky Conservatoire in Moscow, the Forbidden City Concert Hall in Beijing, Walt Disney Concert Hall in Los Angeles, and Weill Hall in New York City. She also appears on chamber music and contemporary music programs throughout the United States and internationally and is associate dean for academic affairs at Chapman University's College of Performing Arts.

Hélène Visentin is professor of French at Smith College. She has authored numerous articles on machine theater and ceremonial entries and three critical editions of seventeenth-century plays: *La descente d'Orphée aux enfers*, by François de Chapoton (2004); *Les sosies*, by Jean de Rotrou, in *Théâtre complet*, vol. 8 (2005); and *Andromède*, by Pierre Corneille, in *Théâtre*, vol. 4 (forthcoming). She also coedited *L'invraisemblance du pouvoir: Mises en scène de la souveraineté au XVII*[e] *siècle en France* (2005) and *French Ceremonial Entries in the Sixteenth Century: Event, Image, Text* (2007). She is developing a collaborative digital edition and translation of Lafayette's *La princesse de Clèves.*

Ellen R. Welch is professor of French and francophone studies at the University of North Carolina, Chapel Hill, and author of *A Taste for the Foreign: Worldly Knowledge and Literary Pleasure in Early Modern French Fiction* (2011) and *A Theater of Diplomacy: International Relations and the Performing Arts in Early Modern France* (2017). She specializes in ancien régime literature with a focus on theater and performance as well as early modern French culture in its global contexts.

Toby Wikström holds a dual appointment at the Graduate School and Centre for Research in the Humanities at the University of Iceland. His work centers on the intersection of globalization, performance, and law in early modernity, with a secondary focus on captivity and religious conversion in the sixteenth- and seventeenth-century Mediterranean. He has published on these topics in *L'esprit créateur* and in the anthology *The Dialectics of Orientalism in Early Modern Europe*, among other forums, and is presently completing a book manuscript titled "Staging and Erasing the Global in Early Modern France."

David Wray is associate professor in the Department of Classics and the Department of Comparative Literature at the University of Chicago. His publications include *Catullus and the Poetics of Roman Manhood* (2001) and the coedited volume *Seneca and the Self* (2009), and he is currently at work on "Seneca's Revenge: A Queer Tragic Study" as well as verse translations of Pierre Corneille's Greek mythological plays.